VOICES
FROM THE
LITERACY FIELD

James A. Draper and Maurice C. Taylor
Editors

Original Edition 1992
First U.S. Printing 1994

Printed and Published by
KRIEGER PUBLISHING COMPANY
KRIEGER DRIVE
MALABAR, FLORIDA 32950

FROM A DECLARATION OF PRINCIPLES JOINTLY ADOPTED BY A COMMITTEE OF THE AMERICAN BAR ASSOCIATION AND A COMMITTEE OF PUBLISHERS:
This publication is designed to provide accurate and authoritative information in regard to the subject matter covered. It is sold with the understanding that the publisher is not engaged in rendering legal, accounting, or other professional service. If legal advice or other expert assistance is required, the services of a competent professional person should be sought.

Library of Congress Cataloging-in-Publication Data

Voices from the literacy field / edited by James A. Draper and Maurice
   C. Taylor.
        p. cm.
    Originally published: Toronto : Culture Concepts, c1992.
    Includes bibliographical references and index.
    ISBN 0-89464-861-6 (U.S.)   ISBN 0-921472-10-2 (Canada)
    1.   Literacy--Canada--Case studies. 2. Elementary education of
adults--Canada--Case studies.   I. Draper, James A., 1930-
II. Taylor, Maurice C. (Maurice Charles), 1952-
LC154.V65   1994
374'.012'0971--dc20
                                    93-21016
                                      CIP

10   9   8   7   6   5   4   3   2

CONTENTS

Section One: Foundations of Literacy

Section Two: Case Studies on Community Building

Section Three: Case Studies Focusing on Special Needs

INTRODUCTION

Voices from the Literacy Field is an attempt to capture the experiences of literacy practitioners and their participating students through observing their interactions and joining in discussions and interviews with them. This selection of case studies is from all regions of Canada (they have been selected from our previous work: *Issues in Adult Literacy and Basic Education: Canada*). This will explain why some of the theme areas in this book have a predominance of one or two authors. In addition in the original study, more case studies were conducted for Ontario (because it is the most populous province) which explains the number of studies documented here. These descriptions and reflections provide a critical and revealing commentary on effective practice in literacy education in Canada.

We found it heartening to see first-hand the number and kinds of services provided through the many literacy agencies, each one uniquely tailored for the delivery of practical literacy education. We also found that agencies differed in some aspects of teaching methodology, in just how students participated, in the ways in which their communities became involved, and even in the ways that paid and volunteer workers were trained. Other differences were noted in the clientele the agencies served, how they were financed and the reasons for their locations. They differed also on how they viewed research and in the ways they assessed their own work and that of their students.

To each of these selected case studies chapters, we have added introductory 'boxes' of information that provide a quick who-what-where synopsis at the very beginning. And we have added discussion questions at the end of each case study to provoke further reflection and perhaps debate.

You will be interested to see that five of the case studies have been translated either from French to English or from English to French because of their importance in understanding the special concerns of cultural groups.

Four of the case studies, written in French, depict literacy programs in the province of Quebec. An English translation immediately follows each. *Please note that this translation is shown as a separate chapter.* Since a case study from Ontario documents some of the issues important to franco-ontarians, it too, has been translated into French, totalling five case studies which attempt to present a francophone perspective on issues. Finally, because of the subtleties of language, the discussion questions at the end of the French and the English studies differ slightly.

Our underlying assumption within the *Foundations of Literacy* is that improving literacy practice and developing literacy professionals, necessitates familiarity with the possible philosophical alternatives, the basic adult education principles, as well as learning theory which underlies and guides good practice. The chapters by Draper, Taylor and Barer-Stein illustrate the theories upon which the case studies are to be interpreted.

Philosophy underlies our work, principles guide our work, and if learning isn't the goal of all literacy programs, then what is?

The *Selected References* are not the only resources. We would like you to know that the agencies themselves can be contacted for further information too.

While we are all aware that the case studies captured in a book will — and should — be in constant change, we hope that what they reveal will be valuable as an educational tool, as a reference, and as a resource for specific issues. Finally we hope that our Epilogue: *Continuing the Debate* will really be examined to provoke your own discussions. You have the last word.

James A. Draper and Maurice C. Taylor

ACKNOWLEDGEMENTS

The case studies constituting the core of this book represent the contributions of literally scores of practitioners who shared their literacy experiences with us. In addition to thanking these practitioners, we are especially indebted to the author-researchers who travelled to various regions in Canada to see for themselves, to listen, to question, and then to write these case studies with care and understanding.

Within the National Literacy Secretariat, Department of Multiculturalism and Citizenship Canada, we sincerely thank Richard Nolan, and Sue Smee for their continuing encouragement and support not only to publish this book but also for supporting the national literacy research project upon which this book is based, *Issues in Adult Literacy and Basic Education: Canada*. We also wish to express our appreciation to Brad Munro, until recently with the Canadian Commission for Unesco, and now a policy analyst with the Department of the Secretary of State, for his long-time support and encouragement of our literacy projects. Within the Literacy Branch of the Ontario Ministry of Education, we continue to be indebted to Harold Alden, Betty Butterworth, and Arthur Bull.

We consider *Foundations of Literacy* to be a valuable contribution which balances the actual practice of literacy education with the theoretical components underlying it. To this end, we thank our colleague Thelma Barer-Stein for her chapter which provides both new and thoughtful material for all teachers, trainers, coordinators, as well as for students themselves.For undertaking specific and important tasks required in manuscript preparation, we express our thanks to Lorisa Stein for French editing; Yingmin C. Xu for her work on the bibliography; and Kathleen Sparacino and Jeanie Stewart both from the Department of Adult Education, the Ontario Institute for Studies in Education, for typing many parts of the manuscript. And at the Faculty of Education, University of Ottawa, special thanks to Gabriel Bordeleau, Bayne Logan and Diane Jackson.

James A. Draper and Maurice C. Taylor

THE CONTRIBUTORS

Major authors

Thelma Barer-Stein

Thelma Barer-Stein, Ph.D. is founder and president of Culture Concepts Inc., the publishers of *Adult Literacy Perspectives* (1989), and *Basic Skills for the Workplace* (1991). Her writing and research is in the areas of cross-cultural understanding, adult education and phenomenology with a focus on the learning process. Her many published articles and chapters include "Reflections on the Universal Learning Process" in Taylor and Draper's *Adult Literacy Perspectives* (1989) and "Experiencing the Unfamiliar: Matrix for Learning" in Cassara's *Adult Education in a Multicultural Society* (1990). She also co-edited the classic book *The Craft of Teaching Adults* (1988).

Her workshops on literacy and learning have been presented to literacy trainers and teachers as well as to the International Reading Association's Conference on Literacy held in Banff, 1991. In 1985 she was invited to participate in the National Australian Literacy Conference in Sydney, Australia, as well as the Australian Conference on Literacy and Community Development. She was also an invited participant to the National Consultation on Literacy organized by UNESCO in Ottawa, 1991.

James A. Draper

Since 1967, James has been a faculty member in the Department of Adult Education, Ontario Institute for Studies in Education, at the University of Toronto, and is cross-appointed to the University of Toronto's Centre for South Asian Studies. It was in 1964, while a faculty member for two years at the University of Rajasthan in India, that he began to work in the area of adult literacy education, advising on the role of universities in supporting literacy programs.

From 1969 to 1990, he was a board member of World Literacy of Canada, serving as president from 1973-78. During his presidency, WLC undertook the first national study of adult literacy and basic education in Canada. In the early 1980's he chaired the Ontario Ministry of Labour's Task Force on Literacy and Occupational Health and Safety. Later under contract with the Ministry of Education, he undertook a review of literature relating to adult literacy which was later published as a book *Re-Thinking Adult Literacy*. In 1987, he was on the planning committee for the International Conference on Literacy in Industrialized Countries, held in Toronto. His many publications include *Adult Literacy Perspectives* (1989) and *Basic Skills for the Workplace* (1991), co-edited with Maurice C. Taylor.

Maurice C. Taylor

As an associate professor at the University of Ottawa, Faculty of Education, Department of Educational Studies, he teaches and supervises graduate students in adult education. During his twelve year tenure with the Adult Basic Education Department of Algonquin College of Applied Arts and Technology, he coordinated the bilingual tutorial literacy program and taught in many of the adult upgrading and college preparation programs. In addition, he has instructed life skills, remedial education, and supervised adult work placements in various basic employment and re-entry programs.

As well as working on projects with the Literacy Branch of the Ontario Ministry of Education in the areas of occupational literacy and a job-related curriculum for colleges, he has participated in national colloquia on skill development and immigration landings, and in the capacity of principle investigator conducted several applied research projects with the National Literacy Secretariat, Department of Multiculturalism and Citizenship Canada. His publications include numerous articles and reports on adult basic education and he is currently chair of a joint Canadian, United Kingdom and Germany youth literacy study. He co-edited *Adult Literacy Perspectives* and *Basic Skills for the Workplace*.

Case study authors

Hélène Blais, La Salle Quebec

Écrivaine, professeure et chercheure, Ph.D. en sémiologie, Hélène Blais travaille dans le milieu de l'alphabétisation des adultes depuis 1980. Elle s'intéresse particulièrement à l'écriture des allographes (ces analphabétes «transformés»), comme moyen d'expression et de libération de leur parole tenue à l'écart, pour aider les adultes qui s'alphabétisent à migrer de l'analphabétisme vers l'allographie.

Richard Darville, Ottawa Ontario

Richard has worked in adult literacy for over 15 years and has taught literacy in community college and prison classrooms. He has been active in practitioners' organizations, and is a past president of the Movement for Canadian Literacy. Currently he is a faculty member in the Department of Linguistics, Carlton University in Ottawa. Before that he worked at the University of British Columbia Centre for Policy Studies in Education, where he wrote extensively on literacy and managerial policy as well as popular conceptions and practices of literacy.

Sheila Goldgrab, Toronto Ontario

She was the project coordinator for the provincial and national studies on issues in adult literacy, both completed in 1991. Prior to that, under contract with the Ontario Ministry of Labour, she recommended communication strategies to increase the awareness of the pay equity legislation among non-unionized women. She has also worked as a researcher for the Centre for Industrial Relations, University of Toronto. Currently, Sheila is doing workshops on the psychosocial and cultural influences of the medical rehabilitation of injured workers, and writing a clear language guide for health practitioners. Somehow she also finds time to pursue a master's degree in adult education at OISE, University of Toronto.

Mary Norton, Edmonton Alberta

Mary Norton has worked in the adult literacy field for about 14 years, as a consultant, tutor, and researcher / writer. She has developed and presented workshops and courses for literacy workers and learners, and has written literacy development materials. She is currently the coordinator of the Learning Centre literacy program in Edmonton.

Tom Walker, Vancouver British Columbia

Tom is a freelance writer and researcher who specializes in educational and social policy issues. He has collaborated with Richard Darville on literacy policy reports for the British Columbia Provincial Literacy Advisory Committee and for the Canadian Council of Ministers of Education. He has also taught a Literacy Instruction Methods course at Simon Fraser University, both on campus and at the Mountain Correctional Institution.

Marion Wells, Saint John New Brunswick

Marion was on the development team of the Saint John Learning Exchange in 1983 and has been executive director of the Exchange since 1984. She has worked on numerous committees and boards concerned with literacy and adult education and is the in-coming president of the New Brunswick Committee on Literacy, which is a provincial, multi-sector advocacy group.

Section One

FOUNDATIONS OF LITERACY

Chapter One

LOOKING AT PHILOSOPHIES FOR LITERACY EDUCATION

James A. Draper

Why should we consider philosophy?

A discussion of our philosophy of literacy practice is more than an academic exercise. We may not be conscious of it but each day we live our philosophy. Philosophy encompasses the principles, values and attitudes that structure our beliefs and guide our behaviours, in our work as well as in the whole of our daily life.

But to what extent do we articulate and understand these values, assumptions, beliefs and attitudes which guide us? A number of case studies in this book do explicitly state their philosophy of practice but whether stated or not, all of them imply an underlying philosophy. Our individual or collective philosophies are the basis upon which we defend and practice what we do. The way in which we perceive and deal with issues are determined by our philosophy.

Many questions which practitioners ask challenge their beliefs. For example:

- On what basis do we argue that one teaching method is preferred over another?

• Why do we believe that developing curriculum materials with the involvement of students, is better than the development of textbooks written by experts?
• Why does the criteria for evaluating our literacy programs, imposed upon us by a funding agency, sometimes conflict with our feelings of how our student-centred program should be evaluated?
• What determines the type of relationships we wish to develop between tutors and students? Between our agency and its surrounding community?
• In our training programs, what determines what we will teach?
• What criteria do we use and what qualifications do we look for when selecting volunteers to work in our programs?
• What determines the words we use to describe our programs?

What this chapter is about

This chapter begins by looking at how our behaviour raises philosophical questions and encourages us to reflect on and articulate our personal philosophy. And how it is expressed in our work.

This is followed by a description and discussion of five general philosophical orientations, all of which are evident in the broad field of adult literacy education: liberal, behaviourist, progressive, humanist and radical. The relevance and practice of these in literacy education is then illustrated. The next section discusses how our values as educators are expressed in our daily behaviour and language. The importance of language and the need to take our words seriously follows. Finally, we see that values and assumptions are integral to the way in which we plan, implement and evaluate our literacy programs, and in the way we distinguish between education and 'learning'.

What do we mean when we talk about philosophy?

It is a human tendency to feel that what we do is rational, that there are reasonable explanations for our behaviour, that we are right in what we think and do. We do not usually articulate these feelings. We just take them for granted. Our philosophy of life, those beliefs and values which guide us in our work and our relationships with others, are an integral part of our identity that we seldom question. But can they also limit our perceptions? Are there other views to listen to and benefit from? Are the assumptions we make about the educational needs of others really a projection of our own values? How do we know?

All of these are philosophical questions. Being able to answer these and many other questions helps us to understand and implement the literacy programs in which we are involved, including the identification of training needs, curriculum planning, delivery, evaluation and selecting teaching materials. Philosophy affects them all. But how?

The *Random House Dictionary* defines philosophy as "a system of principles for guidance in practical affairs; the rational investigation of the truths and principles of being, knowledge, or conduct." Articulating our personal philosophy helps us to understand why we behave and think the way we do.

Furthermore, it helps us to understand the consequences of our behaviour and the influence our philosophy has upon others, such as those we come in contact with through the educational programs in which we are involved. It helps us to be consistent but also challenges us to question our inconsistency. It can help us in communicating with others, providing we take care to openly express our values and assumptions. It may help us defend our actions: "I use this teaching approach because it expresses the philosophy I believe in."

Being able to articulate our preferred philosophy also helps us to be more professional as adult educators. That is, it helps us to describe our behaviour from a thoughtful and theoretical point of view. The generalist practitioner is often only able to describe what is done, not why. Understanding the Why illuminates our practice.

Articulating our beliefs and values also helps us to bridge theory and practice; to more clearly see the relationship between education and society, and the various social, economic, political and cultural forces which influence education. Our philosophy influences our practice, and practice illuminates our philosophy. Rooted in our individual history and the history of our society, our philosophy is always personal yet it identifies us as members of a group. Focusing on our explicit beliefs helps us to both utilize and create knowledge, especially when we are open to the beliefs of others.

The following section describes five philosophical orientations, all of which are evident in the field of literacy. The reader is also advised to refer to the table which compares these approaches.

Labelling our Philosophies

In their book, *Philosophical Foundations of Adult Education*, Elias and Merriam (1984) discuss five philosophies: liberal, behaviourist, progressive, humanist, and radical. What follows is a brief description and comparison of each and their link to literacy education.

Looking at a liberal philosophy

Arising out of early Greek thinking, the purpose of liberal education was to develop a person's intellect and morals (the distinction between right and wrong) and to develop the ability to make wise judgements. The intent was to liberalize the human spirit through the development of rational and critical thinking capacities. This is still the intent of liberal arts programs in universities today. The student was usually guided by an authority figure, a teacher who was conversant with the content. Being teacher-centred, the dominant teaching method was the lecture. The liberal tradition was intended to be a discovery of the self with external assistance, and what a person learned was expected to be reflected in their everyday life. The early history of Western literacy education for instance, often had a moral overtone, focusing on the reading of the holy scriptures.

The relevance of this orientation to literacy programs is the value which it places on the quality of the "philosophical" content which is being read, presenting to the reader new and relevant ideas which often go beyond the classroom. The liberal tradition attempts to teach people to think, to reason, to question, and to engage in timeless reflections and discussions about justice, truth and goodness.

Looking at behaviourist philosophy

Growing out of the stimulus-response work of B.F. Skinner and others, this philosophical orientation aims to change behaviour in the direction of pre-determined stated objectives. The goal of behaviour modification or conditioning is teacher-directed and teacher-rewarded.

The student is led through a sequencing of learning modules toward an ultimate goal which can be measured. Competency based training is a prime example of this philosophical orientation, where the outcome and the means for reaching it are pre-programed. Reaching this end goal is all important. This philosophical orientation is sometimes criticized since the student gives up a degree of freedom, putting himself or herself in the hands of another person in order to reach a pre-determined goal which, it is presumed, has some value to the student. While the student and the teacher enter into a kind of contract with one another, this task-oriented approach to education often ignores the previous experiences of the student and the choices of learner response may be limited.

This approach to education is practised in many traditional literacy programs where, for example, the student's goal is to prepare for an examination leading to a formal certification or where one is taught to master specific sequentially arranged skills such as learning to use a computer.

Looking at progressive philosophy

Beginning in the early part of this century, this philosophy grew out of a socio-political North American context characterized by: industrialization, utilitarian values, the expansion of vocational training, capitalism, citizenship and language training of new immigrants, as well as the increasing predominance of the scientific method and rational thinking (left brain) in objectively explaining human behaviour. These values were reflected in the public schools which were often isolated from the daily life of the community and characterized by an authoritarian approach to education, focusing on facts and memorization.

A reaction against this was an attempt to progress towards education which would introduce new attitudes, ideas and teaching methods. The intention was to free students to value the experiences they already had; to make education relevant and applicable by developing skills of problem solving and by using a scientific method to discover knowledge through field trips and projects. The teacher became the organizer and guide. Education became more democratized and more focused on the pragmatic, and was seen to be both experimental as well as experiential.

This progressive approach had a profound influence on the practice and theory of adult education. Experiences were valued and encouraged. Participation in one's own learning, with degrees of control over what is learned, and the idea of human developmental potential took on a new depth of meaning.

This philosophy also helped to raise questions about the social responsibility of institutions such as schools and private industry. Beginning with an assessment of learner's needs, this approach to education was seen as an instrument of social change. Much of the spirit and practice of this progressive philosophical approach is seen today in many literacy programs, especially those which are community based.

Looking at humanist philosophy

The progressive philosophy focused on the social context of individuals and their ability to promote social change. The humanist philosophy differed because it focused on personal growth and self actualization. It arose out of an 18th century reaction against the authority of traditional institutions and the anonymity of industrialization which was thought to dehumanize the individual. Viewing individuals holistically, humanistic philosophy valued the intrinsic, intuitive (right brain), ethical sense of people and their willingness and ability to take responsibility for their own learning through a process of self-direction, self-evaluation and self-actualization.

With a view that each individual is a universe, this approach focused on encouraging people to explore the depths of their feelings, building self-concept, and valuing each human life. The goal was to maximize the human potential, building on the innate goodness of the individual, with the support of empathetic teachers as facilitators and partners in learning who were themselves on the quest of self-discovery. This philosophy is especially evident in literacy programs today which value learning as a process (see Barer-Stein's chapter) and which encourage discussion and self-discovery.

Looking at radical philosophy

Based initially on Marxist-socialist ideas, the radical educational philosophy sets out to produce free and autonomous persons by liberating them from their oppression. The first step is to 'raise their consciousness' about their daily life experiences. In doing so, people describe their 'world' (their community and surroundings), exposing those forces which they believe prevent them from reaching their potential. To free themselves from oppressive elements, it is important for people to discuss these elements in groups.

First they articulate and critically examine their world (for example their workplace), then they plan actions to gain greater control (power) over their lives, thus changing the system which they believe to be the cause of their oppression. Being involved in the process of change provides people with a shared vocabulary which can become the basis for the content of their own literacy education (for example the words they use to read and write).

The radical philosophy more than any of the other orientations, acknowledges that the process described above is a political one. The goal is to change the power relationships between individuals and groups.

Groups which gather to discuss their social issues are examples of this philosophical orientation and out of this process people may realize the need to develop their literacy skills. On the other hand, literacy programs are sometimes used to bring people together to discuss political and economic issues and literacy becomes a secondary focus. This philosophy attempts to democratize and humanize society by questioning its assumptions and myths. The process is often guided by a participating facilitator-teacher. Dialogue and the development of a critical consciousness are essential elements in the process. Improving the quality of life and extending the choices in people's lives is another goal.

This philosophy is one that is frequently misunderstood in both its interpretation and application. Too often people think of this as a method only and not as a philosophy. In fact, it is both. One can practice radical philosophy in any human situation, for example, in examining the sources and form of power in one's family or one's workplace. Depending on the tolerance level of those who have power, this process can lead to mutually constructive and peaceful changes, which in themselves may extend the tolerance for change.

The radical philosophy makes reference to the 'colonizing of the mind' which refers to the labels which are often used to describe people, such as troublesome, inferior, unintelligent, lazy, immoral, stupid. These labels are frequently internalized by those who are labelled, often resulting in negative self-concepts. Sadly, there are all too many examples of the dehumanizing effect of blaming the victim, of labelling people who are on welfare, illiterate, unemployed, poor or disabled. We are reminded that often the first task of an educational program is to begin, not with the teaching of content or skills but to focus on eliminating negative internalized labels, in order to revive individual self-esteem and dignity. Only then can education provide an open door to learning.

Philosophically where do we stand?

Given the above descriptions of the five philosophical orientations applicable to education, an instructor in a literacy program might begin by asking which one best describes my approach to education? "Do the methods I use in my work match with what I say I am doing?

A similar question can be posed as well for the employers, planners and managers who are associated with these programs. Quite naturally, these persons may see themselves in more than one of the philosophical orientations, depending on the context in which they are working. "Sometimes I do things this way but at other times another approach seems more appropriate."

In practice there are seldom clear and rigid boundaries between them. It becomes obvious that the application of these philosophies are situational, often determined by educational goals (which may conflict with each other), the resources and time available, and especially by the content, skills or attitudes to be learned. The comparative value of the five orientations can be useful to those responsible for the different parts of an educational program. Each orientation is determined by the purposes to be achieved. As one can see from the following table, there are specific expectations of students and teachers in each orientation. Each is also characterized by predominant methods for teaching and learning and is described by key concepts.

Understanding our own philosophical orientation

In an attempt to understand the essence of each philosophical orientation and as a way of assessing one's own teaching philosophy, the literacy educator might ask:

- What is the role of social change in each orientation?
- Does our philosophy focus on perpetuating the status quo or in bringing about constructive change? Change from whose point of view and to what ends?
- Does the literacy program value experiential learning, questioning and exploration, and the interaction with others in working toward the achievement of educational goals?
- Are these processes stated explicitly as intended outcomes of the program? Or is the program focused on the achievement of pre-determined end goals, such as in a behaviourist philosophy? Or both?
- How is the individual (as compared with the group) valued in the program? Is the focus of the program on individuals competing with each other or are individuals encouraged to interact, share, cooperate and support each other in their learning?
- Is individual learning assessed consistently with the stated goals of the educational program? Is the evaluation done by the student or by an authority figure? Or is evaluation a cooperative effort?
- Finally, is the program built on a model which Barer-Stein (see *Learning about Learning*) calls Rote Internalizing as compared with Reflective Internalizing? That is, are individuals expected to learn solely through rote memorizing, (expected to repeat what has been presented to them) or are they encouraged to submit their accumulated learning to a process of personal and critical reflection?

Gaining a familiarity with the alternative philosophies, educators can understand more clearly what they are doing and why. They may become more aware of and

Table I

	LIBERAL	BEHAVIOURIST
PURPOSE	To develop intellectual powers of the mind; make a person literate in the broadest sense — intellectually, morally, spiritually, aesthetically.	To bring about behaviour that will promote behavioural change through predetermined objectives.
STUDENT	A cultured continuous learner who seeks theoretical understanding and knowledge rather than just information.	Learner takes an active role in learning, practicing new behaviour and receiving feedback; strong environmental influence.
TEACHER	The expert; transmitter of knowledge; an authority who clearly directs learning process.	Manager; controller; predicts and directs learning outcomes.
KEYWORDS / CONCEPTS	Learning for its own sake; rational, general intellectual education; traditional knowledge.	Stimulus-response; behaviour modification; competency-based; mastery learning; behavioural objectives; feedback; reinforcement.
METHODS	Dialectic; lecture; study groups; critical reading and discussion; contemplation.	Programed instruction; contract learning; teaching machines; computer-assisted instruction; practice and reinforcement.

Summary Chart of Philosophical Orientations in Adult Education

PROGRESSIVE	HUMANISTIC	RADICAL
To transmit culture and societal structure; promote social changes; give practical knowledge, problem solving skills.	To enhance personal growth and development, self-actualization.	Through education, to bring about radical social, political and economic changes in society.
Learner needs, interests and experience key elements in learning. People have unlimited potential to be developed through education.	Learner is highly motivated and self-directed; assumes responsibility for learning.	Equality with teacher in learning process; personal autonomy enhanced; people create history and culture by combining reflection with action.
Organizer; guides learning through experiences that are educative; stimulates, helps to evaluate.	Facilitator; helper; partner; promote but does not direct learning;	Coordinator; suggests but does not determine direction for learning; equality between teacher and learner.
Problem-solving; experience based education; lifelong learning; pragmatic knowledge; social responsibility; needs assessment.	Experiential learning; freedom; individuality; self-directed; cooperation; authenticity; feelings; holistic.	Consciousness-raising; noncompulsory learning; autonomy; critical thinking; social action; deinstitutionalization; political.
Problem-solving; scientific method; activity method; experimental method; project method; inductive method.	Experiential; group discussion; group tasks; team teaching; self-directed learning; individualized learning; discovery method.	Dialogue; problem-solving; maximum interaction; discussion groups.

value alternative approaches to planning educational programs. If nothing more, an awareness of these orientations
might minimize contradictions while at the same time clarify
goals and outcomes of a program. Each philosophical orientation has its place within the rich diversity of educational
practice. With experience, the educator will know when to
use a particular method or practice a particular philosophy.

Sometimes it might seem that there is a contradiction
between a person's general philosophical approach to literacy teaching (which may be humanistic) and the need to
apply a different philosophical approach (behaviouristic) for
a particular situation. Sometimes short term goals such as
acquiring basic knowledge and preliminary skills can be
achieved best through "behavioural objectives" yet the long
term goal may well be to make use of those acquired skills in
creative ways.

Being flexible is more important than rigid adherence to
a particular philosophy or method. The effective educator
is able to orchestrate all the variables of a literacy program
without losing sight of the overall goal of holistic human
development.

The Importance of Language in Expressing a Philosophy

A philosophy is expressed through people's attitudes and
behaviour but also through the language which they use to
describe what they do. Is the practitioner's language gen-
uine? That is, are current terminologies being used but neither understood nor practiced? For example, it is relatively
easy to use current terminology, such as "learner centred" or
"community based" or "self directed learning" without
really knowing the meaning of these terms or the implications of practising them. The words used by the radical
philosophical orientation, words like "power", "social
change", and "critical consciousness" are in vogue today but
are they understood in the context of local action?

A literacy program might encourage its participants to
become more self-directing, to offer their suggestions on
how things might be done differently, to value and encourage creativity (which begins with constructive criticism
about how things are currently done), and to build a "team
environment". The achievement of such goals exposes the

power and political relationships between people and nurtures individual critical faculties, helping to bring about degrees of social change.

Each philosophical orientation has key words that describe its main focus. For example, what are the different meanings of such words as facilitator, teacher, guide and tutor? In addition to speaking of power, cultural identity and revolution — Botkin, Elmandjra and Malitza (1979) speak of anticipation and participation as the basis for a conceptual framework for innovative learning processes, and talk about "Liberation of the Fifth World Literacy". Note again the words which are being used. Critically examining the words we use is more than a matter of semantics.

Much of the vocabulary used today in adult literacy is now taken for granted. Some has been rediscovered from past usage and some has come from a radical philosophy within a Third World or developing nations context. For example we speak of equity and justice as the real end goals of literacy. Value laden words such as freedom, exploitation, struggle are also used. Illiteracy may be seen as a form of violence or oppression. The end goal of literacy education may be the empowerment of the individual or literacy may be seen as a synonym for self-reliance, for liberation, for independence. Although seldom stated explicitly, all educational programs are expressions of an ideology, a philosophy, a value system, and a kind of vision.

From the language we use and from the goals we develop, we can speak of generic and philosophical goals for literacy education. In an educational program, we know that not only content and subject-matter are being taught. We know that adult students are also reacting to the environment within which the program is taking place. They are also developing attitudes about the subject matter, reacting to the teaching methods being used and becoming aware of how they are perceived and treated.

A generic approach to literacy training and teaching

In the midst of this discussion of philosophical stances in literacy education, it may be useful to pause and describe some generic approaches and goals:

- the development of communication skills of listening,

speaking and writing
- the valuing of learning as a life-long process
- the development of skills to retrieve and store information
- the building of positive attitudes about oneself as well as developing the skills of critical thinking

The practitioner needs to consciously teach for these goals. They will not automatically come about. All too often the absence of an articulated philosophy tends to narrow rather than broaden the stated goals of education. Referring again to the chart and comparing the different approaches to education, the literacy practitioner can imagine:

- Perceiving the student learner as one who is dependent on others for direction compared to one who is interdependent/independent and self-directing;
- An educational program which is subject-matter centred compared to one which is task, problem or self-centred;
- A program which students enter because of external or imposed forces as compared with one in which the student voluntarily and enthusiastically participates;
- A program which has been planned by an authority figure or expert, such as a teacher specialist, as compared with one in which the planning is democratized and includes wide participation, including the involvement of the intended students in the program.

Which philosophy does your program portray? How does one balance short term and long term goals? An educator's philosophy of teaching and learning can be enhanced by being more precise with the vocabulary we use to describe what we do. A precision based on our own clear understanding.

Improving Teaching Practice: Education versus Learning

In the attempt to improve literacy teaching practice, it is also important for practitioners to be more precise about the meaning a person gives for 'education' and 'learning'. Learning can be seen as the process whereby we interact with and absorb from our environment. Education can be referred to as a process of organizing or planning for learning to happen. Education is intentional learning. Barer-Stein (1985) (also see *Learning about Learning*) refers to education as the "providing of support and resources for learning." Learning, she notes, is "the partaking of opportunities for extending and enhancing what one already knows."

A literacy program is only one of many places that provide the opportunity for learning. We know that learning is personal, complex and dynamic and a part of daily living. It is important for educators and others to know something about education and learning in order to be more effective in planning and implementing educational programs — for others and for themselves.

Concluding Comments

By re-examining their statements of goals and strategies, literacy planners, policy-makers, educators and administrators can present themselves as learners, engaging in a process of self-growth.

> The choice of [philosophies] shapes our thinking about the issues of the strategy, the tactics and the logistics of adult education. To which of the philosophical systems otherwise expounded in our country shall we commit ourselves? (Kallen, 1962:34)

This chapter has emphasized how all aspects of an educational program are influenced by one's philosophical orientation. Literacy education has often focused on the learning of specific skills for specific immediate purposes. There is now a trend from a narrow focus on skills training to a broader focus on education towards human development.

Literacy case studies vary in their philosophies

Within this book, each of the case studies expresses a dominant or a combination of philosophies. For example, a learner-centered (essentially humanist) approach to education is expressed in such case studies as *Collaborative Learning and Times of Change* by Marion Wells and *Native People Regaining Control* by Sheila Goldgrab. The latter study also expresses the belief that education which goes beyond literacy is an example of a holistic (also humanistic) approach to education. The case study *Training Literacy Practitioners* by Mary Norton points out that a strong community-based (essentially progressive), learner-centred philosophy of literacy development is used in this program and that these values were nurtured over a number of years. The words used in the titles of other case studies illustrate different value orientations, such words as: sharing power and authority (radical), active student participation (humanistic-progressive), collaboration in workplace literacy and peer tutoring. The words which are used are important clues to the philosophical stance of an educational program and becomes the basis upon which the program is to be assessed.

An important point which needs to be made is that the intention of reflecting on our personal philosophy (or that prescribed by the programs with which we are associated) is not to attach labels. Few if any of the five philosophical orientations cited in this chapter will be ideally practiced. We need to accept that our behaviour usually reflects characteristics of more than one orientation. As educators it is important to be aware of the alternatives. Education is a concept which goes beyond the learning of only skills, but views individual learning more holistically. Such a view also acknowledges that what is learned in literacy classes may (should) stimulate further learning outside of these classes and vice versa.

A discussion on a philosophy of education in literacy education applies to all those in the program. The focus is not just on those that need literacy but to all others in the program, since all are learners. Cross (1981:227) makes this point by saying that "...if an educator wants to know how to help a learner learn, he needs to know how teachers should behave in order to facilitate learning".

What philosophical statements exist in your program which enhance the continuing education of tutors? As literacy becomes a specialized focus within the broader field of adult education, there is a need to extend the specialized body of knowledge in this field, based on research, experience and reflection. As always, theory and practice complement each other and extend the meaning and understanding of practice.

The need for a dialogue on philosophy

A number of questions further help to focus on the need for a dialogue on philosophy. For example, how do we account for differing cultures which provide differing orientations, differing perspectives and perhaps differing philosophies in any organization and in any classroom? (see Barer-Stein, 1988) Where is the place of the tutor as learner in the educational program? Is literacy education to focus only on learning immediate skills or does it include goals which help people become more socially responsible and more critically reflective? Does our educational philosophy help people to reflect on possibilities and to make choices?

There are a number of things that we do know. We know that education is not a neutral enterprise but involves both political and philosophical decisions. We know that our philosophy influences all aspects of an educational program from its original inception to the methods we use in teaching and the way we evaluate. We know that particular philosophies, based on particular assumptions about human nature, can help to democratize a literacy program and society. Also, we know that there needs to be a compatibility of management and infrastructure with the philosophy which we expound and want to emulate in the classroom.

We know that our philosophy, like culture and values, is learned. Our philosophy may encourage us to seek partnerships with student learners, with the community, and with other organizations. Or it may encourage us to remain closed.We know also that the forces which influence our behaviours are real and may conflict with our preferred way of behaving. For example a funding agency may impose a quantitative model of evaluation upon a literacy program which values qualitative outcomes of learning. Similarly, within a given organization, policies may be incompatible with the philosophy of a workplace education program. How do we philosophically handle these and other contradictions?

Finally, we know that our philosophy is an expression of an ideology. All of the case studies in this book express, in one form or another, particular ideologies, beliefs, values and principles (see Taylor's *Understanding the Principles Guiding our Practice*). But we have a tendency to take these for granted. We need to rethink the meaning of literacy (Draper

1986) and to pause, reflect on, and articulate our philosophies. By understanding our values we maximize the rationality of our behaviour. Our philosophy is the foundation upon which we act. These are the rudders which steer us through our daily life and which determine how we will teach and behave in countless other ways. A philosophy is not a theoretical thing that other people have. It is the understanding which provides meaning for each individual.

Notes

1. This section has been adapted from _Basic Skills for the Workplace._ Maurice C. Taylor, Glenda R. Lewe and James A. Draper (eds) Toronto: Culture Concepts Inc., 1991.

Chapter Two

UNDERSTANDING THE PRINCIPLES GUIDING OUR LITERACY PRACTICE

Maurice C. Taylor

The quality of literacy services

In the last few years there has been a great interest in adult literacy as the realization grows that knowledgeable adults are key to the social and economic success of our country. As a result of regional public awareness campaigns, attention has tended to focus on the number of adult illiterates, the number of programs and the number of people in those programs. However, numbers are not enough. In building on this information we must now shift our attention to the effectiveness and quality of the literacy services that we provide.

We need to be asking questions like: How has a community been strengthened as a result of literacy services? What works in encouraging active student participation? How is language, culture and literacy connected? What can the workplace offer in meeting the needs of adult learners? These types of questions move us toward a clearer understanding of how best to support adult learners in attaining literacy skills.

One approach that is showing some promise is to document ways through which practitioners in adult literacy and basic education perceive and deal with issues that characterize the field. And in a similar vein is the important link between the way people grapple with issues and the connection of those issues to some of the guiding principles of adult education. The integration of these two avenues of inquiry may shed some light as we begin the search for answers to help move us along the path to greater effectiveness.

What this chapter is about

The purpose of this chapter is to link the actual literacy practice currently in motion with some of the well-founded principles in adult education. Based on the seminal work by Brundage and Mackeracher (1980) entitled *Adult Learning Principles and Their Application to Program Planning*, this chapter will demonstrate how various literacy issues can be understood through a prismatic frame of adult learning principles. Since learning occurs not only as a result of the student's activities but also as a result of the interactivity between instructor and student, this chapter is divided into two parts.

The first section *Characteristics of Adult Learners*, discusses the salient characteristics of the adult literacy student especially those of self-concept, the role of past experiences and learning styles. Under each characteristic a brief statement is made which includes its importance to literacy practice, an adult learning principle which is inherent in the characteristic, and a description of events in two case studies (presented in this publication) illustrating that particular learning principle.

In the second section *Characteristics of the Learning Situation*, three variables are chosen for discussion: teaching behaviours, the design of the teaching process and characteristics of the teacher of adult students. Although the characteristics chosen for this chapter are certainly not exhaustive, they are intended to give practitioners a sense of what we do that works and why.

Characteristics of adult learners

About self-concept and self-esteem

Most educators would agree that how adults interpret perceived feedback both from within themselves and from others defines the self. As this information is interpreted it involves both cognitive and emotional elements. The cognitive element of the individual's description of himself or herself is often referred to as the self-concept. And the way the individual feels about himself or herself in comparison with others or the emotional element is usually called the self-esteem. The knowing or cognitive element then, is called self-concept, while the feeling or affective element is called self-esteem. Both of these personality dimensions play an important role in terms of learning especially for literacy students. As Brundage and Mackeracher suggest:

> Adults learn best in environments which reduce potential threat to their self-concept and self-esteem and which provide support for change.

In the case study *Psychiatric Patients in London Psychiatric Hospital's Literacy Programs and Their Preparation for Independent Living*, students often entered the sequenced literacy programs with a very low self-esteem. Adult students usually had a combination of psychiatric problems, social skill problems, anxiety and a lack of education. But one of the factors that contributed to the success of the small groups literacy class in the hospital was the regular positive reinforcement given by tutors to encourage the students to think independently.

This constant building of the self-concept was set in a classroom environment where blackboards, desks, quiet time, discussion and individual attention worked positively to convey a clear message of what was expected from the student. The small size of the group and the individual attention given to the learners helped alleviate their fear of failure and increase their ability to think positively.

Another learning principle associated with self-concept that is mentioned by Brundage and Mackeracher is that:

> Adults react to learning experiences or information as they perceive it, not as the instructor presents it.

This principle is related to the notion that adults have already developed organized ways of focusing on, taking in and processing information. These qualities are sometimes referred to as cognitive style and are often assumed to remain relatively constant and consistent throughout adulthood. Connected to this is the fact that if an adult thinks that formal learning is only for children, he or she will likely not participate in formal learning activities.

An example that illustrates this notion can be found in the case study *Collaboration in Workplace Literacy: The Vancouver Municipal Workplace Language Training Program*. In conducting a five-week needs assessment which resulted in the learner-centred workplace language literacy program, the project consultant realised how earlier efforts to set up a program had been unsuccessful. Part of the reason for this lack of success was that students had been sent to a private training company with computerized assisted instruction and found the training patronizing. They had felt like children dealing with cartoons and had difficulty taking ownership of the learning activities. Although this type of instruction has proven to be valuable in other literacy settings, here the students perceived the learning experiences very differently than had been anticipated.

Effects of adults' past experiences

Adults who participate in basic skills training bring to the program the pragmatic experiences of life. They have developed ways of perceiving and understanding their daily life experiences and have a well organized set of personal meanings and values. Past experiences act as a frame and help to structure the ways in which an adult will approach new experiences. This reservoir determines what information will be selected for further attention and how it will be interpreted. In discussing the learning principle related to past experience, Brundage and Mackeracher mention that:

> The past experience of adult learners must be acknowledged as an active component in learning and respected as a potential resource for learning.

A good example of this learning principle in a literacy setting can be found in *Promoting Language, Literacy and Culture in an Arctic Community*. In this setting an attempt was made to develop a literacy program for aboriginal students based on an English tutor-based model. However, this met with limited success. One of the reasons for lack of participation in the program was due to the inadequacy of printed resource materials related to the local Inuktitut community.

In a second attempt the coordinator decided that activities which incorporated the learner's experience were a key component of the program, and initiated an elders' syllabic writing project. By going around visiting the elders and recording what they had to say and later transcribing the stories, songs and rhymes, these materials then became available for the community and served as a foundation for the instructional material for the program. In other words, adult learning was facilitated when the student's representation and interpretation of personal experience was accepted as valid and acknowledged as an essential aspect influencing change in the Inuktitut community.

The focus of adult learning

In a similar vein, Brundage and Mackeracher explain that:

> Adult learning focuses largely on transforming meanings, values, strategies and skills derived from past experience. This process requires more energy and more time than learning based on the formation of new learnings.

For example, many adults cannot perceive connections between past experiences and current problems. They only see some parts of past experience as relevant. And in such instances, it is important to develop learning strategies that will help the student reinterpret the experience in new connections. The case study *Promoting the March of Words Around a Lake and on the River Banks: Literacy Training in the County of Roberval and Sept-Isles* (pages XXX) illustrates this principle.

In providing literacy services to native people, it is important to remember that these learners have kept their traditional life styles and view the reservation as an artificial habitation. It is this dual style of living which at times impedes the connection between past experiences and current problems . Also related to this is the belief that native people have a different approach to learning in relation to non-native people. For example, the concept of time for native people does not hold the same value as it does for other groups of people. Therefore, in helping native literacy students to make the connections to past experience, one must be receptive to their differing time frames and their style of living which follows the natural seasonal rhythms. Such cultural sensitivity should be extended to all students.

About learning styles

One of the popular themes in the adult education literature is on how adults learn. Much has been written on topics like how adults take in information, or select certain information for further processing or to create new meanings. Some of these topics relate to the notion of learning style. A style is the preferred way an individual organizes experiences and a learning style is the individual way of changing meaning, values, skills and strategies. Over the years much debate has ensued as to how constant learning styles and preferences are during adulthood. This discussion continues. One of the reasons why this characteristic is so important to literacy instruction is that it is a trait which could affect everything else the individual does in the learning process. Brundage and Mackeracher maintain that:

> Adult learners each have an individualistic learning style for affecting change in their behaviour and an individualistic cognitive style for processing information.

A case in point is *The Preservation of the Franco-Ontarian Language and Culture*. What the reader finds in this case study is a description of the program Le Centre d'Alphabétisation de Prescott, and a wide variety of activities. Each facilitates a different cognitive style.

For example, recovering the franco-Ontarian popular history through story-telling or discussing the regional educational and economic developments, or taking action to meet with a member of Parliament to understand the national issues all provide different and effective ways for adults to learn. And as illustrated throughout the case study, adult literacy students learned most productively when their learning styles matched those of the teacher.

Another general principle described by Brundage and Mackeracher that relates to learning style is that:

> Adults tend to be proficient at self-selecting those learning situations and teaching-learning interactions which

best enhance their own learning or cognitive style.

This ability seems connected to the fact that adults experience a need to learn quickly and to get back to their work, family activities and other responsibilities. In the case study *Literacy Training in the Workplace: Ensuring the Future of Bread Winner* a program was designed to provide employees of a bakery with the skills required to function in a new factory equipped with the latest high technology. Since most of the recruits were older, with many years of work experience but little formal education, it was crucial to develop a program that could bridge aspects of their current work to the newer types of responsibilities.

As most of the students found the training program quite novel, the teaching-learning interactions were developed to provide the opportunity to review the skills and knowledge — that had perhaps been buried — with job specific tasks related to the new technology. In this way their learning style was connected to their working style. By designing learning activities such as understanding the basic operations of an electronic calculator, reading instructions in order to complete a task, understanding production plans and filling out production reports, trainers were allowed to discover the direct relationship between the learning situation and the new types of job tasks. Both the content and the process had an immediate and practical application to their life.

Characteristics of the learning situation

Looking at teaching behaviours

Information on how to teach adults is plentiful. Brundage and Mackeracher indicate that there appears to be three basic modes of teaching: directing, facilitating and collaborating. Each mode has advantages and disadvantages and is probably best viewed as parts in a continuum. As evidenced throughout this book literacy teachers use each mode in response to different situations.

Using the collaborating mode means that student and teacher share. They are co-learners in the discovery and creation of meanings, values, and skills. This mode seems to work best with material in which all co-learners have a stake and through which they can grow both individually and as members of a team. In other words, it is the best method for building a community of learners. With regard to teaching behaviours, Brundage and Mackeracher mention that:

> Adults learn most productively when the teaching mode matches their needs and preferred learning behaviours and styles.

A good illustration of this learning principle which depicts a collaborating teaching mode can be found in the case study *Outreach*. Providing effective literacy services to a wide range of students in a rural county is a constant challenge for programers.

One method that has received some success is the development of a mobile Family Literacy Unit.This mobile unit is able to travel to isolated meeting places to deliver services. Underlying the success of the program has been the collaborative teaching mode used by the educator. This mode seems to suit the goal of the program which is to empower the parents.

As well, through a collaborative mode parents experience their importance as deliverers of their own children's play and learning activities. By using this teaching mode the educator is able to encourage effective parent and child interaction to discover and to create new values and skills in the process of parents reading to children.

There is no one best teaching style

Another learning principle associated with teaching behaviours which Brundage and Mackeracher discuss is that:

> There is no best teaching style for use with adult learners. Each style is appropriate for some learners, in some settings and for some content.

In the case study *Tearing Down Paper Walls: Participants in Quebec City Open a Dialogue with Social Decision Makers* the reader will find the practice of the three teaching modes of directing, facilitating and collaborating. These modes have been used in varying combinations depending on the materials, the students and the setting of the learning activities.

Of particular interest in this case study is the closing conference for International Literacy Year called the *Grand Dialogue*. The purpose of the conference was to sensitize the general public to the literacy issues and to bring together students from different regions. What the reader finds is a rich example of the meaningful type of learning that can take place when exhibits, murals, mini plays, and collective writings are the products of the different teaching styles.

Each of these teaching modes in their own right have provided adults with the opportunities to propose concrete and practical solutions to better their lives.

Design of the teaching process: some models

Practitioners who are interested in reading the literature in adult education on methods for designing the processes through which a student can be assisted to learn would find a very wide range of articles. Brundage and Mackeracher have stated that much of the literature can be summarized into three basic types of models of teaching: information-processing models, programed learning and person-centred models. These models are not exclusive and tend to overlap in actual practice. They can be used in various combinations and can be adapted for group or individual learning.

The information-processing models focus on the cognitive dimension of learning. They assist the adult in acquiring and extending knowledge and in developing cognitive skills and strategies. Programed learning models assist students to acquire standardized knowledge or skills which are consistent with a set of expectations and objectives which can be evaluated according to specific criteria.

Person-centred models are most relevant to the affective dimension of learning and lead to attitude change, to an understanding and awareness of personal meanings and values and to changes in both self-concept and self-esteem.

In reading through this book the practitioner will discover numerous examples of these three models of teaching. For instance in the case study *Sharing Power and Authority: Student Control in a Community-Based Program* the reader will find the practice of a person-centred model. The objective of this type of teaching process is to facilitate the student's discovery and the creation of personal meaning and skills which are used to encourage further learning.

Within the process of a person-centred model, adults must already have some awareness of themselves and be able to focus on meanings and values through self-reflection. Such capacities are facilitated in an environment based on trust relationships as demonstrated in the board formation activities of trainees in the "Journeys" program. In that example, involvement on the board and within committees prompted learning and development in many areas of the student's lives.

In the process of preparing to interview potential staff, students learned how to review resumes, what to look for in applications, and how to plan and ask appropriate questions. Being involved in such procedures gives adults good practice on how to handle themselves in their own job interviews, expressing themselves more effectively, speaking directly to an issue rather than around it, and learning about the importance of listening.

Helping adults to comprehend learning relationships

Brundage and Mackeracher also explain that a learning principle relevant to personal meanings and values or the affective dimensions is that:

> The adult learner needs to be able to comprehend the various relationships between experience, persons, things, processes, concepts and strategies.

In the case study _Linking Literacy and Health: A Popular Education Approach_ the coordinator combined health education with English language and literacy practice in a Northwest territories Inuit community. Interesting to note was the identification of learning topics such as how to care for sick kids and how to help children learn which provided beginning readers with the links to previous experiences and strategies for problem solving. This type of teaching design allowed participants to become more comfortable in believing in their own abilities and in making decisions about the health of their children.

Characteristics of teachers of adults

In describing the basic characteristics of teachers of adults, there are several sets of characteristics that seem to be prevalent in the adult education literature. One group of characteristics is concerned with the teacher-student relationship. According to Brundage and Mackeracher, teachers need to be aware of their interpersonal style and skills and how these attributes affect students. Along with being empathetic, caring and understanding, the teacher must also value and respect the individual.

As well, the teacher needs to be committed to the learning of others and to be able to step aside to allow students to discover, to acquire, create and test out personal meanings, values, skills without imposing or demanding. In other words, a positive teacher-student relationship is facilitated by the teacher who is aware, accountable, committed, open and responsive to the student.

A good description of these various characteristics can be found in the case study _Peer Tutoring in the Classroom_. The teacher's role is described as a guide, coach and facilitator. She is not always someone with the answers. She is there to talk with students, explore strategies, and help set goals for the needs they have identified. She gives encouragement when a student is stuck or ready to quit. As a facilitator, she can learn something about how students overcome difficulties and share these with the class. As a co-learner in the instructional process, she is willing to give up the control and power that many teachers have in the classroom. Acting in this capacity she is better able to encourage the peer tutoring process and to empower the students to seek control of their own situation.

Another learning principle outlined by Brundage and Mackeracher that is related to the characteristics of the teachers of adults is:

> Adult learners require a teacher who has knowledge and expertise in both the subject area being taught and the teaching function.

As suggested by the authors, the teacher needs to be able to use a wide range of directing, facilitating and collaborating processes as well as to understand the characteristics and nature of adult students and to respond to individual styles and needs. As a teacher, the person needs to be able to guide both individual and group learning activities and to utilize several different models of teaching.

A good illustration of this learning principle can be found in the case study *Training Literacy Practitioners for Community-Based Settings.* In developing a three-level certificate program in response to practitioners' requests to work toward certification, the case study provides an account of how the trainer has responded to individual styles and needs using her subject-matter expertise. Being in a good position to know about emerging policy developments which may affect training, the instructor was able to deliver workshops to help practitioners develop listening strategies, to set boundaries and to develop awareness of referral networks. In addition, marrying her subject matter expertise with her teaching skills, she was able to help practitioners explore their own learning styles and methods to help their own students develop awareness about learning strategies.

Concluding Comments

Let's take a look at what has been described in this chapter. First, there appears to be a basic set of learning principles drawn from the knowledge base in adult education that can be applied to the on-going activity level in the literacy field. As perceived by literacy workers, there are certain issues that characterize our practice and how people grapple with these issues is directly related to a core set of adult learning principles which reflect guidelines towards particular goals, and that can be useful tools to help literacy practitioners move along the path to greater effectiveness. By describing what we do in the field and connecting it to some of these guidelines, we begin to understand the why behind our actions.

Secondly, there emerges from our practice a number of important generalizations. We know that learning basic skills is usually less difficult when learned in a real life situation. We know that the content of any kind of literacy service should be directly related to the student, the community and / or to labour market needs. We also know that developing partnerships with the various stakeholders helps to ensure that literacy services are responsive to the changes in the community and that adults are served as well as possible.

Indeed we have travelled many miles in the last decade — mobilizing, developing, involving, searching. Now by providing an opportunity for people in the field of basic education to reflect upon their concerns and see their links with the body of adult education principles, we can strengthen and improve our existing efforts.

Chapter Three
LEARNING ABOUT LEARNING

Thelma Barer-Stein

Sharing the literacy dream

Most literacy educators and literacy students share the same dream. They hope that the use of newly acquired literacy skills will eventually become as natural as breathing. As educators, we spend a lot of energy on the content and the goals of literacy programs but rarely concern ourselves with understanding the most important outcome of education which is learning.

- What do we really know about the steps of the literacy student's learning journey?
- What is that learner experiencing, what is that learner's perceptions of their own learning, and how can we help them?
- What draws them to learn, what holds them within a learning program, and what influences their lifelong curiosity to learn still more?
- And how can we become more effective in our own learning?

These are the questions that lie at the heart of all teaching and all education, not just literacy learning. These are the questions that tend to be shunted aside because they are too subjective, too personal and too difficult to answer. It is only when we recognise and accept that learning is an inner, personal experience that we see the validity and the necessity of understanding learning from the point of view of the learner, rather than from some researcher who is on the outside, so to speak, observing that learner.

In this chapter, we will look at how learning happens and what the learning process feels like from the learner's perception. But having revealed these steps, we will also include comments of observations from literacy tutors and practitioners as they observe and work with their students moving through these learning steps. In other words, what is different here is that we are going to go deeper than the usual discussion of learning styles and learning strategies to reveal and expose the underlying structure of individual learning steps that learning styles and strategies should be based upon.

All learning is influenced by past experiences and present emotions and concerns. The steps of the Learning Process, can be visualized as actual steps upon which the learner may move ahead or regress or sometimes remain fixed for a period of time. Above all, they are steps that reverberate with feelings. Here as we look at the steps of the Learning Process we will also keep in mind that we are all learners, whether we are reading this chapter as a student, a tutor, or a literacy administrator.

The 'Learning Process'

Learning as a Process of Experiencing the Unfamiliar is a universal structure of the human learning process that emerged from my own recent phenomenological research. In this work, I will refer to it as the Learning Process. It is 'universal' because it depicts the bare bones, so to speak, the underlying structure of any and all learning at any time, for any person. It is 'universal' in the same sense that our own bones are universally similar to the bones of all human beings anywhere in the world, although the surface details of what covers those bones certainly do differ and help to distinguish one person from another. Similarly all learning rests on the same underlying structural 'steps' that make up the Learning Process. What differs from one person to another, from one culture to another are the myriad of surface details.

What this chapter includes

In this chapter we are going to expose that underlying bare-bones structure of what learning is about, the 'steps' that each learner can choose to move upon, upward (progressing) or downward (regressing) or even jumping off (exiting). But here we are going to discuss that learning process structure with a special focus on the literacy learner: student and tutor.

In any program such as learning to be literate and numerate, each separate aspect to be learned becomes a separate learning process. Each of these separate but related learning processes proceed, or have the potential to proceed through the same "steps" that comprise the full Learning Process. It is this underlying structure of steps that I have named Learning as a Process of Experiencing the Unfamiliar. And each time we take the first step towards something unfamiliar, we are entering the steps of a process that has the potential to make the unfamiliar familiar, and even to make the unfamiliar habitual. I insist upon using the word "potential" because the learner usually has the choice of whether or not to proceed, and at what speed. (Timing between or on steps could be moments or years)

For example, learning to read involves much more than just learning about reading. That is to say that a person is not just engaged in the process of learning how to read, but they are also engaged in learning how to relate to their tutor, learning how to relate to other students, learning to fit this literacy learning into their previous experience, learning to develop their own confidence, and so on — to a hoped-for integration with their accumulated learning to date.

As complex as these many interwoven but separate Learning Processes are, each of us is engaged in countless such processes every day. Perhaps that is why we take this matter of learning for granted and seldom trouble to question just what is going on. Learning is happening all the time.

This chapter begins with a general exploration of some commonly asked questions about learning. This will be followed by a brief discussion of Learning: A Process of

Experiencing the Unfamiliar. Because it depicts the learner's viewpoint of learning, it provides a framework and a vocabulary to discuss learning. This Learning Process has been shared with tutors and literacy administrators as well as with many literacy students over several years and it has been extended through their thoughtful reflections and dialogues. In particular, Regina Muetze, a literacy tutor and administrator from Sudbury Ontario, followed my presentation of this process with her own case study of Becky (not her real name) a literacy student, in a workshop held in Toronto in 1991 for the Ontario Literacy Issues Study Group. The literacy tutors at that workshop saw themselves as learners too, and the comments they made as they looked at their own learning are condensed into a brief table.

A subsequent presentation of our joint work was given in a workshop for the International Reading Association's North American Conference on Adult and Adolescent Literacy, held in Banff, Alberta 1991. The responses from the Banff participants formed the basis for the literacy practitioner's comments on some implications of this Learning Process for literacy planning, teaching and evaluating, and these too are collected here. The chapter will conclude with some collected reflections on the importance of understanding learning from the learner's viewpoint in order to develop practical implications for students, tutors and administrators in literacy programs.

Becoming consciously aware of learning

Learning is what we do when we need to become more familiar with something.

Learning is also something that takes place almost subconsciously as we notice things in our daily life, find them useful and incorporate them as part of our common everyday doings. So learning can be planned and deliberate (formal learning) or it can be accumulated seemingly with little effort (informal learning or rote learning). It is this latter type of learning accumulation that we find so difficult to articulate to anyone else. Sometimes we call this our cultural learning: it is so much a part of us, so common and habitual that we are scarcely aware of knowing what we know.

Learning is what each of us have done all our lives and so it is not surprising that when we are asked to think about what learning is — like any other habitual practice — we are at a loss for words. It is so commonly a part of our daily life, we just do it. But only when we need to. Here, I am making a case for the critical importance of each of us becoming consciously aware of every possible aspect of this habitual practice of learning if only for the reason that such conscious awareness cannot help but impinge in an illuminating way on every aspect of what we do. But especially what we do as literacy educators.

It is only when we stop taking something for granted, that is, doing it without thinking about it, that we can then entertain some openness to critically examining it as a phenomenon and reflecting on what we find.

Trying to understand what learning is

Learning can be described as the personal need to acquire knowledge or skills differing from what we previously knew. Learning something — whether that learning seems negative or positive at the time — is always an extension to the learning we had previously acquired. It may seem obvious, but it is worth repeating some truisms about learning: People learn because they want to or need to. People learn what is personally relevant and retain the learning that is useful and meaningful for them. Learning is never really 'lost' nor can learning be 'unlearned'.

What is not of immediate importance to us becomes what I have called Submerged Knowledge. We can differentiate between Surface Knowledge and Submerged Knowledge. This latter forms part of our vast lifetime storehouse, sometimes only retrievable by a persistent deliberate effort to do so, and often only with the support of a Significant Resource who may be a friend or a therapist; Surface Knowledge includes knowledge that we have and can use without the effort of retrieval from deeply past accumulations.

Exploring some meanings of learning

Some of the confusion that exists about learning has to do with the fact that in our culture, learning can be both a noun and a verb. That is, learning can be a name and an action. In this chapter, we not only examine learning as something that can be acquired (noun) and something that we do (verb); but we also examine the process through which we do it and eventually acquire it. But first let's look briefly at these differing meanings of learning:

> LEARNING (noun): The attitudes, knowledge or skills acquired through informal experience or systematic study.
>
> LEARNING (verb): The action of acquiring attitudes, knowledge or skills through informal experience or systematic study.
>
> LEARNING PROCESS(noun): The steps through which attitudes, knowledge or skills are acquired either through informal experience or through systematic study.

Of course there is nothing new about the fact that people have been learning things all their lives. Nor is the notion of learning unusual. It is a common, everyday and universal occurrence. What is different at this moment, is that we are pausing to examine this ordinary everyday occurrence, not because it is unfamiliar to us, but because we want to become more consciously aware of it and because we want to understand it. There are some good reasons for doing so.

- Understanding the Learning Process provides us with a non-threatening framework or underlying structure and a vocabulary to talk about learning.
- Understanding the Learning Process can help to expose modes of thinking, how habits are formed and how change can occur both internally and externally to the learner
- Any re-examination of familiar things can often reveal new insights.
- Just discussing the differences between learning as an action and learning as an outcome, and the process through which this is accomplished, can enhance rapport between teachers and students, helping them to anticipate difficulties and to work together on possible solutions.
- Teaching, planning and even assessing literacy programs can become increasingly effective when we do so against an explicit framework of the steps in the Learning Process.

Further, by making a conscious decision to retain that conscious awareness of learning as a sequential process, we gain better control over its progress. Control, or at least a sense of it, helps to lessen anxiety. Prodding ourselves frequently to recognise where we are within that Learning Process helps to give us a concrete grasp of our progress. This could increase the likelihood of success. Knowing what is ahead helps us to anticipate problems. Recognising that learning progresses through sequential steps, provides us with a kind of map that can be consulted. And we will have the choice to do this on our own, or with someone else.

In other words, instead of just focusing on the topic of literacy learning, this chapter introduces the notion that there must be an explicit understanding of learning itself before undertaking any particular focus on the topic of learning.

This understanding of the interrelationship between what is learned and how that learning sequentially progresses should, ideally, be shared by everyone in any educational program. When the attitudes, knowledge and skills (learning as a noun) and the action of acquiring them (learning as a verb) can move sequentially through familiar steps (the Learning Process) then any program of education will be increasingly collaborative, effective and exciting.

Teachers, tutors and administrators as well as their students can base their discussions about learning on this common framework and common vocabulary. In fact, the awareness of the Learning Process and the ability to discuss it may be an important new adjunct to any educational program.

The steps of the Learning Process (briefly)

Each one of us is engaged in countless Learning Processes at any given moment. The learning of any one thing always encompasses many Learning Processes because each thing that we learn is related to everything else. Because the Learning Process for each of these learnings consists of steps, it is possible for us to be engaged not only in many Learning processes at the very same time, but also to be on differing steps of each. Each new process moves sequentially through five possible steps. The steps of Learning: A Process of Experiencing the Unfamiliar include:

1. Being Aware
2. Observing
3. Participating
3a. Rote Internalizing
4. Confronting Perceived Risk or Perceived Challenge
5. Reflective Internalizing

Since we do not learn what we already know, learning is always a movement in the direction of increasing knowledge or increasing familiarization. That is to say, when we feel familiar with something, the only reason we may review it is to extend our knowledge or to focus on some aspect of it that has freshly invoked our attention. What begins with curiosity — that desire or need to know — holds the potential to move from the unfamiliar to the habitual.

In re-examining something that we thought we already knew, as we are doing now with the topic of learning, we are making a deliberate effort to explore new aspects, unfold new possibilities, and open fresh critical paths for reflection and possible change.

We can direct our reflections inwardly or outwardly. Questioning our own assumptions and our own practices provides a model for self-exploration and personal enhancement and provides the possibility of inner change. Applying the same process of Reflective Internalizing to matters external to ourselves, provides the possibility for change in those external matters. For example, changing our own perception of what learning is about, is a change within our inner world; innovation in our mode of teaching is a change that will affect our students who are part of our external world.

Some factors that affect how we learn

Past and present experiences

Each of us is unique. Past learning experiences are very much a part of any new learning. Each learner brings their own life experiences, values, emotions and concerns as background to the new learning. There may be past experiences that excite and provoke curiosity. But there may also be experiences that smother curiosity with anxiety and even fear. In any learning situation, it is helpful if these past experiences, whether pleasant or unpleasant,can be explored either through private or small group discussions and their significance for further learning discussed. For example, it is a great relief to many adults to discover that their literacy learning will not be like their memories of authoritative 'schooling'.

Some barriers

Other problems sometimes combine to form seemingly impenetrable barriers that prevent people from attending or remaining in literacy programs. Many of the case studies in this book affirm this but also describe the many special efforts communities and individuals can make to meet personal and local needs. In attempting to find out just what is necessary, outreach efforts in each community may differ, but in their differing ways they help to develop awareness of literacy programs. These may be provided in small groups or on a one-to-one basis not only in homes but also at workplace sites as well as meeting rooms and classrooms. But physical barriers are easier to overcome than economic or psychological ones, and many of the studies in this book provide innovative yet practical suggestions that have worked for particular communities and may be helpful for others.

The interconnectedness of learning experiences

This chapter, like others in this book, emphasizes the interconnectedness of every aspect of a person's daily life. Recognition and support for the whole person includes consideration for the physical and mental, the rational and the intuitive as well as the relational and spiritual aspects that impinge on the successful outcome of learning. Learning is crucial to human development, adaptation and survival and while learning is an individual activity, it is always socially embedded and culturally influenced. Because of this, learning itself can be neither studied nor facilitated without taking into consideration every aspect of a person in a particular environment or social setting. The literacy program that focuses solely on the content of lessons will not last, especially with adults who come voluntarily to any adult learning program.

Despite the many factors — culturally and socially bound — that affect learning, the actual process of learning, from initial awareness to reflective internalizing, remains consistent and constant universally. What differs from one person to another, is their choice of what they are learning (although there may not always be a choice), how far to proceed along the steps of that process, how long it will take them to do so, and how much of the learning that is offered is personally relevant.

About learning styles

Within any setting and with any topic of study, adults have preferred ways of learning things and this is called learning styles. Depending on what is to be learned, individuals often like to select between choices of visual, kinetic, or auditory materials and activities. These preferred ways of learning vary according to what is being learned and may even vary on different steps of the Learning Process.

That is, a person may have a preference for learning something by seeing it, by doing something with it, or by listening to something about it. For some people, or for the learning of some things, a combination of these styles may be most effective. Learning styles involve people's preferences for using various sense organs and effective teachers often reinforce learning by providing materials and using teaching methods that appeal to various senses. Such teaching flexibility and sensitivity not only enhances individual learning, but helps to provide useful repetition in interesting ways.

Learning styles are not just affected by sensory preferences, they are also affected by past experiences. These past experiences represent an accumulation of knowledge (cognitive experience), skills (psychomotor experience) and feelings (affective experience). Again we can see the importance of recognising the complexity of learning and the factors that impact upon it.

The universality of learning

Learning is something that everyone does. Yet how can

learning be considered universal when each person is so unique and cultures seem to differ so much? This can be answered with a brief reflection showing that we already know and accept many commonalities about learning:

- Each person is capable of learning
- Learning occurs at every age
- What we learn is cumulative
- Learning cannot be 'unlearned', but it may be submerged as newer learning becomes more relevant
- Submerged learning (memory) can be retrieved, and this too follows a learning process that begins with Awareness and moves to Reflective Internalizing
- Learning is intrinsic to most human activities.
- Learning is the essence of all cultures and the means of cultural transmission and cultural transformation (or cultural dynamism)
- Learning helps to transform the unfamiliar into the familiar and eventually into habitual behaviour.
- All learning that has become entrenched as habitual, whether through Rote Internalizing or through Reflective Internalizing reflects the paradox that the more we know something, the less we are aware of knowing it.

Common and universal though learning is, there is still much that perplexes us. What draws us to unfamiliar things? How do we conquer risks and jump into challenges in learning? What drives some people to deliberately seek out such learning challenges? And conversely, why do some people choose to remain at a certain place in their learning and seem to avoid anything new or different? While much perplexes us, we still have some deceptively simple answers to some learning questions:

- Why do people learn? Because they want to.
- How do people learn? As they need to.
- What do people learn? Only what is relevant.

Learning: a process of experiencing the unfamiliar

Looking at the steps of a process

Long ago someone said that the answer to Why is always Because, but the answer to How always involves a complex answer describing a pattern or a process. Understanding how we learn then, also involves a complex answer describing a process of the possible steps along the way. However the notion of "steps" should not be taken as a stolid staircase, rather "steps" should be seen as they are perceived by the individual: sometimes long and sometimes short, sometimes smooth and sometimes rough, and at times seemingly more like a landing than a step. And overall, we should not lose sight of the sensitive structures that link the steps with other Learnings Processes, and spiral in ongoing movements.

Learning equals experiencing

How do we learn something is to ask, How do we go about experiencing something that is new for us? What actually happens to transform something unknown into a common everyday part of our lives? What steps do we take to shift from unfamiliar to familiar and eventually to a habit? What feelings do we have along the way? Recognising that the steps of learning are like the steps of a staircase, and making choices about stepping up or down or remaining for a while in one place, or even jumping off the staircase are choices that we can usually make.

The knowledge that learning can be described as a series of sequential steps, can also be as helpful as a detailed map or directory to unknown territory or to unfamiliar information. We can make reference to our progress in learning in the same way that we can locate ourselves in unfamiliar territory. It means we now have some guideposts. Looking at the Learning Process in this way provides us with possibilities of alternate directions, possible resting points and important territorial information. We can better anticipate what lies ahead, we can move with greater confidence. But it cannot lay out for us either exciting distractions, frightening disruptions or unpredictable events. We must meet challenges and risks as we confront them. At least, we will see that we have that choice. Now let's look at the Learning Process in more detail.

Before moving on to a more detailed discussion and examples of the steps in the Learning Process, I want to insert a cautionary word about models attempting to depict human processes. No model, no matter how deftly drawn, can show the ebb and flow or the intricacy of reality. This model is no exception and it is here (readers of previous papers on my work will recall differing versions) only as a guide.

Movement within the process

Like most other human activities and characteristics, there is no stasis except death, and some of us aren't even sure about that. Like life itself, learning is always in movement.

> "Learning is really no-fail, because knowing that I can jump on again when it is more comfortable or relevant for me makes me feel good"

Literacy practitioners should be acutely aware of how important this single factor of movement may be to their students. Knowing they can "jump off" may be the incentive to get started. Knowing they can "jump on again" may be the motivation to lifelong learning. It also highlights the importance of discussing this Learning Process because it helps both tutor and student to articulate their place and movement within the Learning Process. Such discussions may help the teacher in reviewing previous steps and ultimately bringing the learner to risk going it alone

How do we take the first step and how do we progress?
Step One: BEING AWARE — WHAT IS THIS?

Being Aware encompasses anticipation and expectation both flickering briefly while as the learner's attention is caught. Internal responses include a combination of Curiosity and Enticement and a brief appraisal of Relevance. Externally the learner may only exhibit a superficial glance, a

LEARNING: A PROCESS

The Steps	Inner Responses & Reactions	Degree of Familiarity
	(italicized responses represent those of critical importance within the step)	
1. Being Aware	* _Relevancy_ * _Curiosity_ * _Enticement_	Unfamiliar
2. Observing (non-threatening)	Watchfulness Marginality	Familiarizing
3. Participating	Increasing comfort & confidence. (Want everyone to know about this)	Assuming total familiarity
3a. Rote Internalizing	Confident Happy Secure	Familiar **Habitual Behaviour**
4. Confronting Risk or Challenge	**Perceiving Risk:** Anxious Fearful Confusion of: *_Accomodating_ *_Conflicting_ *_Withdrawing_ - - - - - - - - - - - **Perceiving Challenge: (opportunity)** Learner shifts directly into Step Five	Abruptly Unfamiliar Dilemma Contradiction Problem / Decision Doubt - - - - - - - - - - - excitement of new possibilities: *Curiosity *Relevance *Enticement
5. Reflective Internalizing	**The "SH'MA"** 1. Listening 2. Dialoguing 3. Critical Recursive Reflecting 4. Doing / Being **Habitual Behaviour**	Familiar Because of discovered relevance & personal meaning, ideas / action become one with the learner.

OF EXPERIENCING THE UNFAMILIAR

Observable Behaviour	Dominant Questions	Teacher's Actions
(Sometimes inner & observable responses & reactions may coincide)	(learner's point of view)	(suggested)
Passive, Superficial & Distanced from Subject	What is this?	Tell about it, show examples & possibilities.
Spectator *Sightseer* *(just looking)*	How does this compare with my previous experiences?	Watch while I do it.
Trying things out. *Acting* *Appraising* *Missionizing* *Cluster-Judging* *Claiming knowledge*	Shall I try it out & see?	You can try doing it. Help each other to do it. (Creating a supportive environment.)
Memorizing Practising Repeating Copying (dependent on external reward & evaluation)	I can do this!	Reinforcements Rewards Support
Defensive behaviours of: Passive / Reconciliatory (Accomodating) or: Arguing / Fighting (Conflicting) or: Withdrawing	What is happening? Do I know this? Do I want to?	Presenting a problem, something new. **Risk**: Learner may exit
Challenged & excited (dependent on inner rewards & evaluation)	How did this come to be? What possibilities are there?	**Significant Resource**
Imagining Creating Innovating Visualizing Reorganizing Changing Improvising Decision-making Problem-solving Learner is intensely focused & concentrated (Note that **change** may be in learner's internal or external world)	(Questions continue recursively as above) **What is the relevant meaning for me, for this situation?**	Acknowledge learner's efforts & energy. Provoke imagining of further possibilities & alternatives. "OK to try & OK to fail." Do! Be!

passive posture, content to see and hear but only from a distance.·

A mode of thinking: the Reflective Pause

This brief and superficial mode of thinking (commonly applied especially in the first three steps of this Learning Process) I have named the Reflective Pause. It encompasses the following sequential steps and may be repeatedly applied as needed:

1. Collecting of information
2. Questioning of what was collected
3. Comparing with what was previously known
4. Selecting what seems important

"My friend has joined a literacy group and he seems to be enjoying it."
"In what ways am I held back by not being able to make sense of what I read?"
"My boss says I have trouble reading reports and because of this I might not get a promotion."

Those early inner responses of Curiosity, Relevance and Enticement may persist long enough to push the learner gently onto the next step. In fact, all the inner responses of each step remain with the learner throughout the Learning Process, alternately or occasionally emerging and submerging in importance.

Summary of characteristics of Step One:
- Begins with flicker of attention.
- Learner is distanced from object of attention.
- Engagement of Reflective Pause: a brief and superficial collecting, questioning, comparing and selecting of information.

Step Two: OBSERVING: WHAT'S GOING ON? HOW DOES THIS COMPARE?

In this step the learner's attention is increasing, and there is a preference to watch what is going on from the sidelines.

The inner responses of Watchfulness combined with a feeling of Marginality indicate a slightly closer approach to the topic of interest than was shown in Step One. Spectator-like attentiveness may with increasing interest gradually shift the learner to focusing rather like a Sightseer who is keen to discover all about one special interest but still from a safe distance.

> "Heck, what have I got to lose by going to one of the literacy classes with Bill. I can just sit and watch what's going on."
> "The tutor seems to take time with each person. School was never like this."
> "Some of these people are about my age. They seem to handle what's going on. They seem to be enjoying this."

Like a snowplough that pushes all accumulations in front of it, the three initial responses of Curiosity, Enticement and Relevance move together and are retained throughout any Learning Process, and now and then one or the other of them seems to emerge more importantly than the rest. Similarly, the responses of Watchfulness and Marginality exhibited on this second step of the Learning Process may emerge periodically as the learner progresses.

Summary of characteristics of Step Two:
- Attention is heightening and focusing.
- The learner remains marginal (Spectator)
- The learner is watchful (Sightseer)
- Previous characteristics of Curiosity, Enticement and Relevance are retained together with the Reflective Pause mode of thinking.

Step Three: PARTICIPATING — SHALL I TRY IT OUT?

Now comes the decision to step into the action and take part. At first the learner's trial participation may just consist of making appraisals of what is going on (Appraiser) then a sense of knowing takes over as excitement and confidence pushes the learner to tell everyone what they are learning (Missionizing). The whole world now seems divided into those who are part of this new learning and those who are not (Cluster-Judging). Increasingly, confidence burgeons with new achievements and the learner feels a sense of ownership while claiming a knowledge of it that she is as yet incapable of assessing as superficial. (This is similar to travellers claiming to have "lived just like the natives") The learner at this point is blissfully unaware of the reality of the complex depths of their newly acquired learning.

"Reading isn't so tough once you get the hang of it."
"Last night I was telling Meg about our newsletter. She could hardly believe we wrote it. I was so excited."
"I can see how important being literate is. Sad for those who aren't."
"We got a good group here and it's more than reading and writing. We talk a lot too, and we find ways to help each other with personal things too."

Summary of characteristics of Step Three:
- Attentiveness has extended to taking part and trying things out.
- Watchfulness has shifted to confident appraisal of what's going on (Appraiser).
- Overwhelming desire/need to tell everyone (Missionizing).
- Clustering people as participants or non-participants (Cluster-Judging).
- Claiming ownership (living like the natives).
- Reflective Pause is retained as the mode of thinking.

Step Three A: ROTE INTERNALIZING with REPETITION AND REWARDS

This step of the Learning process is more like the landing part way up a staircase rather than a separate step. It is really an extension of Step Three. For here the learner's confidence is built on repetition of what has been copied, memorized modelled and repeated. This learning has been warmed by the support of the teacher and other students. There is a lot of pleasure in memorizing and repeating, copying and reciting. Mistakes aren't common if the learner is careful and besides, everyone is doing the same thing. There is a sense of camaraderie here and the confidence is buoyed by external reinforcements and rewards. Rote learners depend on that and also on external assessments and approval.

"I showed my husband and he was so proud of me."
"I read it so many times I almost knew it by heart."
"really watch my tutor and the other guys and do it just like them."

The step of Rote Internalizing may be so comfortable that the learner may be content to remain here. Such responses are not uncommon when the teacher has provided a safe environment where mistakes can be made and where each effort is duly recognised. In fact Rote Internalizing frequently leads to habitual behaviour, attitudes and routines which then become so commonly taken for granted that they slip into a way of life.

But the realities of everyday life are neither routine nor habitual. Abrupt unfamiliar happenings confront the learner frequently and may shatter previous complacency and confidence.

Summary of characteristics of Step Three A:
- This Step is an extension of Step Three.
- Rote memorizing, copying and reciting are central.
- Sense of confidence and camaraderie.
- Learner dependency on external reinforcements, rewards and assessments.
- Reflective Pause is still the mode of thinking.
- Rote Internalizing leads to habitual behaviour, attitudes and routines.

Some reflections on the first three steps

These first three steps of the Learning Process provided the entry to new learning. They served to transmit knowledge, skills and attitudes. In these steps, the learner gradually moved closer to the new learning and repeated and practiced what had been transmitted (verbally and through modelling) accepting the new skills and information almost without question. The content of the learning had been transmitted but not changed in any way.

Dependent on external modelling and support, external reinforcements and rewards, the learner's success was determined according to the accuracy of repetition. The accurate repetition of rotely learned knowledge and skills, and approval of peers were the criteria of success.

With sufficient practice, the learner began to 'internalize' what was learned, and the learning slowly became habitual and routine. This habitual behaviour derived from repetitive imitation rather than from personal reflection. This distinction is important.

Step Four: CONFRONTING: PERCEIVED RISK
& PERCEIVED CHALLENGE

Here Confronting takes on the literal meaning of coming face to face with something different or unfamiliar. Essentially the term has neither a positive nor a negative meaning; and whether Confronting is perceived as a Risk or as a Challenge depends on the experience and the perception of the learner and to a lesser degree, the influence of Significant Resources (others or things) in the learner's life.

Confronting occurs when the learner faces an abrupt unfamiliarity. We only notice the formation of the words we are reading or writing when they are unfamiliar Similarly, habitual behaviours and routines only come to a sudden halt when we notice that there is something about them that is suddenly different. Another way to explain the step of Confronting may be to describe it as coming face to face with a contradiction, a dilemma, a problem, a decision, or any change from what the learner knew previously. Or more bluntly, what worked before suddenly isn't working anymore and making sense is difficult.

Within this Learning Process, there are several ways that the learner may choose to handle this Confrontation: by perceiving it as a Risk, by perceiving it as a Challenge (opportunity), by regressing to the previous Step Three A and continuing the Rote Internalizing or by exiting altogether from this particular Learning Process. For the literacy student, this would mean opting out of the program.

Perceived Risk:

> "Up until now I've been mostly reading, but now the tutor expects me to write my own short story for our class book."
> "I want to write a letter to my aunt, but what if I make mistakes?"
> "I thought I could read government documents O. K. but this one is not like the one we had in class."

The confidence built up through the first three steps of the Learning Process is too often short-lived. The real world contains problems, doubts, incongruities. When things appear differently than we expected them to, when something totally unfamiliar looms before us, we may see it as impenetrable as a brick wall. The learner may be unwilling or even fearful to tackle that wall.

Risk, and the possible disruption of familiar ways, routines and habits may be enough to bring the learning to an abrupt and sometimes startling halt. This is a common step for a learner to jump off the Learning Process. Or it may be a point in the Learning Process of a confused 'dance' between responses of Accommodating: being passive or ignoring difference, Conflicting: engaging in verbal or physical abuse to defend the status quo, and Withdrawal: a physical or psychological retreat from what seems to be too formidable a challenge to risk.

Perceived Challenge (opportunity):

> "Hey how did this happen?"
> "Something here is different, This is getting exciting."
> "I wonder what ways there are to solve this?"

One final possibility of action remains. Sometimes by seeking help and support from a Significant Resource (which may be a person, book, film or anything that inspires) or through what we may call intuition or inspiration, the learner may plunge into a questioning reflection. Reflective Internalizing is here depicted as a separate step but for the learner who perceives confronting as an opportunity rather than a risk, Steps Four and Five may be almost indistinguishable. In fact, for the person who experiences Confronting as a challenge, there is a direct path that draws them immediately into Step Five.

> "Maybe Ben and I can work on this together and figure out what makes a story a story. Just imagine what it would be like to see our story in print!"
> "I wonder if we could try filling out different kinds of forms. I'd really like to do my own banking and income tax."
> "Maybe my tutor would help me find words in the dictionary so I could really write a letter by myself."

Summary of characteristics of Step Four:
- Confronting means to come face to face with something unfamiliar.
- Step Four has two main aspects: Perception of Risk and Perception of Challenge.
- Learner's responses and behaviour are dependent on which of these they perceive.
- Learners perceiving Risk engage in Accommodating, Conflicting and Withdrawing behaviours and responses, or they may regress to a previous Step or exit the Process.
- Learners perceiving Challenge will excitedly progress immediately to Step Five and this may be aided by a Significant Resource.

How does change happen?

Examining two kinds of change

There are two kinds of change that we mean here. The first is change in knowledge itself and the second is change in the learner's internal or external world.

Changing knowledge

In the first three steps of the Learning Process, knowledge

is communicated or transmitted to the learner, but the learner does not change that knowledge in any way. In the last step of the Learning Process, the learner decides to extend or transform the accumulated knowledge by taking ownership of it, and by enhancing or transforming it in some creative way. Knowledge itself has the potential for change through the reflective actions and new practice of the learner. We call such change by various names such as creativity, or cultural dynamism for example. Changing knowledge can also affect change in the learner's internal or external world.

Changing the learner's internal or external world

In the first three steps of the Learning Process, it is true that a learner can be said to be 'changed' because at this point, the learner *knows something more*. But the accumulation of knowledge does not necessarily lead to a change in behaviour, attitudes or routines. (Health professionals can attest to this.) Through persistence, reinforcement and rewards, the learner may acquire changed habits simply through repetition. As we have seen, habitual behaviour can result from Rote Internalizing. This is how much of our daily learning occurs and how cultural mores are acquired. Because such learning is often (but not always) at a subconscious level, the learner performs because of dependency on external approval and evaluation. Nonetheless, habits are formed, routines are established. The learner *knows*, but may not *understand*.

When the learner accepts Confronting as a challenge or opportunity and sifts through accumulated knowledge with the intent of discovering personally relevant meaning — whether for oneself (internal world) or for one's work or project external world) — the deliberate and conscious Reflective Internalizing results in a consciously-acquired change of or for the self. The learner now performs (is or does) independent of external approval or evaluation. The learner now has transformed mere *knowing* into *understanding*.

Often such progress requires or is supported by a Significant Resource which may be a person, or could be the stimulation or inspiration one may gain from a film, a book, a chance remark or incident. For the learner who is more accustomed to perceiving problems, dilemmas and decisions as opportunities, and finds them exciting, that Significant Resource may be within themselves.

Step Five: REFLECTIVE INTERNALIZING

"When I have to figure things out for myself, then I take ownership."

Reflective Internalizing is characterized by a deliberate and concentrated reflection with a committment to achieving change. The change may be in many forms and may be called innovation, problem-solving, decision-making, reorganization, improvisation or creativity. The outcome is always a transformation or enhancement of the learner's previous knowledge and/or skills or as we have just discussed, a change in the knowledge itself.

This is of critical significance. The learner who is a habitual 'Reflective Internalizer' is one who understands that any extension of their own previous learning is always an enhancement to themselves, or to their world whether the actual change is negative or positive, the learning has been extended. Whether developing change within one's internal or external world, or within knowledge itself, Reflective Internalizing represents a no-exit immersion in the concentrated effort of the mode of thinking which I have named as a fourfold process: The Sh'ma.

The SH'MA

What to call a complex four-fold mode of thinking that forms the essence of Reflective Internalizing? I chose Sh'ma from the Hebrew word Shema which means literally to listen but which also implies the responsibility that resides in listening. For having listened, one cannot plead ignorance. Similarly, there is no exit from The Sh'ma. Once engaged in, it is not external rewards or reinforcements that propel the learner, it is the inescapable importance of those three forces apparent from the very first step of the Learning Process: Curiosity, Relevance and Enticement.

The four-fold process of The Sh'ma includes the following sequential steps: (only briefly noted here)

1. Listening: attentive and responsive openness to what is seen and heard. A collecting of knowledge both immediate and past (surface and submerged knowledge).

2. Dialoguing: a further opening of oneself to accept and consider differing views, underlined by a willingness to 'see differently' and to exchange ideas and to collect them.

3. Critical Recursive Reflecting: represents the analyzing (separating) and interpreting (reassembling) of possibilities to discover their personally relevant meaning. This may involve imagining, visualizing, inferring, projecting into differing patterns and possibilities of all that has been collected. It may also involve a recursive returning to further collections of 'data' and to further 'research', with each piece of knowledge being submitted to the same intensively critical appraisal in order to make sense and find meaning.

4. Doing/Being: Doing in a new way or Being somehow different is the outcome. It represents the embracing of change as a part of oneself and one's identity. It may also refer to change in the learner's external world.

Summary of characteristics of Step Five:

- Reflective Internalizing can only occur following the Confronting of something abruptly unfamiliar and involves deliberate and concentrated effort and committment to change.
- 'Change' can be improvisation, reorganization, innovation, problem-solving, decision-making or creativity.
- Whether change is negative or positive, the learning achieved is always an extension to what was previously known.
- The essence of Reflective Internalizing is the mode of thinking encompassed in the four-fold Process of The Sh'ma: Listening, Dialoguing, Critical Recursive Reflecting and Doing/Being.

Further reflections on Learning as a Process of Experiencing the Unfamiliar

Following along in the exploration and discoveries that emerged throughout this work, you likely found yourself nodding, "Well of course" at many points, as your response attested to the familiarity — from your own experience — of what was exposed. But this simple utterance is so important, because it gives credence and validity to all that has been shown. It is this very simple response that denotes the universality of this Learning as a Process of Experiencing the Unfamiliar and its meaningfulness for each person.

How shifts in reactions and behaviours became apparent

Throughout this Learning Process, the subtle shifts in attitudes and behaviours and the learner's inner responses and reactions became apparent by asking three questions:

1. What is the learner really doing?
2. What differing behaviour marks each shift?
3. What feelings could the learner express?

The first three steps were characterized by intensifying attention and proximity of the learner to the topic of the learning. The content of the learning was not changed in any way, but it was transmitted from the teacher to the student. Eventually with repetition and practice, what was learned became habitual. Throughout the first three steps of this Learning process, a mode of thinking called the Reflective Pause, brief and superficial, was used by the learner to collect, question, compare and select information.

Confronting as the critical decision point

This was the point in the Learning Process where an abrupt unfamiliarity emerged. The learner could perceive this either as a Risk or as a Challenge. If the learner perceived further engagement in learning as a Risk, then he may choose to engage in a confusing 'dance' of responses including Accommodating, Conflicting or Withdrawing. If however, the learner perceived this unforeseen unfamiliarity as a Challenge, then she would immediately become engaged in the kind of Reflective questioning that would draw her directly into the fifth step.

Differing modes of thinking

A differing mode of thinking differentiated the fifth Step from the first three Steps. The Reflective Pause characterized the first three steps of the Learning process, while The Sh'ma formed the essence of the last step of Reflective Internalizing.

Differing paths to habituation

We saw too, that there were two paths to habituation: through Rote Internalizing and through Reflective Internalizing. Nor was any effort made to distinguish either of these two paths as being inferior or superior. In fact, in any person's life, each of these has a place. It is not necessary to develop creativity in everything; many things in life can be safely relegated to robotic routine, and most of our cultural learning has been acquired through Being Aware, Observing and Participating. Acquiring habits through Rote Internalizing did not require problem-solving, decision-making, improvising, imagining, inferring, innovating, reorganizing or change of any kind. It only required attentive imitation. Developing habits that differed from what had been rotely acquired could only be achieved through the intensive concentrated effort of The Sh'ma.

Charting the intensifying reactions & behaviours

The following chart of intensifying attitudes and behaviours may help to shed further light on Learning as a Process of Experiencing the Unfamiliar:

CHART OF INTENSIFYING BEHAVIOURS

Steps	Behaviours & Attitudes:		
	Interest Level	Depth of Knowledge	Commitment & Responsibility
1. Being Aware	Apathetic	Aware/Seeing	Uncommitted & not Responsible
2. Observing	Attentive	Knowing About	
3. Participating	Really Interested & participating	Knowing & Sympathizing	
3a. Rote Internalizing	Interest sustained & participating		
4. Confronting	Risk = Confused & defensive Challenge = peak of interest	Risk = Confused & defensive Challenge = Intensive Curiosity to expand knowledge	Risk = Confused & defensive Challenge = Increasing committment & responsibility
5. Reflective Internalizing	Involved	Understanding Appreciating Empathizing	Committed & Responsible

The case study of Becky, a literacy student

Regina Muetze, a literacy tutor and administrator in Sudbury, Ontario has long been concerned with some elusive questions about literacy programs and her own role as a tutor:

- How can this role be most effectively directed to helping a person learn?

- How does one deal with the fine lines separating an adult's work world, private world and their new world as a literacy learner?
- What is the tutor's role in the support and development of an individual's feelings and self-esteem, and how do these impact on their literacy learning?
- How can we help literacy learners accommodate to their own changing social context?

It was with these questions in mind that Regina decided to return to her own journal notes of Becky, a literacy student who had captured her interest for more than two and a half years. After a review of her own notes and a meticulous study of my work on Learning as a Process of Experiencing the Unfamiliar, Regina decided to share both her own journal notes and her own understanding of this Learning Process in a lengthy dialogue with Becky. The following represents a summary in Becky's words as she described her own movement through the steps of the Learning Process and her feelings and behaviours within each.

Becky's progression through the learning process steps

Step One: Being Aware:

Becky became aware of the literacy classes through a flyer from her child's school. Her Curiosity was "intense", the Relevance for her was her need for independence, and the Enticement was the promised non-typical class environment. Becky described her feelings as "shame, disbelief, distrust and aloneness" and she felt herself to be "indecisive and stupid". On hearing about the literacy classes for adults, she admitted to a sense of relief that perhaps a second chance existed for her, yet shame seemed to overwhelm her as she told Regina:

"How can you understand how I am feeling? I'm an adult. I should be able to read and write."

Step Two: Observing

Regina invited Becky to come and see the class. The flow of Becky's feelings are evident:

> "I watched you work with others. I had to learn who you were."
>
> "I had to let go of insecurities of who I wasn't...had to let you in...that wasn't easy."
>
> "I could learn, you believed that I could learn! They were strong words for me and now I couldn't backtrack."

Step Three: Participating

For Becky this was a happy step, it was where "I wanted to be: learning." She went on to describe this step as "feeling good", Fascinating. I could question..." "Safe, secure, my confidence and my committment steadily rising."

Step Four: Confronting Perceived Risk or Challenge

Regina had decided to present Becky with a challenge: to write a letter describing her elation at learning to become literate. There was also to be a mall display on literacy and perhaps if Becky wrote that letter it may even be in the display. But Becky perceived Risk. She was scared and feared being disowned by her family and friends because her letter may not be good enough. As she danced through a confusion of feelings, she said:

> "They would all know who I am through my writing...uneducated. It's not a good feeling."

But watching others writing letters, and gaining support from other students and her own daughter, Becky decided to write a letter and when it was chosen for the literacy display in the mall, she said she felt like she was "Stepping out!"

Step Five: Reflective Internalizing and The Sh'ma

> "I don't need to latch on to other people anymore."

" ...uncomfortable feelings are all gone now."
"Now I could write to a stranger. I could reveal myself
through writing."
"I used to think that I could only make friends (and be
someone) if I was educated. Now I know that's not true."

The tutor's observations of her student's progress through the learning process

Step One: Being Aware:

On meeting Becky, Regina noted that she was withdrawn,
distrustful and accustomed to having her husband do everything for her. She expressed her own shame and her sense of
being " very, very stupid". Regina told her: "Our environment is different. I'm your friend, don't look on me as a
teacher..."

Step Two: Observing

Becky finally did come to sit in on a class, and then returned many times. But often she separated herself from the
others, and sometimes even left the class crying.

Step Three: Participating

It is often hard to distinguish just where one step ends and
another begins. But I noticed her practicing more, expressing
her fascination more and more and her excitement in learning itself. She engaged more with others. There was no
evident insecurity, no crying. "I was there for her. I was
always there for her."

About the Reflective Pause:

"To help Becky on a daily basis, we would deliberately use
reflective time on what she had done, collecting, questioning, comparing and selecting what seemed most important."

Step Three A: Rote Internalizing

Becky's energy was expressed in her own words, "I wrote and wrote and wrote and felt confidence."

Step Four: Confronting

I acted just by gut level and decided to give her a challenge to write a letter and perhaps have it displayed at the mall for the literacy exhibit. Only her husband I knew about her literacy classes at this point. She said, "I can't do that." Eventually she wrote the letter, and even slipped over to the mall to watch other people reading her letter. When she told her daughter about the letter, her daughter told her, "I still love you Mom."

Step Five: Reflective Internalizing

In Step Four, I realised that Becky's whole person was at stake, she took the Challenge, even though she first felt it to be a Risk, and with great fear shifted into thinking and doing for herself.

Overall now as Becky and I talked, we realised that her learning literacy had been very cyclical, with frequent stalemates, regressions and often long stretches with little progress. But she is on her own way now...while Becky's dependency/independency is always an issue, she no longer asks for my opinion anymore.

Other Tutors' Comments & Perceptions of the Learning Process

The following remarks and reflections are those of the tutors who participated in the Toronto Workshop. Their comments followed presentations of the Learning Process and the case study of Becky. It was interesting how each tutor fell quite naturally into discussing learning using the vocabulary and the steps of the Learning Process, even though this was their first exposure to it.

How literacy tutors see their own role in facilitating each student through their own Learning Process

Step One: Being Aware:

> "I know what I want to do: not act like a school teacher."
> "Make sure they always have a choice; a second chance even here."
> "There is a feeling of drawing towards the learner with a mix of empathy and anxiety. Am I going to be able to teach this person?"

Overall: There is an indefinable art that each of us has developed about what's needed in literacy teaching. There is a sense of equality because there is so much to learn on both sides. We are attempting at this point (step) to define our relationship, a sense of shared responsibility.

Step Two: Observing

> "I had a sense of discomfort in being watched by the new students, but I didn't want that discomfort to transfer to the student."
> "I know there is a mutual watching and apprehension. I want to ask a lot of questions and to draw them out."

Overall: Our own feelings can go into different steps of the Learning Process, depending on the person we are working with. Important to be reinforcing, encouraging.

Step Three and Three A: Participating and Rote Internalizing

> "I am feeling excited for the learner"
> "Closer. A real connection is growing between us."
> "There is a rhythm now, a participating and I really have to use my intuitive tools."
> "This person needs a lot of reinforcement...encouraging them to continue...."

Overall: Our own feelings can go into different phases, depending on the person we are working with. Important to be reinforcing, encouraging.

Step Four: Confronting Perceived Risk or Challenge

"It is a time to intensify our relationship, to realise there is something special that we share."

"If our bond is strong enough, we can encourage them to take the risk of a challenge, to take it as an opportunity."

"There is a changing balance of power now — transferring Confronting in literacy learning to the step of Confronting in other aspect's of one's life. More than literacy is being learned."

Overall: Supporting now rather than instructing. The realisation that it is the student who is in the forefront of choice-making. But the tutor's attitude now is, "I am behind you but I won't press."

Step Five: Reflective Internalizing

"Hard for us to step back and let them work it through on their own."

"I had to physically step away from them. I have anxiety about letting them go. Because I very much don't want them to fall."

"I have a fear for them. We are their last chance. Where do they go from here?"

"I feel to reach this point is a success story. It is a good feeling to see them making choices about their own life, even if they may not be the right choices."

Overall: Later more than one tutor laughingly remarked, "Don't we sound like parents...?" The ambivalence that tutor's feel about the Learning Process of their own students is rarely talked about. They are also acutely aware that the literacy learner's future choices will impact on their whole life. Both the tutor's and the student's feelings at this step are so intensely personal, they are rarely exposed.

Practitioners suggest Implications of the Learning Process for Literacy

The participants in the Banff Workshop found the

Learning Process useful as a framework and a vocabulary to discuss literacy learning, this time, from the literacy practitioner's point of view. The participants in this workshop included tutors, trainers, and administrators. Here is a condensation of their key points in their own words:

- We need this Learning Process as a framework to make our teaching philosophy and our own learning explicit.
- As tutors, trainers and administrators, we need to learn this Process so that we can make daily use of it in our own literacy practice.
- The Learning Process together with an understanding of the student/learner's viewpoint provides us with the structural tools we have needed.

About evaluating literacy programs and students

- We need to be aware of this Learning Process in order to set our own goals, to allow for individual student's 'exits' and lingering plateaus, and to make us realise not to be hasty in assessing anyone.
- There is a need for us to take the time to identify where both a student and a tutor is in their own learning, before acting.
- We are always evaluating the outcome or the end product. Maybe an understanding of this Learning Process is showing us that we need to spend more time evaluating learning as a process.
- We need to be patient with our evaluative observing and identify ourselves as part of the Learning Process: "How have I done?"

About Planning Literacy Programs & Projects

- Student-based, open-ended planning makes sense.
- Understanding the Learning Process provides a sense of inner direction, predictability and control. "Gives me a sense of power for myself."
- Planning needs to allow for being stuck, for moving backwards, and for re-entry.

About Teaching literacy

- There's an appropriate 'season' to learn things, and we always need to consider the other forces in people's lives.
- We need to forget feeling responsible for other's learning, and get busy developing an attitude and creating an atmosphere that helps students to develop increasing committment to and responsibility for their own learning.

Collected Reflections

This chapter has provided an opportunity for the re-examination of something that we usually take for granted: how we learn. *Learning as a Process of Experiencing the Unfamiliar* provided a basic framework and vocabulary for learning, discussing and reflecting on the underlying structure of all learning. The Learning Process provided a way to map our own learning progress and to understand the learning steps of our students. What was important here, was that this Learning Process provided insight into what learning is for the learner.

In order to make our mutual dream come true, to make the skills and the knowledge of literacy and numeracy as natural as breathing, we need to understand and apply this Learning Process to our own learning and our own work, and to share it with others including our students. Between tutors and students, between trainers and administrators, and deep within ourselves, an opportunity for a more effective means of planning, evaluating and teaching has been opened.

The process of learning had often seemed like a laborious climb up a dimly lit staircase. Knowledge and skills so often listed as "objectives to be achieved" failed to take into account the learning that occurs between relationships or even the emotions that accompany learning. Our awareness of the inter-relatedness of all types of learning has been opened and awaits further study.

Learning styles and learning strategies have their place, but we have seen that subjective perceptions, social obligations, physical barriers and ordinary but complex human relationships each played a role as instigators or as inhibitors in a person's Learning Process. Further, we saw that each thing that is learned 'occupies' a Learning Process. because of this, each person is engaged in countless such Learning processes at any given moment. Such aspects of a person's daily life could not be shunted aside for they impacted on every aspect of learning.

In a tangible way, these subjective aspects of learning needed to be taken into account in any learning program, and especially an adult literacy program where memories of schooling may prove to be one of the most ponderous barriers. The learner's perceptions and feelings need to become a basis for discussion and a bridge to further learning.

Further we saw that there were two ways to achieve habitual behaviour. Through Rote Internalizing, the learner could accumulate knowledge and skills and with repetition and encouragement, such knowledge could become habitual. Throughout the first three steps, the learner applies a mode of thinking called The Reflective Pause; it is brief and superficial, but for the most part satisfactory. There is no question that rotely accumulated knowledge provides change both in the learner's internal and external worlds, but the knowledge itself as an entity remains unchanged, and this process differs from the kind of change resulting from Reflective Internalizing in several important ways.

Reflective Internalizing is the final step in any Learning Process and it is the step where the accumulated knowledge becomes transformed in order to discover personally relevant meaning for the learner. This may result in changes in the learner's internal or external worlds, or in the knowledge itself. We may call this latter change research.

This happens only through the efforts of the learner, but may be facilitated or encouraged through a Significant Resource. Such transformation of accumulated knowledge can only be achieved after Confronting something unfamiliar and recognising it as an opportunity to discover new possibilities. Such transformation is only achieved through the application of The Sh'ma.

In short, while each step of the Learning Process is important, Rote Internalizing makes habitual use of knowledge and skills that have been transmitted. Reflective Internalizing makes habitual use of knowledge and skills that have been accumulated and transformed into new possibilities by the learner. Whenever the Learning process is presented, in any context of interest to the participants, implications and inferences explode as each participant recognises how deeply imbedded learning is as a part of almost every human experience. While supportive and patient teaching, and abundant resources of every kind are important in every aspect of learning, perhaps what stands out most clearly, is the critical importance of exposing the learner to something abruptly unfamiliar. In confronting the unfamiliar lies the challenge of creativity and change and the opportunity to take ownership, to discover personally relevant meaning. All participants concluded that at this step lay the heart of human development and the enhancement of self esteem.

Retaining a deliberately conscious awareness that learning is a process, to be taken a step at a time, is valuable. The fact that adults have more choice and more time and can more clearly recognise the Learning Process, may well be factors that help to distinguish adult learning and adult education from that of children.

Section Two

CASE STUDIES ON COMMUNITY BUILDING

INTRODUCTION

James A. Draper

A theme which runs throughout the case studies in this section, and which is touched upon in other theme sections as well, is the importance of cooperating with others in undertaking adult literacy education. Such cooperation can build community support for literacy education programs. This support is required in order to sustain the program over a period of time and to maximize its effective use of resources.

For the city of St. Mary's, community involvement was necessary to integrate adults with disabilities back into the community. In order to carry out its community-based literacy program, Killaloe developed a network with other organizations, professionals and the media. In the Northwest Territories, schools were controlled by the community, and Community Education Councils were set up. Training programs in Manitoba built on a community of interests felt by literacy education tutors.

Authentic community building practices cooperation in concrete terms. In a spirit of non-competition, those interested in and committed to adult literacy education come together to develop strategies for working together in order to exchange information, to coordinate activities, to effectively use resources including limited funding, and to create political support. Coalitions frequently have more political influence than actual political power.

The term community can refer to a geographical location or to a community of shared interests. Both of these uses apply to literacy education. Such shared interests occur within a geographical or municipal context. By acknowledging this, literacy programs actively reach out to government and non-government agencies for support and communication links. To varying degrees then, a function of literacy programs is to develop connections to the resources of other agencies.

This frequently occurs informally but may also be formalized, as in the case of the Killaloe outreach program. Here, one or more persons are actually designated as outreach workers, whose functions are to build a support base within the community. One way to build such support is to plan and implement special projects. All the case studies in this theme area give examples of such events or activities. However, liaison with the community, as well as cooperation and coordination, do not just happen. There must be an effort to bring these about.

Literacy education is also characterized by a community of interests shared by those who understand, or wish to understand, the issues relating to illiteracy. Members of this kind of community are self-designated and can potentially include anyone, not just those working within the literacy field. For example, a community of this kind would include adult students, people from government, the media, other professions, libraries, those from business and industry and many others.

Literacy education agencies put a great deal of effort into building a community of trust and dedication. Both meanings of community, the geographical and the community of shared interests, integrate with and complement each other, developing a support base within and from their respective communities. The metaphor of building bridges to the community can only come about by making an effort to create sound foundations.

Literacy programs and the communities associated with

them are characterized by a particular cultural, social, economic and political context. Context is a very key concept within the field of adult education. For instance, those individuals or agencies who make up the membership of a coalition will likely reflect the context within which the coalition emerges and functions. In developing coalitions, formal or informal, it is important to develop broad representation, commitment and action. One way to assess the representation of a coalition is to ask: Who is missing from the context or the fabric that makes up this community? For example, many of the case studies in this section point out the special function of the public library in literacy education.

The context of communities is dynamic and changes over time. It is important for literacy workers to be aware of the changing character of their communities — changes which they help and create and those which they inherit.

Any discussion on community building must give serious thought to the kind of structures which are most appropriate. What kind of informal or formal structures are being built with other literacy agencies? With government? With the media or with industry? In the case of the Saskatoon Literacy Coalition, it began as an informal network and only later did it emerge as a more formal structure.

In the case of the St. Marys' community-based program, a one-to-one 'community' between the student and a tutor seemed most appropriate for students who needed special attention. The Killaloe outreach program located the literacy program in its community centre, as the most practical setting. As literacy programs attempt to develop working relationships with other programs, it is essential that the intent and the unique circumstances guiding the building of community relationships are compatible with the existing structures.

The ways in which people are asked to express their commitment to literacy education is raised in a number of case studies. People need choices in the ways they can express their commitment to literacy education. The Saskatoon literacy coalition, for instance, gave careful consideration to its membership categories. They took into consideration the knowledge a person might have about literacy issues, their available time, energy, and level of current interest. Variations in membership categories reflect these degrees and interests in participation.

In community building, people also need room to feel their way as they move through a discovery and learning process, from the point of initial awareness of illiteracy issues to a point where they can express commitment and familiarity (see *Learning about Learning* in Section One). Gradations of membership (for individual, for agencies, or for both) are therefore desirable. However, each membership category, representing degrees of formality, should be spelled out, clearly expressing the coalition's expectation in order to avoid misunderstandings at a later date. A coalition of mutual benefit occurs when both the members and the coalition give and receive. Through a membership that provides choices, there is wide opportunity for sharing information and ideas.

Each case study in this section shows ways of involving people in a process of social change. Increasing awareness is one of the first steps in both the learning process and in community building. Broadening one's view of learning and the variety of settings within which it can occur (not just the classroom) can have wide repercussions. Developing self-confidence can be a first step for students who are learning to speak for themselves. Particular skills and attitudes are required to accomplish this.

The interrelationship between involvement, commitment and self-reflection are now seen to be self-evident. Helping people to define education for themselves encourages them to believe in their own abilities. Relating learning to student interests and involving students as equals in undertaking surveys can provide credibility to a literacy program. Involving students in planning a program and helping people to teach themselves further emphasizes that literacy programs often go beyond merely reading and writing. Such activities not only give the student (or the tutor or the coordinator) an opportunity to advocate but also to serve as a role model to others, as in the case of the Saskatoon case study where students went into local schools to encourage young people to remain in school.

Most of the case studies in this section defend the traditional use of volunteers in literacy programs and illustrate a number of basic principles and ideas for training volunteers and paid staff persons.The principles of teaching and learning which are expounded for students in literacy programs should be applied as well to the training of literacy educators. These principles apply to the content, skills and attitudes being taught, and also to the human relationships developed through the learning process.

The essence of what is imparted through training programs is generic to any and all such programs. These include up-to-date information on the recent and relevant literature in adult education, changes in policy developments, and improvement of tutor skills such as teaching, assessing and counselling. Generic content would also include a basic understanding of the learning process, philosophy and principles of adult education (see Section One).

Many of the above points raise a number of serious questions about the trend toward the professionalization of literacy tutors, a fairly recent issue. The case study on Training Literacy Practitioners speaks to this issue.

The training of volunteers and paid staff is another way to achieve community building. Through these case studies, many of the concerns to build support systems for students also apply to creating such systems for volunteers and paid staff. Examples of this would include:

- Providing transportation and child care services;
- Conceptualizing programs with a local as well as a regional framework;
- Acknowledging the cultural, social and other contexts within which a training program takes place;
- Encouraging peer tutoring, that is, tutors teaching other tutors; involving tutors (and students) in community building;
- Building a program (for students or for tutors) on an assessment of their needs; stimulating discussion, with self-reflection, on the learning process;
- Making the program learner-centred, whether the learner refers to students or to tutors;
- Encouraging each participant to reflect on their preferred learning styles;
- Encouraging people to become involved with their own education, and developing self-confidence and the desire to be life-long learners; and
- Respecting the privacy of the individual.

Several other factors emerge from these case studies as

being important to the broad view of the meaning of community building. Seeing and making linkages is also part of this building process, such as linkages between literacy and health education, between literacy and community building, or between the education of the child and the adult.

Building community support systems also requires direct contact with whatever group is the focus of attention at any given moment. It requires flexibility in terms of hours when organizing an educational program; and it requires acknowledgement of what people already know and need to learn. Finally, it is essential to accept people for the potential which they seem to have, both for learning as well as for teaching.

In conclusion, a number of principles of adult education and community development are highly relevant to planning, implementing and assessing adult literacy programs and to community building. Reflecting together on why things work, and sometimes do not work, involves a process of networking and building on the strengths which individuals and agencies together have in effectively maximizing coordination and cooperation for the cause of adult literacy education.

Chapter One
TRAINING LITERACY PRINCIPLES THAT GUIDE OUR PRACTICE

Mary Norton

Place: *Literary Office, Manitoba*
Participants: *Practitioners in community-based literacy
            programs*
Issues: 1. *Pluralistic literacy development*
        2. *Community-based literacy*
        3. *Training*

Training for adult literacy practitioners in Manitoba has been provided by provincial government staff since the mid-1980's. Present provision has been shaped by the employment in 1988 of an Adult Learning Specialist to plan and deliver workshops, by an emphasis' on community-based and learner-centred literacy programing, and by a broad variation in practitioners' backgrounds. Challenges which practitioners face in accessing training include funding, terms of employment, and distances to training sites.

I prepared this case study by speaking with the following people: Gayle Halliwell, a director of continuing education who administers a literacy program; Robin Millar, the Manitoba Literacy Office Adult Learning Specialist who is responsible for practitioner training; and also to Jonine Anderson, Diane Eastman, Sam Klippenstein, Shirley Skogan, and Betty Watkins, practitioners who work in a variety of community-based or other learner-based settings.

Background
Most of Manitoba's approximately one million people live

in the province's urban centres, with over half of the population living in Winnipeg. The rest of the population lives in smaller communities, on farms or on Native reserves across the province. Population density decreases in the northern part of Manitoba where distances between communities grow, and travel by road becomes more difficult.

Aboriginal[1] people account for 20% of Manitoba's population, and First Nation languages are spoken in some communities, particularly in northern Manitoba. Descendants of Manitoba's early settlers mainly speak English, although about 4% are francophone. Recent immigrants who speak languages other than French or English also account for a portion of the population.

Provision of adult literacy education in Manitoba during the 1970's and early 1980's, was available through academic upgrading programs offered by the province's three colleges and some school division-sponsored continuing education departments. Laubach tutoring was also available in Winnipeg, through the Volunteer Reading Aides.

In 1985, the Post-Secondary, Adult and Continuing Education (PACE) Branch of the Manitoba Education and Training department employed a Literacy Officer. Her role was to encourage and support the development of adult literacy programs across the province. A strong community-based, learner-centred philosophy of literacy development was nurtured over the following years.

This philosophy was affirmed by the Manitoba Task Force on Literacy, which in 1989 recommended a strategy of programing to address the literacy development needs of Manitobans. The Task Force's first recommendation was that the Government of Manitoba develop a literacy policy based on, among other factors, "a commitment to pluralistic literacy development that is learner-centred and across Manitoba."[2]

The Manitoba Literacy Office

The Manitoba Literacy Office opened on September 8, 1989 with the task of providing leadership in the development and delivery of adult literacy programs.[3] The Office is still a part of the PACE branch, and its staff includes a director and a provincial program coordinator, two community developers, based in Brandon and The Pas, and an adult learning specialist. The Literacy Office funds a number of community-based programs and provides support and coordination for literacy programs which are funded through other sources.

Community-based programs

Currently, many of Manitoba's community-based literacy programs operate as learning centres staffed by paid instructors. Learning is related to individuals' interests and needs, and centres may be open a combination of morning, afternoon or evening hours to accommodate students' schedules. Volunteer tutors assist instructors in some centres, and in some cases, off-site volunteer tutoring is offered as well. Programs which are entirely volunteer-based are in the minority. The colleges and some school division sponsored continuing education departments continue to offer academic upgrading programs, which are generally curriculum based.

Participants in the community-based programs may be at any stage of literacy development, but most can read at least at a beginning level. Some want to develop their literacy for specific reasons, while others are preparing to enroll in academic programs or to write General Equivalency Diploma (GED) exams. In some programs, a large percentage of students is aboriginal. English may be their second language, or they may speak a variety of English which reflects the first language of their communities.

Practitioners in the community-based programs have varied backgrounds. Some have teacher training and experience, but teacher training is not a requirement for employment in these programs. As Robin Millar explained, "We felt it was important for the practitioner to come from the community and to be living there as part of the community." Literacy practitioners may be hired on the basis of their own reading and writing ability, their interest in reading, and their potential to work with adults.

Practitioner training needs

Betty Watkins, who started as a volunteer tutor and is now employed part-time as a paid tutor, felt that she couldn't "presume to teach someone without having some [teaching] skills." And as Robin noted, people in any field need continuing education. Even experienced workers need to improve and their skills, and"carry on developing as persons and as teachers." Shirley Skogan mentioned the need for professional development as well.

Sam Klippenstein approached the topic of training needs by saying,"there's something that kept [adult literacy students] from learning to read and write when they were in school." Gayle Halliwell stressed that it is "critical that we do the right thing by these people now." As well, Sam said, "learning to read and write is a pretty complicated process [so] we need all the knowledge and advice we can get." Doing the "right thing" requires an understanding of adults as learners and of how to work collaboratively with them. At this stage in Manitoba, few literacy workers start out with training or experience in these areas. Although some practitioners are trained as elementary school teachers and have experience teaching reading and writing, other teachers and those without teacher training do not have a background in this area.

As well as needing to understand adult learning theory, practitioners need to be able to apply it. need to be able to help adults use their prior experiences to learn, and need to be able to facilitate learning and literacy development. As Robin suggested, this requires an understanding of reading and writing theory and having a range of strategies to help students to "teach themselves" and to become independent learners. Practitioners also need to understand and be able to address learning styles, language differences, and learning difficulties.

Counselling-related skills were also identified as a learning need for practitioners. Because of the nature of adult students' lives and livelihoods, Diane noted that they may be coming with "problems which they have to solve before they can get on with learning." Often, as Diane, Robin and others pointed out, the literacy worker offers the first sympathetic ear for some adults.

Gayle also identified some training-related needs from her perspective as an administrator. As learners themselves, practitioners "may have questions about what they do, but they may not know what those questions are." One of her roles as an administrator, she says, is to help her staff clarify their questions and find ways to address them. Gayle also suggested that program managers may need training in order to understand the nature and importance of practitioner training and what their roles are in supporting it.

Challenges in accessing training

Practitioners face many challenges to access the training they need. Each of these challenges seem to be related to the economics of literacy work. Literacy teachers and administrators may have other jobs or responsibilities which may make it difficult for them to attend training sessions scheduled on their days off. Nor are there usually any funds to hire a substitute to take over their literacy training. "Very often", Diane said, "If people go to a workshop, the centre has to close down. You have to think, is it more important for me to go to that workshop, or stay here?"

Further, costs of travel and accommodation to attend a workshop, as well as costs of childcare while away, affect access for practitioners who do not have this program support. Travel costs are particularly high for practitioners in the north, who have to drive five or more hours to attend workshops in Winnipeg.

Addressing needs and challenges

Providing training through the Literacy Office

The Manitoba Task Force on Literacy recognized the importance of practitioner training in its 1989 recommendations, affirming training activities that had been initiated through the PACE branch. Practitioner training, which is now provided through the Literacy Office, supports learner-centred programing and is open to literacy practitioners from any setting.[4]

As an employee in the Literacy Office, Robin is able to keep abreast of new programs and keep in touch with people involved in the field. She is also in a good position to know about emerging policy developments which may affect training. A disadvantage to having a government-based program is that people in the field sometimes expect more than government workers can provide; Government employees can advocate and recommend action, but they do not make the global decisions which affect literacy provision in the province.

The Literacy Office requires that communities interested in applying for funding establish Literacy Working Groups. These groups develop the program, provide practitioner support once the program is started, and manage funds. The two community developers who are employed by the Literacy Office work with these groups.

In planning and scheduling workshops, Robin cooperates with the Literacy Workers Alliance of Manitoba (LWAM). Founded in 1988, and funded by a Federal Government Secretary of State grant, LWAM is open to all literacy workers in the province. Among other activities, LWAM organizes training events to meet specific needs, such as a summer institute on materials development, and workshops held in conjunction with its Annual General Meeting. When Robin schedules training events in conjunction with an LWAM event, LWAM may be able to pay travel costs for participants.

The Certificate Program

Robin developed a three-level certificate program in response to practitioners' requests to work towards certification as well as participate in training. The Level I certificate has been in place for a few years and Levels II and III were introduced in 1990.

The Level I certificate may be awarded for participation in an 18-hour Introduction to Literacy Workshop. The Level II certificate, Competence in Literacy Training, may be awarded to practitioners who have completed 12 workshops, and the Level III certificate, an Advanced Certificate in Teaching Literacy to Adults, requires completion of a 90 hour course.[5]

The people I spoke with recognized advantages and disadvantages to having a certificate program. Some saw the certificate as helping to professionalize the field and provide credibility for workers, particularly for those who do not have formal teacher qualifications. People did stress however, that the certificate program should not become a barrier or a means of excluding workers. The level III certificate in particular, Robin noted, is "academically rigorous" and requires a major commitment of time.

At this point, the certificate does not offer possibilities for job advancement or pay increases. Finite resources mean that practitioners will continue to be employed part-time, and that their wages and benefits are not likely to increase, regardless of the extent of their training. However, some suggested that having a certificate may offer an advantage in actually getting a job in the field.

Currently, the certificates are issued by the Literacy Office and it was suggested that they might carry more weight if they were granted by a post-secondary institution. The level III certificate, for instance, is equivalent in work and content to a graduate level university course, but does not carry the same credit. Jonine Anderson suggested that while the course content would be more useful for a literacy practitioner than credit courses which might be available, some may opt to take a credit course in order to work towards a more marketable certificate.

A concern was raised that the certificate program could legitimize a recurrent focus on entry level workshops, with little provision for people beyond that level. Turn-over in workers in existing programs, along with the development of new programs each year, create an ongoing demand for new practitioners' training. Experienced practitioners are generally concerned that their needs for continuing training may not be met because of new practitioners' training needs.

Robin is well aware of the challenge of addressing more experienced workers' needs at the same time as meeting the ongoing requirement for training new practitioners — she had recently conducted five Introduction to Literacy workshops in three months! One way to address this challenge, she suggested, is to train others to conduct the introductory workshops, so that she may focus on the other levels of training. The Literacy Office community development workers are beginning to facilitate local network development and region-based training. As well, Diane has started assisting with the introductory workshops, and LWAM has funds to facilitate training for trainers.

Planning courses to meet learning needs

The workshops which are offered through the Literacy Office are on topics related to practitioners' identified needs. For instance, since she has some training in counselling, Robin is able to conduct workshops to help practitioners develop listening strategies, to be able to set boundaries, and to develop awareness of referral networks. These workshops are not intended to train workers as counsellors, which would require a much fuller course, but to assist them in helping students deal with issues which they face.

To address questions of learning difficulties, Robin has introduced workshops on two prerequisite topics: learning styles and language awareness. Workshops on the first topic help practitioners explore their own learning style as well as to explore ways of helping students develop awareness about their learning strategies.

Language awareness workshops help practitioners understand how students' first languages or language varieties affect their English literacy development. This understanding is proving essential in programs whose aboriginal participants speak varieties of English. The aim is to facilitate students' awareness of the origins of their languages as a basis for understanding written English. To develop these workshops, Robin combined her background in language awareness developed in Britain, and local research on aboriginal language structure.

For the past two years, Robin has published a schedule of training events, based on a needs assessment carried out in the spring. As Sam noted, practitioners are now able to plan their professional development in relation to their program and personal responsibilities. The workshop descriptions also help practitioners clarify their training questions.

Innovations in delivery

Practicums

A focus on learner-centred literacy education places particular demands on literacy practitioners. Learning how to facilitate learning and literacy development requires practice and feedback, as well as demonstration and exposure to ideas. Practicums have been incorporated into the Introduction to Literacy Workshop to address these needs.

The introductory workshops are arranged so that theoretical concepts and practical activities are presented in the morning, and afternoon sessions are devoted to practising the activities with students. Robin is able to observe and critique practice, and afterwards, address questions. As well as giving people a firmer grounding in using the activities, the practicums orient new practitioners to working with adult students. Betty noted that "It makes you examine where you're coming from. They give you real insight about where the learner is coming from."

The practicums also serve to ground learner-centred principles as students take on a teaching role. For instance, a student from Diane's program took part in an introductory workshop practicum. Afterwards, when people were discussing ways to put students at ease, he asked what he could do to help his nervous tutor.

Observation and apprenticeship

Although Robin would like to incorporate practicums into all the workshops, she recognizes that this isn't possible. In current practicums, practitioners and students may be meeting each other for the first time, and "for some things you need to know the students you're working with." Robin would like to provide more on-site training, where she can both model learning approaches and observe practitioners at work. Practitioners also recalled that when they had started in their roles, they had benefited from visiting an existing program to observe an experienced practitioner at work. They suggested that such visits would be of ongoing use.

An apprenticeship model is a related alternative which Diane introduced in her own program for an worked individually with students, and finally worked with a small group who wanted to obtain their drivers' licences.

Literacy Office staff had intended to establish a base for apprenticeship at Journeys, a community-based program in Winnipeg. The plan was for new practitioners to come and work in the program for two weeks, as well as attend sessions about program organization and teaching strategies. Although funding was obtained to support Journeys as a centre for workshops, it hasn't been possible to fund new practitioners to work in the program for any length of time.

Distance education

The availability of more trainers will address some issues of distance as more workshops can be offered on a regional basis. Technology also offers possibilities for reaching workers at a distance, and Robin is undertaking a pilot project to explore these possibilities. Making use of community cable TV and interactive teleconferencing, she will deliver training to a number of communities in northern Manitoba. The workshop will be conducted with a group of practitioners in a Winnipeg studio and community participants will be able to watch the workshop and join in by teleconference. The outcome of the project will help the Literacy Office determine how to allocate training resources in the future.

Concluding comments

In Manitoba, the challenges of practitioner training are being addressed by providing training through a government office. With a focus on supporting community-based programs, training is evolving to help practitioners develop learner-centred approaches through practicums. The advantages and disadvantages to a certificate program are being weighed, and barriers to access are being addressed by training additional trainers, by working with the Literacy Workers Alliance of Manitoba, and by exploring distance education possibilities. Economic barrier remain part-time work, short contracts and uncertain long term program funding are continuing challenges.

Notes

1. The term aboriginal is used to include all people who might identify themselves, or be identified as Treaty, Status or Non-Status Indians, or Metis.
2. Manitoba Task Force on Literacy. *Recommendations of the Manitoba Task Force on Literacy*. Winnipeg. Manitoba: Manitoba Education and Training. April 1989.
3. Gabor, D. "What Is Being Done in Manitoba to Address the Issue of Illiteracy? *Manitoba Education* 17 (4), 1990.
4. Gayle suggested that open participation can create difficulties when full-time, salaried staff attend training alongside community-based practitioners who work part-time for hourly wages.
5. Manitoba Literacy Office. *Certification of Training*. Winnipeg, Manitoba: Manitoba Literacy Office.

Discussion Questions

1. What do you think should be the basis for developing and training programs for practitioners?
2. What are some of the essential elements which should go into such programs?
3. Distinguish between those elements in a training program which would be appropriate for training practitioners anywhere, as compared with items which would be unique to communities in Manitoba?
4. What are the advantages and disadvantages for using part-time practitioners to teach literacy programs? What are some ways of overcoming the limitations?
5. What are the advantages and disadvantages to having a practitioners' training program run by a government office?
6. Do you think that a certificate should be awarded when a practitioner completes a training program?

Chapter Two
COMMUNITY STRENGTHENING

Sheila Goldgrab

Place: Public library and museum, St. Mary's, Ontario
Participants: Adults in the community, developmentally
        handicapped adults
Issues: 1. Community-based literacy
       2. Community outreach
       3. Re-integrating people with disabilities back into the
          community

Background

Community members are active participants of many of the activities of St.Mary's community-based adult literacy program. The library, local museum, the Association for Community Living, and the program volunteers have all been involved in integrating the literacy student more fully into the community. The literacy program has, as a result, built and strengthened the community.

St. Mary's is a city of 5,000 located 26 miles northeast of London, Ontario. It has an industrial base composed of companies such as Campbell's Soup, Domtar, Hayes Dana and a cement plant. The number of unemployed is currently small. Americans, English, Irish, and Scots first settled there. The Italians came to work the railroad in the early 1900's, and the Dutch settlers came before World War II and again in the 1950's. Since then, a small number of Chinese have moved to the area.

Over 41% of the residents have high school diplomas and many of them have university degrees. The size of families is

93

larger, the number of home owners and stay-at-home mothers are more numerous than the provincial average. St. Mary's beauty, small size, and proximity to Stratford's thriving theatre scene has also attracted many retired arts people.

St. Mary's Library and literacy education

St. Mary's community-based literacy program began in 1986. Prior to that time, the Board of Education's program of English as a Second Language and the evening literacy course were not successfully attracting students. The classroom setting was thought to have been a reason for the low enrollment. St. Mary's Library then offered space to hold a literacy program on their premises. The Board of Education still advertises its course in the academic calendar, and all those who are interested are referred to the community-based literacy program in the library. The recently renovated, attractive library is in a central location that provides a welcoming environment for one-to-one literacy instruction.

The literacy program's coordinator administers the program on behalf of the library board. The Ministry of Education funds the literacy program, although the library provides space, a phone, photocopier and reading materials. The library has shared the responsibility of confronting illiteracy in their community.

Marilyn Haywood, a co-coordinator of the literacy program, believes that the library has a special community function in St. Mary's:

> The library is really a community centre, where you go to get information you want. It's an information clearing house for the town and the rural community. The library is open, bright, and there is nothing intimidating about it. Everyone in the area, I believe, feels this way about it.

Barbara Taylor, the chief librarian of St. Mary's Library, views community involvement as an important aspect of the partnership that exists between the literacy program and the community:

> We want the community to take part in the literacy program. Some are aware of illiteracy, others find it difficult to believe that it exists here. The newspaper

covered our Victorian Walk which was a literacy program event that invited the community to participate in
the Oral History Project launch. This event was supported by the library. We'd like this written tour of the
community to be read by visitors and those interested
in moving here.

Barbara commented about the inclusion of literacy students, many of whom are first time library users, as part of
the library's community:

Libraries generally have had a certain population that
we didn't have to go out and find. Now that we know
that there is a major illiteracy problem in Canada we
have to do more outreach and make libraries more
accessible. Four years ago, no one knew that illiteracy
was a large problem. Suddenly we were made aware
that it was a problem, and one that exists in our community. Many adults had poor experiences in the school
system so they didn't want to return to a school for help.
Instead, we've begun a literacy program here. If we at
the library want to have people read lifelong then we
have to be prepared to teach them to read. The library
places less articulate and visible users now on an equal
priority with other users of the library. We have not
received an increase in funding in two years. If funding
was available and we didn't already have a community
program, we would put one in place and fund it.

Through the library's committment, community awareness has expanded to include those people with difficulties
reading and/or writing.

The electronic age has meant that accessing information is
made easier. Whereas teachers of young children formerly
delivered a presentation to their class about a number of
current topics, the emphasis is now, more than ever, that the
students are instructed to do the research about the topic
themselves. The new school curriculum has been influenced
by the availability of the computer and the new accessibility
of information. This, in turn, has meant that the library has
been able to meet the new demands by school-aged children
and literacy students for information that technology is able
to provide. Easily accessible information is now available to

those who, until recently, did not participate fully at all in the library. Videos, pamphlets and fact sheets are currently made available by the library.

In order to support the adult literacy program in St. Mary's, the library has been working to offer special collections, instruction, and support services for these new library users. Barbara described the library materials that are being used by tutors and literacy students, and the library's plans to offer more materials in the near future:

> We have material supports such as books and Adult Basic Education computer packages. It's also a wonderful self confidence booster for a literacy learner to work on a computer. We also have a computer package developed by The London Literacy Program and the school boards for tutors to teach students reading skills and computer skills. We would like to have more materials available for learners. We have books on cassette and videos and we have reading materials for all levels. It is becoming much easier now to get materials for the new adult reader and The Metropolitan Toronto Reference Library will have a library of literacy education materials that we'll be able to order from and make use of.

Gladys Watson is the manager of Alpha Ontario, the Literacy and Language Training Resource Centre in Toronto. She, with others, is developing a collection of adult literacy and immigrant second language training resources for Ontario. The collection and services will be available to literacy practitioners, adult students, libraries, and the general public. The staff at the Centre has plans to discuss the needs of users like St. Mary's Library, in order to find out which services it will offer the library. Videos, cassette tapes, oral history transcripts, and educational software will be available. An Inter-Library Loan network will move the collections, and workshops on there sources will be given upon request.

Community volunteers

With the exception of two part-time coordinators, the St. Marys Literacy program is run by volunteers. Finding volunteer tutors has not been difficult. The literacy program staff is able to find individuals in the community who are interested in being tutors for the program. As well, students and others show their interest in getting involved by approaching the program on their own.

For Marilyn, the participation by a wide variety of community members has meant that the program is truly community-based. In her view, relying on volunteers in St. Marys community-based literacy program helps to build a sense of community spirit. This does not at all mean that the program, by virtue of relying on volunteer tutors, follows a charitable model of service:

> We disagree with that equation. While there certainly is a need for professionals, we make use of volunteers as a way of giving people a chance to contribute to the literacy program. This doesn't just strengthen our community, it builds it. In a small city like ours, we don't think that doing something for someone else is a model of charity. Volunteers gain a lot from their involvement.

Many of the literacy students are also clients of the Association for Community Living (ACL), formally the St. Marys Association for the Mentally Retarded. The volunteer tutors of the literacy program do more than teach people with disabilities in the program literacy and numeracy skills, they enable these people to re-integrate fully into the community that they have returned to. Marilyn explains the important role that these volunteers play:

> Most of the people with disabilities that are currently supported by this community have been away in institutions for a number of years. When people came back to this community, connections had been weakened. Their introduction to the community happens primarily with general professionals, so the person's connection to the community is weak if it is there at all. When people come to the literacy program, they're meeting someone who is a member of the community and who may be their first real connection way to facilitate this is through the use of volunteers. Sometimes volunteers start as literacy tutors and end up as friends of people that they've begun to know. Either way, people re-entering the community have still

made a connection.

Marilyn's work experience in both literacy education and the area of mental retardation has allowed her to compare the issue of professionalization in both fields. The question of professionalization of literacy tutors is a relatively new issue that has recently surfaced in the province:

> Current thinking by some in adult literacy education is similar to the cry for professionalization that took place a number of years ago in the field of mental retardation. It was strongly believed then that the thing that disabled people needed most was to learn skills and the best people to teach those skills were no longer volunteers but college or university graduates with a specialization in the field. Ten years have gone by, and we have lots of people who have lots of skills, but they are missing involvement in or connection with people from the community they live in. So now we're busily trying to figure out how to help people to develop relationships, make acquaintances and friendships. Many agencies are no longer hiring professionals but instead are hiring people from the community with skills gained from life experience. For example, a single person on a single income is able to help someone else with a disability on a single income make meals that are nutritious for little money.

Marilyn concluded that what is needed is a balance in both fields between professionals training volunteers, professionals teaching students, and true community membership involvement. She refutes the often stated argument that volunteer participation in literacy programs is unreliable. High volunteer turnover does not occur in St. Marys literacy program:

> Volunteer longevity is incredible. Many volunteers have been here longer than paid staff. Some have been here for four years...we've never kept any of the paid coordinators in that time.

As well, changes between a volunteer tutor and student are made easily when they are required. Marilyn added that

"We have flexibility to change a match if it doesn't work, we can fix it without being strangled by a bureaucracy."

St. Mary's District Museum and local history

Mary Smith, the curator of the St. Mary's District Museum, is happy to get involved in the library's literacy events: "Happy to encourage anything that has to do with history and research." A guided walking tour of the area's limestone buildings was organized by the group. After the walk, there was a reception at the library and a Victorian Tea. In Mary's view, this public kick-off of the oral history project "was a way to get the community interested in the project and the literacy program. It combined promotion of local history and encouraged literacy."

Re-integrating people with disabilities into the community

Many of the students in the literacy program are also clients of the Association for Community Living (ACL). ACL gives one-to-one support, such as home care, to people who are developmentally handicapped. Their mandate is to reintegrate their clients into the community so that they may lead normal lives and contribute to the community. Their major goal is to help people meet their dreams and desires by providing planning and supports.

Often the staff of ACL discover that their clients have difficulty writing only when they can't write letters or grocery lists. Charlotte Rosehart, the Manager for Community Involvement for ACL, recognizes that having low literacy skills is a barrier for her agency's clients. Jennifer Young, the Coordinator for Services Support has had direct contact with clients where she has learned of their need for literacy upgrading. During the framework meetings where the client's family and a staff person develop a plan of direction with the client, the need for literacy learning is often raised by the family. Although a formal relationship between the literacy program and ACL does not as yet exist, the staff at ACL regularly refer their clients to the literacy program.

A few general information meetings have taken place at

ACL to inform clients about the literacy program. Often, Stella Howett and Marilyn Haywood who currently share the responsibilities of coordinating the literacy program, have found that there is an absence of ongoing contact between the literacy program and ACL about a student who is also a client of ACL. The provision of information to literacy tutors about their student's health condition is felt to be necessary should the student need their tutor's assistance.

As Marilyn was formally employed by the ACL, information about a number of adult clients is often communicated in an informal way to the literacy program through her. She is familiar with the disabilities of adults in her community that are served by the Association and shares this information with the program.

Both Charlotte and Jennifer of the ACL felt that the small size of the community meant that many had seen a community member experience seizures of one sort or another in public. Although they concluded that most people were knowledgeable about what to do if a seizure should occur, Stella has asked ACL to develop a package and prepare an educational workshop for the literacy tutors about illnesses and disabilities. Stella would like the workshop to include information about what assistance a tutor can offer their student should the need arise. This would formalize the relationship and the literacy program.

Concluding comments

For the St. Mary's Literacy Program, being a community-based educational program has meant involving members of the community, and connecting with other community associations and organizations to improve their services to students. In this way, they are able to root the literacy program in the fabric of the community.

Discussion Questions

1. *Give some examples of how an adult literacy program can help to strengthen a community?*
2. *In what ways can a public library prepare itself to provide literacy programs for adults?*
3. *What does community-based literacy really mean?*
4. *Integrating a person with a disability into the community can sometimes lead to dependency on a tutor. How can we prepared for this situation?*
5. *What is the contribution professionally trained persons can make to a literacy program? What is meant by "professional"?*

Chapter Three
LINKING LITERACY AND HEALTH: A POPULAR EDUCATION APPROACH[1]

Mary Norton

Place: Community Education Council in Araviat, North West Territories
Participants: Inuit
Issues: 1. Integrating relevant content into education programs
2. Home-based education

> *My definitions of health is very broad. I don't see it in narrow terms of physical wellness, but in mental and spiritual [terms as well]. Being literate...is part of being healthy.*
>
> **Linda Pemik**

This broad view of health was one of the foundations for a health and literacy project that Linda Pemik coordinated in Arviat, an Inuit community in the Northwest Territories.[2] Another foundation of the project was a belief in community development and popular education principles. According to Joy Suluk, an Adult Educator trainee in Arviat, popular education means "getting people to do things for themselves in their own way, with their own abilities, and their own skills."

This case study is about the health and literacy project and the principles in which it is rooted. To research this case study, I spoke with Linda and Joy, and with Stu MacKay, the Adult Educator in Arviat. Facilitating some project follow-up activities.

Background[3]

With a population of about 1300, Arviat is a major settlement in the Keewatin Region of the Eastern Arctic. Although Inuit comprise 95% of the population, and Inuktitut is widely spoken,[4] English is generally needed for employment, education and training, and for communication outside the community.

In Arviat, English is the language of instruction in the upper elementary grades and high school, and Inuktitut is one of the languages of instruction for the first four years (k-4). The school system is aiming to help young people maintain their identity while preparing them for the new way of life in their communities.[5] Still, Joy says, there are young people leaving the school system without full fluency in either English or Inuktitut.

An elected Community Education Council (CEC) oversees the school's programs and facilities, and along with a more recently formed Community Training Advisory Committee (CTAC), the CEC also relates to the Community Learning Centre. This Centre was started in the early 1970's as part of a territory-wide move to provide upgrading and employment training for adults. It is now affiliated with the recently formed Arctic College.[6]

Enrolments in Community Learning Centre courses have been increasing steadily since 1986 when about 36 people took part in a full-time Adult Basic Education (ABE) program and a few other courses. In 1990, 228 people enrolled in one or more of the 23 part-time and full-time courses provided in the areas of ABE, Personal Development and Career Development. Stu, who began his job as adult educator in 1986, attributed the increased participation to a community development approach: "We've gone out and sought community involvement, not only in the programs but in the whole planning structure."

Adult education as community development

The federal government was responsible for schooling in the NWT from the 1950's until 1970, when the newly-formed Government of the Northwest Territories assumed that responsibility. A 1972 GNWT Department of Education report recommended community control of schools, and this led to the development of Community Education Councils such as the one in Arviat.[7] However, Joy suggested that while people have been told for several years that they have control of education, "most of the people younger than myself have never experienced control of education."

Referring to traditional ways of child rearing, Joy explained that at one time "parents had full control of their children's education [and] overnight that control was gone." Joy's generation was the first to attend the federal government schools, and she recalled that when she started school, her grandparents" Now, Joy suggested, "people are relying too much on the schools" and they have to start defining education for themselves.

Helping people define education for themselves has been a goal of adult education in Arviat in recent years. Prior to being engaged as the adult educator, Stu worked as an economic planner for the Arviat Hamlet Council. In this role, he had identified community members who had a strong interest in adult training programs, and who were concerned about the ways in which training decisions were being made. As Stu described it, they were "sick and tired of Canada Employment putting courses in without telling us anything about it."

Stu helped these people organize the Community Training Advisory Committee, and helped them to articulate and direct their concerns. This initiated a process of change so that instead of "everything happening to you [it's now] happening because you initiated it. Once people have a taste of that", Stu said, "then they're on their way." Stu's role in this process reflects his view that "it's far more important for the adult educator to be the facilitator of training and development, than [to be] the actual deliverer."

Stu was introduced to community development principles when he worked with Canadian University Services Overseas (CUSO), and as adult educator he sees his role as helping people identify community needs and "enabling others to meet the needs. " In keeping with these principles, Stu has been working with Joy, who will be assuming the role of adult educator.

Joy has always "had this dream that I wanted to be an educator. " Although she was able to go only as far as grade

six at the Arviat school "that was the highest grade offered
at the time." Joy never let go of the dream. She worked as a
classroom assistant and later, for ten years, as the secretary
of the Community Education Council. When the Adult
Educator trainee position was developed, Joy applied for
the position and was hired. Joy has also been continuing her
education. She attained a GED certificate in Arviat, and,
through a distance education program, she earned a Diploma in Adult Education.

Joy will be one of the first Inuit to fill the adult educator
position, and as a person from the community, she will be
attuned to issues in a way that an outsider could never be.
However, she said that she was a "little nervous" about how
the community would accept her in the adult educator's role.
They are used to having "qablunaat"[8] in the position, and as
Linda explained, there are "people [who] have lived here for
years who are convinced that qablunaat know everything,
that they know nothing..." Helping people change this
attitude is a goal that Joy and Linda share.

Community development and public health

Linda has learned "basic" Inuktitut over the years that she
has lived in Arviat, but there is one expression which she
would rather not hear. "When [my students] make a mistake," she explained, "they say,'Inugupta' [meaning] 'because I'm an Inuk', that's why I make a mistake." Linda says
that people may have learned this attitude at some point
through their schooling, but she also sees it as a reflection of
the "whole system" which evolved with northern development. She cited health care as an example:

> The health care system does everything for people. It
> doesn't allow people to make decisions about them-
> selves or their bodies, and it doesn't listen to people
> when they try to communicate what they think.

Linda said that she is proud to live in a country where
there is financial and social support for people, but she noted
that there are different ways to help:

> There's help that robs people of their independence and
> their abilities and their belief in themselves, and there

are ways that give it to them.

Linda sees popular education as a way to help people and to encourage people to change "in a way that they choose and in a way that's positive rather than negative." Linda was introduced to popular education through her involvement with the Arviat Health Committee and meeting public health workers. Her interest in the approach took her to a workshop in northern Manitoba and, more recently, was the impetus behind organizing a course on popular education methodology for Community Learning Centre staff.

The Arviat Health Committee was formed about five years ago, Linda said, by people who were "fed up with the quality of health care and [who] wanted to do something about it." Determined to make some changes, the Committee tackled the issue of understaffing at the community nursing station. Linda said that the Committee "made [their] voices heard," and when staffing was increased, they felt that they had contributed to the change. With this success behind them, the committee was ready to take on the challenge of reinstating midwifery services.

Although nurse-midwives had enabled Arviat women to have their babies at the nursing station until the early 1980's, midwifery services were phased out and pregnant women had to be flown out of Arviat to have their babies in a hospital.[9] The Health Committee conducted a survey about midwifery and the results showed that 99% of the women interviewed wanted to have their babies in the community, and that this desire crossed all boundaries of age, culture and education level.[10] Until the survey was completed, there had been an assumption that the interest in midwifery service was mainly among older women. Linda said that the survey helped the health committee gain credibility: "[it] really made the medical profession stand up and take a look at us."

The survey was also designed to collect information about general health issues, and the results demonstrated a need for health education in the community. The Health Committee concluded "that many people in Arviat, especially children, could be healthier if mothers had a better understanding of health and sickness."[11] The committee's next task was to raise funds to carry out health education with young mothers. Through her involvement with the Community Learning Centre[12], Linda learned that there were grants available for literacy programing, and the idea of combining health and literacy education emerged:

> At first it was a way to get money, but as we sat down and planned it, and looked at it more seriously, we came up with a model that worked...

Linking health and literacy education

The model which Linda developed combined health education with English language and literacy practice, and the community was able to obtain funds for a four-month pilot project.[13] To start the project, Linda surveyed young mothers about their knowledge of health, and about their interest in taking part in home learning about health issues. She visited 31 homes and talked to 23 people. Twenty of the women Linda talked with said they would like to take part in the project, and fifteen did participate in home-based lessons. From her observations, Linda estimated that the majority of project participants were at a "developing" stage of English literacy ability.[14]

As part of the survey, women chose the topics they wanted to learn about and Linda prepared printed information which the women could use during the lessons and which they could refer to afterwards. (The most popular topics in the project had included "how to care for sick kids", and "how to help your children learn".) Linda explained how literacy and health education were connected in the lessons:

> I see literacy entering in many ways. One way, of course, is that we did have some written materials [about health], and I did involve learners in some writing if they wanted that. So people practised reading and writing skills in English.

Linda also felt that having written course material generally enhanced the project by helping people feel that they were learners: "I don't think they thought they were learning unless they were reading and writing and doing things they had done in school." There were a few cases, however, where she felt that people were a bit intimidated by the formality, and she adjusted her approach.

Practising oral English was also seen as an important

aspect of the project, but as Linda explained, she "didn't sit down to tutor English." Rather, English was the vehicle for learning health: "[I] tried to incorporate both oral and written language in every lesson." Sometimes she and the student dispensed with the prepared lesson and just talked in English.

Linda completed 30 home tutoring sessions over the six weeks that instruction was taking place and the home visits proved to be an important aspect of the project. Linda did explore possibilities for group learning, but the first meeting at the Community Learning Centre was, she said, "a disaster" — only two people came, one on time, and the other two hours late.

A number of factors may have contributed to the poor turnout for the group session, including a difficult-to-read notice and the fact that the weather on the meeting day was exceptionally nice. In the project evaluation questionnaire, women reported that they didn't attend the group meeting because they were too shy, because they were afraid to talk in front of others, or because they didn't have a babysitter.

In completing the evaluation questionnaire, women also said they liked learning at home, and that they would participate if the home visits were to continue. Linda sees an ongoing need for home learning.

As well as having people complete individual evaluation surveys, a group evaluation was conducted in conjunction with a Christmas party. Again, the interest in home learning was strongly supported, but the women also indicated that they thought they would enjoy learning at home with a friend. Small group home-based activities were being introduced as a follow-up to the literacy and health project. The plan was for three or four mothers and their children to gather in a home and take part in activities aimed at helping children learn. Linda had noted that her most successful tutoring sessions were those that involved participants in an activity, and the small group activities are being planned with this in mind. The week before I visited Arviat, participants had gathered at Cindy Fleishman's home to make "jello candy" and learn to sing "jelly in the bowl" and other rhyming songs. While taking an active part in their own learning, mothers practised English and helped their children learn.

In her report on the health and literacy project, Linda noted that from talking with project participants it "became clear that many people depend on others to tell them what to do when there is sickness in the family." She recommended that future programs try to encourage learners to believe in their own abilities to make decisions about their health and the health of their children, and that all teaching be done with this in mind. She went on to suggest that "groups which are already working toward improving community health should also be helped to grow stronger within the community."

Practising popular education

As chair of the Arviat Health Committee, Linda is committed to helping the group grow stronger by applying popular education methodology. In her view, the most important aspect of popular education is

> ...the emphasis on the teacher as a facilitator rather than as a boss who's telling everyone what to do. It becomes a means of enabling, or empowering — whatever term you want to use — the student or learner.

Linda noted that practising the role of facilitator was hard sometimes, because she is "a very directive person." As well, Linda said, Inuit traditionally learn by listening and observing others, so while "as a teacher I'm always looking for ways to minimize what I say" it is not always easy to draw people out.

Linda also recalled that when she was first teaching adult upgrading classes she "struggled with ways to use the new [popular education] ideas in the classroom" and found it difficult because "no one knew what I was talking about." However, she said that adult education has "changed so much in the past five years":

> We've gone from a one-man show to a team approach...It's very exciting to work with a group of people who share the same philosophy, and to learn from each other.

Through a community development approach to adult education, and by practising popular education principles, the understanding of literacy has also changed. In Arviat, literacy no longer means just reading and writing. Rather, as Joy suggested,

> ...the way I think about literacy is many things, skills, how you control your life, and what control you have in society...It's learning how to make your life easier in different ways.

Notes

1. The Government of the Northwest Territories requires that all research in the territories be done under licence from the Science Institute of the NWT. Prior to carrying out the research for this report I was granted a 1991 Scientific Research Licence, number 11109.
2. The community has also been called Eskimo Point. Arviat is the preferred Inuktitut name and is now the official name.
3. More background about Arviat is included in another report in this book, titled *Language, Literacy and Culture in an Arctic Community*. This report describes the development of an Inuktitut literacy program in Arviat.
4. Inuktitut is also used in its written form. For a discussion of Inuktitut literacy development, see the case study referred to above.
5. Shouldice, M. "Making Education Work for Inuit in the Modern World." *Inuktitut* 63, 60. Summer 1986.
6. In most communities, the equivalents of the Arviat Community Learning Centre are called Adult Education Centres. Adult educators are hired to work with the community to plan and coordinate upgrading, pre-employment training and other courses of interest. In many situations, the adult educator also teaches the courses.
   Arctic College was formed under the Colleges Act in 1985, and campuses have been established in six regions of the NWT. The community Adult Education Centres, which were under the direct jurisdiction of the GNWT Department of Education, are now part of the college system; the Arviat Community Learning Centre relates to the Keewatin Campus, headquartered in Rankin Inlet.
7. Patterson, D. "The Challenge to Northern Education." *Inuktitut*, 63, 51. Summer, 1986.

8. "Qablunaat" is an Inuktitut term used to refer to non-Inuit people.

9. Linda explained that until the early 1980s women were generally flown out to have their first baby in a hospital, and unless there were complications with that birth, they could stay in the community for subsequent births. Restrictions on hiring British-trained nurse-midwives were among the factors contributing to the phasing out of this service.

10. The health committee conducted the survey and sent the results to the University of Manitoba for analysis. A University of Manitoba anthropology professor helped the committee arrange for this support.

11. Pemik, L. *Learning for a Healthier Future: A Pilot Project in Health and Literacy*. Arviat, NWT: Arctic College. 1990.

12. Linda has taught ABE and other courses at the Community Learning Centre. When I met her, she was teaching a course to prepare home care workers.

13. The project was funded through grants from the GNWT Community Literacy Projects and the Walter Duncan Gordon Charitable Foundation.

14. Linda used a model for literacy assessment which had been introduced in tutor training workshops in Arviat. People at a "developing" stage would have basic reading and writing skills, but might not be able to manage the range of reading and writing tasks which are a part of daily life.

Discussion questions

1. *From this and other case studies, give examples of how literacy programs can be community-based?*
2. *How can health concerns be built into a literacy education program?*
3. *What are some steps that can be taken in order to give people a choice of attending educational programs?*
4. *How does the definition and practice of popular education compare with other case studies in this section?*

Chapter Four
OUTREACH

Sheila Goldgrab

Place: Community Resource Centre, Killaloe, Ontario
Participants: Community members
Issues: 1. Community outreach
       2. Family literacy
       3. Rural education

Killaloe's literacy program is the only community-based adult basic literacy program in all of Renfrew County. It serves a large area in eastern Ontario. In order to promote awareness of the program, it has developed a network with the organizations, professionals, and the media of the region. Its location, its Comment Card designed to promote clear language, and its Oral History Project are other examples of how the literacy program promotes itself in order that potential students will learn about the program.

Background

Killaloe's Community Resource Centre Literacy Program serves a population of 10,000 people in an 800 square mile radius in the southwestern area of Renfrew County, Ontario. Renfrew county is the most rural county south of Sudbury, and the delivery area for the literacy program covers the most rural part of the county.

An economically depressed area based on traditional slow

growth industries, and with relative isolation from major markets, the region is also experiencing plant closures and lay offs. The aging population and the outflow of youth to the region's more prosperous urban centres has meant a low local tax base that has not been able to finance the full provision of essential services in the area. By southern Ontario standards, this is an isolated region with limited available social services.

The Algonquins were the first residents of the area. Later, in the mid 19th century, Europeans, particularly the Irish, Germans, and Poles, settled in the area. It was then that the Opeongo settlement road was built from the Ottawa River west to Barry's Bay to encourage settlement of immigrants for the booming logging industry. Until recently, the main sources of employment have always been traditional. These were wood products, agriculture, clothing, and textiles.

More recently, the major sources of employment have expanded to include cedar homes, magnesium, thermostats, electronic switching devices, large scale turbines, and tourism. In the late 1960's, many Canadian and American urban dwellers moved to the area. Most of these newcomers were back-to-the-landers who built small businesses and contributed to the small but renown craft community. Recently, many older people have moved to the area to enjoy their retirement.

The Community Resource Centre's (CRC) literacy program is run by the management committee of Women Initiating Responsible Change (WIRC). WIRC is an incorporated non-profit organization with a mandate of providing resources to meet the personal and social needs of both sexes. As well as establishing a Woman of the Year award to a woman in the area and providing a scholarship to a number of grade 12 high school girls, the members of WIRC founded and developed a community resource centre. The objectives of the resource centre are to provide access, support and space to the community at large. The literacy program is but one of the centre's many programs and activities which serve to provide support for the community.

As transportation and travelling great distances are major problems in this region, WIRC developed a storehouse of useful information that could easily be accessed by the region's residents. When the first Woman of the Year award recipient, herself a literacy instructor working for the

Renfrew Board of Education, told the community centre of the need for private literacy tutoring, WIRC was interested in knowing more. When the funding for a literacy program became available, the centre pursued it. There is currently a part time program coordinator and a half time support staff person working in the literacy program.

Preparing for outreach - becoming visible

When the literacy program participants were asked whether the literacy program would be more effective if it were autonomous. Presently it was subject to the WIRC appointed management committee, the resource centre, the literacy program staff, the coordinator for the community resource centre (CRC), and the president of the board of directors. But each listed several advantages to the existing cooperative relationship.

Operating as part of a resource centre has meant that the centre has been able to share its resources with the literacy program. Funding from a federal Job Development program has enabled the centre to hire a support staff person. Since the program shares an office with the resource centre, it is able to share the support person on staff. In times when the literacy program's activities require additional staff time, the support person is able to work out an arrangement to spend more time working with the literacy program.

Often the community centre applies for funding for the literacy program to ministries other than the Ministry of Education which is responsible for providing funds to literacy programs. Much of the funds for the literacy program's new family literacy pilot project was, for example, secured by the centre from Ontario's Ministry of Community and Social Services (COMSOC), the same Ministry that funds the resource centre. COMSOC has funded the purchase of books and toys and a mobile bus that will be driven throughout the region to encourage family reading and literacy.

The literacy program is able to share the resource centre's volunteer force and as a result, the program benefits from a broader volunteer base than if it were on its own. Residents of the area surrounding Killaloe who may not know about the literacy program are drawn there to learn about the literacy program, and often end up volunteering their time to answer the phones for both the centre and the program.

Being located in the centre of Killaloe is an advantage to this literacy program's promotional efforts. The joint facility with the resource centre serves a valuable purpose by protecting the students' privacy. An individual with literacy problems is able to inquire about the program without the stigma of going to a location that offers only programs or activities that are literacy related. Many literacy students who receive literacy tutoring have successfully kept their activities hidden from others, if they so desired, and they have appreciated the anonymity gained by going to a community centre involved in many other publicized and unrelated activities. To begin, the literacy program was able to share the network mailing lists that the CRC had developed.

When the Killaloe library had no room for their storytime activities, the community resource centre helped by providing space for mothers and their children. This meant that mothers were aware of the literacy program in the centre long before the family literacy program had been designed.

The central location of the resource centre in Killaloe, the variety of services it provides, and the community organizations that use the rooms in the centre, all serve to reinforce the presence of the literacy program in the community.

Reaching out into the community

Diane Nicholls' spelling difficulties were noticed when she attended the resource centre's life skills program. As a result, she was referred to the literacy program and was in turn approached to work as a support staff member at the resource centre with the literacy program. Diane's salary is funded by the Canada Employment Centre. Diane welcomed the idea of working on her spelling "on the job" because it is easier for her than doing homework alone at home. Diane believes that "it would have made me more nervous (to study at home). " Diane offered her view of the community and its approach to new programs and to change:

> People around here find it hard to welcome anything at first. I find that later on, when they find that it is what they need and what the community wants, they will welcome it. It usually gets rejection at first.

Kathy Lampi, the executive director of the resource centre, agrees that the community is resistant to change:

> Killaloe is a static community. As such, it is slow to accept what people's grandmothers didn't have...It is, however, better now than it was 20 years ago.

In order to be accepted and known by the community, the priority for the program's first outreach worker in August 1987 was to raise community awareness of the problem of illiteracy and to inform people working in the social services about the existence of a literacy program in the region. Letters sent and follow up meetings were made with service clubs, women's institutes, the legal system, doctors, public health nurses, the clergy and others who would have come into contact with adults who had problems with reading and/or writing stimulated awareness.

Referrals are responsible for many of the literacy student participants. Patty Shore (not real name), a retired teacher who is now a volunteer tutor with the literacy program, works with a student who was referred to the program by Avoca House, a shelter and outreach program for women and children in crisis. A number of women who have needed the services of Avoca House have literacy problems as well. Some of the Avoca House staff are also volunteers of the resource centre and both staffs work toward a common purpose. According to Patty, "many who arrive to Avoca House need more education. Often [their] studies have been interrupted by family responsibilities."

The Pembroke Canadian National Institute for the Blind (CNIB) helped Diana Hasler by referring her to the literacy program. Mis-diagnosed by the teachers in her early years of school as an attention-getter with no motivation and no interest in reading, Diana did not learn to read. Encouraged years later by her own family to make a visit to the CNIB, it was discovered that Diana was legally blind. The CNIB referred Diana to the literacy program and she presently receives private tutoring in her home by Lynne Gillespie. The program received money to purchase a low-vision machine to help people like Diana who have sight problems. The funding came from the Ministry of Education's literacy branch through "special support" to improve services for people on social assistance.

Oral History Project and outreach

The Oral History Project is another way in which the literacy program has attempted to reach the community at large. The program advertised their Oral History Project in the newspaper and asked people to call and suggest women who they knew to have interesting stories that they remembered their mothers had told them about settling in the area. Literacy students participated in writing letters to those people who were suggested and, in some cases, made a telephone call to find out if these women were interested in telling their stories.

Next, students and their tutors tape recorded their interview with the story teller, and in at least one instance, one advanced level student transcribed the oral interview onto paper. Some interviewers brought along a brochure about the literacy program to spark an interest in those who would benefit from literacy instruction. Although the Oral History Project is still young, it is already known that the students have benefited greatly from this learning experience. This was an opportunity for students to practice their listening and writing skills. It has also been discovered that most seniors from the area who have been interviewed, had left public school before graduating.

Jenifer McVaugh, a professional writer, editor and the literacy program's Outreach and Volunteer Coordinator, has promoted the Oral History Project to the Renfrew County Board of Education. She has emphasized the benefits of participation in the Project to school children in her written communication with the local Board of Education. Here is a sample of a letter she wrote to them:

> ...if you were interested I would like to come to a PD day [professional development], to a classroom or school assembly and give a workshop explaining the principles of oral (anywhere from grade 6 up) to hear the stories of their forebears, and to put them into the young and old people in producing a "story" is valuable for everybody concerned. Youngsters can work with family members or neighbours, or in cooperation with a seniors' home, or seniors group. The story teller doesn't have to be old, either. Oral history has been used as a way to help communication in housing

projects, racially mixed classrooms, etc...

Jenifer has made the program's goals for the Oral History Project known to the local Boards of Education. By appealing to them for volunteers, she is able to continue the program's intention of working at building bridges between readers and non-readers, and between memories and written records. Providing the community with an opportunity for dialogue among people is one of the objectives of the program. As well, promotion of the project has encouraged a program to be started in St. John Bosco School in nearby Barry's Bay.

This dialogue is also taking place in the pages of a local newspaper. By approaching all the local papers, such as the Eganville Leader, the intention is to bring the literacy issue forward. The literacy program has placed a year-long ad in the local paper to publicize the program. In addition, Jenifer has inquired about writing a regular column on plain language. The first column established plain language as an issue for everyone and debunks the myth about illiterate adults:

Plain English

Everybody can read a little.
Most people can read a stop sign.
But many people cannot read enough to read
a newspaper.
As for reading a letter from the Government
— Forget it!

People who cannot read and write are not stupid.
They just never learned how to read and write.
Now they want to learn how.
It is easier for adults to learn than it was for children.
But it still takes work.

Adult learners need things to read that are easy.
This story is easy to read.
IT is written in Plain English.
It has short words. It has simple sentences.
It is in large type.

But it is written for adults.
We want to show you what Plain English looks like.
That is one reason we have this column.
Here is another reason:
Not everybody who takes the Leader is a good reader.
Some people just look at the pictures or read the ads.
It is not they cannot read —
But all that small print looks pretty hard and too boring.
This story has big print, short words
and lots of white space.
We hope it will be fun to read for adult learners.

In conjunction with the newspaper publicity about the program and Jenifer's articles about literacy and clear language, Jenifer has developed a "plain English Comment Card". These letters have been distributed to tutors and students and are distributed to the general public on a regular basis by the Community Resource Centre. It is meant as a convenient way for the community to make writers aware that their written material may not have been readable to many readers and asks them to reconsider the complexity of their language.

It begins by explaining the reason for a comment card. "I want to comment on this piece of writing you produce. I think you could have said what you meant in much simpler words." Then it draws the writer's attention to the International Year of Literacy (1990, a year dedicated to literacy awareness) and to the complicated language of the written material. Finally, it invites the writer to reply to the readers' comments.

Reaching out to other literacy organizations

Kathy Lampi, the Community Resource Centre Coordinator, believes that outreach to other literacy programs and organizations is imperative for a small poorly funded program, such as Killaloe's. "As a small program, we can't remain insular, untouched by what else is going on out there."

The tutors of the literacy program have received two tutor training workshops from groups outside the program and the area. The People Words and Change program in Ottawa, a 12 year old non-profit organization committed to adult literacy, was contracted by the Renfrew County Board of

Education to give a tutor education workshop. They are used as a resource for tutor training and new methods of teaching. Laubach's structured educational methodology, was taught to the volunteer tutors by the Laubach instructors. Patty Shore is one tutor, among several, who expressed the desire to receive more feedback and encouragement about her teaching skills. The literacy program administrators agree, and would like to receive government funding to implement an ongoing tutor training program. Applications for funding this activity have been made, but funding has yet not yet been approved.

Literacy Link of Eastern Ontario has shared information and given advice to the literacy program. From to run ads and have made a financial contribution to help pay for tutors' transportation costs.

Ontario Literacy Coalition has supported the literacy program by answering questions, sending information, and by helping the staff complete a Trillium application for a bus for the program's Family Literacy activities. (This application has been since turned down.)

Family literacy

The literacy program did receive funding from the Ministry of Education to staff a pilot mobile Family Literacy Unit. The bus will be able to travel to isolated meeting places too. Jenifer was able to clarify the goals of the family literacy program. They include "empowerment of the parents, fostered by a feeling of ownership of the program. This program will help parents experience their importance as directors and deliverers of their children's play/learning activities.

The Family Literacy Program will include lending library for toys which will make high quality educational toys available to families throughout the area. It also will provide families in many areas with weekly play groups. These play groups are for children and their care-givers. They will be directed by a highly trained and experienced educator who will model and encourage effective parent/child interaction.

The centre has chosen not to advertise the program as literacy-related but it will stress the importance of parent-reading to the child. This will be done in order that the mobile van and program will not be stigmatized by the literacy label. "We don't want to paint this bus with the brush of illiteracy. There's no point to that. It won't help us." Kathy Lampi said. As well, the literacy program is hoping to produce brochures with good ideas about how to get a child interested in reading at a young age.

Concluding comments

Outreach to such a large rural area is very difficult. Kathy Lampi summed up the successes and the difficulties:

> The agencies and professionals that we've contacted about the literacy program have helped us to reach people who are receiving physical, mental or emotional assistance. That's great, but there are many people out there that we have so far not been able to reach.

Discussion Questions

1. *What were the advantages of the literacy program's association with the Community Resource Centre?*
2. *What are the necessary steps required to build a community linkage between services that lasts?*
3. *What does Family Literacy mean to you?*
4. *How can an oral history project help to create an interest in literacy education?*

Section Three

CASE STUDIES ON SPECIAL NEEDS

INTRODUCTION

Maurice C. Taylor

Developing in adults the power and freedom to control their own lives and to meet the demands of a changing society now seems to be a commonly held goal of most literacy interventions. The degree of effectiveness in reaching this goal is often determined by how adult learning is facilitated to focus on special needs. As the reader will discover, all of the different theme areas and sections of this book actually explore this dynamic issue. One thing is true about the facilitation of adult learning, it is a complex and exhilarating phenomenon. And adults needs seem always to be special.

Although there exists a rich literature on specific instructional techniques and practices, there is little discussion on the intrinsic principles which guide the facilitator in regard to special needs. For these reasons special attention was given to this topic as a theme. In this section the various case studies serve to illustrate some major principles inherent to facilitating adult learning focusing on special needs: self-esteem issues, enhancing literacy proficiencies, building supportive and challenging learning environments and the significance of praxis. Together they provide the beginnings of a philosophical rational for deciding which facilitation skills to use with special needs of literacy groups.

Self-esteem issues

One basic principle that has a far-reaching influence on this special focus is recognizing the importance of self-esteem issues. For many, self-esteem simply refers to how one feels about oneself. There are many accounts in the educational literature which suggests that adolescents and adults with high esteem take risks, care deeply about humanity, are confident and appreciate their own worth. On the other hand, there are a similar number of literacy studies that describe adult learners who have entered a program with intense feelings of fear, a background of experience in repeated failure and with low self-esteem. For some of these people such emotions lead to further negative thoughts like "I'll never be able to read" or "I never have enough time to do my work." Often the end result means withdrawal, more failure and continued low esteem.

A recurring theme evident in the following program descriptions is the importance given to the nurturing of self-esteem. There are examples of how instructors have helped develop positive self-attitudes by focusing on a person's strengths, reinforcing positive self-talk and rewarding improvement and work toward a student defined goal. Other ways to nurture self-esteem is to encourage students to use their support systems. As illustrated in the two case studies *Peer Tutoring and Psychiatric Patients and Their Preparation for Independent Living*, instructors provided opportunities for socialization so students could build a support system within the learning environment. These as well as others describe the effectiveness of co-operative learning and how peer coaching can teach students to use supportive skills that will serve them well long after literacy classes are completed.

Enhancing individual proficiencies

Understanding that adults engage in literacy activities in order to enhance their proficiencies whether it be reading, writing, job or life skills is another principle to keep in mind.

Many experts believe that understanding the differences between current and desired proficiencies of a student can be useful in many ways. As part of the program development process a needs assessment can help specify such a discrepancy. *Psychiatric Patients and Their Preparation for Independent Living* describes how various students, aware of their desired proficiencies such as being able to break up medication and being able to tell the time to take medication, were actually motivated to persist in the learning activities.

Building supportive and challenging learning environments

Inherent in the facilitation of adult learning is the importance of building supportive and challenging learning environments. Many adult educators would agree that even though the major influences on motivation and learning are within the students themselves, there are many ways in which instructors can help adults become committed to a literacy program.

Common to all case studies is the fact that early in the program participants got to know both the instructors and other group members. This supportive interpersonal setting helped students to feel secure, welcomed and accepted. In each of the following program descriptions the literacy staff demonstrated respect for the learning potential of each student. They were also cognizant of the fact that educational facilities influence learning. For example, in *Peer Tutoring* classrooms were transformed into centres for literacy activities with lounge areas and places for socialization. This provided students with a place where supportive interactions could take place and risk-taking behaviours could be practised.

Another common thread in most of the program descriptions was that a challenging setting was created to enhance learning. The idea of 'challenging' helps to make the distinction between information given to the students, versus information that they are 'challenged to discover on their own.' For example in *Psychiatric Patients and Their Preparation for Independent Living*, program staff developed non-threatening learning activities that promoted worthwhile achievements and at the same time helped participants understand their problems and search for ways to find effective solutions.

The meaning and significance of praxis

Another intrinsic principle underlying the facilitation of adult learning with a focus on special needs is the significance of praxis. What this actually means is that it is important for both students and instructors to be involved in a process of activity followed by time for reflection on that activity. Experts in literacy would agree that this notion of praxis is central to adult learning. This exploration of new ideas or skills does not take place in a vacuum but is connected to the student's past, current and future experiences. A good example of action and reflection (or praxis) is where students and staff, in a popular education session, discuss barriers to participation, how to eliminate the barriers and develop new ideas for program change. Again, taking time to reflect becomes a worthwhile habit.

Critical to the practice of this principle is the selection of materials and the use of educational methods by the instructor to help students interpret, understand and assign new meanings or insights in the context of their own experience. As evidenced in several of the case studies, understanding the importance of this principle of action and reflection — praxis — can help adults further develop the power and freedom to control their own lives.

Chapter One
PEER TUTORING
IN THE CLASSROOM

Sheila Goldgrab

Place: *St. Thomas School in Sudbury Ontario*
Participants: *Retired citizens, laid-off miners, unemployed*
                 youth
Issues: 1. *Promoting peer tutoring*
           2. *Changing roles of teacher and student*

According to native teachings, human development is based on the physical, mental, emotional and spiritual aspects of the person. This holistic approach takes the idea of learner-centred education one step further. The learner-centred philosophy is based on the idea that a person will learn to read and write more successfully if the learning materials are reflective of that person's interests. Many of the students in the Niin Sakaan Literacy Program in Sault Ste Marie have many special needs with which they need assistance. The Indian Friendship Centre offers services to help meet those special needs.

Background

The current population of the city of Sudbury Ontario is about 100,000 people. The major employers in the region are Inco, Falconbridge, the Sudbury Board of Education, the Sudbury Roman Catholic Separate School Board and the Provincial Government. In 1991 the current rate of unemployment was 11.9%. English is the mother tongue of 64% of residents, French is the mother tongue for 23%. And 13% have another language such as Italian, Finnish, German, Ukrainian or Polish as their mother tongue(Statistics Canada, 1986).

The Sudbury District Roman Catholic Separate School Board (SDRCSSB) runs a literacy program at five sites in the Sudbury area employing eight certified teachers. The literacy programs at St. Thomas School are the only programs offered by the Board within the city of Sudbury. Thirty students are enrolled in three day classes and one evening class. A full day program and a half day program is offered free of charge to the student.

Many of the adult students in the literacy programs at St. Thomas School have worked in mines and were laid off because their low literacy skills impeded their advancement in the company. Most have raised families and some have retired. Others are unemployed youths, some of whom are collecting disability pensions. A number of students are francophones and many Italian Canadians are in the program as well.

Why pairings in a classroom?

Until four years ago, literacy instruction by the School Board was done on a one to one basis. Then in 1988 the Ministry of Education requested that instruction be changed to small group settings. As a result private one to one instruction is no longer available. The large size of the class has made it more difficult for the teacher to provide individual attention to each of the students. Where the small group process is encouraged, the teacher is able to give individual attention to students on a regular basis while others in the class are learning with their peers.

Regina Muetze, the literacy teacher and Teacher Coordinator of Literacy Programs at the St. Thomas School for the Separate School Board, promotes peer tutoring, that is students teaching students, in her advanced class. Regina orchestrates her classes into group sharing sessions where she, as the teacher, initiates instruction and then bows out. For Regina, the most important reason for using this approach is that students learn the skills to learn reading, writing and numeracy independently. Regina begins the learning process by helping each student develop their own learning program. Then she encourages the process to continue by asking the students in the group to look upon their fellow classmates as peers, and to go to them for assistance. They are responsible for assisting their peers and each student is held accountable for their own learning.

The teacher's role

When new students join the class they are shy, sometimes angry, and often believe that they are unable to offer assistance to other students. Regina tells them that they "don't have to be that far above someone else's level to help." She believes that in many ways, the students have more to offer one another than she does as the teacher:

> The learners all have a common ground of understanding. They can understand someone else's difficulties. They share the process of overcoming their difficulty with their peer, and it then becomes their unique experience. When it comes from the peer, it becomes more clear and meaningful.

Regina's role in the classroom is to act as guide, coach and facilitator. She's not always someone with the answers. She is there to talk with the students, explore strategies, and help them set goals from their identified needs. She gives encouragement when a student is stuck or feeling at the point of quitting. Regina is also a co-learner with the students:

> As the facilitator, I learn something about how two students overcome a difficulty and I am able to share it with the class. There is a cycle of learning that goes on in the classroom.

As the co-learner and facilitator in the learning process, Regina is willing to give up the control and power that many teachers wield in the classroom. She explains how the peer tutoring process differs from traditional styles and dynamics of education delivery:

> The peer tutoring process implies a shift of emphasis. You're empowering the student to take control of the

process. The teacher isn't identifying needs, but instead is drawing out learners' specific needs and working from there. As a result, learning becomes more relevant for them.

Expectations, low self-esteem, and learning in public view

The first noticeable obstacle to peer tutoring in a large group is the anger and lack of self-confidence that is experienced and expressed by new students. Often these students are angry about life's disappointments, about not being able to read and write, and angry at the schools they believed have failed them. Ironically, most of these students demanded a more teacher-directed approach when they first began the class. According to Regina, these adults wanted and expected the classic classroom relationship between student and teacher in their adult literacy class:

> Adult learners join the class with firm constructs of the role of teacher and students. Some want me to be the teacher who teaches the class from the front of the room. They want what they missed — but that's not how adults learn. They learn more from their common experiences, by identifying their own learning needs, taking ownership of their own learning, and taking an active role in evaluation. Adult learners come in with many life experiences and I draw on those experiences.

For Nancy (not her real name), returning back to school after many years, school memories seem to return most sharply when a group process is emphasized:

> Being in a group in a classroom? When I first started, it bothered me at the beginning. I felt that I was going to kindergarten again.

Her expectations about school were anticipated by her former experiences there. Johanna, a student not unlike others in the class who felt reluctant to admit their literacy problem, felt afraid when she first began to attend the class. Her shyness about being in public surfaced again in the classroom:

> At first I thought I was stupid. I was ashamed, embarrassed and insecure. I was afraid of being introduced to

guests in the classroom, the principal and new students. I worried that people would notice that I was uneducated. I wondered if people would speak for me.

Laughing at your own mistakes and moving on

Johanna is a student who has undergone a change of attitude about making mistakes in front of the group:

> Regina asked me to read aloud during class. She probably thought that I had nothing to be afraid of and that making a mistake is OK. I thought people were going to laugh at me if I made a mistake.

After time with the group, and a lot of encouragement from the other students who play an active role in Johanna's learning, reading in full view of others is no longer an obstacle for her:

> Now that I've been here for 2 years, I have more confidence. We all encourage each other. When one person sees the other person asking for help, they think that's it's OK for them to ask too. They were just interested and would be encouraged by my efforts. It's encouraging when the other students listen to one another. Now I know that I can learn. I always thought I couldn't.

Regina emphasizes that when the students read aloud or write in the classroom, they do it for themselves not for the teacher. New students, who are unanimously reluctant to read aloud in a group, are encouraged by a peer's efforts to do the same. Their confidence to learn in public view is reinforced when they learn to trust that their fellow students won't make fun of them when they make mistakes.

For Annette Simpson, who enjoys the opportunity for discussion and the exchange of ideas, the group process provides a variety of necessary supports:

> I like being in a group a lot. When I'm stuck, I ask someone for an answer. If they don't know, I go to someone else. I'm more relaxed and I know I'm here to learn from others and not to work all alone by myself.

For Alfred Gascon, a student who does a lot of tutoring,

working with others has made him feel relaxed. Although Alfred genuinely likes his teacher, he admits that he feels more comforted by his peers:

> You can go at your own pace. The one who is behind can pick up a lot more from their peer than from the teacher. I feel more comfortable with my peers than a teacher. Teachers from the past represented authority. I guess it's a drawback from that.

Cooperation

All the students share the roles of tutor and student at different times throughout the class. Arthur (not real name) worked with his father when he was very young and never had the opportunity to attend school as a young boy. Solving a problem is approached in a similar way to how it is done outside school. Arthur described how the process of peer tutoring works on an informal basis:

> If I have a problem with something I can't do, I'll go to Fred and I'll learn how to do it. I know that Fred will know the answer. Larry comes to me to get help. This took time. Larry acted like a funny clown in class and made people feel comfortable. Everyone's friendly, we get along and we all help each other.

The tutoring role is a rich learning experience for a student. Agnes Frank, a former student in the class who has continued her education in the retail floral program at Cambrian College, spent a lot of time tutoring Betty, another student in the class. They became good friends, both gained more confidence in themselves, and are more at ease with other people in and outside of school. An advocate of peer tutoring, Agnes reflected about what she has learned from the experience:

> Peer tutoring should happen in every class. I learned a lot from helping Betty. I learned that she is an understanding, loving, quiet, shy person. I understand her for who she really is. I learned that I liked to teach. By helping her, I got to learn the meaning or the spelling of a word that I didn't know before.

Agnes didn't find it difficult to criticize her peer. "You make a joke of it," she said "You make it a fun thing. It's a cooperative effort. She's not asking that I not give her criticism, she's asking me to help her."

Teachers choose their own teaching method at the literacy programs run by the Sudbury District Separate School Board. Although Helga Butcher, a literacy teacher with the Board, did not use the peer tutoring method with her class, she noticed while substitute teaching for Regina, that information sharing among students happens naturally when students are on their own:

> I noticed that Harvey, a new student to the class, and Larry often had discussions about spelling. Larry was practicing word spelling on the board and was telling Harvey the techniques he used. Harvey then considered each technique and decided if he would use it himself.

Her observations about the self-directed learning, peer tutoring and small group work that happens in Regina's advanced class are positive:

> I think it's an excellent technique to get bonding and support from peers. In fact, it probably can prevent people from dropping out of the program. All learners will seek support from the teacher, but they learn that the most important bonds are with the other students themselves. They have common problems, struggles with learning, fears, motivation to stay in the class and feelings of success about what they've learned.

Fred Gascon, an independent learner from the start, described an occasion that in his view best illustrates how students in his class have taken responsibility for their learning:

> Regina had to leave the room to answer the phone. Before she left, she was reciting and writing words on the blackboard. Three words had been written on the blackboard. When she left, someone in the class continued to read other words aloud. Some of us wrote the words she was dictating. We took off where Regina left off and without her there.

Fred often gives credit to those students in the class who, like him, show initiative and work hard to learn literacy skills.

Group activities

Regina's students often ask to read aloud in the classroom. People read stories from books they enjoy and from the newspaper. The students want to know if they're pronouncing the words correctly, and they want to practice their fluidity and rhythm. They want to learn from listening to others read.

Students also initiate writing on the blackboard. They learn the patterning of sentences and words, they enjoy the immediate feedback that they receive from the other students and the teacher, and they enjoy the kinetic experience of writing in large print on a surface other than paper. Betty thinks that the activity is helpful because "it has helped me to be open to others and not just work inside my head." Making mistakes doesn't prevent her, or any of the students from correcting their mistakes. "Betty," they say, "Look at the word again." So she erases the error and starts over.

Many group discussions take place spontaneously. Occasionally, one student or a number of them will approach Regina and raise an issue that they would like to discuss in the classroom. Topics such as politics and learning are often discussed. As well, what goes on in the classroom, complaints, requests to have a party, sending a greeting card and inviting a guest speaker are initiated by the students.

Students' suggestions

I asked the students for their ideas about what is necessary for the peer tutoring process to be a success. This is the list that they developed in a brainstorming session with their teacher who acted as a facilitator:

- Peer tutoring should be encouraged in a class where the teacher is comfortable using it.
- Everyone should give positive feedback.
- An attitude of equal treatment should exist among co-learners.
- The learners should be willing to work together.

- The structure of the program is an evolutionary process.
- Both the teacher and the adult students learn from one another.
- The teacher must be committed to encouraging this process and use it
- Trusting the teacher and other learners is important.
- The teacher should understand the limits of the learners and not push

The students in this class told me individually that they all were enthusiastic about the peer tutoring and small group process. They enjoyed the opportunity to evaluate their learning on a regular basis as an alternative to being tested by another person. They liked choosing their own work assignments and reading materials for their learning plan. They especially looked forward to receiving support from their peers.

Johanna described the group feedback she's come to expect from her classmates. If someone has made a mistake reading or writing, the students give an encouraging comment such as "the next time, you'll get it." In response to a person who has done well, "scream and yell to them that we knew they could do it." It's giving them a compliment, it helps them learn and it improves their self-esteem."

Discussion Questions

1. What kinds of team building exercises can you facilitate to prepare students for peer teaching?
2. Describe the characteristics of a good coach for a peer-teaching process.
3. How could you initiate a discussion with your students about the perceived authority image of an instructor?
4. Discuss the following student comment "Peer tutoring should happen in every class."
5. What kinds of assessment opportunities would you provide for students who are involved in peer tutoring?

Chapter Two
LITERACY, WELFARE AND POPULAR EDUCATION

Mary Norton

Place: *Journeys Community-Based Literacy Program in Powerview, Manitoba*

Participants: *Former Journey's students who developed and performed* Under the Line, *together with the Popular Theatre Alliance of Manitoba.*

Issues: 1. *Involving people in their own education*
2. *Working individually and collectively to address challenges of living on welfare*

> *It's just how they make you feel. Like you have to be praying all the time for something. Just crossing your fingers and hoping it'll come through. It's a never ending thing.*
>
> **Lisa Nelson**

Lisa is talking about living on welfare. In 1990, she was one of the 25,000 people in Winnipeg who had to support themselves and their dependents with income from the provincial or municipal social assistance programs.[1] For some, welfare provides temporary income between jobs. For others, it is a longer term necessity.

For Lisa finishing school offers possibilities for getting a job and increasing the income she needs to support herself and her son. This is one of the reasons she's attending Journeys, a community-based literacy education program in Winnipeg. But Lisa is also learning that she doesn't have to rely on prayers or luck to get the benefits that she is entitled to. At Journeys, students can work individually and collectively to address the challenges of living on welfare.

139

Journeys students have worked on obtaining funds for child care, they have lobbied for bus passes and they attend public meetings to learn for instance, about their rights as tenants. In collaboration with the Popular Theatre Alliance of Manitoba, a group of Journeys students wrote and produced a play, *Under the Line*, to inform people about welfare rights and to raise public awareness about living under the poverty line. Through these and similar activities, students learn about the welfare system, they practise communication skills, and they develop the confidence to keep on working for their rights.

To prepare this case study, I spoke with the following people[2]: Kathleen Walsh, Journeys' Teacher-Coordinator, and Brian Orvis, a teacher at Journeys; Margo Charlton, the Artistic Director of the Popular Theater Alliance of Manitoba; Doreen Ducharme, Bernice Hall, Isabelle Hall, and Arlene Sandy, former Journeys students who developed and performed in *Under the Line*; Walda Anderson, the receptionist at Journeys; and Avril Chartrand, Yvonne Lemky, Lisa Nelson, and Lilian Zagonchuk, Journeys students. Avril Chartrand assisted me by arranging interviews and doing interview follow-up work.

Background

Journeys

Journeys originated in 1984 as adult evening classes at Rossbrook House, a youth drop-in centre in Winnipeg's inner city. Rossbrook House staff, who were generally recruited from among youth who participated at the centre, asked for classes because they were having difficulty writing shift reports. The evening classes soon expanded to include community participants, and the name Journeys was chosen to reflect the journey that students and teachers embark on together. According to Kathleen Walsh, the aims of the program are to help people with adult education and literacy, to develop self-esteem and respect for themselves, and to work together with one another. Community building "getting along in and contributing to a community" is a priority.

In 1988, Journeys was incorporated as the Journeys Adult Education Association. The fourteen member Board of

Directors includes 10 students and four people from the community. Journeys has since moved to more spacious accommodation in downtown Winnipeg, and staff now include a teacher-coordinator, a part-time teacher, a receptionist, child care worker, caretaker and bookkeeper who also work part-time. The Winnipeg School Division One and the Federal Government Secretary of State Department are the program's major funders.

Journeys operates two afternoons and two evenings a week, and about 100 students from all over the city attend.[3] Students work with either of the two part-time teachers or with one of the 25 volunteer tutors. Some students are employed or are retired from employment, but income for the majority is from municipal or provincial social assistance, unemployment insurance, or Workers' Compensation.

The Popular Theater Alliance of Manitoba

Under the direction of Margo Charlton, the Popular Theatre Alliance of Manitoba (PTAM) has been promoting and producing theatre for social change since it was founded in 1984. Rooted in popular education and community development work, PTAM operates through two avenues. In the professional program, actors develop issue-oriented plays for presentation in community or formal theatre settings. In the community outreach work, PTAM staff work with people who have something which they want to say, and for whom theatre provides a means of saying it. This work reflects Margo's understanding that "popular education involves people in their own education" and that popular theatre is one method for doing this. The community outreach work may be supported by professional script writers, directors and others.

PTAM became involved in the adult literacy field through the annual Manitoba Learners' conferences which PTAM staff organize and facilitate. PTAM made the connection with Journeys at the first of these conferences.

Addressing challenges

Childcare
The need for free on-site childcare emerged early in Journeys'

history, when the program was still located with Rossbrook House.[4] As Bernice Hall explained,

> Welfare won't help you in certain areas like daycare or bus fare or things like that. We couldn't get that even for going to school, we were doing it on our own.

Some students were able to get "special needs" allowances to pay for childcare, but when this money was used up, they had to drop out of the program.[5] Funds were raised from various service clubs to pay a monthly honorarium to a woman who minded students' children at a nearby site, but stable funding was more difficult to secure.[6] Social service agencies claimed that childcare was an educational issue, and education agencies responded that it was a social services concern.

About this time in 1985, Journeys students attended the first Manitoba Learners' Conference. As part of the conference, students identified barriers to attending literacy programs, and Kathleen explained how their program was funded. Prior to the conference, students had been well aware of the consequences of the funding problems "such as no childcare" but had not fully understood the sources of these problems.

Following the Learners' Conference, Lib Spry, a popular theatre facilitator who was visiting PTAM, conducted a "rehearsal for reality" to help Journeys students prepare for a meeting with representatives of potential funding agencies: Winnipeg School Division One, the Winnipeg Core Area Initiative, and Manitoba Education. The meeting itself was the "show" and the preparation beforehand was the "rehearsal."[7] The Winnipeg Core Area Initiative provided funding for childcare. As well, said Isabelle:

> ...the first thing we learned [was] that many can do wonders, one alone, it's hard. And we found that out. A group can do an awful lot, because each of us has a talent for something [and] can do something. You're very powerful when you're together.

The Wednesday Welfare Workouts
The rehearsal for reality paved the way for further

collaboration between PTAM and Journeys. A series of workshops, dubbed "The Wednesday Welfare Workouts" was initiated when Margo Charlton offered to do some more issue-oriented work with Journeys students. No one knew how far this four-month project was destined to grow.

During the fall of 1986, a group of Journeys students got together every Wednesday afternoon to identify and address issues of being on welfare. Margo, another popular educator (Marjorie Beaucage) and Kathleen planned and facilitated the workshops. Margo explained that the purposes of the workshops were to "help people figure out the welfare system, how to be able to live within that system, and how to access as much within the system as they could. " Participants also wanted to work on communication between themselves and their welfare workers. Bernice, who participated in the project, explained, "...you're not used to talking to people like that...like the people that give us the money every month. When we talk to them we get kind of scared."

Initially the Wednesday meetings drew people together because, as Bernice said, "we were able to share what happened to us on welfare." By listening to others, Bernice found out that she was not the only one "that's having these problems, that they're doing it to everyone." Doreen Ducharme agreed: "That's how it started...to help each other." A mixed group at first, the men gradually dropped out and the group evolved into one for women only.

Margo drew from her knowledge of popular education methodology to facilitate people's development as a group, and to help the group identify and clarify issues. As a facilitator, Margo said, her role was to come with "some tools and some skills and try to make yourself as available to the group as possible." She stressed, however, that popular education methods and techniques are only tools, and that "sometimes the best thing to do is simply sit down and talk." Margo added that people can "get hung up on the tools, worried more about what game to use than the purpose of why everybody is there."

Often the information to answer questions was available in the group and Margo's role was to help people sort out and see it in terms of the bigger picture. As they identified questions which they couldn't answer, group members undertook research assignments. Resource people were not brought in to answer questions because, Margo explained, (the group needed to find out answers "they didn't have a resource "figuring it out together." Because some people found it very hard to make phone calls to their welfare workers, they role-played the phone calls and received group support as they made them.

By researching welfare policies and guidelines, the group learned, for example, about special needs and "excess special needs" allowances.[8] They found out that when welfare workers come to your house without letting you know, you do not have to let them in. Bernice recalled that "we were always scared of that, they would never phone to let you know." Doreen added, "They're not just supposed to walk in like that and open your fridge and cupboard."

Towards the end of the Wednesday Welfare Workouts the group played a game called "Have a Wish".

One woman wanted to know how much special needs money she had left. She rehearsed what she would say, then called her worker and got the information she wanted. Another woman phoned and secured a special needs allowance for herself, and another was able to get a bus pass. Kathleen recalled:

> This was just a high, everybody in the group got their wishes. This is incredible, when we stick together, we can really get something. They saw the power of the group, the support that they weren't alone, and that they could ask for what was their right.

Through the workshops, the women gained a better understanding of the welfare system and developed confidence to speak to their social workers. They also grew and developed as a group and weren't ready to disband at the end of the project. They wanted to do something with all the information they had, and decided to do a play. This decision initiated a two year process of the development and production of Under the Line.

Under the Line

Margo and Kathleen continued to work with the group, and Kathleen secured grants from the Manitoba Arts Council and the Federal Government Secretary of State Department to support the development of the play. The group chose the title *Under the Line* because, as Isabelle explained, living on welfare means living under the poverty line. They named themselves the "No Name Brand Clan" for reasons implied in a scene from the play — one of the characters who is lined up to pay for her groceries comments to herself:

> No name corn flakes. No name crackers. No name peanut butter. No name tomato soup. I'm a walking advertisement for No Name Brand. If they paid me to do their advertising, I'd be a rich woman now.[9]

Development

The group decided to address two audiences. They wanted to inform people on social assistance about their welfare benefits and rights, and they wanted to tell their stories to people who had never been on welfare. Over the weeks, they identified the information and issues which were eventually worked into the play: living on welfare, welfare benefits, myths about people on welfare and the need for assertiveness to get those benefits. They also wanted to say something about how they should be treated by their workers, and, as Isabelle said, they wanted to show "the strength and dignity of people that are living on a low income."

As an example, the play explores the stigma of being on welfare: "Hey Harry", yells the cashier in Scene 3, "How do you process a welfare voucher?" Bernice referred to this scene when she talked about:

> ...the stigma you get when you're on welfare, like the Safeway scene where the checker holds up the voucher...That's the prejudice, because you're on welfare its OK to embarrass you. People who have jobs, they think, "Oh, they're on welfare, it doesn't matter how you treat them."

A number of themes are addressed in Scene 4. When all but one of the elements on her stove burns out, "Linda" calls her worker for special needs assistance to have it repaired. "Mrs. Roberts" arrives unannounced at breakfast time,

Linda holds her ground, gets approval for the needed repairs, and tells Mrs. Roberts to phone the next time she visits. The following words are exchanged as Mrs. Roberts leaves:

> Mrs. Roberts: You know Linda, you were a lot easier to deal with before you started visiting those welfare rights groups.
>
> Linda: You mean I was a pushover.

The No Name Brand Clan drew mainly from their own experiences and previous research to develop each scene, although in some cases, additional research was needed. Bernice explained that they checked their facts because "we had to make sure that we didn't put things in there that would make them sue us." In one instance, to prepare for her role as a welfare office receptionist, Isabelle observed how a receptionist in a welfare office dealt with clients. And when developing a scene about welfare workers on their coffee break, Bernice asked a niece who worked in a welfare office to review the script.

This particular scene was used to present some perspectives on welfare workers. "Mrs. Popinsky" is a worker who was "so horrid" that when Isabelle first played the role she worried about how the audience would react. But "Mrs. Livy" is portrayed as a worker who believes that "it's our job to make things as decent for them as possible." The group worked on presenting this balanced picture, because, as Isabelle explained, "there were people in the group who were satisfied with their workers." Bernice added, "some of them really do try to help." Margo emphasized that it was the group's decision to show both sides, and added that the balanced portrayal reflected their earlier research and understanding of the complexity of the issues.

Scripting

When it was time to prepare a script, the group improvised dialogues, and Tanya Lester, a professional writer, was hired to work their improvisations into a script. Isabelle was elected to work with the writer to make sure that the dialogue would be authentic. As she explained, the writer was a middle class person who "had no idea of what this person would say." Each week the group reviewed the script that had been written from their improvisations of the week before.

Rehearsing and performing

Kathleen attended and co-facilitated development sessions, and according to Margo, Journeys staff were invaluable in helping the actors practise their lines. Kathleen recalled how one woman actually learned to read by participating in the script development and rehearsals. After weeks and weeks of re-reading the script, she had learned enough words to start reading a book.

The No Name Brand Clan gave their first performance to their community. A 200 member audience responded with a standing ovation and sent them on their way to read or perform the play 23 more times to a total of more than 1300 people.

After each reading or performance, the women responded to questions from the audiences. While audience response and interest was generally very open, Margo remembers one occasion where some members in the audience tried to offer tips about how to juggle and stretch their money. She suggested that the audience wasn't prepared to just "accept the gift of information" which the No Name Brand Clan was offering, "that they felt something was needed of them" in return.

Isabelle, however, recalled that the play was "an eye opener, especially for some of the middle class people in the suburbs who don't come to the inner city." She added that these audiences views had often been shaped by dramatized media portrayals. They hadn't realized "that inner city people are very strong and they do have dignity."

Branching out and moving on

After their last performance, the No Name Brand Clan participated in a retreat. During that weekend, they wrote the following poem:

A group of women working together
Breaking down their fears
and combining their strengths and differences

and using their creativity
and growing
and having the courage to branch out
for something better for themselves
and for others
and bringing out their spiritual selves.

The group's parting poem speaks to what they learned over the time together. They learned about the welfare system, but more important to each of the women interviewed, they learned about themselves and their potential. Bernice explained that "we couldn't open up before, you used to feel if you get close to people, soon everyone knows your business." Isabelle, who went on to work and act in another play said, "It made me aware of the things I could do." And Doreen recalled that:

It took time to share and speak out, but now I do that. [Whether] it is a friend or a worker, I speak out, I stand my ground, whether this person has power and money, I speak out and I just say my thing, my side, my story. That's what I'm doing today and I'm quite happy about that.

In these ways the process of developing the play was as important as the play itself. And as Margo commented, the process of group building, issue analysis and confidence development is a long one that can't be measured in "terms of how good the show was or the applause that they get at the end of the show."

Carrying on

The No Name Brand Clan learned about the welfare system and developed skills and confidence to deal with it and to branch out in many ways. Audiences learned about welfare recipients' rights, and the play raised awareness among audiences who've never experienced life "under the line."

But the welfare system carries on and learning to deal with the system is an ongoing need. Brian Orvis, who teaches at Journeys, suggested that people on welfare often develop a "feeling of hopelessness...that nothing can be done" and added that, at the same time, people may feel that "some place, somebody with magic can solve the problems."

There is no magic, of course, and at Journeys people learn the process for dealing with their problems themselves, a process which Brian calls being "militant in a personal way." Personal militancy often means writing a letter to a Member of the Legislative Assembly, for as Brian explained, MLA's "can investigate in a way that no one else can." Lisa, for example, was having difficulty getting the bus tickets which she needed for her and her son to make the trip to Journeys.[10] Apparently the social worker didn't want her to go to school before she had gone for educational counselling. With Brian's encouragement, Lisa wrote to her MLA, and within a few days the bus ticket problem was solved. Lisa said:

> I wouldn't have thought of doing it myself, but now I know what I'm going to do in the future if something should come up. It's an option for me to take and I wouldn't hesitate to do it again.

Although individuals write their own letters, Brian emphasized that there is an acceptance at Journeys that "we're all in this together." It's not a matter of one person solving the problem, but a process that everyone needs to get involved in. Often, one person's experience with a problem will help others address theirs. And he added, "we try to get people involved not only in things that have a very close personal meaning but also in community-based kinds of things."

For instance, one Journeys student had lived for years in a particular apartment because she had been told by her social worker that she couldn't move. An example Brian said, of the "kind of control that is there in the lives of people on welfare [which] people in better economic situations do not have to endure." When the student attended a public meeting on housing, she raised the issue and within a month she learned that the regulation had been changed.

At the time of her interview, Yvonne Lemky had just returned from a meeting about the closing of some public library branches. The first time Yvonne had applied for a library card, she was told "I couldn't have one" they said I wasn't "eligible because I was sitting on welfare and not attending school." She added that "It didn't make much sense to me but I didn't know too much so I didn't argue with them." Now a card holder and an avid library patron, Yvonne is preparing to argue. She and another student will represent Journeys at the next meeting about the library closures.

For Yvonne the library is one of the few free cultural activities available. After paying for rent, food and other necessities, there is little left from a welfare allowance to pay for leisure activities. Journeys tries to provide cultural experiences for students who couldn't afford them on their own. One year, the program obtained a grant for a couple of hundred dollars to buy tickets for the symphony or ballet. Another year, they managed to buy tickets for a play.

At Journeys, addressing welfare challenges is linked with literacy and educational development. Writing letters to MLA's provides obvious writing practice, and issues raised at public meetings provide impetus for discussion and learning about civics. For Brian, this just makes good teaching sense.

Notes

1. In Manitoba, social assistance is available through a provincial or a municipal program. The Income Security Branch of the Manitoba Department of Family Services administers the provincial welfare program which is generally for adults who are considered unable to work because of family responsibilities or disability. Each of the approximately 220 municipalities in the province administer a municipal welfare plan ("city welfare") which is for adults considered eligible to work. In Winnipeg, the municipal plan is administered by the city's Social Services Department.

    The 24,152 people who received social assistance in 1990 account for about 4% of Winnipeg's population. Of the total, 15,766 people received provincial assistance and 8,396 received municipal assistance. In 1990, the unemployment rate in Winnipeg was 7.9%, and the numbers of employable people on assistance increased by 12%. (Sources: City of Winnipeg Social Services Department and Province of Manitoba Department of Family Services.)

2. Many of the people with whom I spoke shared their experiences of life on welfare. Their stories and insights deepened my awareness and underscored the need for continuing

advocacy and teaching for "personal militancy" regarding welfare rights:

Lisa is working towards a GED at Journeys. Although a "top student", Lisa left school in grade eight because of pressure and threats from other students who wanted her to do their work for them. She married at 16 and had a child and found it very hard to cope when she and her husband moved to Winnipeg from a Native reserve community. After separating from her husband, Lisa decided to turn her life around. She concentrated on being a good mother, and is now rebuilding her confidence as a learner.

Lilian started at Journeys as a tutor and is now working on a GED herself. She left school in grade seven and worked steadily until 1986. Work ran out in 1989, and she "had to go on social assistance for the first time in my life". Lilian recalled that she was treated "very clinically" when she applied for assistance, and that there was no acknowledgement that her situation was not her fault. She hopes that finishing a GED will open some doors for employment or job training.

Yvonne left school in grade eight because she was pregnant and was 15 when her son was born. She has since had a daughter, and her sister currently cares for both children during the week. Yvonne decided that "if I ever want to get off welfare, I need at least a grade 12 to be able to find a job." She is working towards that and towards having her children back with her full-time. Walda is the secretary at Journeys.

Walda finished high school despite being pregnant in her last year, but had to give up plans of going to university when her son was born. She worked part time, married, and had to apply for welfare when her husband left her with two children and a new baby. Social workers tried to dissuade Walda from attending a secretarial training program, saying that she would not be able to cope with school and her young children. With support from her parents and boyfriend, and with her own determination, she did.

3. Two students actually attend from outside the city, one of whom drives one and a half hours to attend.

4. Although the name "Journeys" was not used until later in the program's history, the name is used throughout the report to avoid confusion.

5. People who receive provincial social assistance may apply for an annual "special needs" allowance of $150.00 The allowance may be used to cover costs of necessary items not covered by the monthly allowance.

6. Social assistance recipients may earn $50.00 a month. Any amount over $50.00 is deducted from their monthly allowances.

7. Later, a group of forty students attended a School Board meeting to request that the Board pay the salary for a second teacher for Journeys. Isabelle Hall, a former Journeys student who participated in the meeting, recalled that the Board of Education "was apparently impressed with the number of students who took the time to go to the meeting."

8. In some instances, people can apply for money in addition to their special needs allowances. This is called "excess special needs."

9. No Name Brand Clan and Tanya Lester. (1990) *Under the Line*. Winnipeg, Manitoba: Popular Theatre Alliance of Manitoba and Journeys Education Association, p. 21.

10. Once a bus pass has been approved, students have to provide their welfare workers with a letter from Journeys every three months to indicate that they are attending the program. As Yvonne, a student, explained, "Trying to keep a bus pass from city welfare is pretty hard. They are getting to the point now where you bring in a letter every three months stating how good you are doing and if you've been attending regularly."

Discussion Questions

1. How would you describe the evolving nature of the Journey's program?
2. What are some facts and some myths about popular education?
3. Is there a Popular Theatre Alliance or a similar group in your community? How could you interest your students in learning more about such a group?
4. In the project Under the Line comment on the process of group building, issue analysis and confidence development.
5. Are you comfortable with the term "personal militancy"?

Chapter Three
PREPARING PSYCHIATRIC PATIENTS FOR INDEPENDENT LIVING

Sheila Goldgrab

Place: London Psychiatric Hospital's Literacy Programs in London Ontario
Participants: Literacy and rehabilitation staff as well as the in and out-patients of the literacy programs
Issues: 1. Literacy as a tool for transition between hospitalization and community re-entry

---

Students in each of the three literacy programs at the London Psychiatric Hospital are improving their reading, writing and numeracy skills so that they can realize their potential more fully. The literacy class itself, as well as other hospital programs help prepare students to make the transition from the hospital to the outside community for their literacy education. Outside support systems are helpful as well.

Background
The first Adult Basic Education (ABE) program in London was established in 1969. Since then, an average of 115 students and 90 tutors are involved in the one-to-one program each year. Classes are held in elementary and secondary schools, in a neighbourhood resource centre, at the Hutton House Workshop for Physically Handicapped Adults, at the Elgin-Middlesex Detention Centre and at the London Psychiatric Hospital (LPH). A Wide Range Achievement Test was conducted in 1985 with clients from the London Psychiatric

Hospital's programs operated by the Vocational, Recreational, and Rehabilitation Services Department. The results indicated there was a need for upgrading among the patients and they expressed a strong interest in doing this. As a result, the Adult Basic Education program at LPH began in 1986.

London Psychiatric Hospital has three literacy programs. The aim of the Basic Education Program is to give all students (including those with limited ability) access to a fundamental education. This is a maintenance program to review the literacy and numeracy skills they have acquired throughout their lives. The students in the Upgrading Program are those who are not able to learn independently or may exhibit learning disabilities. These students have not succeeded at high school, and are returning for either literacy upgrading, personal satisfaction or better employment opportunities.

Students in the Independent Studies Program have academically specific goals, are motivated, and can study independently. Some have a grade 12 diploma. These students have the potential of succeeding in community literacy programs, community college and university. Others are acquiring accreditation through correspondence courses from The Independent Learning Centre in cooperation with the G.A. Wheable Centre for Adult Learning.

The literacy upgrading programs were first intended for those in-patients who would be discharged from the hospital in one and a half years. There was also a need for continued education for those who had already been discharged. Most literacy students in all of the programs are currently out-patients who return for the literacy class and one other hospital program. Each literacy program session lasts one and a half to two hours three to four times a week. Students' ages range between 17 and 57.

Carol Barrett, the chief educator of the literacy program at LPH, has done post-graduate work in education, guidance and counselling. She plans and teaches student programs and also supervises volunteer tutors who teach in all three programs as well as the English as a Second Language class.

Reasons for poor literacy skills

Many psychiatric patients exhibit a diminished ability to tell time, write a letter, or find phone numbers in the phone book. An illness in early school years, the disruptive nature of moving to different locations and changing schools, deprived or abusive home situations during childhood, and learning disabilities may each have caused or contributed to the reasons for poor literacy skills. In addition, for a number of out-patients of the hospital, a loss of literacy and other life skills may have been due to their previous stay in a hospital.

Donna McManus, a rehabilitation counsellor, explained the process by which institutionalization may contribute to the lack of ability to perform basic skills such as reading and writing and she is supportive of the literacy program which helps clients live on their own. Lengthy hospitals admissions often de-skill patients over time. Activities of daily living such as washing laundry, grocery shopping and meal preparation are largely done for them.

Once patients leave the hospital, these basics are difficult for them to do and have to be re-learned by some patients. In the literacy program, Carol is able to improve the numeracy skills for some patients so that they can more efficiently budget their money and improve their reading skills for practical purposes, such as following sales ads in the newspaper. Carol has taught one student the basic skills required so that she can understand how to break her pills (for medication) in half when she is living on her own. Carol has also taught her how to tell time so that she knows when to take her medication. Literacy skills are necessary for independent living.

Michelle Walker, a former literacy tutor at LPH, a teacher's aid, and a group home counsellor, concurs:

> Living in group homes and hospitals has made them dependent on those institutions and the professionals. They no longer have their own independent thoughts.

In recent times, the trend has been to decrease patients' hospital stay and to reintegrate them into the community to the degree that is feasible and as early as possible. Donna McManus described how the hospital provides support to that end:

> Some patients are able to continue going to work or school while they are in hospital. It is very important that they do not lose their support systems or their skills. Social workers keep the families involved where

possible so that they do not lose touch with their loved ones. The rehabilitation counsellor helps them to interface with the community. In order to increase their options we let them know what is available. We explore the variety of vocational, recreational and educational programs in their community, and through counselling, help them to make an educated choice.

Benefits to the students

The rehabilitation counsellor works closely with Carol and the student to develop an educational program plan which may include preparation for further education upon discharge. It often includes the literacy program for those whose writing and reading skills need to be refreshed, improved or learned for the first time.

At LPH, the rehabilitation counsellor is part of a multidisciplinary team of psychiatrists, nurses, psychologists, occupational therapists and social workers. The benefits of the literacy program for the patients is recognized. In some cases, the literacy program increases the student's opportunities in the area of employment. Donna explained:

> We use literacy training to enhance the employability of our clients. Without education, many of our patients will work in low paying jobs. Literacy education is often necessary for meaningful employment and independent living. The combination of a work conditioning program and literacy classes help us to assess the readiness of the client for further vocational training. It's very important for our patients to have assistance during the transition period between hospitalization and community re-entry.

As a literacy tutor, Michelle Walker was aware of her students' low self-esteem. She knew that this would have to be overcome for the students to return and fit comfortably into their community. To that end she encouraged her students to take a chance in the classroom. She gave them regular positive reinforcements to encourage them to think independently:

> I've noticed a lot of people down about themselves.

They lack self-esteem and there is little positive thinking. Students have a combination of psychiatric problems with social skill problems, nervousness and lack of
education. Together these factors may create a barrier
for those who hope to attend a school like Wheable
(high school), Fanshawe College or a university. They're
afraid that they won't fit into the community. Many
students will get positive reinforcement from me or the
other tutors but they don't take credit easily for anything they've done themselves. Their transition to the
outside would be harder if we didn't encourage them to
succeed on their own in the literacy program.

While sharing concerns and solutions for academic problems, the student and teacher have time to build a trusting
relationship necessary for this educational endeavour to succeed. Carol explained:

I think that one of the important aspects of communication skills is respect for the individual. When students
and I work together there is mutual respect for one
another. I can take the time to value and listen to their
opinions. This is one of the advantages of being a
teacher in this facility.

In the literacy class, students are able to get acceptance and
reinforcement for their work. Elsewhere somebody's work
would be clinically assessed, whereas Carol and the tutors
review it, accept and reinforce the creativity. Here too, clients
are able to talk about things other than their problems.

The classroom setting of a blackboard, desks, quiet time,
discussion, and individual attention works positively to convey a clear message of what is expected of the students. Not
unlike many other adult students, literacy students at LPH
may be paralysed from fear. Carol has accepted that "many
times there is an anxiety problem not a problem with their
intellect. There is a fear of failure." The small size of her
classroom and the individual attention from a tutor puts
"their fears to rest."

Donna believes that the classroom situation is a place where
students can learn respect for others and practice social skills:

Social skills learned elsewhere can be enhanced and practiced in the classroom. There are certain acceptable classroom behaviours. For example, a student must wait for the teacher's attention. I've seen students who may act rude to other people be very polite and sit and listen to Carol.

Donna suggested that the patients' exposure to members of the outside community is positive. The literacy tutors are all members of the outside community and are not considered as hospital staff. She believes that working with the volunteer tutors gives the students an opportunity to develop a supportive relationship in a friendly atmosphere with a member of the community.

Literacy education and other hospital programs

Many of the students in the literacy program return to the hospital for other programs as well. In one such program called Anger Management, patients learn how to express anger. The literacy program is not formally connected with the anger management program, but the two complement one another in some cases. Some patients who have been referred to the literacy program bring their personal journal to class. In these journals students are able to express their anger in written form. Carol and the student work on expressing feelings and writing skills in the journal. Carol offers grammatical instruction. Together they work on the mechanics of writing.

In Occupational Therapy where patients learn life skills such as budgeting, cooking and grocery shopping, patients learn the use of money. The mechanics of adding is taught in the literacy program. Carol explains the relationship of the skills taught in both programs:

I think that life skills and literacy skills are intertwined. In the literacy program we teach the individual why something is the way it is and the process by which they get the answers. It's my view that the literacy classes also teach students to value their own opinions. It gives them confidence in their own thought processes. The life skills programs give the student opportunities to use their skills in various practical applications.

Another program that many literacy students attend is the Vocational Workshop, that is part of the Vocational Recreational and Rehabilitation Services Department. There patients work in manufacturing and woodworking. Often this is the first vocational training for these individuals. They learn to work under supervision and with other patients in the workshop. This serves to prepare patients for the routine of employment. The literacy classroom and the individual workshop can work on preparing them for the transition to their community, whether they decide to pursue employment, further their education, or both.

The transition to literacy education outside the hospital

For many students, hospital staff support can help them to make the transition to community education. Nursing staff often take the time to talk with the students about their literacy classes and reinforce what is learned. The literacy program at LPH provides the student with a safer environment then they could presently expect from a larger community classroom setting. For some a sudden or ill-prepared transition can result in re-admission. A carefully planned transition from the literacy program at LPH to community educational programs is developed for those who are ready to make such a move.

Although returning to the hospital for a literacy class after discharge may not necessarily slow down a student's reintegration into the community, attending an outside literacy program is a viable option. One obstacle to the integration of ex-psychiatric students into the community is the pervasive societal myth that those with a psychiatric illness have a low level of intellect. According to Carol, there is a lot of confusion about the ability and the capacity of people with psychiatric illnesses to learn:

> Many times the psychological and the reading problems are intertwined. It's hard to determine if the reading problem has caused the emotional problem or vice versa. The literacy classes are able to deal with the learning problem itself while other difficulties are dealt with by the appropriate professional staff. People equate psychiatric problems with the inability to learn.

Because someone has an illness of the mind, often others presume that the mind doesn't function. The truth is very different. Many of my students are very intelligent and need only to refresh specific skills.

Learning outside a sheltered environment

If these people are indeed able to learn, could they learn outside a sheltered environment? Is such an environment necessary? The hospital rehabilitation counsellor, and the literacy tutors, felt that a community literacy program would be a good place for hospital clients if they were well prepared. A number of concerns surfaced about how this would operate successfully. Since private medical records are confidential and could not be shared with community literacy tutors, they suggested that tutors in a community literacy program should learn to recognize psychiatric illnesses and disorders. In this way, they would be able to identify the symptoms. It was also suggested that a resource list of medical professionals should be compiled to answer their questions when needed.

Low income and community re-entry problems

Many of the out-patients in the literacy programs at LPH complained about the hardship of living on a low income. Finding accommodation and paying the bills, after living as an in-patient at the hospital without employment, are often barriers to a successful transition.

One community-based organization that concerns itself with community re-entry, housing and rehabilitation of those with a chronic psychiatric history is the Western Ontario Therapeutic Community Hostel (WOTCH) located in London. Wally Parsons is a program director at WOTCH responsible for both rehabilitation and housing for those with mental illnesses. WOTCH's permanent housing program consists of 12 single family residences with places for 36 individuals. Here residents are secure that they will not lose their housing due to absence (return to the hospital or a loss of employment) caused by their psychiatric illness.

WOTCH also provides Rehabilitation Housing. There are four group homes with seven to eight residents in each. Here, people are taught life skills, co-operative living skills, and the daily rhythm of living. Finding decent, affordable housing is difficult in London. Wally summarized the situation by remarking that "decent housing in London is available but often this housing is not affordable. Often what is affordable, is often not decent."

There are 420 members of WOTCH. Members participate in rehabilitation programs, receive subsidized housing and may attend ongoing social programs and activities. According to Wally Parsons, although the organization believes it is meeting the needs of the community, it is unsure about how many people presently in hospitals are ready to make the transition to the community and would need their services.

WOTCH's mandate is to facilitate community re-entry, improve the quality of life, develop life, social and relationship skills as well as pre-vocational and work skills for those with mental illnesses. Over the last year, the staff has begun to think about expanding their mandate. The organization is beginning to reshape the role that they play in re-integrating people into the community. Attention to developing people's capabilities, has recently been addressed. Wally explains:

> De-institutionalization has traditionally meant placing people into the community. Recently, we in the mental health field have begun to look at people's capabilities and ask ourselves how we can realize them. Our concern is how we can maximize those potentials. Literacy is basic to this. If we expect to contribute to a person's development in the area of education and vocational training without ensuring that they have literacy skills, we're missing the boat.

Presently, WOTCH does not pay a lot of attention to the literacy needs of their members because the problem of illiteracy has only recently been raised as an issue.

Suggestions for the future

For those who are able to make the transition from the literacy program at the London Psychiatric Hospital to one in the outside community, their needs are more highly specialized. In Carol's view, a support system must be in place in order that students can receive the benefits given to other students in the community:

We [in society] should be taking a holistic approach much like the one that is emerging for adolescent learners. A guidance counsellor, pre-vocational training and other services that are available to the adolescent learner should be available to the adult learner. There is a definite need for a support system within the community for people with learning disabilities or psychological difficulties. If we're going to provide the place and the time to learn, we need to furnish a support system. When you have a child in high school, the parents support them emotionally and financially. Adults need that same sort of support. Some of us have family and friends that support us in our academic endeavours, but most of these people do not. Carol made these further suggestions:

I would like to see teacher training, one-to-one literacy sessions in small sized rooms, more staff, and more communication among educators who work with high risk populations such as those who have had substance abuse problems or psychological problems. A support group of people of similar difficulties would be helpful.

When literacy educators begin to recruit people with psychiatric illnesses to their programs, more options will be available for the ex-psychiatric patient and hospital outpatient. The program would be able to enhance what the student already knows, and assist in developing self-reliance and self-confidence.

Organizations whose mandates are to help people with mental illnesses re-enter and integrate themselves into the outside community, are beginning to look at literacy education as an important step in that process. By considering the importance of literacy education to their members and taking action, they can develop the potential and improve the lives of those who are making the transition to independent living. Developing the potential of someone with a psychiatric history will enable them to live and thrive in their own community.

Discussion Questions

1. How have the different programs fostered independence?
2. Describe the philosophy in using a multidisciplinary team approach for educational planning.
3. What kind of supportive mechanisms does one establish for patients who are moving from a hospital-based literacy program to a community-based literacy program?
4. What are the advantages of using informal assessment methods in hospital-based programs?
5. What agencies in your community would make up a network to support the transition to independent living?
6. Underlying life skills are literacy skills. Discuss.

Chapter Four
LES PAS DES MOTS

Hélène Blais

Lieu: Le Centre d'alphabétisation de Roberval Lac Saint-Jean,
Quebec
Participants: Formatrices-terrain
Autochtones
Thèmes: 1. Les groupes d'alphabétisation formés en région
éloignée
2. Les pratiques d'alphabétisation auprès des
autochtons

---

*Creuse le dense. Creuse la danse d'espace aux paroles aérées
de sève.*

*Creuse l'orbe d'être au plus large de ces deltas. Parle de nos
cimes au tourbillon de grandir, et d'épeler en grandissant, et
de germer en formulant ces mille feux qui nous explosent en
l'orbe d'être plus large — aux marnes — et sel broui — aux
phrases de mer durcie dans le feu véritable —*

le feu véritable feu véritable

Yves Préfontaine, «Le septénaire des espaces» dans Parole
tenue, Poèmes 1954-1985, *Montréal, L'Hexagone, 1990.*

Pour mieux comprendre ce qui fait la spécificité des actions
d'alphabétisation des adultes vivant hors des grands centres
urbains québécois, je suis allée dans le comté de Roberval,
autour du Lac Saint-Jean. Je suis aussi entrée en contact avec
une personne-ressource de Sept-Iles, qui s'est rendue chez

167

nous à Montréal. Nous avons recueilli son témoignage pour avoir plus de données sur l'alphabétisation des autochtones.

Avec les personnes-ressources de Roberval et de Sept-Iles, nous avons abordé les questions suivantes : le recrutement des participants, l'hétérogénéité dans la formation des groupes d'alphabétisation, l'harmonisation possible ou difficile des réseaux d'alphabétisation institutionnel et para-institutionnel et enfin les pratiques d'alphabétisation auprès des autochtones.

Caractéristiques socio-géographiques

Le comté Roberval

Autour de Lac Saint-Jean, lac qui se déverse par le Saguenay dans le fleuve Saint-Laurent et qui mesure 1,060 kilomètres carrés, l'alphabétisation des adultes du territoire administratif du service de l'éducation des adultes (SEA) Louis-Hémon se pratique dans les municipalités suivantes : Chambord, La Doré, Pointe-Bleue, Roberval, Saint-Félicien, Saint-François de Sales, pour ce qui est du secteur sud; Dolbeau, Mistassini, Normandin, Saint-Thomas Didyme, Albanel, pour ce qui est du secteur nord.

La région de Sept-Iles

Située à 930 kilomètres de Montréal et à 670 kilomètres de Québec, Sept-Iles est une ville portuaire de 30,600 habitants sur la rive nord du Saint-Laurent, face à la Gaspésie. Petit village de pêche au début du siècle, Sept-Iles a connu des périodes de grande prospérité grâce à son rôle dans l'exportation du minerai de fer du Nouveau-Québec. L'effondrement du marché du fer dans les années 80, jumelé à la récession économique, a causé des torts considérables : taux de chômage élevé, exode des travailleurs. Naguère florissante, Sept-Iles ressent, encore plus aujourd'hui, son isolement géographique et son éloignement des grands centres décisionnels. La région manque de ressources au plan socioculturel, au plan de la santé et de l'éducation.

Je me suis particulièrement intéressée aux pratiques d'alphabétisation auprès des populations autochtones, dans la ville même de Sept-Iles et dans le quartier amérindien de Uashat, situé à l'extrémité ouest de la ville de Sept-Iles ainsi que dans la réserve montagnaise de Malioténam, située à environ 15 kilomètres à l'est de Sept-Iles.

Le recrutement des participants

Au Centre d'alphabétisation du comté de Roberval Inc., environ 15 personnes, dont une coordonnatrice à plein temps, onze formatrices employées à temps plein ou à temps partiel selon les besoins et rémunérées par le SEA du territoire Louis-Hémon, trois employés à des projets ponctuels de développement, en plus d'une conseillère pédagogique, sont impliquées dans l'alphabétisation de quelque 300 participants inscrits par année. Le Centre offre des services d'alphabétisation à la population du territoire, recrute des participants, accueille, réfère les adultes et leur offre des activités d'alphabétisation, c'est-à-dire de la formation de base en français et en mathématiques. En plus, on organise des pièces de théâtre, des colloques d'apprenants, on invite des personnes-ressources sur des sujets de pointe, par exemple, des spécialistes en sexologie, en toxicomanie. Toutes ces activités dites «sociales» visent l'information des participants et leur intégration sociale. Ces activités «sociales» ont une portée soit locale, soit régionale, soit provinciale.

La population-cible visée par le Centre est constituée des habitants des quartiers de roulottes, de quartiers de Habitations à loyer modique (HLM), de locataires. On recrute aussi de futurs participants en alphabétisation parmi les habitants de vieux quartiers non rénovés et parmi la population rurale vivant du travail de la ferme, de l'agriculture et de la forêt. Le mandat d'un groupe d'alphabétisation populaire consiste à recruter en périphérie d'autres adultes pour pouvoir offrir des services d'alphabétisation en dehors des territoires ratissés où des actions d'alphabétisation ont déjà lieu. En périphérie, les activités d'alphabétisation ont lieu à temps partiel seulement.

Des moyens très concrets sont déployés pour recruter des participants. On voit à la publicité et à la promotion des services d'alphabétisation en ayant une présence visible lors d'événements majeurs qui ont lieu sur le territoire desservi. On passe aussi par le réseau de la télévision communautaire, par les stations de radio. On place des affiches dans des lieux susceptibles de regrouper des participants potentiels : Centre de travail Québec, commissions scolaires, bureaux d'aide sociale, associations caritatives, publicité par le bouche à oreille. Des animatrices-terrain font aussi des incursions au sein de coopératives d'habitation. Elles pratiquent le port-à-porte dans des HLM où habitent souvent de jeunes couples avec enfants qui auraient besoin de services de garderies pour pouvoir assister aux activités d'alphabétisation. Elles s'adressent à des entreprises commerciales du comté, des centres locaux de services communautaires (CLSC), des centres de femmes, des maisons de jeunes, des centres culturels, des clubs de l'âge d'or, des associations de familles monoparentales, des associations de fermières, des associations féminines d'éducation et d'action sociales.

L'hétérogénéité dans la formation des groupes d'alphabétisation

Les groupes d'alphabétisation formés en région éloignée sont encore plus qu'ailleurs sujets à une grandes hétérogénéité: participants d'âges variés, groupes mixtes composés d'hommes et de femmes dans des proportions diverses, des niveaux multiples d'apprentissage et d'analphabétisme. Ainsi, un groupe d'alphabétisation typique d'une région couvrant un vaste territoire peut être formé de personnes âgées, présentement à la retraite, qui n'ont pas eu la chance de fréquenter l'école; de personnes handicapées au plan intellectuel ou physique; de jeunes qui ont décroché du système scolaire sans diplôme ni formation professionnelle. On y retrouve aussi des femmes mères de famille à la maison, non intégrées au marché du travail, des travailleurs manuels, des travailleurs forestiers, à qui l'on demande d'améliorer leurs connaissances en lecture et en écriture, soit pour accéder à un nouveau poste, soit tout simplement pour être en mesure de conserver le poste qu'ils occupent déjà, compte tenu de la compétition très vive du milieu de travail actuel. Des agriculteurs peu scolarisés qui aujourd'hui sont obligés de passer par le biais de l'écrit pour mener à bien leur entreprise familiale joignent eux aussi les rangs des groupes d'alphabétisation en région éloignée.

Au plan de la formation, les personnes engagées sont confrontées à des problèmes de distance, à des impondérables dus au climat nordique québécois. On manque aussi d'un réseau d'informations consolidé et de temps pour que toutes les formatrices soient au même diapason. Souvent, les formatrices dites «en périphérie» ou «formatrices-terrain» se doivent de transporter leurs outils de travail dans leur automobile. On leur assigne trois ou quatre groupes à temps partiel. Les formatrices se rendent donc sur place en transportant tout le matériel qui leur est nécessaire dans leur laboratoire roulant.

De façon générale, les groupes d'alphabétisation populaire en région éloignée se forment ainsi : on entre dans le milieu ciblé à l'aide d'une personne qui y est dynamique et influente, par exemple, une dame faisant partie du club de l'âge d'or dans une paroisse. Ensuite, on élabore une petite enquête-maison auprès de membres de la petite communauté pour connaître leurs besoins de formation, leur disponibilité. Par la suite, il ne reste plus qu'à trouver un local bien situé, central, accessible, pas trop dispendieux, et le tour est joué. Parce qu'il y a très peu de services éducatifs dans des municipalités à très faible densité de population, il est habituellement facile d'intéresser les gens aux activités d'alphabétisation pour adultes. On mentionne aussi le manque d'expertise pour alphabétiser des adultes immigrants. Hors des grands centres urbains, on manque d'outils pour répondre à leurs besoins spécifiques. De toute façon, l'immigration en zone rurale est un phénomène nouveau, un peu marginal.

Harmonisation des réseaux institutionnels et para-institutionnels

Pour que les actions d'alphabétisation survivent en région éloignée, il faut qu'il y ait concertation, ententes entre les divers responsables des réseaux des groupes d'alphabétisation populaire et des commissions scolaires.

C'est le cas du groupe LIRA inc. de Sept-Iles qui collabore avec la commission scolaire (CS) de Sept-Iles. Groupe populaire crédité en 1983, LIRA inc. se donne pour mandat de sensibiliser la population à l'analphabétisme, de recruter des gens pour former des groupes d'alphabétisation et, par la suite, d'assumer la formation. Avant 1987, la CS de Sept-Iles ne s'impliquait pas dans le domaine de l'alphabétisation des adultes. Après une entente avec la CS de Sept-Iles, huit formateurs sont engagés en 1987. La CS administre l'argent nécessaire au paiement du salaire des professeurs et à l'approvisionnement en matériel pédagogique. Jusqu'en 1989, la CS subventionne même les locaux de LIRA inc.

nécessaires à l'alphabétisation exercée en milieu populaire. Depuis 1990, l'entente de service liant la CS à Lira inc. n'a pas été renouvelée.

Au plan de l'encadrement des ateliers d'alphabétisation et des formateurs, le fait d'alphabétiser dans des locaux de la CS restreint l'autonomie à laquelle tous s'étaient habitués. Par exemple, si dans le groupe populaire, on décidait de faire une visite à la bibliothèque, on n'avait pas d'autorisation à demander contrairement à maintenant où c'est plus «administratif» et «réglementé».

Souvent, on invoque comme argument que l'on ne peut maintenir deux réseaux de services parallèles dans une petite ville. Il est avantageux pour un groupe d'alphabétisation populaire de s'affilier au réseau des commissions scolaires au plan salarial. Dans un groupe populaire, le salaire moyen des formatrices est de 17$ de l'heure, tandis qu'une formatrice rémunérée par une commission scolaire obtient un salaire de 33$ de l'heure, tarif établi selon la convention collective des professeurs de l'éducation des adultes. L'attrait d'un salaire décent pour exercer un travail identique à celui qui se fait dans les commissions scolaires ne met cependant pas fin à l'ère du bénévolat au sein des groupes d'alphabétisation populaire. Pour ce qui est des désavantages, on craint dans les groupes populaires d'alphabétisation, de devenir plus «scolarisants» à cause, entre autres, des cadres plus rigides qui existent au sein même des façons de procéder des commissions scolaires.

Les pratiques d'alphabétisation auprès des autochtones

> Le Blanc dit vrai quand il dit : «L'Indien n'a pas de livres». C'est vrai, l'Indien n'a pas de livres mais voici ce que je pense : chaque Indien possède des histoires dans sa tête, chaque Indien pourrait raconter la vie que nous vivions dans le passé et la vie des Blancs que nous vivons à présent, il pourrait dire à quel point le Blanc nous a trompés depuis que c'est lui qui nous administre. À mon avis, aujourd'hi c'est plutôt à nous qu'il revient de prendre la parole dans les journaux et à la télévision parce qu'ici, sur notre territoire, il n'y a aucun Blanc qui sache mieux que l'Indien comment les choses se passaient avant l'arrivée du premier Blanc dans le Nord.

Il devrait y avoir plusieurs Indiens qui soient rémunérés pour contribuer à l'enseignement en indien aux enfants, autant qu'il y eut de Blancs rémunérés pour leur enseigner le français. Il devrait y avoir plusieurs livres écrits en indien que les enfants puissent lire. Et on ne devrait pas faire dans chacune des réserves indiennes.

Anne André, *Je suis une maudite sauvagesse*, Montréal, Leméac, 1976, p. 37-39 et 93.

Depuis 1986, dans le comt'ae de Roberval, tant bien que mal, des activités sont offertes dans la réserve de Pointe-Bleue. Des intervenants amérindiens évaluent que le tiers de la population habitant Pointe-Bleue est analphabète. Le recrutement des participants autochtones pose de sérieux problèmes. L'alphabétisation en français ne parvient pas à surpasser l'importance qu'ont pour les autochtones les activités de chasse et de pêche en forêt. Pour beaucoup d'Amérindiens qui ont conservé leur mode de vie tradition-nel, la réserve est un lieu qu'ils n'habitent pour ainsi dire que quelques mois par année. Un lieu d'habitation artificiel, une réserve-dortoir sporadique. Quand on passe l'hiver en forêt, la stabilité des groupes d'alphabétisation est précaire.

Les problèmes d'absentéisme sont aigus : souvent, les participants n'ont plus le téléphone. Des problèmes sociaux, financiers, familiaux, des problèmes d'alcoolisme, font en sorte que souvent toute la famille ou les proches des partici-pants en sont affectés. Cela remet en question la survie des groupes d'alphabétisation qui a pour fondement l'assiduité et la continuité, critères éducatifs et administratifs blancs. Les autochtones ont leurs propres services communautaires. Les Amérindiens habitant la réserve peuvent avoir recours à des services d'écrivains publics à même leurs propres services éducatifs, de traduction, de santé. Les Amérindiens savent qu'ils peuvent obtenir de l'aide de façon ponctuelle quand ils sont confrontés, par exemple, au monde des formulaires. Cela les rend tout à la fois dépendants et réfractaires devant l'effort à fournir pour apprendre la langue et les lois de l'autre, du Blanc. Ils remettent en question des exigences avec lesquelles ils ne se sentent aucunement solidaires. Les Amérindiens qui vivent dans le bois viennent chercher leur courrier une fois par mois. Donc l'information par écrit ou la publicité que l'on peut produire pour promouvoir des activités d'alphabétisation auprès d'eux est véhiculée une fois par mois et se perd dans le monceau d'autres choses sur papier qu'il leur faut régler.

Enseigner auprès des Amérindiens

Une formatrice blanche ayant une connaissance des Amérindiens parce que son propre grand-père était fréquemment en contact avec eux, nous a généreusement donné des indications sur ce qui fait à ses yeux leurs principales caractéristiques. Pour elle, les Amérindiens sont des personnes secrètes qui vivent encore aujourd'hui très près de légendes et des croyances qui expliquaient et réglaient la vie des ancêtres. Ainsi, les Amérindiens traditionnalistes, qui recréent la même vie que celle de leurs ancêtres, s'opposent aux façons de vivre et de penser des Blancs, des «capitalistes».

À Pointe-Bleue, par exemple, en situation de relation pédagogique, il faut toujours se placer à leur côté. Dans la culture amérindienne, quelqu'un qui se place en avant se situe dans une relation de défi. Les Amérindiens ont aussi un rythme d'apprentissage lent par rapport à l'efficacité obligée de la civilisation blanche. La notion du temps pour un Blanc et pour un Amérindien n'a pas la même valeur. Il faut donc, en assumant la responsabilité de leur alphabétisation, être en mesure de s'ajuster à leur horaire, à leur façon de vivre à travers les rythmes naturels saisonniers, bref négocier avec eux des façons de faire et d'être qui puissent satisfaire les deux parties. Quand on travaille avec des autochtones, il faut aussi prendre en considération le temps d'apprivoisement mutuel nécessaire. Trop souvent et longtemps écrasée par la population blanche, la population autochtone prend du temps avant de faire confiance aux Blancs, mais une fois que cette confiance est acquise de part et d'autre, une relation pédagogique est possible. Ainsi, dans la mesure où la communication andragogique s'établit au plan oral, il faut tenir compte du fait que pour les Amérindiens le français est une langue seconde qui exige de leur part un effort de traduction de concepts dans leur langue maternelle.

Quand l'alphabétiseure a fini de parler, les Amérindiens gardent silence par respect et parfois aussi parce qu'ils ne sont pas sûrs d'avoir bien saisi les subtilités de la langue française. Les Amérindiens apprécient beaucoup aussi le fait que les formatrices blanches s'intéressent à leurs traditions et les insèrent au processus d'alphabétisation. J'ai questionné la nécessité ou la pertinence d'organiser une alphabétisation en montagnais qui précéderait ou serait concomitante à une alphabétisation en langue seconde, c'est-à-dire en français. La question a été soulevée, semble importante comme piste de réflexion à approfondir. Il y aurait des structures organisationnelles et du personnel qualifié à mettre à contribution.

Pour exercer une pratique d'alphabétisation auprès d'adultes autochtones, il faut être sensibilisé au fait que l'analphabétisme chez Amérindiens nécessite une attention particulière quant au temps à y consacrer, aux difficultés particulières qu'ont les Amérindiens avec l'apprentissage d'une langue seconde qu'ils se doivent de lire, écrire et parler. On doit donc exercer un suivi ponctuel : l'assiduité est essentielle sinon l'effritement des groupes sera inévitable. D'autres règles de fonctionnement engagent à la fois les formatrices et les étudiants insérés dans un processus d'alphabétisation : par exemple, la régularité des horaires, l'heure des dîners, du coucher des enfants, le temps alloué aux cours. De façon générale, dans la ville de Sept-Iles, les groupes d'alphabétisation non exclusivement autochtones comportent cependant 20% d'étudiants autochtones et cela, sans avoir à faire d'efforts de recrutement spécifiques.

L'alphabétisation des autochtones accessible à même les réserves est liée au respect et à l'acceptation de la part des animatrices de travailler de concert avec des gens qui ne partagent pas la même culture qu'elles. Les Amérindiens vivent parfois plusieurs mois de l'année en forêt, aux racines de leur propre histoire. On leur demande de s'adapter à la façon blanche de comprendre et de faire les choses. En montagnais, «katshishkutamatsheutshuap», mot qui signifie «école», se traduit de la façon suivante : «la maison où on enseigne». Mais avant que les «écoles» en tant que telles existent pour les Amérindiens, ceux-ci ne comprenaient pas la signification même du mot. Les distinctions à établir d'un point de vue grammatical entre le genre féminin et le genre masculin posent aussi des problèmes aux formatrices blanches. Elles éprouvent de la difficulté à faire assimiler cette notion aux étudiants amérindiens. Il ne semble pas y avoir d'équivalent de ce concept en langue montagnaise. Le point d'ancrage pour que cette notion soit comprise et saisie par les autochtones semble difficile à déceler.

Conclusions, prospectives

En faisant le bilan des actions d'alphabétisation de Sept-Iles et des environs, on se rend compte que les plans d'alphabétisation dans les réserves se moulent aux plans d'alphabétisation des autres centres d'éducation pour adultes. Ainsi, on met de l'avant des programmes de formation individualisés, sans s'interroger sur leur impact particulier auprès d'étudiants amérindiens. L'alphabétisation auprès des autochtones n'est pas une priorité, mais la perspective d'une alphabétisation des autochtones assumée par une formatrice amérindienne pourrait, semble-t-il, faciliter les apprentissages, surtout au niveau de la langue. Souvent les formatrices attitrées à la formation des montagnais éprouve des difficultés à faire comprendre certains mots et expressions qui n'ont pas leur équivalent dans la langue maternelle amérindienne. Responsable du groupe d'alphabétisation populaire LIRA inc., Louise Leblanc admet bien humblement qu'il n'existe présentement pas de programme d'alphabétisation qui soit adapté aux Amérindiens. Les Amérindiens ont suggéré de trouver un groupe d'analphabètes de la région de Montréal pour être en mesure de communiquer par voie épistolaire avec eux afin de mettre en pratique leur apprentissage de l'écriture dans des situations de vie réelles.

À la réserve de Pointe-Bleue, on alphabétise hebdomadairement depuis trois ans. Très peu de temps semble être consacré à l'alphabétisation, soit de la mi-novembre jusqu'en mars. Les autres mois sont consacrés à la chasse, à la pêche ou au trappage. De la mi-décembre à la mi-janvier, c'est le temps des Fêtes, alors pas question de penser recruter de gens ou de donner des activités d'alphabétisation durant cette période. Ce sont surtout les femmes qui recourent aux services d'alphabétisation. Les filles montagnaises ont des enfants très jeunes et abandonnent donc leurs études très tôt.

Quand les Amérindiens abandonnent leur processus d'alphabétisation, ils abandonnent à deux ou à trois : «Je venais aux cours avec ma soeur ou mon conjoint...nous ne vient plus.» À l'inverse, la grande force de la solidarité familiale amérindienne peut faire en sorte que si le mari ou la soeur d'une étudiante est disponible pour garder les enfants à la maison, la femme autochtone a la voie libre pour poursuivre ses activités d'alphabétisation. Dans la bouche des autochtones, on entend rarement le «je». Quand une décision se prend, elle implique très souvent deux ou trois personnes. La vie communautaire des Amérindiens est intense.

Questions de discussion

1. *Quelles difficultés rencrontrez-vous parce que vous vivez en milieu rural?*
2. *Quel est votre "vecu" d'alphabétiseurs ambulants?*
3. *Comment instaurer des activités d'alphabétisation en région éloignée?*
4. *Au plan du recrutement et de la continuité dans les services offerts, l'alphabétisation auprès des autochtones est-elle un problème pour vous?*
5. *Comment voyez-vous l'alphabétisation auprès des Amérindiens du point de vue de la langue d'alphabétisation, des horaires, de l'organisation socio-économique et familiale, de la culture spécifique, de la relation pédagogique à l'intérieur de laquelle l'alphabétiseur est un Blanc ou lui-même un autochtone, etc.?*
6. *Comment adapter les programmes actuels d'alphabétisation aux attentes et besoins d'une population autochtone?*

Chapter Five
PROMOTING THE MARCH
OF WORDS

Hélène Blais

Place: Literacy Training Centre in Lac St-Jean, Quebec
Participants: Field work teachers and native learners
Issues: 1. Literacy services in outlying regions of northern
       Ontario
     2. Native literacy training practices

In order to better understand the uniqueness of literacy training efforts for adults who live outside large urban centers in Quebec, a study was conducted in the county of Roberval, around the shores of Lac St-Jean. A contact person was also enlisted from Sept-Iles to help in this case study in order to have more information on literacy training for natives. With the contacts from Roberval and Sept-Iles, the following subjects were discussed: recruiting of participants, heterogeneity in the literacy groups, the possible harmonization of literacy groups — institutional and para-institutional and literacy training practices for native peoples.

Socio-geographic characteristics

The county of Roberval
Around Lake St-Jean, a 1060 square-kilometer lake which flows into the Saguenay and St-Lawrence rivers, literacy training for adults in the Louis Hemon territory is offered in

179

the following municipalities: Chambord, La Dore Pointe-Bleue, Roberval, St-Felicien, St-Francois de Sales, all in the southern sector; and in Dolbeau, Mistassini, Normandin, St-Thomas Didyme and Albanel in the northern sector.

The region of Sept-Iles

Sept-Iles is located 930 kilometers from Montreal and 670 kilometers from Quebec City. It is a port city of 30,600 people on the northern shore of the St-Lawrence, across from the Gaspesie. From a small village at the turn of the century, Sept-Iles has seen periods of great prosperity due to the exporting of iron ore from New Quebec. But the collapse of the iron market in the 80's coupled with economic recession has caused high unemployment and an exodus of workers. The once flourishing Sept-Iles area feels its geographic isolation and its distance from decision-making centres even more keenly now. The region lacks resources at the socio-cultural, health and education levels. This case study focuses on the literacy training practices for the native populations within the city of Sept-Iles and in the Indian sector of Uashat on the western outskirts of the city and on the Montagnais reserve of Maliotenam, located some 15 kilometers east of Sept-Iles.

Recruiting the participants

At the Roberval literacy training centre, there are about 15 people on staff: one full-time coordinator, 11 teachers working full or part time and paid by the Adult Education Service of the Louis-Hemon territory, three employees for development projects, and one pedagogical counsellor. This team is involved with the literacy training for some 300 participants who register every year.

The centre offers literacy training for the population in the area. The staff recruits participants, welcomes them, refers adults and offers literacy activities such as basic training in French and mathematics. As well, the centre organizes social activities such as plays, workshops, and guest speakers on key topics, all aimed at facilitating the participants' social integration. These activities have either a local, regional or provincial impact.

The centre's target population is made up of inhabitants of

trailer parks, low-income housing neighbourhoods or rental areas. New participants for literacy training are also recruited from older, not yet renovated neighbourhoods and from among rural inhabitants who make their living from farming, agriculture or forestry. The mandate of the training group also involves recruiting other adults in peripheral regions outside of those areas where literacy training is already established. In these regions, literacy instruction is on a part-time basis only.

Some very concrete strategies were used to recruit participants. For example, publicity and promotion of the literacy training was gained with literacy field workers creating a visible presence at all major functions and activities in the areas to be served. Community television and radio stations were also visited. Signs were placed in locations most likely to attract potential participants such as the Quebec employment centres, school boards, social services office. Every effort was made to increase word of mouth publicity. Field workers were also sent directly into housing cooperatives. They went door-to-door in low-income housing projects where many young couples with children were in need of daycare services before they could attend literacy training activities. The field workers also contacted commercial organizations in the county, local community centers, women's centres, group homes for youths, cultural centres, senior's clubs, single parent organizations, women's farm associations, and women's educational and social action centres.

Heterogeneity in the formation of literacy groups

Literacy training groups in outlying regions are even more subject to a greater heterogeneity than in urban centres. In these regions it is common to find participants of various ages, groups made up of both men and women, and with differing levels of ability and illiteracy. Therefore, a typical literacy training group in a region which covers such a vast territory may be composed of retired seniors who never had a chance to go to school; of mentally or physically handicapped people; young drop-outs who left the school system without a diploma or professional training; stay-at-home mothers who have not been integrated into the workforce; manual workers, and forestry workers who have been asked to brush up their skills either to get a better job or to simply keep the one they have because of the keen competitiveness in today's job market; or farmers with little schooling who have been forced to become more literate in order to succeed on the family farm.

From the training standpoint the staff must face the problem of covering great distances and unpredictable temperatures due to the northern Quebec climate. There is also the lack of a consolidated information network to keep all teachers updated on their different activities. Often, those teachers who are termed 'peripheral' or 'field work teachers' must transport their teaching materials in their cars. They are assigned three or four groups on a part time basis, and arrive at their assigned destination carrying with them all the necessary material in their 'laboratory on wheels'.

Generally, literacy training groups in outlying areas are formed in the following way. First, access to the target group is gained with the help of a dynamic and influential person within the group for example, a lady who is part of a golden age club in a parish. Then a simple home survey is set up to determine the needs of the group, and their availability. All that remains is to find an ideal facility, centrally located, accessible, and not too expensive. Because there are so few education services in such low population density municipalities, people are usually eager for adult literacy training activities.

The lack of expertise for literacy training of adult immigrants is also noted. Outside of the larger urban centres, there is a lack of tools to meet this group's specific needs. At any rate, this type of literacy instruction for immigrants in rural areas is a rather new phenomenon.

Harmonizing institutional and para-institutional networks

For literacy training efforts to survive in outlying regions, there must be dialogue and agreement between the administrators of the different literacy groups and various school boards.

Such is the case with the LIRA INC. group in Sept-Iles which collaborates with the Sept-Iles School Board. Established in 1983, LIRA INC.'s main objectives are to sensitize the population to the problem of illiteracy, to recruit people to begin literacy training groups and to later assist in the

formation of those groups. Before 1987, the Sept-Iles School
Board was not involved in the area of adult literacy. However,
after an agreement with the school board, eight teachers were
hired in 1987. The board manages the funds necessary to pay
the teachers and to supply materials. Up until 1989, they also
subsidized the classrooms where LIRA INC. held its literacy
training activities. But since 1990, the service agreement bind-
ing the school board to LIRA INC. has not been renewed.

In some respects, literacy training within the school board
facility has curbed the autonomy to which most of the
teachers had become accustomed. For example, if the literacy
group had decided to visit the library, there was no need to
request authorization. However now things are more administrative and regulated.

In the issue of salaries it appears to be advantageous for
the literacy group to be affiliated with the school board
network. In the literacy training group, the average salary for
a teacher is $17 per hour, while a teacher paid by school
board rates is paid $33 per hour. This is the rate set by union
contracts for adult education teachers. The attraction of a
decent salary for a job identical to that being done in the
school board network does not put an end to volunteer work
within community literacy groups. As for the disadvantages,
there is a fear within community literacy groups of being too
scholarly because of among other things, the rigid framework of procedures within school boards.

Literacy training practices for native peoples

> The White Man speaks the truth when he says: "The
> Indian has no books." It is true, the Indian has no books
> but this is what I think: each Indian has stories in his
> head, each Indian could tell of the life that we lived
> before and of the White Man's life that we live now, he
> could tell how much the White Man has cheated us
> since he administers to us. In my opinion, today it
> should be us speaking up in newspapers and televi-
> sion, because here on our land, there is no White Man
> who knows better than the Indian how things were
> before the arrival of the first White Man in the North.
>
> There should also be many Indians who are paid for
> contributing to the teaching of Indian languages to

children, as many as there have been Whites paid for teaching them French. There should be many books written in Indian so that the children could read. And we shouldn't have Indian books on just one reservation, they should be on every Indian reservation.

Anne Andre, *Je suis une maudite sauvagesse*, Montreal, Léméac, 1976.

Since 1986, in the county of Roberval, activities have been offered in the Pointe Bleue reservation. It has been estimated that one third of all inhabitants of the Pointe-Bleue reservation are illiterate. But recruiting native participants poses serious problems. Literacy training in French cannot surpass the importance of hunting and fishing for natives. For many Indians who have kept their traditional lifestyle, the reservation is their home base for only a few months out of the year. It is an artificial, sporadic habitation. When participants usually spend winter in the forest, the stability of literacy training groups is precarious.

Absenteeism is a major problem. Often, participants no longer have a telephone. As well, social, financial, family and alcohol problems may affect the family and friends of the participants. These incidents threaten the survival of literacy training groups which are based on the assiduity, continuity, administrative and educational criteria of the non-native society.

Since the natives have their own community services on the reservation, they can make use of the writing services within their own educational translation and health services. The Indians know that they can count on help being available when they are confronted, for example, with forms to fill out. This makes them both dependent and rebellious towards the efforts they must make to learn the language and the law of the other — the White Man. They question the pre-requisites with which they feel no solidarity. In addition, the Indians who live in the woods come in to get their mail once every month. Therefore, written publicity to promote literacy training aimed at this target group is circulated once a month but is quickly lost in the mass of other written documents they must deal with at that time.

Expressing sensitivity to native cultural characteristics

One non-native teacher whose grandfather had had frequent

dealings with Indians was kind enough to share with us what she believes are their principal characteristics. According to her, Indians are secretive people who still today live very closely to the legends and tales that explained and regulated the life of their ancestors. As such, traditionalist Indians who have re-created the ancient lifestyle for themselves are opposed to the way of living and thinking of the White Man, the 'capitalists'.

At Pointe-Bleue, for example, in a teaching activity, it is important to stand next to them. In Indian culture, someone who stands before you is placing themselves as a challenger. As well, the Indians also have a slower speed for learning in relation to the efficiency required by non-native civilizations. The concept of time does not have the same value for natives as it does for 'whites'. Therefore in taking on responsibilities for literacy training, one must be ready to adjust to their schedule, to their way of living with the natural seasonal rhythms, and to negotiate with them a procedure for the activities which can satisfy both parties. When working with natives, it is also important to consider the necessary time for mutual familiarity to develop. Too often and too long oppressed by the 'white' population, native society is slow to trust non-natives. However, once this bond is created on both sides, a pedagogical relationship is possible inasmuch as oral communication, for example, takes into account that French is a second language for Indians and requires them to translate concepts from their mother tongue.

When the literacy teacher has finished speaking, the Indians keep silent, as a sign of respect or, sometimes, because they are not sure they have fully grasped the nuances of the French language. The Indians also appreciate the fact that non-native teachers take in interest in the native traditions and integrate these traditions into the literacy training process. Questions were also raised as to the necessity or pertinence of organizing literacy training in Montagnais and which would precede or be concomitant with the literacy training in French. This question seems worthy of further reflection bearing in mind that organizational structures and qualified personnel need to be given a priority.

In order to develop effective literacy training for native adults, one must be sensitized to the fact that illiteracy within native populations requires a special approach both in the time allotted and in the difficulty that Indians have with learning a second language which they have to read, write and speak. Therefore there must be a careful follow-up. Assiduity is essential, otherwise the break-up of the group is inevitable. Other rules of operation apply to both teachers and students; for example, the regularity of schedules, meal times, children's bedtime, and the time allotted to classes. Generally, in the city of Sept-Iles, the literacy groups which are not exclusively native are still made up of about 20% native students even without specific recruiting efforts.

In other words, literacy training for native adults on the reservation is linked to the teacher's acceptance and respect of people of a different culture, who live for many months of the year in the forest, close to the roots of their history and who are asked to adapt to a non-native way of understanding and of doing things. In the Montagnais language, 'katshishkutamatsheutshuap', a word meaning 'school', is translated as 'the house where there is teaching'. But before the 'school' as they know it today existed for the Indians, they did not even understand the meaning of the word. As well, there are many other distinctions from a grammatical point of view between the feminine and masculine gender which also pose a problem for non-native teachers. As can be expected teachers often have difficulty in getting their Indian students to grasp the concept of gender in the Montagnais language. The point at which this concept is understood by natives is elusive.

Concluding Comments

In preparing a synopsis of literacy training activities in Sept-Iles and the surrounding area, one realizes that literacy instruction in the reservations resembles strategies used in other adult education centers. That is, that individualized training programs are put forth, without questioning their particular impact on the Indian students. Literacy training for natives is not a priority. However, the possibility of this type of instruction for natives by a native teacher could facilitate learning, especially of the language. Often, the instructors assigned to teach the Montagnais groups have difficulty explaining certain words and expressions which have no equivalent in the Indian mother tongue. Louise Leblanc, who is in charge of the LIRA INC. literacy admits humbly that there is presently no one literacy program adapted for Indians.

The Indians have suggested finding a literacy group from the Montreal region so that they may communicate on an epistolary basis with them in order to better practice their writing in real life situations.

On the Pointe-Bleue reservation, there has been weekly literacy training for three years now. There seems to be very little time allotted for literacy, from mid-November to March. The other months are spent fishing, hunting or trapping. From mid-December to mid-January is the Christmas season during which recruiting or literacy activities are out of the question. It is especially the women who make use of the literacy training services since the Montagnais girls start having children at a very young age and dropout of school early.

When the Indians drop out of literacy training, two or three drop out together. "I used to come to school with my sister or my spouse — we are no longer coming." On the other hand, the great strength of the solidarity of the Indian family often makes it possible for a native woman to come to class because her sister or spouse are willing and available to babysit children while she pursues literacy training. The word 'I' is rarely heard from the mouth of a native person. When a decision is taken, it involves two or three people. As can be seen, the communal life of Indians is intense.

Discussion Questions

1. What are the different recruitment strategies used in literacy services? How do they differ for an urban literacy program?
2. How does a "field work teacher" differ from a tutor in an inner city program?
3. Is there a professional committee in your program addressing the issue of salary? If not, how can one be organized?
4. What are some important cultural aspects to be mindful of when teaching native learners?
5. Literacy training for natives in a rural area is not a priority. Discuss.

Section Four

CASE STUDIES
ON ACTIVATING
STUDENT
PARTICIPATION

INTRODUCTION

Maurice C. Taylor

How to reach more people?

Many people would agree that literacy programs in Canada must reach a far larger number of people than they have been able to reach in the last few years. Along with this belief, there has also been a growing awareness that literacy students prefer active roles as users of education rather than recipients of education. Based on this need for learner-controlled literacy efforts, practitioners are now involved in a more intense discussion on how to encourage active student participation. Often this discussion is prefaced by concerns such as How do I deal with resistance to active participation? How do I help students take responsibility for their own learning whether it be in program instruction or program management? and How do I decrease the feelings of failure for students in unfamiliar activities?

Although these questions are not easily answered, a framework to guide a much fuller debate may be useful at this stage. In this section several principles are discussed which may help point the way for increasing opportunities for active student participation — examining a program's statement of purpose, providing consistent student support, developing student training opportunities and communicating feelings of ownership.

The importance of a statement of purpose

For practitioners who want to encourage active student participation, a basic principle may involve examining the manner in which the program's statement of purpose has been written. Taken together, statements of mission, philosophy, expected results for its learners and expected community results makeup a statement of purpose and can provide a framework to build student involvement into program instruction and management.

In the CORE program described in "Active Student Participation and the Dialogue Project" in *Tearing Down Paper Walls* a clearly written statement of purpose included what the learner population needed and wanted and how they were going to be involved in the operation and management of the program and the literacy activity. Through such guiding statements, students were provided with opportunities to become engaged as partners in the learning process. They were consulted in the selection of evaluation methods, the content of tutor training, the development of learning plans and the range of community awareness activities.

In the case of the Dialogue Project, a statement of expected community results provided the fuel to activate student participation. It referred to the results both the community and a specific constituency group of social decision makers were to experience. A statement of purpose can be viewed as a building block for actively encouraging student involvement. And as indicated in the case study *Sharing Power and Authority*, some of these statements changed over time to invite and nurture student participation in program management. Once the program had developed its own personality, it followed that students could realistically become involved in its ownership, control and purpose.

The importance of consistent student support

Another key ingredient for encouraging active participation is the importance of consistent adult student support.

This may be done in a variety of ways. In the case studies *Literacy Training as a Key* and *Activating Student Participation,* the overall design of the structure and operations of the program ensured that the concerns of the students were central. In some respects job descriptions describing the student's role on the different committees helped them to define what was expected of them and their co-workers.

A similar situation occurred in *Sharing Power and Authority* where students were well aware of their responsibilities on the various standing committees. The reader will observe that in both the CORE and the CLE program mechanisms were built in to encourage the participation of students in all phases of program planning and operation.

Developing opportunities for interaction

As described in all case studies, another way of providing consistent adult student support is through the development of opportunities for interactions with other students, instructors and managers. Such activities included the grand dialogue in *Tearing Down Paper Walls,* the Christmas Party Committee in *Sharing Power and Authority* and the newsletter "The Write Stuff" in *Activating Student Participation.*

In these types of activities the program staff and instructors supported the students by accompanying them as advocates on relevant issues or by extending their friendship. On this same point of providing consistent support as a means for encouraging participation, the importance of recognizing the achievements of students as they take the risk of becoming further involved in a program is also critical. As students begin to feel a readiness for literacy advocacy for example, staff should take every opportunity to acknowledge their commitment, their good rapport with others or their skills in managing time.

Developing training opportunities

Developing training opportunities for students who take on new roles is another guideline for encouraging student participation. If active participation in literacy education enhances the personal development of individuals and extends such development to initiate change in their own communities, some type of training is required for this to occur. As students move through different roles in a program, providing an orientation or pre-service or in-service training may be necessary. Many of the obstacles for actively becoming involved in literacy education may well relate to a lack of training.

Depending on the skill level of the individual and types of desired roles, various training orientations might provide opportunities to learn about program purpose and expectations of involvement. It may also allow students to make an informed choice about whether to commit their time and energy to the program. As well, pre-service training could also include public speaking, fund development, recruiting and other program responsibilities. In three case studies *Tearing Down Paper Walls, Activating Student Participation,* and *Sharing Power and Authority* there appears to be a need for student in-service training. This type of on-going exchange of ideas is important for maintaining skills and morale, for the exchange of ideas, for problem solving and for learning new skills.

With such an approach to staff development, students may have the opportunity to incorporate such practical skills and be able to deal with the reading and writing requirements of board meetings and working with differing backgrounds and experiences that become exposed in committees.

Engendering a sense of ownership

Another principle which encourages active student participation is creating the kind of communication among participants that engenders feelings of ownership of the program and its outcomes. The reader will note that each of the case studies demonstrate how feelings of ownership are enhanced when participants are included in decisions that affect them, when a feeling of quality prevails, when people get what they need and when the purposes of the program or literacy activity are fulfilled.

Feelings of ownership stem from a variety of planned actions such as an avoidance of the traditional top-down form of management. As can be seen from the description of CORE, Journeys and CLE, these programs purposely set out to empower adult students to share in the governance of the literacy initiative.

Chapter One
SHARING POWER
AND AUTHORITY

Mary Norton

Place: *Journeys Adult Education Association in Winnipeg,
    Manitoba.*
Participants: *Staff, students and board members*
Issues: 1. *Ownership*
    2. *Control*
    3. *Purpose of a community-based program*

Adult literacy programs may be called "community-based" for a variety of reasons. The term may imply that a program is not based in an institution such as a school or college. It may mean that a program is close — geographically or psychologically — to the people it serves. But the essence of a community-based program has to do with its ownership, control and purpose: Who owns the program, who controls it, and whose interests does it serve?[1]

The Journeys Adult Education Association in Winnipeg is based in a community of students, tutors and staff who have a common interest in literacy development. As well as serving the interests of students, Journeys is addressing questions of community ownership and control. The program's fourteen member board of directors includes ten students, and many more students are actively involved on various decision-making committees and task groups.

When I visited Journeys, some students and staff were in the midst of organizing a press conference and others were preparing for the annual Christmas social. Still, students, teachers and board members made time to meet with me over lunch, during breaks, and on the weekend. We talked about the evolution of the board, about the roles of staff and board and committee members, and about having and sharing ownership and control.

The people I spoke with were: Kathleen Walsh, Journeys' Teacher-Coordinator; Brian Orvis, a teacher at Journeys; Yvonne Lemky, a Journeys student; Rachel Hofer, a Journeys board member; and Wayne Bell, Avril Chartrand, Larry Kowbel and Peter Zashlae, Journeys students and board members. Avril Chartrand assisted me by arranging interviews and doing interview follow-up work.

Background

Journeys originated in 1984 as adult evening classes at Rossbrook House, a youth drop-in centre in Winnipeg's inner city. The classes were started when Rossbrook House staff asked for help to upgrade their writing skills and basic education. Kathleen Walsh developed and obtained funding for the original classes, and has taught in and coordinated the program since.

The evening classes soon expanded to include other participants, and the name Journeys was chosen to reflect the journey that students and teachers embark on together. Journeys has moved from its first location to more spacious accommodation in downtown Winnipeg, and in addition to Kathleen and a part-time teacher, staff now include a receptionist/secretary, child careworker, caretaker and bookkeeper, all of whom are employed part-time. Journeys operates two afternoons and two evenings a week, and about 100 students from all over the city attend. Students work with either of the teachers or with one of the 25 volunteer tutors. The Winnipeg School Division One and the Federal Government Secretary of State Department are the program's major funders.

As Kathleen described them, the program's aims are to help people with adult education and literacy, to help people develop self-esteem and respect for themselves, and to help people work together. Community-building "getting along and contributing to a community" is a priority.

Journeys was incorporated as the Journeys Adult Education Association in 1988. According to Kathleen, incorporation was initiated mainly for funding purposes; as an incorporated association, Journeys can apply for and manage funds independently, rather than working through a sponsoring agency.Membership in the Journeys Adult Education Association is open to current or former students, tutors and staff, and to anyone from the larger community who supports the association's aims. Membership, which costs one dollar for students, includes the right to nominate and vote for board members.

Board formation

With incorporation, the Journeys' board gained legal status, but the board had been formed before the program was incorporated. Avril Chartrand, who has served on the board since it started, recalled that "a group of twelve students wanted to pitch in and help with running the school. Kathleen saw the board as providing a forum for students' ideas and decision-making, but she also supported the board's formation because a board "could run the school better than I could." Having responsibility for every aspect of the program was too much for one person.

The impetus for forming a board seems to have emerged naturally from the program's general bent towards addressing students' interests and encouraging students to share responsibility for addressing them. For example, early in the program's history, a group of students lobbied successfully for childcare funding — students rehearsed for and attended a meeting with funders. Students took part in this activity because Kathleen had informed them about program funding problems, and their meeting was successful because a facilitator helped them plan how to act on the information they had.[2]

Information and support were also provided for students who wanted to have a larger role in forming a board. A board development workshop was included in a Manitoba Learners' Conference, and participants were introduced to concepts and processes of board operations. Avril recalled learning how to make and vote on motions, and that after the conference, a group of Journeys students met weekly to continue learning about board functions and meeting procedures. A group of ten or twelve students who attended the meetings formed the core of the Journeys' board.

The board now includes ten Journeys students and four peo-ple from the larger community. People who fill the later positions are sometimes nominated because of their exper-tise in certain areas. For instance, a lawyer who currently fills one of the positions may be called on by the board for advice on constitutional matters. Community board members are also able to help with board and committee paperwork as needed.

The board is legally responsible for making sure that the program runs as it is supposed to, but as Journeys teacher Brian Orvis noted, "Board members don't do all of the work themselves." Sorting out responsibilities and relationships between the board and staff is an ongoing process, particu-larly as board members gain experience in their roles.

Sharing control: roles of board and staff

Who is responsible for running the Journeys program? Student board members' response to this question were mixed. Peter's view was that "We are not running the school, the teachers are running the school. We are on the board and part of that is education for us." Avril suggested that this education was two way:

> The teachers are learning from the students, and the students are learning from the teachers. That's why we got on this board, so everyone can learn from each other.

Wayne Bell emphasized that the board makes the decisions. He explained that the board has been "slowly taking control more" as members have been learning and growing.

When asked how they saw the coordinators' role, Larry Kowbel noted that the role of the founder was a question currently before the board. Kathleen's history with the program is longer than any of the current board members, and it is apparent that she has been instrumental in encouraging and supporting board development.[3] Avril explained that Kathleen herself posed the question about her role because when we didn't have a board she "did everything." What is her role now that a board is in place? What decisions can she make and which should be left for the board?

The board had yet to address these questions officially, but Larry suggested that although Kathleen "still puts ideas in our head, [she's] backing out as we're getting more developed." Avril suggested that the coordinator's role was "like an advisor", and added that "she knows what's going on at the school, so we really need her at the meetings."

As coordinator, Kathleen sees herself as responsible for the day-to-day management of the program. She reports to the board and facilitates decision-making as necessary. When her help isn't needed, she withdraws:

> Another thing I learned is that at a certain point the group wants more power. They grow and they understand things and they want more say. That's where I pull out of the group, when I feel they can do it on their own.

Sharing control: board and community

Questions about decision-making are not limited to the coordinator-board relationship. For whom does the board make decisions? Whose interests do they serve when they decide? These questions came to the fore during the process of declaring Journeys a smoke-free environment.

When Journeys moved to its current location, a room was set aside for smokers. However, the smoke which wafted out of the room caused discomfort for non-smokers. The board addressed the issue by conducting a poll, and of the eighty people who responded, fifty voted in favour of no smoking in the program. When the poll results went to the board — many of whom smoke — there was considerable debate about whether they should be accepted. As Avril explained, "the board has since learned that in fact the poll results were not debatable. The board asked for students to vote on the issue, and the vote results stand on their own."

This is one example of how board members learn their roles through experience. They also attend board orientation workshops, and the board is set up so there is always a mix of experienced and new board members. According to Avril, she and other experienced board members have a responsibility to teach new members. Rachel Hofer, now the board secretary, recalled that when she first joined the board:

> I was as green as grass. For the first three or four times at
> board meetings, I was very bewildered. I could see how
> involved [Wayne and Avril] were [and] was really
> admiring them for their involvement. I gave myself
> time, and now I understand.

Sharing responsibility on committees

In addition to attending board meetings and carrying out
related responsibilities, board members also serve on various
standing committees. For instance, as a member of the personnel committee, Avril was involved, with Kathleen, in
hiring Brian as a teacher for the program. Then, along with a
community board member — but without Kathleen this time
— Wayne and Avril hired the program secretary and
caretaker.

As well, students work together on specific tasks and ad
hoc committees are formed from time to time to manage
projects or events. Board members and other students from
the program serve on these committees. As a fund-raising
project, Larry and Wayne worked together to design and
order crests for the program. They developed the design,
sought estimates for making them, and brought the information to the board for a decision. The crests are sold to raise
funds and to promote Journeys.

Yvonne Lemky has been a student at Journeys for about a
year, and was involved in two ad hoc committees when I
spoke with her. In one committee, she was involved in
organizing the annual Christmas party. In the other, she was
helping with a press conference which Journeys called regarding the close of International Literacy Year and the students
and staff involvement in everything from social events to
political action.

Yvonne explained that Kathleen chaired the Christmas
committee meetings and recorded the minutes, while committee members planned and carried out necessary tasks.
For instance, Yvonne and another student prepared invita-
tions — with some computer instruction from Kathleen —
and one of the committee members was to cook the turkey.
Yvonne had written a letter to Winnipeg Harvest asking for
food donations, and the whole committee was to be involved

in decorating the room.

The Christmas party is an annual highlight for the Journeys community and one of the social events that is important to community building. The press conference was aimed at involving the larger community, to call attention to the need for ongoing action for literacy. According to the press release, "the press conference will be aimed at reaching all Manitobans who have not yet been involved in the struggle to eliminate illiteracy."[4]

As acting president at the time, Avril was responsible for overseeing press conference planning, but Brian, as he said, was "working behind the scenes." For efficiency at the time, Brian drafted the press release which went out over Avril's signature, but the writing was completed in consultation with the committee. The committee also discussed what needed to be said at the conference and who would speak.[5]

Literacy development

Students who attend Journeys are at various stages of developing their literacy, and differences in reading and writing ability have to be accounted for in board and committee meetings. At the same time, involvement in the meetings and related activities is a vehicle for literacy development.

Currently, differences in reading ability are addressed by having minutes read out at the start of the meeting. This process has become so natural for Kathleen that she surprised herself at a meeting of another organization by asking who was going to read the minutes. However, reading minutes aloud does take meeting time, and some board members noted that the procedure can be frustrating.

Avril pointed out that all of the people on the board work according to the abilities they have — she, for instance is "good at bringing people in." If fluent reading had been a criteria for board membership, she might not have been eligible to stand for election. Still, she speculated about whether some reading ability should be a requirement or whether a buddy system might address the needs of less able readers. Avril added that since she needs time to read for herself, she reads all her minutes before meetings.

When asked about reading requirements, Brian answered that the minutes can become "reading material for school." Committee work and related activities also provide content for literacy development. Larry noted that he had to give a speech about why he was standing for election to the board, and said that writing the speech was a useful experience[6] And Brian suggested that students would be reading about the press conference in the paper and writing their own versions and views of what happened.

Avril did point out that some of the board material is confidential, and cannot be brought to a tutor for help. She also noted that some of the board reading and writing demands are "way higher" than what she is comfortable working on. So while some of her board work provides content for literacy development, she has to manage her time so she can practise reading and writing at more comfortable levels as well.

Personal development

Being involved on the board and committees promotes learning and development in other areas as well. In the process of preparing to interview potential staff, Wayne and Avril learned how to review resumes, what to look for in applications, and how to plan and ask appropriate questions. Wayne said that since being involved in the hiring procedures, he had a better idea of what to say and how to handle himself in job interviews.

Avril has been on the board since it was formed and is currently the Vice President. She said that being on the board had helped her "come out of her shell" and express herself more easily. She could now speak directly to an issue rather than around it, and was learning about the importance of listening. As acting President for a time, she was also learning how to make sure that everyone in a meeting had a turn to speak and how to control the time that was taken to discuss any one issue. Overseeing the press conference planning was a chance to learn and practise delegation skills.

When Rachel started in a nursing program, she lacked confidence, even though she had completed the necessary upgrading for admission. She was referred to Journeys and the "first thing [Kathleen] did was get me onto the board." Rachel felt that being on the board had been of great benefit to her. As well, she said, she's developed an awareness of what's going on in society. Although pressed for time because of her own studying, she hopes to be able to contribute to Journeys in other ways at some point.

When Yvonne started at Journeys she didn't talk to anyone. In her second year she got to know people,felt more comfortable, and became more involved. She also mentioned learning how to organize things and said, "You never know if you are out on your own, and you have to organize something and you have nobody else around." Yvonne also saw her committee work as a her way of contributing to the program:

> The school is giving me my education, and I thought the most I could do, seeing that I couldn't provide anything, is...help and get involved in some committees.

Concluding comments

As community-based literacy programing grows in Canada, the questions of control and ownership are being raised increasingly in terms of students' involvement on program boards. Whenever this topic is discussed the inevitable questions seem to be: How do you deal with reading and writing requirements of board meetings and how do you deal with differing backgrounds and experiences with meetings and committees?

At Journeys, these questions are recognized, but they do not seem to be central ones. Brian has worked with a variety of non-profit groups, both voluntarily and as a civil servant in the Manitoba government, and from his perspective, there is really no difference between the process for teaching board procedures to literacy students and the process for teaching them to any other group. He recalled that even new Members of the Legislative Assembly often had to be coached in parliamentary procedures.

The central question for any group concerned about community ownership and control has to do with whether those in control really want to share ownership. Brian suggested that:

> Authority and power are curious things. Power is terribly sweet, and very often people who get power don't want to give up one iota of it — certainly not to someone who is uneducated...

At Journeys, there has been a commitment to sharing authority and power, and rather than looking for barriers to student participation, there has been a basic belief that given the opportunity and support, people from the community can manage their community.

Notes

1. Dr. Carlos Torres made this point during a discussion in an adult education course at the University of Alberta.
2. For a description of these events, see the case study in this book called *Literacy, Welfare and Popular Education*.
3. Prior to Journeys' incorporation, Kathleen worked in the program on a two-thirds time basis and was paid through the Winnipeg Core Area Initiative. In March, 1989, following incorporation, the Journeys board hired Kathleen to work full-time. She reports to the board.
4. Press release issued by Journeys Education Association Inc. November 29, 1990.
5. The press conference resulted in television news coverage and an article on the first page of each of Winnipeg's two daily newspapers.
6. Larry's speech was subsequently included in an article about Journeys which was published in the January 1990 issue of Manitoba Education.

Discussion Questions

1. *What is your definition of a community-based literacy program?*
2. *How could you organize a board development workshop for your students?*
3. *In your opinion, who is responsible for running the Journeys program?*
4. *What criteria would you suggest for board membership?*
5. *As students become more involved on program boards, how do we deal with differing backgrounds and experiences with meetings and committees?*

Chapter Two
LES MURS DE PAPIER

Hélène Blais

Lieu: Le Centre Louis-Jolliet de la Commission des écoles catholiques de Québec, Ville de Québec, Québec.
Participants: Les étudiants en alphabétisation et le comité de l'Année internationale de l'alphabétisation et des décideurs politiques
Thèmes: 1. La sensibilisation du public en général
2. L'implication des personnes analphabètes elles-mêmes

> *On s'est dit : si on donnait une chance aux deux bords de se rencontrer et de se parler, peut-être que cela permettrait de faire des pas dans la bonne direction? À tout le moins, toutes ces personnes qu'on réunirait ne pourraient plus continuer à faire semblant puisqu'elles auraient parlé ensemble. On a misé sur le dialogue. (Labrie et les mots de bien du monde, 1990).*

Les origines du projet-dialogue

Pour soulinger l'Année internationale de l'alphabétisation (AIA), le comité organisateur de l'AIA à la Commission des écoles catholiques de Québec (CECQ) élabore un plan d'action qui vise un cheminement éducatif de sensibilisation et de dialogue sur l'analphabétisme vécu par les citoyens de la ville de Québec et des environs, par exemple, dans la ville de Vanier en banlieue de Québec. Par ce projet échelonné sur toute l'année 1990, on veut impliquer de façon directe les étudiants en français de base du Centre Louis-Jolliet de la CECQ pour qu'ils sensibilisent la population à ce qu'ils vivent et dialoguent ouvertement avec elle. Des membres du comité étudiant pour l'AIA s'expriment ainsi :

Nous voulons parler, vivre une expérience de groupe positive, apprendre à tenir nos engagements, être informés et informer les autres, nous adapter mieux à l'école, améliorer notre orthographe, nous conscientiser, savoir ce qui se passe à l'étranger en alphabétisation, soutenir le monde, amener les gens à vivre du respect autour d'eux...

Il serait très intéressant de rencontrer des enfants en train d'apprendre à lire et à écrire...

On veut être appelés «étudiants» et pas «élèves» mais on aimerait changer le nom «d'Alpha» pour «Français de base» ou quelque chose de semblable...

Nous aimerions avoir plus d'informations sur qui a décidé de l'AIA et pourquoi. Ici, il va y avoir une pièce de théâtre, un colloque et de la sensibilisation. Il faut que les gens qui ne viennent pas à l'école arrêtent d'avoir honte. Il faut que nous puissions parler de nos problèmes et de nos efforts. On a besoin de plus de 2 000 heures pour tout apprendre. Pendant l'AIA, c'est à notre tour de se faire entendre partout.

Le comité organisateur de l'AIA pour la CECQ est constitué des membres suivants : deux adultes en alphabétisation, une formatrice en alphabétisation, la conseillère pédagogique en alphabétisation et un conseiller pédagogique des services de l'éducation des adultes, en plus d'une stagiaire en service social engagée spécialement pour ce projet spécifique d'intervention. Formés en comité étudiant, les adultes en processus d'alphabétisation sont partie prenante du programme d'activités. Entre autres, ils prennent en charge leur situation de porte-parole ou de porte-voix de la majorité silencieuse analphabète, en donnant des suggestions aux représentants de l'AIA et en faisant circuler l'information dans les groupes-classes. C'est ce comité étudiant qui délègue les deux représentants étudiants au comité organisateur de l'AIA pour la CECQ. Bref, on désire, dans le cadre de l'AIA, éduquer tous les adultes de Québec «par et pour les personnes analphabètes».

Pour parvenir à ses fins, le comité de l'AIA planifie

différents types d'actions en vue de sensibiliser divers groupes sociaux. Tout d'abord, on invite des décideurs politiques de la ville de Québec à une conférence de presse où on leur donne des suggestions afin qu'ils saisissent l'importance, pour eux, de s'attarder au problème de l'analphabétisme vécu dans l'environnement urbain. On suscite aussi leur collaboration et une implication concrète de leur part, pour faire en sorte que l'AIA soit une année-pivot pour les personnes analphabètes. Un document pédagogique produit par Vivian Labrie[1] est aussi distribué à tous les directeurs et directrices de toutes les écoles primaires et secondaires de la CECQ afin que les élèves du primaire et du secondaire prennent conscience de l'importance de l'écrit. Accompagné d'une conseillère pédagogique du Centre Louis-Jolliet jouant le rôle de présentatrice-modératrice, une jeune adulte analphabète rencontre tous les élèves de l'école primaire Saint-Pie-X de la CECQ, classe par classe, pour leur parler de sa réalité en tant que personne éprouvant des difficultés avec l'écriture et la lecture et pour répondre à leurs questions.

Dans un premier temps, la CECQ offre aux adultes poursuivant leur formation de niveau secondaire au Centre Louis-Jolliet, l'opportunité d'assister à un spectacle théâtral interactif intitulé «Rayons de nuit», conçu sur commande pour la CECQ, afin qu'ils soient informés de ce que vivent les personnes analphabètes qui fréquentent le même lieu de formation qu'eux. Le texte de la pièce de théâtre est de Gilles-Philippe Pelletier et il est interprété par la troupe de théâtre Sans Détour. «Rayons de nuit» rejoint, dans dix quartiers de la ville de Québec, des groupes communautaires et le grand public afin de les éveiller à la réalité complexe de l'analphabétisme.

Dans un deuxième temps, grâce à la création du Bureau de consultation en alphabétisation animé par Noé Dufour et Vivian Labrie, un dialogue s'initie entre les étudiants en processus d'alphabétisation (à la CECQ et dans d'autres organismes) et des intervenants, des représentants sociaux ou décideurs politiques engagés de quelque façon que ce soit dans différents secteurs d'activités touchant les cinq blocs thématiques suivants :

1° l'école et la famille;
2° les revenues (travail, chômage, aide sociale);

3° les services municipaux;
4° la santé;
5° la culture et les médias.

Dans un troisième temps, on clôture le «projet dialogue» — et du même coup l'intervention de sensibilisation menée tout au long de l'AIA — par un colloque, un «grand dialogue». Celui-ci regroupe à fois toutes les personnes qui ont participé à la prise de parole suscitée par les personnes analphabètes sur les cinq thèmes ci-haut mentionnés et les spectateurs qui ont été rejoints par les représentations théâtrales.

Bref, toutes les démarches proposées visent deux objectifs principaux : sensibiliser le public en général et impliquer les personnes analphabètes elles-mêmes au fait que l'on entende enfin la riche tessiture de leurs voix trop souvent et trop longtemps inécoutées ou tenues coites.

Comment on procède pour «arrêter de faire semblant que tout le monde sait lire et écrire»

En planifiant l'AIA, après sa deuxième réunion du 23 novembre 1989, le comité étudiant élabore les quatre projets d'action suivants :

1°   Une journée de «jeûne» de lecture et d'écriture, en janvier 1990, pour des personnalités connues jouant un rôle important dans un des cinq champs thématiques retenus :

   1° L'école : la directrice générale de la CECQ, un représentant du milieu universitaire;
   2° Les revenus : le ministre québécois du revenu, la vice-présidente de la Centrale des syndicats nationaux (CSN), la directrice du Centre Travail-Québec;
   3° Les services municipaux : le maire de la ville de Québec et son équipe;
   4° La santé : le ministre québécois de la santé, des médecins travaillant dans des Centres locaux de services communautaire (CLSC), des «bobo macoutes»[2], etc.;
   5° La culture et les médias : des journalistes, des animateurs-radio, l'éqéque de Québec, un représentant des Centres d'orientation et de formation pour

immigrants (COFI).

L'idée d'une journée de jeûne de lecture et d'écriture dans un lieu institutionnel ne sera finalement pas retenue par les autorités de la CECQ. Cette expérience dépaysante aurait visé à briser des routines installées souvent sur un socle presque exclusivement scripturaire. Chacune des personnalités choisies serait restée dans son milieu de travail tout en étant accompagnée par une personne analphabète visitant l'entreprise «jeûnante». La personne analphabète aurait joué le rôle d'une personne-ressource ou d'une «surveillante» des déplacements du décideur ou de l'intervenant social sur son lieu de travail. Après cette journée ou demi-journée de jeûne de lecture et d'écriture, on aurait invité les «jeûneurs» à un dîner sobre, humble et simple, à l'image des repas typiques des personnes analphabètes où l'on aurait pu, entre autres, servir de la soupe à alphabet ou présenter le menu du repas offert dans une graphie étrangère, complètement illisible pour les participants «jeûneurs».

Pousser des gens à jeûner de lire et d'écrire, ne serait-ce quelques heures dans des lieux où prédomine presqu'exclusivement l'écriture, se voulait aussi élément déclencheur à une prise de conscience de la façon dont l'écrit conditionne la vie quotidienne de tout un chacun. On voulait essayer, par cette diète insolite, de dégager les avantages et inconvénients de l'utilisation massive actuelle de la lecture et de l'écriture par rapport à l'oralité qui engage les communicateurs dans d'autres types d'échanges humains. Suite à un refus des gestionnaires de la CECQ, le comité étudiant et celui de l'AIA abandonneront cette parite du projet.

2°   Une pièce de théâtre présentée à dix endroits différents sur le territoire de la CECQ, de janvier à mai 1990.

3°   Cinq discussions portant chacune sur un des thèmes retenus, au centre où les adultes pratiquent leurs activités d'alphabétisation puis avec des personnes du milieu, le tout suivi d'une rencontre entre les deux groupes, c'est-à-dire entre les participants en alphabétisation et les intervenants sociaux, de février à novembre 1990.

4°   Un colloque avec tous ceux et celles qui auront participé aux «exercices» de dialogue, dans le but de produire un document de sensibilisation sur «la charte des droits des personnes analphabètes», à la fin novembre 1990.

Pour se préparer à rencontrer des intervenants sociaux et des décideurs, pour entamer avec eux un dialogue, les adultes en processus d'alphabétisation explorent d'abord en profondeur chacune des thématiques proposées. Ils expriment sous diverses formes toute l'importance et toute la place qu'occupent pour eux les difficultés à déchiffrer l'écrit dans des situations de vie collées à leur réalité et auxquelles ils se butent quotidiennement.

Par la suite, des personnes intervenant à divers niveaux pour chacune des thématiques se rencontrent et échangent sur les problèmes que peuvent poser la surabondance et la surimportance de l'écriture par rapport à leur domaine d'intervention respectif.

En dernier lieu, on réunit les étudiants en alphabétisation et les intervenants. Chacun présente son point de vue, sa vision du phénomène. On cherche ensuite ensemble des façons de régler certains problèmes liés à chacun des domaines thématiques et des principes d'action. Un rapport-synthèse de ces solutions et suggestions d'actions à entreprendre pour faciliter les tâches et la vie des personnes analphabètes est distribué dans le milieu d'intervention sous la forme d'un document écrit, de lecture facile, au moyen de caractères typographiques d'une grosseur appréciable, d'accompagnement visuel important, d'illustrations humoristiques, fantaisistes, qui font images — une image ne vaut-elle pas mille mots?

Des moyens de se rendre audibles et visibles

Pour que les adultes analphabètes puissent entamer un dialogue sur les thèmes de la famille, de l'école, du monde des revenus, des services municipaux, de la santé, de la culture et des médias, on a d'abord cherché à sensibiliser les représentants des organismes approchés, au fait qu'il y avait fort probablement des personnes analphabètes parmi le personnel, les membres ou les usagers des services de ces dits organismes.

Par le biais d'activités d'animation diverses, on a aussi pensé à mettre en lumière les situations concrètes et parfois pénibles auxquelles sont confrontés les analphabètes ayant recours aux institutions sociales incontournables. À chaque fois, à travers la mise en pratique du dialogue, on a proposé des solutions pour que l'accès aux services offerts par les différents organismes soit facilité, par exemple : simplifier une procédure administrative, offrir la possibilité d'obtenir des renseignements oralement, de vive voix ou par téléphone; prévoir que les employés préposés aux renseignements soient conscients qu'il leur faudra parfois lire à haute voix des directives, des consignes.

On devrait aussi accorder plus de temps pour la formation à l'intérieur même de l'organisme quand on introduit de nouvelles tâches au sein d'une équipe de travail, utiliser des pictogrammes, des supports auditifs ou visuels et valoriser de façon générale la mémoire, cet outil indispensable et si fortement développé chez les personnes analphabètes. Toutes ces mesures pourraient contribuer à faire disparaître les stigmates paralysants associés à l'analphabétisme.

On se demande également si les organismes rejoints n'ont pas tendance à fortifier l'usage de l'écriture pour leurs propres employés, leurs membres ou leurs usagers. On outille aussi les intervenants sociaux pour qu'ils puissent identifier des moyens, des astuces, quelques signes ou comportements qui simplifient les dédales d'écriture et de lecture que doivent traverser les personnes analphabètes.

Une visite à l'Hôtel de ville de Québec

J'ai eu le grand plaisir d'assister à une rencontre-dialogue ayant pour thèmes la ville et l'accès aux services municipaux pour les personnes analphabètes. Cette rencontre a eu lieu au Centre d'interprétation de la vie urbaine dans l'édifice de l'Hôtel de ville de Québec. Lors de l'animation, les participants alphabétisés et les adultes en processus d'alphabétisation se sont questionnés sur les endroits qu'ils fréquentent ou qu'ils ne fréquentent pas dans la ville de Québec. On a pu inventorier des lieux distinctifs selon que l'on était analphabète ou alphabétisé.

Après une brève mais éloquente «tempête d'idées», nous en sommes venus à la conclusion que «la ville où je vais» correspond grosso modo, pour l'adulte analpbabète, aux lieux urbains suivants : centres commerciaux, pistes cyclables, bars, endroits où l'on peut pratiquer ou regarder des sports (le Colisée, piscines, arénas, etc.), les promenades aménagées au bord de la rivière, les quartiers préférés («endroit proche de chez nous, où je me sens bien», où la fierté d'habiter sa ville se vit dans son quartier immédiat), les supermarchés (Provigo), la pharmacie Chez Jean Coutu, le Vieux-Port de Québec, les parcs, les Plaines d'Abraham, le Musée, l'Aquarium, le Jardin zoologique.

«La ville où je ne vais pas», quant à elle, correspond aux lieux suivants : le Vieux-Québec, les tavernes, le bord de la rivière et la Haute-Ville. Lieu institutionnel incontournable, la Haute-Ville n'est fréquentée qu'au moment des festivités : Carnaval d'hiver, Festival d'été, etc. Le Mail Saint-Roch et la bibliothèque sont d'autres lieux chargés émotivement. Ils sont fréquentés ou pas, c'est selon.

Les apprenants se distinguent des intervenants sociaux dans leurs choix de moyens de transport, selon les propro-tions suivants :

Moyens de transport	Nombre d'apprenants	Nombre d'intervenants
Automobile	5	14
Autobus	11	3
À pied	8	10
Taxi	1	3
Vélo	5	3

La personne analphabète fonctionne dans la ville à l'aide d'indices faisant un grand appel à sa mémoire. Elle voudrait vivre dans une ville où les maisons et les parcs soient pro-pres, calmes, tranquilles. On a aussi pu mettre le doigt sur quatre peurs vécues par elle dans la ville :

1° la peur de se faire attaquer (mail Saint-Roch, bord de la rivière);

2° la peur de se perdre : quand elle veut se rendre à un nouvel endroit, elle doit y aller avec quelqu'un et mémoriser le parcours;

3° la peur de demander de l'information;

4° la peur d'avoir l'air folle parce qu'obligée de lire les pancartes pour se conformer aux règlements munici-paux, aux lois de la circulation. Les personnes ana-lphabètes demandent aussi aux élus qu'ils s'adaptent à leur façon de voir la ville, la vie. Selon elles, les dirigeants municipaux n'ont pas la même vision que le «monde ordinaire», ils ne «pensent pas comme les pauvres».

En soirée, les étudiants assistent à une séance du Conseil municipal de la Ville de Québec. Comme ils ont l'intention d'intervenir lors de la période de questions adressées aux membres du Conseil, les étudiants se sont préparé une série de questions. Leurs représentants pourront finalement en poser quelques-unes :

Pourquoi le marché Saint-Roch n'est pas à la même place qu'avant, au Parc Victoria? C'était plus accessible.

Pourquoi il n'y a pas de panneaux indicateurs à la bibliothèque pour mieux indiquer les étages où sont les catégories de livres?

Pourquoi pas des spectacles gratuits du Festival d'été partout dans la ville, y compris dans la Basse-Ville? (Bénéficiant généralement de revenus très modestes, la plupart des personnes analphabètes habitent les quartiers populaires de la Basse-Ville, la Haute-Ville étant réservée aux gens à l'aise, plus fortunés).

Il y a beaucoup d'accidents sur les pistes cyclables. Pourquoi il n'y aurait pas plus de surveillance, de sécurité, de protection sur les pistes cyclables?

Pourquoi pas transformer les édifices vides de la Basse-Ville en :

- Logements à prix modique ou subventionnés;
- Locaux pour divertir les jeunes;
- Maisons de réhabilitation (alcooliques, toxicomanes);
- Refuges pour personnes démunies.

Pourquoi ils font pas des habitations à loyer modique (HLM) sur Saint-Joseph, St-Vallier, de la Couronne et la Côte du Palais à la place des maisons et des magasins qui sont abandonnés?

On n'est pas informés sur les spectacles, les loisirs, les services qu'il y a dans la ville. Pourquoi pas passer des messages à la radio et dans le journal du quartier aux 15 jours? Il y aurait plus de monde partout.

Une mémoire de ce qui a été fait et dit

Le colloque de clôture de l'AIA, le «grand dialogue» au Musée de la civilisation réunit avant tout la population étudiante en alphabétisation de la CECQ et les groupes d'alphabétisation populaire Atout-Lire et Alphabeille. C'est un moment chaleureux qui redonne la parole en direct, un maximum de visibilité, de place aux personnes analphabètes et leur permet en tout liberté, sur leur propre terrrain parolier — par le biais de diverses mises en situations et différents jeux de mots, devinettes, écriture collective d'un conte — de proposer de nouvelles pratiques et des solutions concrètes qui pourraient faire consensus et améliorer leur sort. Ont successivement lieu :

> une mini-exposition d'objets en rapport avec l'analphabétisme (chaque participant était invité à apporter un objet représentant pour lui l'analphabétisme);
>
> la lecture de rapports rédigés par des étudiants en français de base qui décrivent leurs expériences vécues lors des dialogues thématiques, en plus de leurs expériences quotidiennes de survie, confrontés qu'ils sont avec le monde de la lecture et de l'écriture;
>
> la distribution du livre issu de ces rencontres-dialogues : Vivian Labrie et les mots de bien du monde, Par-dessus le fossé des lettres, Des lieux pour des personnes fières, Dialogues entre des étudiants-e-s en alpha et des intervenants-e-s, Bureau de consultation en alphabétisation, Québec, Commission des écoles catholiques de Québec;
>
> la mise à la disposition, pendant le souper, d'un «bout de mur», afin de permettre une expression encore plus libre autour du thème de l'analphabétisme, par le moyen de graffiti;
>
> enfin, la rédaction d'un texte collectif, d'un conte, coanimée par Alain Bouchard, journaliste au Soleil, et le dessinateur Serge Gaboury sur le thème «Notre planète est miniscule».

Prise de parole unique, le colloque a été rempli d'émotions et d'imagination. Jeux de mots, d'idées, écriture collective. Des objets, des gens, personnages privilégiés de bandes dessinées. Des graffiti, gestes un peu sauvages et illicites, en dialogue avec les mots tracés des autres. Une soirée de fête, un gala des mots, des lauriers sur les têtes des adultes qui franchissent des pas, abattent des murs, brisent des silences, font entendre courageusement leurs voix.

Des moyens pour faciliter la vie des personnes analphabètes

> Je lis. J'écris au son. Il refuse de remplir la formule pour moi. Moi je barbouille dessus comme je peux. Quand j'ai fini de tout barbouiller, il prend sa bouteille d'encre blanche et efface tout ça. Ca prend 20 minutes, ça en aurait pris deux. [...] Il faut que tu lui poses des questions. Si t'es gêné t'auras pas la réponse. Si tu comprends pas, faut que tu dises : donne-moi un terme qui est plus facile à comprendre. [...] Quand t'es nerveux, tu sais encore moins lire! (apprenants cités par *Labrie et les mots de bien du monde*, 1990).

Pour faciliter la vie des personnes analphabètes, de nombreuses pistes restent à ouvrir. On doit se baser sur les expériences difficiles auxquellles ces personnes sont confrontées, c'est-à-dire sur les situations où elles ne sont pas totalement en mesure de répondre à des exigences de fonctionnement social ayant pour fondement l'écriture et la lecture. Par exemple, pour amener des personnes analphabètes à assumer plus facilement des fonctions dans des groupes, afin qu'elles soient en mesure de participer à des réunions à titre de bénévoles, on propose les solutions suivantes :

> être discrète quand une personne nous confie sa difficulté, miser sur les rapports de vive voix, défendre les personnes devant des commentaires mal intentionnés, faire confiance à la mémoire, se passer de papier quand ce n'est pas nécessaire, montrer que c'est normal qu'il y en ait qui ne savent pas bien écrire et lire, avoir des tâches concrètes à proposer. (*Labrie et les mots de bien du monde*, 1990)

Conslusions, prospectives

Les personnes analphabètes sont les mieux placées pour

parler d'analphabétisme. Après toute la démarche de l'AIA et le dialogue en profondeur qu'elle a suscité, les personnes analphabètes sont en mesure de proposer des signes qui permettent de les distinguer et de les décrire dans leurs façons particulières de fonctionner, de se débrouiller dans le monde de l'écrit. En guise d'exemple, voici une liste de signes, extraite de *Labrie et les mots de bien du monde*, 1990 :

Des signes qui aident à reconnaître qu'une personne a peut-être de la misère à lire, à écrire ou à compter

- Arriver beaucoup d'avance à un rendez-vous.
- Répondre sans écouter qu'on l'a déjà fourni quand on nous demande un papier.
- Par la signature qui a l'air tracée avec difficulté.
- Avoir peur de signer et de se faire avoir en signant.
- Arriver avec une enveloppe pas ouverte.
- Dire qu'on a pas ses lunettes.
- Dire qu'on a pas lu le papier parce qu'il fait pas clair chez soi.
- Se moquer des pousseux de crayon.
- Ne pas avoir fait ce qu'on nous avait écrit de faire.
- Ne jamais se proposer pour des tâches qui demandent de lire ou d'écrire
- Refuser un poste, une promotion.
- Arrêter de venir à une activité qui demande de lire ou d'écrire.
- Dire que tout est correct et qu'y a pas de problème.
- Demander de pouvoir remplir un papier chez soi.
- Oublier de la documentation qu'on nous aura donnée.
- Demander des explications alors que tout est écrit sur un document qu'on a en main.
- Prononcer beaucoup de mots de façon non standard.
- etc.

À notre connaissance, ce travail d'ethnographie de la culture des personnes analphabètes, cette liste de signes, peut aider les intervenants à être plus attentifs aux besoins et attentes spécifiques des personnes analphabètes. Ces signes sont la preuve qu'il existe des moyens tangibles, des solutions, des ponts-levis pour enjamber la douve du château fort de l'écriture.

Le projet de dialogue de la CECQ a ouvert la voie, a permis aux personnes analphabètes de prendre la parole. Les intervenants et décideurs sociaux peuvent maintenant leur faire une place au pays des papiers, en empruntant des raccourcis qui suivent le chemin de l'oralité.

Notes

1. Labrie, Vivian (1990) *a b c douze activités à vivre en classe pour souligner l'Année internationale de l'alphabétisation o p q r s t u v w x y z!*, Bureau de consultation en alphabétisation, Québec, Commission des Écoles catholiques de Québec, document polycopié, non paginé.
2. «Bobo macoutes» (ou «Boubou macoutes») : (Dérivé du créole haotien, «tonton macoute», agent de la répression sous le régime Duvalier.) Agents de prestation du ministère québécois de la Main-d'oeuvre et de la sécurité du revenu. Sous le régime libéral du premier ministre Robert Bourassa (appelé familièrement «Boubou»), ces fonctionnaires contrôlent mensuellement, par l'intermédiaire d'enquêtes, de contre-enquêtes et de questionnaires, le statut marital des assistées sociales. L'expression «boubou macoute» est apparue dans le lexique québécois en 1985, quand ces mêmes agents ont brimé les droits fondamentaux de certaines assistées qui se sont alors liguées contre ces pratiques inacceptables en pays dit de «démocratie». Laissons l'une de ces femmes, qui a été «visitée», décrire sa situation :

Alors, si t'as un chum [ami, copain, (prononcer tchomme)] eh ben tu risques tout simplement de te faire couper ton chèque. On va te dire : «Je regrette, mais vous n'êtes pas seule chef de famille puisque je vous trouve avec un homme. Désormais, vous serez coupée.» Et crac!...

Quand l'inspecteur arrive et qu'il n'y a pas d'homme à la maison, c'est la fouille dans tous les racoins [recoins]. L'inspecteur regarde tes armoires et tes garde-robes pour voir s'il n'y a pas de vêtements d'homme. Il regarde même dans ton lit! On sait jamais, ton chum est peut-être caché dedans ou dessous!...Ou bien, il a pu oublier son pyjama ou sa crème à barbe dans la pharmacie...ou sa pipe dans le cendrier...

Le comble, c'est que certains inspecteurs essaient de te faire comprendre que tu aurais beaucoup d'avantages à être «gentille» avec eux...C'était comme ça il y a des années et c'est encore comme ça aujourd'hui. Tout le monde le sait, mais rien ne change pour autant! (Turcot, 1987, p. 146-147)

Dans le cas qui nous intéresse, les participants en processus d'alphabétisation, qui analysaient leur rapport à la santé, ont joué avec l'expression «boubon macoute» pour la transmuter en «bobo macoute», «bobo» désignant, dans le langage enfantin, une plaie, un endroit du corps où l'on a mal ou une douleur physique.

Questions de discussion

1. *Quelles sont les actions concretes qui peuvent provoquer un dialogue entre les participants en alphabétisation et les décideurs et intervenants sociaux?*
2. *Quelle importance accordez-vous à la lecture et a l'écriture dans votre organisme? Un jeune de lecture et d'écriture serait-il envisageable en son sein comme moyen de sensibilisation a l'analphabétisme?*
3. *D'après vous, que faudrait-il pour "penser les pauvres," pour se rapprocher des personnes analphabètes?*
4. *Comment apporter des changements quant aux moyens de diffuser les informations pour faire en sorte que la dimension orale et la memoire des alphabètes soient mises a profit?*
5. *A quelles signes reconnaissez-vous les adultes eprouvant des difficultés a lire et a écrire?*
6. *En suivant le chemin de l'oralité des alphabètes, comment réussir a leur des pas dans la pratique et la connaissance de l'écriture?*

Chapter Three
DIALOGUE WITH SOCIAL DECISION-MAKERS

Hélène Blais

Place: Centre Louis-Joliet, Quebec City Catholic School Board in Quebec City, Quebec.
Participants: Students International Literacy Year Committee members and city officials.
Issues: 1. Sensitizing residents of Quebec City about literacy
2. Involving the students so their voices may be heard.

We told ourselves: What if we gave a chance to both parties to meet and to talk, perhaps this would be a few steps in the right direction? At the very least, all these people, once they had been brought together, could no longer pretend, since they would have spoken to each other. We took a chance on dialogue.

(Labrie et les mots de bien du monde, 1990, p.11)

The dialogue project

To mark the International Year of Literacy, (ILY), the ILY committee at the Quebec city Catholic School Board (Commission des écoles catholiques de Quebec — CECQ) prepared a plan of illiteracy sensitization and dialogue among residents of Quebec city and surrounding areas such as the city of Vanier. Through this project, they aimed to directly involve basic French students at the Centre Louis-Jolliet of the CECQ, so that they could explain how they live with illiteracy through open dialogue with the population. The members of the committee explained it as follows:

> We want to talk, to have a positive group experience, to learn to keep our commitments, to be informed and to inform others, to do better in our schooling, to take stock of what is happening elsewhere in literacy training, to support others and to foster mutual respect...

> It would be very interesting to meet with children who are just learning to read and write...

> We want to be called "students," not "pupils," but we would like to change the name from "literacy" to "basic French" or something...

> We would like more information on who decided on the ILY and why there is going to be a play, a conference and sensitization. Those people who do not come to school should stop being ashamed. We must be able to talk about our problems and our efforts. We need more than 2,000 hours to learn everything. During the ILY it will be our turn to be heard everywhere...

The ILY organizing committee of the CECQ is made up of the following members: Two students in literacy training, one literacy teacher, one literacy training guidance counselor, one guidance counselor from adult education services, and one apprentice social worker hired especially for this project. The adults in literacy training were set up into student committees to become the main participants in the activity program. Among other things, they took to heart their position as spokespersons for the silent majority of illiterate adults, making suggestions to the ILY representatives and circulating information through the class groups. It is this student committee which delegates two student representatives to the ILY organizing committee of the CECQ. In short, the aim was to educate all of the adults in the Quebec city area about illiteracy.

To accomplish this, the ILY committee planned various types of actions aimed at different social groups. First, political decision-makers of Quebec City were invited to a press conference to develop awareness and understanding of the problems of illiteracy in the urban environment. They were asked for their support in making ILY a pivotal year for illiterate adults. Also, a paper prepared by Vivian Labriel was distributed to all primary and secondary school principals of the CECQ so that students at both levels could be informed. With a guidance counselor from Centre Louis-Jolliet as presenter and moderator, a young illiterate adult met with all the students of Saint-Pie-X of the CECQ, classroom by classroom to talk to them and to answer their questions about his life as a person with reading and writing difficulties.

The CECQ offered adults in the secondary program of Centre-Louis Jolliet a chance to attend an interactive theatre production commissioned specially by the CECQ to sensitize them to the problem of illiteracy. The play *Rayons de nuit* was written by Gilles-Philippe Pelletier and interpreted by the Sans Détour theatre group. *Rayons de nuit* reached, through ten neighborhoods of Quebec city, community groups and the general public to awaken them to the complex reality of illiteracy.

Also, thanks to the creation of the "Bureau de consultation en alphabétisation" (literacy training consultation bureau) staffed by No Dufour and Vivian Labrie, a dialogue was opened between the literacy training students (those of the CECQ and of other organizations) and representatives and decision-makers from the following five areas of activity:

1. School and family,
2. Income (workforce, unemployment insurance, social assistance),
3. Municipal services,
4. Health,
5. Media and culture.

Finally, the "dialogue project" — as well as the sensitization activities carried out throughout the ILY — were capped by a conference, a "grand dialogue." This included all those who had participated in the activity generated by the comments of the illiterate adults in the five aforementioned areas and all those were reached through the theatre presentation.

In short, all the proposed actions had two principal objectives: To sensitize the general public and to involve the illiterate adults themselves so that at least their voices might be heard.

How we proceeded to "stop pretending that everyone knows how to read and write"

In planning for ILY, after its second meeting on November 23, 1989, the student committee prepared the following four plans of action:

1. A day of abstaining (fasting) from reading and writing, in January, 1990, for well-known personalities in the five selected areas.
    1) School: the director-general of the CECQ, one representative from a university.
    2) Income: The Quebec minister of revenue, the vice-president of the CSN, the director of Centre Travail-Quebec.
    3) Municipal services: the mayor of Quebec city and his staff.
    4) Health: The Quebec minister of health, doctors in local community service centres — (CLSC), etc.
    5) Media and culture: Journalists, radio commentators, the archbishop of Quebec city, one representative from immigration training and guidance centres— (COFI)

The idea for a day of abstaining from literacy in an institutional setting was eventually abolished by the authorities of the CECQ. This disconcerting experience would have been aimed at breaking the traditional routine rooted in literacy. Each of the chosen personalities would have spent the day in their work environment, in the company of an illiterate person. The illiterate participant would have played the role of a 'supervisor' for the chosen personality, responsible for the movements of the other in the workplace. After this day or half day of abstaining from literacy, the "fasters" would have been invited to a sober meal, humble and simple, much in the image of the typical meal for many illiterate people where the abstainers would be served, among other things, alphabet soup or presented with a menu in completely unreadable type.

To force people to abstain from literacy, even for a few hours, in an environment where reading and writing is paramount, was intended to expose the way in which literacy affects our daily lives. The intention was, through this experiment, to understand the advantages and inconveniences of the many uses of reading and writing in relation to oral exchanges. Following the refusal of this idea by the CECQ, the ILY and the student committees abandoned the project.

2. A play presented in ten different locations within the CECQ jurisdiction from January to May 1990.
3. Five discussion groups, one for each of the five selected areas of activity at the centres where literacy training is offered followed a meeting with personalities from each sector and finally a meeting between both the literacy training students and the decision makers from each sector of society, from February to November 1990.
4. A conference involving all those who had participated in the dialogue, in the hopes of producing a working paper on "the Charter of Rights of illiterate people" by November 1991.

Before meeting the decision-makers, the literacy training students explored each of the proposed themes. In many different ways they expressed the importance of the problems they face each day in trying to deal with a literate world. Later, people from various levels of the five areas of activity met to discuss the inherent disadvantages of the overabundance and overimportance of writing in their respective fields.

Finally, both groups were brought together. Each presented their point of view and their interpretation. Together they tried to find solutions to the problems in each of the five areas. A synopsis of these problems and possible solutions and suggestions to better the lives of illiterate people was distributed in the form of a written document, easy to read and in large type, dotted with humourous illustrations. One picture is worth a thousand words.

Ways to become audible and visible

So that illiterate adults could begin a dialogue on these topics of family, school, income, municipal services, health, media and culture, it was necessary to first sensitize the representatives from the different organizations to the fact that most likely there are illiterate adults among their own employees, their members, or the users of their services.

Some consideration was also given to demonstrate the concrete and painful situations which illiterate people must face in dealing with indispensable social institutions. Each time, through the use of dialogue, suggestions were made to render the different organizations more accessible. These included such simplifying administrative procedures as offering information orally in person or by telephone and understanding that information officers may sometimes have to read directions or rules out loud. There should also be more time allotted for training within each organization when new tasks are being assigned. The use of pictograms, auditory and visual reinforcement and a general re-evaluation of memory skills — the indispensable tool of illiterates, could help remove the crippling stigma associated with illiteracy.

The question was raised: Do some organizations have a tendency to increase the use of writing among their own employees, their members or the users of their services? The social decision-makers were also asked for any techniques or shortcuts to simplify the intricacy of reading and writing procedures which illiterate clients must face.

A visit to Quebec City Hall

I had the great pleasure of attending a dialogue-meeting on the subject of the city and access to municipal services for illiterate adults. This meeting took place in the centre for urban living in the Quebec City Hall building. During the discussion, literate and illiterate adults exchanged notes about the places they go in the city. People were able to take stock of different locations depending on whether they were literate or illiterate.

After a brief but eloquent brainstorming session we concluded that for illiterate adults the city includes for the most part: Shopping centres, bicycle paths, bars, sports facilities (pools, the 'Colisée' arenas) river-side parks, favorite neighbourhood ("some area near my place where I feel good", where pride in one's city is expressed through the neighbourhood), supermarkets (Provigo), Chez Jean Coutu pharmacies, the old port of Quebec, parks, the Plains of Abraham, the museum, the aquarium, and the zoo.

Parts of the city where illiterate people tended not to

venture included: Old Quebec City, taverns, the area along the river's edge and the high part of the city. One visits there only for the necessary festivities like the Winter Carnival or the Summer Festival. The Saint-Roch mall and the library can be emotionally provocative. There seemed to be a clear pattern of frequenting or avoiding specific areas.

There was also a distinction between the two groups present in their choice of transportation in the following proportions:

Method of Transportation	Adults in Literacy Training	Social Decision Makers
Car	5	14
Bus	11	3
On foot	8	10
Taxi	1	3
Bicycle	5	3

Illiterates must navigate through the city mostly using memory clues. They would like to live in a city where parks and homes are clean and quiet. We were also able to identify four common fears:

1. The fear of being attacked (Saint-Roch mall, the area along the river);
2. The fear of getting lost when going to a new place, they must first go with someone else and memorize the way;
3. The fear of asking for directions;
4. The fear of being ridiculed because they were unable to read municipal regulations or traffic signs.

The illiterate adults asked the rest of the group to try to see life and the city through their eyes. According to the illiterate group, municipal leaders don't have the same view as "ordinary people," they cannot "think like poor people."

Later that evening the literacy training students attended a Quebec City Council meeting. They were ready with their questions during the public question and answer period. Here are some of the questions they asked:

• Why is the Saint-Roch market not in Victoria Park

anymore? It was more accessible.

- Why are there no signs at the library to show which kinds of books are on each floor?
- Why not have free Summer festival activities all over the city, including lower town? (Being generally low-paid, most illiterate adults live in working class areas such as lower town, the high part of the city is the higher-income area.)
- There are frequent accidents on bicycle paths. Why not more security, surveillance, protection on bicycle paths?
- Why not transform empty buildings in lower town into:
  — Low rent or subsidized housing units
  — Youth recreation facilities
  — Rehabilitation facilities (alcoholics, substance abusers)
  — Shelters for the destitute
- Why don't you build low rent housing on Saint Joseph, St-Vallier, de la Couronne and on Côte du Palais in the place of those abandoned houses and stores?
- We are not informed enough about upcoming festivities, shows, recreation, services available within the city. Why not publicize those on radio and in the neighbourhood newspaper every 15 days?

A memoir of what was said and done

The closing conference of the ILY, the "grand dialogue" at the Musée de la civilisation brought together the literacy training students from the CECQ and other literacy training groups, Atout-Lire and Alphabeille. Illiterate adults had the centre of attention and the chance to propose concrete and practical solutions to help better their lives. Using their own familiar means of expression such as riddles, sketches and puns, this is what took place:

- A mini-exhibit of objects relating to illiteracy. Each participant was asked to bring an item which to them represents their illiteracy;
- A reading of reports by basic French students or their experiences in the dialogue sessions and of their daily

experiences in surviving in a world of reading and writing;
- The distribution of the book which resulted from these dialogue sessions: *Vivian Labrie et les mots de bien du monde, Par-dessus le fossé des lettres, Des lieux pour des personnes fieres, Dialogues entre des étudiants en alpha et des intervenants*, Bureau de consultation en alphabétization, Québec, Commission des écoles catholiques de Québec.
- During the dinner, a part of the wall was made available to allow total freedom of expression, in the form of graffiti, to the theme of illiteracy;
- Finally, a collectively written story, with the participation of Soleil reporter Alain Bouchard and illustrator Serge Gaboury on the theme of 'Our planet is minuscule'.

The conference was a unique platform, filled with emotions and imagination, word games, ideas, collective writing. There were objects, people and star cartoonists. The illicit graffiti was in dialogue with the straight-laced words of others. It was a party, a gala of words with laurels for those brave adults who are breaking the silence, tearing down the walls so that they may be heard.

Ways to facilitate the life of illiterate adults

I read. I write phonetically. He is refusing to fill out the form for me. I scribble on it as best I can. When I am through scribbling, he grabs his bottle of white-out and covers everything. It takes 20 minutes, it could have taken two. You have to ask him a question. If you're shy you won't get the answer. If you don't understand, you have to say: tell me in words I can understand. ...when you're nervous you can read even less!
Literacy students quoted in
Labrie et les mots de bien du monde. 1990

Many avenues are still to be opened to help illiterate adults. We must first consider the many difficult situations these people face — situations where they are not completely competent at meeting those requirements of society which are based on reading and writing. For example, in order to allow illiterate adults to function fully in a group situation as volunteers, the following solutions were put forth:

Being discreet when a person confides his problem, trying to deal more in verbal exchanges, defending such people against hurtful comments, trusting memory, doing without paper whenever possible, showing that it is normal that some people can't read or write, having concrete tasks to propose.

Labrie et les mots de bien du monde, 1990

Concluding comments

Illiterate adults are the most qualified to speak about illiteracy. After this International Year of Literacy and the dialogue it has generated, they have suggested signs and clues to describe their way of functioning in a world of writing. Here is a list, from Labrie et les mots de bien du monde, 1990:

Clues to recognizing that a person may have difficulty reading, writing, or counting:

- Arriving much ahead of time at appointments;
- Answering that it has already been given when asked for a document;
- By the signature which appears painstakingly written;
- Fear of signing one's name;
- Arriving with an unopened envelope;
- Claiming to not have glasses;
- Saying the paper could not be read at home for lack of light;
- Mocking pencil-pushers;
- Not having accomplished instructions given in writing;
- Never volunteering for tasks which include literacy;
- Refusing a job or promotion;
- Dropping an activity after it requires reading or writing;
- Saying that everything is OK and there's no problem;
- Asking to fill out a form at home;
- Forgetting to bring documentation that was given;
- Asking for explanations when they are already written on a document in hand;
- Pronouncing many words in a different way.

In our opinion, this list of clues to recognizing illiterate adults may help to make others more aware of the needs and expectations of illiterate people. These signs are proof that there are ways and solutions possible to conquer the forbidding paper walls of reading and writing. The CECQ's dialogue project has paved the way in allowing illiterate adults to speak up and be heard. It is now up to society's decision-makers to make room for them in the world of papers, by using shortcuts based on verbal communications.

Notes

Translator's note:
There is a play on words which was not translated into the English text. The French text contains an explanation of the background of the term 'tonton macoute' (Haitian secret police under the Duvalier regime) and how it came to be applied to welfare fraud investigators under Quebec Premier Robert Bourassa as 'bouboumacoute' with quotations from unnamed participants. In regard to the document at hand, one adult in literacy training, when discussing health services, translated the word 'bouboumacoute' into 'bobomacoute', 'bobo' being in the language of children, a sore or some part of the body where there is pain or discomfort.

Discussion Questions

1. *What were some of the different steps taken by the ILY Committee to prepare for the launching of the "grand dialogue" project?*
2. *How could you encourage a group of students to begin talking about school and family, income, municipal services, health and media, and culture?*
3. *The crippling stigma associated with literacy is slowly changing. Do you agree with this statement?*
4. *Is there an interest from your students in attending a City Council meeting. How can the student group be prepared?*
5. *What clues for recognizing that a person may have difficulty reading, writing or counting are frequently demonstrated by your students? Are there other clues mentioned in the case study?*

Chapter Four
ACTIVATING
STUDENT PARTICIPATION

Sheila Goldgrab

Place: CORE Literacy, The Working Centre in Kitchener
   Ontario.
Participants: Students and staff at CORE Literacy.
Issues: 1. Sharing program management responsibilities.

The CORE Literacy program's statement of purpose promotes "learner-based literacy learning". CORE staff and students are exploring ways in which students can fully participate in their learning both with their tutor and in program management. Full student participation in the areas of self-evaluation, tutor training, the learning plan, promotion, outreach, funding, and program management are all encouraged.

Background

Situated in The Working Centre in Kitchener, CORE Literacy also provides extension services in the Waterloo Detention Centre and the Elmira Public Library and is presently intending to begin new services to the area. The majority of students in Kitchener's community-based literacy program have been paired with tutors to receive one-to-one literacy instruction. The remainder of the adult students are involved in a group learning situation.

The Kitchener Waterloo area has a population of 250,000 composed of many ethnic and regional groups including German, Portuguese, Italian, East European, West European, and Eastern Canadians. Recently, Southeastern Asians, East Indians, Central Americans and West Indians have settled in the area. Primary and manufacturing industries employ most of the residents. Textiles, food, construction, plastics and furniture are among the many other industries in the region. Many of these plants employ non-skilled labourers who have a difficult time searching for and finding work when they are unemployed.

The character and structure of the program began as a six month pilot project of English in the Working Environment (EWE) where small-group literacy instruction took place at the St. John's Soup Kitchen in downtown Kitchener. The Kitchen is a single meal drop-in centre that serves an average of 250 meals to adults per day. Once the pilot project funding was finished, Doug Rankin was hired to coordinate a fully funded literacy program in November 1987. The program became incorporated with a budget of its own in September 1989, and the connection with St. John's Soup Kitchen has been maintained. The Kitchen is managed by the Working Centre, a self-help employment resource centre, located upstairs from the literacy program.

Of the 35 students in CORE literacy, 60% are unemployed. The Working Centre refers people with low literacy skills, which may act as a barrier in finding or maintaining employment, to CORE as a place to improve their reading and writing. As Chris Mockler, the manager of the Working Centre explained:

> We're a community project and we saw the CORE Literacy program as a community project that fits well with our idea of the services people needed and didn't have access to. Now someone can get related with different services in the same building.

Chris pointed out that because of their shared location he has learned a lot about how to identify people with low literacy skills and has been able to refer them to the literacy program. As well, the two programs share a focus that facilitates collaboration among them: "The learner-centred approach (at CORE Literacy) is the same as our approach.

We let our clients define our role for them," Chris said.

Self-evaluation, tutor training and the learning plan

Application of the student-centred approach begins with training tutors in student self-assessment. Assessment occurs throughout the adult students' learning, not just at the time the student begins and ends the program. The continuing basis of the self-evaluation process is seen as an important part of the students' learning plan. The design and the implementation of this process are left to the student and tutor.

Students play an important function in the tutor training process. Once the prospective tutors have been interviewed by a staff member, they attend an initial 14 hour training program. During one of the sessions, tutors meet a student, listen to the student's suggestions about what works and what doesn't, and what it means for them not to be able to read and write. Tutors are encouraged to trust a student's opinion that a particular method of teaching is not working for them. The importance of listening and the importance of student participation in developing an agenda is also stressed. Perhaps most importantly, the students have the opportunity to explain to the tutors how they can be most effective.

Larry Leis, a student who attends tutor training sessions, feels that it is important that he represents the student's point of view in the initial training program:

> I think it's important that tutors get to meet a student and get their fears and hesitations out in the open. Tutors often have hesitations and they talk to me about them. They can face these before they get matched up the first time. They've never done it before and they're nervous just like the students are. I like to tell them to be flexible. Go the way a student wants to go. Students know what they want to do. "I know when I'm learning because I can read and understand something that I couldn't before." Tutors need to hear that this kind of reflection and evaluation is important. It's better than testing.

The learning plan is a joint project between the tutor and

student. When the CORE staff was asked why activating learner participation is important in this area, the program coordinator Anne Ramsay responded simply that "we couldn't have a program without them." Staff researcher Don Duff-McCracken spoke about the practical advantage of this approach: "It's easier to ask what learners' needs are than to figure out their needs by guessing."

In fact, learner participation was an integral part of the early development of the program when a needs assessment took place. Doug Rankin, the coordinator of CORE who carried out the first needs assessment explained:

> When the program began at St. John's Kitchen, we went into it with the philosophy that we were trying to provide learning for people who were not able to access other adult education programs. We thought it was important to ask people who were interested in improving their reading and writing skills how they would best be able to do that. I asked about the best times to meet during the week, and whether or not people wanted to meet in a group or individually with a staff person or tutor. We also asked adults what their learning goals were. Why they wanted to read and write.
>
> Most of the adults responded with short term goals like reading mail, prescriptions, completing application forms, etc. From there, I began to research what teaching methods and materials were available that would allow us to pursue a student-centred direction. We found that in the program at St. John's, adults felt they were being listened to and they were able to learn some literacy skills that were relevant to their daily needs. This initial approach has been the direction we've taken.

In each case the tutor and student discuss the student's long and short term goals. Like many of the students in community literacy programs, CORE students generally have short term goals. They remain motivated by determining their own learning direction. In turn, the learning plan is flexible enough so that the tutor can adjust the educational methodology to the students' learning style.

Tutors are encouraged to be flexible about the kinds of exercises and activities that students work on. If a learner is uncomfortable with certain activities, tutors are encouraged to try ones that are more effective. This allows students to determine the direction of the learning and it allows for the learners' goals to change as they develop their literacy skills. A student may enter the program wanting to fill out application forms, and later they may want to write a personal letter to a friend.

Leslie Lack's long term goal is to improve his writing and so he and Lauri Middleton, his tutor, have chosen several short term goals to work on. All of them reflect Leslie's interests. Turned off by big classes after attending an adult education literacy class elsewhere, Leslie appreciates the privacy and individual attention he gets from his tutor at CORE. Lauri, quoting her student Leslie, voiced her attitude about the individualized approach when she said: "People are people, people aren't projects."

Promotion, outreach and funding

Promotion and outreach is always an important and particularly challenging job for a literacy program. People with poor literacy skills who would benefit from a literacy program are most often left untouched by written campaigns. Doug Rankin believes that word of mouth is still the most effective means of getting new students to the program. In addition, flyers in clearly written language are developed with the help of students.

When putting together the newsletter *The Write Stuff*, and in-house produced reading materials or pamphlets, staff member Don Duff-McCracken asks for student input. Although the students have no training in design, all student writers are invited to participate in the layout and design process. Speaking of the students' strengths, Don said: 'What's the old saying? I may not know publishing, but I know what I like. It's easier than researching which is the most readable typeface to use. Instead I ask the learners." Student writers decide by consensus on type size and style, graphics and photographs as well as the overall look of the publication. In short, the student writers exercise control over the publication.

The students who write for *The Write Stuff* are always aware that the audience is other adults in CORE Literacy and in other literacy programs. Their goal is to make their stories readable, and they understand first hand what clarity means.

When CORE is asked to make a presentation about the program to other social agencies, the staff invites students to join them. "They're the best people to communicate what it feels like to learn reading and writing at an older age," Anne Ramsay said. When Reaching Our Outdoor Friends (ROOF) approached CORE Literacy to give a workshop on building self-esteem among transient youth, one of the CORE students was invited by the staff to describe how gaining literacy skills helped him to express himself. The benefits for students are numerous. The reason for student involvement in outreach is that students can communicate to groups directly about what it's like to be a student of a community-based literacy program and they gain self-confidence speaking in public about a subject they know well.

Students are actively involved in the preparatory work required before grant proposals are written. The objective of a project called New Initiatives is to improve the access of literacy programs to social service recipients and the "unem-ployable." Neighbourhood community workers felt strongly the community would be resistant to a ready-made literacy program. They recommended that CORE ask for the com-munity's input to develop a program.

CORE students were approached by the staff to do the initial outreach in low income neighbourhoods. Students began by relating their experiences of learning to read and write at the CORE program. Anticipating resistance to par-ticipation in a literacy program, the speakers emphasized that their literacy instruction did not take place in a tradi-tional school setting and that students and tutors jointly plan a curriculum to suit a student's needs. Larry Leis explained why he believed it was important for him to speak to a neighbourhood group:

> When I first came into the program I didn't know what to expect and I was scared. You see, when I went for help I had to break my code of silence about having trouble reading and writing. Not even my wife knew. That's a big step. There's a lot of people in that situation. I think if new students can talk to someone who has been in the program it makes it easier for them.

The student group is now discussing the obstacles that people may be facing that prevent them from joining the program.

Program management

It was the staff's intention from the very beginning of the program to get students involved in program planning because a community-based literacy program meant more than being located in a community. It meant that, among other things, students participated in program management and the CORE board of directors.

The initial staff of the CORE program did not want the lack of skills necessary to be a Board member to be a barrier to students who were interested in making a contribution. Their desire to develop and run the literacy program was considered sufficient. The staff felt that students involved on the Board would develop new skills of communication, consensus-building, planning and financial management that would put their literacy skills to practical use.

Marlene Zakrajsek, a student at CORE, feels that sitting on the Board is satisfying but complains that sometimes the discussion is hard to follow. To facilitate more understanding, the Board has agreed to follow a structure that would add some regularity to the meetings. As well, two versions of the minutes are written. One is clearly written with students in mind and contains less detailed information than the original. The absence of details in the summarized version is a problem for the students who require all the information about an agenda item. This remains a challenge for the Board as a whole.

CORE Literacy has applied for a grant to do research about student participation in program management. The objectives of this federal-provincial shared grant for research in student participation in program management, are to identify barriers to participation and to research ways in which other programs have met these challenges. The program planners intend to spend a lot of time talking to students about how they would like to be involved. By consulting with literacy students they hope to get new ideas about overcoming those barriers.

Recently Larry Leis, a student at CORE, has become inspired by the Ontario Literacy Coalition's Learners'

Network. Students from diverse regions of Ontario travelled to Toronto for a conference to discuss ways in which they could involve learners in literacy program activities. Larry enjoys the exchange of information that takes place at these regular meetings. His volunteer job as Learner Representative of Southwestern Ontario is to set up meetings, encourage the formation of learners' committees in literacy programs, and to visit other programs. When he was asked about all of these responsibilities, he spoke of the social and personal benefits of greater student involvement:

> ...the busier I am, the more I like it. It gives me a chance to meet more people, feel more relaxed and get more sociable. It's like when I fill out my own cheques and do the banking. Instead of letting other people do things, I do them for myself.

Active learner participation has resulted in the staff's perception of students as colleagues. Doug Rankin views future employment of students by the program as part of a natural and desirable evolutionary growth of CORE:

> If a learner can go and speak to someone in an Ontario Housing Complex and tell them of their experiences of the program and what that person should expect, they'll be believed a lot more than I am because those people may distrust staff. They may distrust my clothes, my middle class upbringing. I shouldn't be paid to do that if a learner is going to be better at it. And I think that we have to accept that.

> We have to be realistic about what functions well...If we want to encourage learners to participate, then we have to think about their future employment by the program. If Larry keeps talking to volunteers and visiting programs we have to recognize that.

Each staff member views students as colleagues. "I think that the learners do really feel in control of the program," Don Duff-McCracken said. The roles of students who participate in the program's management are less predictable and limited. Marianne Paul, the staff researcher and writer working exclusively on CORE Literacy's extension services to

Waterloo Detention Centre, commented approvingly that
the rigid roles of the participants at the Kitchener program
have indeed been blurred.

Challenges to full participation

The staff have willingly accommodated the way they work
in order to realize their aim of full student involvement. Staff
support and staff time are important factors, so they can be
supportive when people call or drop in. Students may also
need staff to provide transportation to events.

For some students, participation in a group setting is new.
In one instance,when a group of students needed help to
decide on a name for the students group, a staff member got
the ball rolling. She suggested that each person pitch in their
ideas and that they choose by process of elimination. Others
contributed with their ideas of consensus and majority vote
until they agreed about one process of group decision making. Teaching new skills always takes time but "Once it's
running," said Don Duff-McCracken "it will be the most
efficient." Marianne Paul added that it is "more valuable than
the staff making decisions and completing the task for the
learners."

Other suggestions were made about how to achieve student participation. The staff said that the support of the
board of directors is necessary in order that the program can
move in one unified direction and pursue the project funding it thinks is necessary.

Doug Rankin added that "It has to be proactive. It might be
easy to say at some point that here is learner participation
happening but unless learners are making the decisions that
effect the direction of the program, that isn't the case."
Spending time to approach students individually to encourage them to get involved has been successful.

There are several obstacles that the CORE program's participants have encountered. One obstacle is lack of time to
provide day to day support for students who would like to
talk about their concerns. Understaffing is viewed by the staff
as an obstacle to full student participation.

Doug Rankin, a senior staff member of CORE Literacy,
holds the view that fully entrenching the student-centred
approach is an organizational matter for the program. Providing "learner-based instruction" is part of the program's

statement of purpose. The staff sees the learner-based approach as including student participation in program management. Without explicitly including this in the statement of purpose, there is no guaranty that student participation in program management will be maintained over time.

Program participants view student organization and a cohesive staff as having benefited the program. Lauri Middleton commented that as a tutor she would like to enrich the students' experiences by participating more fully in the program:

> There is no real liaison in this program between tutors. You get your training and then are matched with a learner. Les and I do fine by ourselves but it would be nice to be [a greater] part of the program.

Tutors sit on the board, play an active role on committees and help out with publications. The program newsletter regularly encourages tutors to get involved. The staff at CORE intend to organize regular tutor training workshops that would be supplementary to the initial training program. In this way tutors would more easily be able to meet and share ideas about what they're doing in their pairings.

Lauri believes that a tutor network in the program and planned tutor/student pair meetings would give students and tutors an opportunity to share their projects with other matches.

Concluding comments

When Anne Ramsay, a former volunteer tutor was hired, she said she was overjoyed that she got the job without a university degree. According to her, the hiring committee's priorities reflected the philosophy that permeates throughout the entire program:

> I like to think that they hired me not necessarily because of what I had on paper but instead, they saw what I could give to the program. And that's an important aspect of the program, to see people as people...that's why we have learner participation. We see learners for what they have to give, their ideas as individuals, and for their life experience and common

sense. It breaks down stereotypes of what a learner is in your mind.

The staff feel that sharing responsibilities among those who are involved in CORE Literacy has led to a greater sense of belonging among students both to the program and to their community. Activating student participation also fosters a sense of ownership in their learning. As well, both the staff and students recognize that it is often the students of the program who are the best suited to take on those duties. Undoubtedly, greater student participation has given students an opportunity to enhance their literacy skills, develop other new skills, and make a profound contribution to the growth of the program.

Discussion Questions

1. *Most programs talk about learner-centredness, but what does it really mean?*
2. *What are the different parts of a learning plan? How can self-evaluation be made more meaningful?*
3. *How can you encourage a student to make a written contribution to a program newsletter?*
4. *How do you know when a student is ready to consider program management?*
5. *Can you think of some critical thinking exercises for students that would enhance their participation on a board of directors?*
6. *Participatory literacy education can be too time consuming. Discuss.*

Chapter Five
S'ALPHABÉTISER
POUR POSSÉDER UNE CLÉ

Hélène Blais

Lieu: Le Centre de lecture et d'écriture, Plateau, Mont-Royal,
    Montréal
Participants: Le comité des participants du CLÉ
Thèmes: 1. Un groupe d'alphabétisation populaire
         2. La place accordée aux participants à l'intérieur
         du groupe d'alphabétisation

---

*Au plan ésotérique, posséder la clef signifie avoir été initié. Elle
indique, non seulement l'intrée dans un lieu, ville ou maison, mais
l'accès à un état, à une demeure spirituelle, à un degré initiatique.
[...] La clef est ici le symbole du mystère à percer, de l'énigme à
résoudre, de l'action difficile à entreprendre, bref des étapes qui
conduisent à l'illumination et la découvert.*
Jean Chevalier et Alain Gheerbrant, *Dictionnaire des symboles*,
Paris, Robert Laffont / Jupiter, 1982, p. 262.

Introduction

    Le Centre de lecture et d'écriture (CLÉ) existe depuis 1982.
Le Centre est installé dans le Plateau Mont-Royal, quartier
populaire montréalais, où près de 30% de ses habitants ont
moins d'une neuvième année de scolarité. Le CLÉ offre des
activités d'alphabétisation à la population analphabète qui
environne son logement de sept pièces sur la rue Mentana.

En 1990, le CLÉ a rejoint une soixantaine de participants.

CLÉ : un groupe d'alphabétisation populaire membre du RGPAQ

Le Centre de lecture et d'écriture (CLÉ) est membre du Regroupement des groupes populaires en alphabétisation du Québec (RGPAQ) depuis sa fondation.[1] La visibilité bien orchestrée du RGPAQ et ses nombreux contacts au plan provincial, national et international ont des répercussions tangibles sur la vie des groupes d'alphabétisation populaire qui en font partie et le Centre de lecture et d'écriture (CLÉ) est de ceux-là.

Les particularités du Centre de lecture et de l'écriture (CLÉ)

Rhéo Desjarins, membre du comité des participants du CLÉ, a déjà suivi une formation dans une commission scolaire en alphabétisation quatre soirs par semaine. Au CLÉ, Rhéo suit des activités d'alphabétisation à raison de deux soirs (6 heures) par semaine et s'exprime ainsi :

> À CLÉ, on apprend moins vite mais mieux. On a une meilleure qualité d'enseignement. On n'est plus seulement un élève, mais un membre actif du Centre. On améliore aussi notre langage. Les animatrices sont spéciales. Elles essaient de comprendre notre côté humain. Elles sont chaleureuses. Ici, j'ai réalisé que j'allais pas juste apprendre à lire et à écrire.

Organisme sans but lucratif, le CLÉ est un groupe d'alphabétisation populaire, c'est-à-dire que l'alphabétisation qui y est pratiquée s'effectue dans un environnement et dans une atmosphère de travail à mille lieues de ceux d'un milieu scolaire. Enraciné dans le quartier populaire où il a établi domicile, le CLÉ offre des services d'alphabétisation entièrement gratuits. On y offre des activités qui tiennent compte du rythme d'apprentissage des participants, de leurs besoins particuliers : entre autres, leur désir de se développer d'une façon autonome, de se sentir soutenus et compris par tout le personnel impliqué qui intervient auprès d'eux à différents titres. Le CLÉ se définit aussi comme un lieu important où chacun a son mot à dire et où les participants peuvent rencontrer des gens, d'autres personnes en processus d'alphabétisation qui vivent les mêmes difficultés. Dans cette optique, les participants son sensiblement en mesure de faire des pas dans le chemin qui mène à la connaissance de leurs droits et à la possibilité de les exercer. C'est ainsi que se créent des liens ténus entre les participants et les intervenants.

Les ateliers d'alphabétisation se donnent en petits groupes d'une dizaine de participants où les intérêts et attentes de chacun sont pris en compte. On essaie aussie d'instaurer des situations d'apprentissage où la compétition entre pairs est remplacée par l'entraide et le respect attentif mutuel.

Par son rayonnement communautaire, le Centre de lecture et d'écriture vise à sensibiliser la population à la réalité des personnes analphabètes pour amoindrir les préjugés défavorables entourant l'analphabétisme. Les participants sont eux-mêmes sensibilisés à cet objectif de démystification de l'analphabétisme. Ils sont partie prenante du CLÉ et y entrevoient la possibilité d'améliorer leur qualité de vie, de promouvoir et de défendre leurs droits.

En pratiquant des activités d'alphabétisation, le CLÉ promeut les milieux populaires et les personnes analphabètes. On permet ainsi aux personnes analphabètes d'exercer des activités de lecture et d'écriture, de s'alphabétiser, pour qu'elles puissent s'exprimer culturellement, politiquement et socialement. Au plan idéologique, l'alphabétsation est ainsi perçue comme une forme d'intervention politique et sociale que amène les personnes analphabètes, très souvent issues des couches sociales populaires, à s'approprier les outils de la lecture et de l'écriture. On tente de développer chez elles une meilleure conscience de leur réalité et situation sociales.

Historiquement parlant, à l'origine du CLÉ, les fondatrices et fondateurs étaient issus et engagés politiquement dans des mouvements populaires, par exemple, des groupes populaires au niveau de la presse communautaire, des organisations politiques et des mouvemnts féministes.

Les pratiques et les réflexions d'autres groupes populaires d'alphabétisation ont été des phares pour CLÉ, en particulier le Carrefour d'éducation populaire de Poite-Sainte-Charles et le groupe d'alphabétisation Le Tour de lire du quartier Hochelaga-Maisonneuve. Ces deux groupes ont eu un impact quant à la perception idéologique de l'alphabétisation, à

l'approche pédagogique, à l'organisation des activités d'alphabétisation et quant au choix des lieux physiques où se
déroulent les activités. Au CLÉ, on alphabétise dans un logement comme pour le groupe Le Tour de lire.

L'alphabétisation pratiquée au CLÉ vise l'acquisition des
outils sociaux essentiels que sont la lecture, l'écriture et la
raisonnement mathématique, mais en prenant en considération les six éléments essentiels suivants :

1. Le développement de connaissances générales (fonc-
   tionnelles, politiques, sociales, personnelles, etc.);

2. Le développement de la pensée critique;

3. La capacité de «prendre» des décisions individuelles
   et collectives;

4. Une approche à l'intérieur de laquelle l'individu est
   intégré à une démarche de groupe;

5. La reconnaissance du langage, de la culture et des
   valeurs du milieu populaire;

6. Le développement d'un sentiment d'appartenance à
   une collectivité, afin d'améliorer la qualité de vie de
   cette population. (Gladu. 1988, p. 18)

L'alphabétisation populaire pratiquée au CLÉ se caractérise par quatre principales constantes : la place accordée
aux apprenants, le lien avec le milieu «naturel», les liens
tissés avec des organismes communautaires et un processus
d'apprentissage et de réflexion visant la globalité des personnes analphabètes, plus particulièrement au sein de leur
espace social, politique, culturel et économique.

Une autre particularité du CLÉ consiste dans le fait que ses
alphabétiseurs sont appelés «animatrices» et «animateurs».
Ces personnes-ressources animent et guident les participants, les personnes analphabètes, dans leurs démarches.
Elles les instrumentent, en les aidant à acquérir des habiletés
visant la prise en charge de leur propre apprentissage. Pour
les animatrices, il est très important que les connaissances
qu'elles possèdent ne soient pas mystifiées. Cela est rendu
possible par des relations égalitaires les plus limpides
qui soient : les animatrices commes les participants sont
impliqués dans la transmission des connaissances, en un

processus d'induction, de découverte.

L'implication des participants

Le CLÉ pratique une alphabétisation populaire qui se caractérise par la place accordée aux participants à l'intérieur du groupe d'alphabétisation. On fait une large place aux points de vue, aux prises de position et aux prises de parole des participants.

Pour les animatrices, impliquer les participants dans leur processus d'alphabétisation comporte plusieurs facettes : on tient autant compte des acquisitions notionnelles en français de base (au plan de la lecture et de l'écriture), et des processus particuliers du raisonnement mathématique que de tout ce que l'on pourrait appeler la para-alphabétisation. La para-alphabétisation est entendue ici au sens de toutes les activités effectuées sur une base volontaire et en dehors des ateliers d'alphabétisation proprement dits. Au CLÉ, les personnes analphabètes son amenées, par exemple, à participer à des assemblées politiques, à des «ventes de trottoir» pour faire la promotion de l'alphabétisation populaire, à sensibiliser la population environnante à leur existence en tant qu'organisme et à exercer la défense de leurs droits au travail, à la santé, à l'information. Les participants contribuent aussi à la distribution de l'organe d'information écrite du RGPAQ, un journal publié à l'occasion de l'Année internationale de l'alphabétisation (AIA) intitulé *l'Alpha Pop*.

L'une des caractéristiques du fonctionnement du CLÉ est la mise en branle de projets pédagogiques collectifs qui intègrent les connaissances et habiletés acquises à l'intérieur des ateliers d'alphabétisation. Ces projets pédagogiques collectifs visent des échanges inter-ateliers pour lier les participants des quatre différents ateliers du CLÉ entre eux. Les projets collectifs mènent les participants à réaliser concrètement des «produits finis» qui tiennent compte des apprentissages effectués ou à effectuer en lecture et en écriture. Ce sont des preuves tangibles du chemin parcouru.

Ces projets sont habituellement échelonnés sur deux sessions de trois ou six mois et sont suggérés, acceptés, décidés et pratiqués par l'ensemble des participants de tous les ateliers d'alphabétisation du CLÉ. La compilation de la correspondance et des échanges de cartes postales avec le groupe d'alphabétisation populaire Atout-Lire de Québec, la production de journaux d'étudiants, de calendriers, d'agendas constituent des exemples de projets pédagogiques collectifs. Le CLÉ produit aussi un album-souvenir de photos de ses activités, pour garder une mémoire de tout ce qui se fait au Centre.

Le comité des participants

Nycole Trudeau, membre du comité des participants du CLÉ, définit ainsi le rôle du comité des participants :

> Un comité des participants, sert à donner une meilleure qualité de vie aux autres participants, à les aider. Ca sert aussi à faire de la sensibilisation : j'ai moi-même participé au Salon du livre de Montréal, où j'ai pu expliquer à une personne c'est quoi l'Année internationale de l'alphabétisation et c'est quoi les groupes populaires d'alphabétisation. Un comité des participants, nous permet d'exprimer nos revendications. Ca sert à aider les animatrices, à les appuyer dans leurs tâches.

Le CLÉ se veut un lieu d'appartenance pour ses membres, c'est-à-dire autant pour les participants que pour les animatrices. Les personnes analphabètes s'y sentent donc à l'aise et jouent un rôle de premier plan dans l'organisme. Au comité des participants, il n'y a pas d'élection. Tout le monde peut en faire partie. Il n'y règne aucune hiérarchie ou rôle défini à l'avance. Les membres du comité des participants peuvent cependant choisir d'assumer des tâches et des responsabilités individuelles, en demandant l'approbation du comité.

Le comité des participants sert, entre autres, à voir à l'organisation de soirées collectives, de fêtes, de sorties, d'activités spéciales de para-alphabétisation. On y prend des décisions, on prépare des éléments de discussion pour les assemblées générales. Un procès-verbal rédigé en langage simple et concret est disponible pour quiconque veut s'informer de ce qui a été discuté lors des réunion du comité des participants. On a même eu l'idée d'enregistrer oralement sur des cassettes ces mêmes procès-verbaux pour en faciliter l'accès aux personnes ayant un rapport difficile avec l'écrit. Ainsi les personnes malhabiles à décoder, à lire, ne seraient plus exclues des informations importantes inscrites dans ces procès-verbaux.

Les participants éprouvant de la difficulté à lire pourraient emprunter la voie d'un support oral. Le comité contribue également à créer un lien, une continuité entre chaque assemblée générale regroupant tous les membres participants du CLÉ. Les membres du comité des participants sont à l'écoute des participants du CLÉ, voient à leur bien-être et à ce que l'ambiance et le fonctionnement du Centre soit des plus agréables. Le comité des participants évalue le niveau de satisfaction des participants en ce qui a trait au choix des cours, des horaires, des activités intégrées ou parallèles à l'alphabétisation proprement dite.

Les membres du comité sont les porte-parole des participants à l'intérieur et à l'extérieur du CLÉ. Le comité des participants compose un noyau solide, mais non pas rigide. On y instaure un minimum de structure. Le comité des participants sert de lieu d'échange, de dialogue, de communication, d'information entre les participants, les employés, c'est-à-dire les animatrices, les autres groupes communautaires du quartier, les autres groupes d'alphabétisation et tout autre organisme qui s'adresse au CLÉ. Le comité des participants du CLÉ donne aussi un coup de main appréciable lors des campagnes de financement, par exemple, en participant activement à l'envoi du courrier.

Un membre du comité des participants doit tout d'abord avoir une grande disponibilité, le désir de rencontrer d'autres personnes analphabètes, de s'impliquer, de prendre sa place et avoir envie de recevoir et de donner. De façon générale, un membre du comité des participants se donne la chance d'évoluer, de faire un pas de plus dans son ouverture à la société, dans sa prise de parole, dans un contact privilégié avec les autres participants. Être membre du comité des participants exige une très grande capacité d'écoute.

Voici quelues échantillons de réponses que m'ont données les membres du comité des participants à la question «Qu'est-ce que votre participation au comité vous apporte personnellement?» :

> Maintenant je m'intègre dans d'autres groupes (coop d'habitation du Plateau Mont-Royal). Je travaille plus l'écriture et la lecture. Je suis moins solitaire. Je prends des cours sur les procès-verbaux. (Richard)

Le comité me donne de l'expérience, il me permet d'assister à d'autres rencontres; j'ai participé à l'assemblée générale du Regroupement (RGPAQ) au Comité d'éducation aux adultes de la Petite Bourgogne et de Saint-Henri (CEDA); je représentais le CLÉ. (Irène)

Le comité m'a permis de participer comme personne-ressource au Forum sur les droites des analphabètes. Je suis plus fier de moi et ma famille aussi. (Rhéo)

J'ai vécu plusieurs expériences intéressantes. J'ai appris un nouveau language (technique). Maintenant, je suis capable de parler en public, d'exprimer mes opinions sans peur. (Nycole)

Je ne suis pas capable d'apprendre si je ne donne pas. Faire partie du comité des participants m'a donné confiance en moi. Je sais que je suis capable d'organiser des activités. Je déteste lire. Lire, pour moi, c'est comme manger du poisson quant t'en aimes pas du tout le goût. Organiser des activités, c'est une récompense pour mes efforts. D'une centaine façon, le comité des participants, c'est la permanence du groupe CLÉ, par rapport au roulement des animatrices. Les membres du comité des participants ont un lien plus proche avec les participants. Ils les comprennent, ils sont dans leur peau. (Alain)

Conscients que les animatrices engagées ne bénéficient pas d'assez de temps pour voir à l'organisation de toutes les activités de para-alphabétisation, les membres du comité des participants prennent la relève, interviennent à titre d'agents d'information et d'organisation de ces activités. Le comité des participants est un lieu favorisant l'expression de chacun des membres. Ceux-ci reçoivent les propositions, les suggestions et les bonnes idées de tous les participants du CLÉ. Ils les soumettent en retour à la discussion et à l'approbation des membres du comité.

Le comité des participants, quant à lui, veille à proposer des solutions pour régler certains problèmes, par exemple, l'absentéisme de certains participants qui peut désorganiser la vie du Centre. D'après l'un de ses membres, le comité des participants aide les participants à s'intégrer à la vie du CLÉ. Le comité prévient aussi, à sa façon, que ne se reproduise insidieusement, dans le milieu de l'alphabétisation populaire, le modèle de fonctionnement de l'école traditionnelle car il a été catastrophique pour la plupart des participants, comme le relate clairement Pierrette, participante au CLÉ :

> Je voulais apprendre, mais j'avais beaucoup de difficultés. Il n'y avait rien qui me rentrait dans la tête. Les classes étaient grosses. La maîtresse s'occupait des plus avancés et me laissait dans le coin. Au lieu de s'occuper de moi qui avais le plus besoin, elle s'occupait des autres. Ca m'a découragé et j'ai lâché en quatrième année.

Conclusions, prospectives

Dans le numéro 11, du mois d'août 1990 du *Bulletin de nouvelles d'action sur l'alphabétisation*, on publiait une déclaration sur la participation des apprenants qui a été préparée lors de la troisième réunion du Groupe de l'Année Internationale de l'Alphabétisation (GAIA) à Chantilly, en France, en décembre 1988. En voici un extrait qui résume bien la vision de l'alphabétisation par un groupe d'alphabétisation populaire comme le CLÉ :

Pourquoi faire participer les apprenants?

- Ce sont les apprenants qui connaissent le mieux leurs problèmes et leurs besoins.

- Les apprenants sont stigmatisés et marginalisés.

- Le processus de participation fait partie intégrante du processus d'apprentissage.

- La méthodologie axée sur les apprenants doit engager leur participation. La participation des apprenants change la relation entre l'apprenant et l'instructeur pour en faire une relation d'apprentissage en commun.

- La participation des apprenants enrichit les programmes et les rend plus efficaces.

- La participation des apprenants favorise l'esprit d'indépendance, l'autodétermination, la dignité et la confiance en soi.

- La participation des apprenants crée des possibilités d'auto-suffisance, de promotion et de création d'un mouvement pour le changement social.

- La participation des apprenants change tout.
  (Groupe d'Action sur l'Alphabétisation, 1990, p. 1)

En bref, l'implication des participants au Centre de lecture et d'écriture est fortement sensible à plusieurs niveaux, entre autres, dans le souci que tout un chacun a de rendre accueillante cette ruche bourdonnante d'activités et d'efforts qu'est le CLÉ. On y stimule les participants à travailler à la défense de leurs droits démocratiques et particulièrement leur droit à l'éducation. On les implique sans détour dans la voie d'une affirmation d'eux-mêmes. Ce que dit Nycole Trudeau, membre du comité des participants du CLÉ, en est un excellent exemple :

Oui, il faut enlever notre masque, s'affirmer. Ne pas avoir peur de dire qu'on s'alphabétise!

Notes:

1. Le Regroupement des groupes populaires en alphabétisation du Québec (RGPAQ) est l'un des trois organismes provinciaux reconnus pour représenter les organisations volontaires d'éducation populaire auprès du ministère de l'éducation du Québec. Les deux autres organismes nationaux sont le Mouvemnt d'éduction populaire et d'action communautaire du Québec (MÉPACQ) et le Regroupement des organismes volontaires d'éducation populaire (ROVEP). Le RGPAQ se voit allouer des subventions du ministère de l'éducation parce que l'on reconnait son action de représentation des groupes autonomes en alphabétisation, son action de promotion de l'alphabétisation et de l'éducation populaire autonome et son rôle au plan de la liaison et de la coordination de ses membres.
Le RGPAG effectue son travail de représentation au niveau provincial, national et international.
Au Québec, le RGPAQ représente ses membres auprès de

différents comités de travail chapeautés par le ministère de l'éducation du Québec (MEQ), tels des comités sur le programme d'aide aux organismes volontaire d'éducation populaire, sur l'alphabétisation, etc. Il représente ses membres et intervient aussi auprès de diverses instances gouvernementales pour favoriser le développement de l'alphabétisation. Il fait partie, entre autres, du comité interministériel sur l'éducation des adultes. Différents ministères et organismes para-gouvernementaux consultent régulièrement le RGPAQ pour son expertise dans les besoins particuliers de certaines populations de personnes analphabètes. Le RGPAQ collabore avec plusieurs organismes, tels que l'Institut canadien de l'éducation des adultes (ICÉA), le MÉPACQ, des organismes non-gouvernementaux (ONG) intervenant au niveau de la coopération internationale, des syndicats reliés au monde de l'éducation (Centrale de l'enseignement du Québec (CEQ), Fédération nationale des enseignantes et enseignants du Québec (FNEEQ), des universités (le RGPAQ est membre du comité de révision du certificat en alphabétisation à l'Université du Québec à Montréal).

Le RGPAQ entretient depuis plusieurs années des relations suivies avec des organismes canadiens qui interviennent en alphabétisation au Canada (The Movement for Canadian Literacy, l'Association des collèges communautaire, le Regroupement ontarien des groupes d'alphabétisation francophones) et aussi avec des groupes locaux francophones hors-Québec (Ontario, Nouveau-Brunswick, Saskatchewan, Alberta, Ile-du-Prince-Édouard), sans oublier sa collaboration régulière avec la Commission canadienne de l'UNESCO. Le RGPAQ reçoit très souvent en son sein des groupes d'alphabétisation canadiens qui veulent développer des services en s'inspirant des expériences tentées au Québec.

Au plan international, le RGPAQ est membre du Groupe international de travail sur l'alphabétisation mis sur pied par le Conseil international d'éducation des adultes travaillant de concert avec l'UNESCO. Le RGPAQ a aussi participé activement à la quatrième Conférence de l'UNESCO sur l'éducation des adultes et l'alphabétisation. Sa collaboration s'étend aussi à différents projets d'alphabétisation dans les pays en voie de développement : alphabétisation au Pérou, projet de formation de formateurs en post-alphabétisation au Nicaragua, etc. Le RGPAQ reoit également des représentants de groupes d'alphabétisation venant d'un peu partout dans le monde : Haiti, Sénégal, Kenya, Amérique Latine, France, Belgique, Angleterre, Écosse, Guinée, Mali.

Questions de discussion

1. Pourquoi s'alphabétiser n'est pas seulement apprendre à lire et à écrire?
2. Comment créez-vous des liens étroits entre les participants et les intervenants dans votre groupe d'alphabétisation?
3. Quel est le rayonnement communautaire, social, politique et culturel de votre organisme?
4. Que faites-vous pour promouvoir les droits des personnes analphabètes au travail, à l'information et à la santé?
5. Considerez-vous que votre groupe d'alphabétisation est un lieu d'appartenance pour les adultes analphabètes et les alphabétiseurs?
6. Comment évaluez-vous le niveau de satisfaction des participants à vos activités d'alphabétisation et de para-alphabétisation?

Chapter Six
LITERACY TRAINING
AS A KEY

Hélène Blais

Place: *Centre for Reading and Writing, Plateau Mont-Royal,
Montreal Quebec.*
Participants: *Participants committee at the Centre.*
Issues: 1. *Popular literacy training groups.*
2. *Meaningful student involvement in program
operations.*

> *On an esoteric level, to hold the key means to have been
> initiated. It indicates not only access to a city or a house but
> access to a state, to a spiritual house, to an initiatory degree.
> The key in this case is the symbol of the mystery to be solved,
> the enigma to be resolved, of the difficult action to undertake,
> in short, of the steps that lead to illumination and discovery.*
> Jean Chevalier and Alain Gheerbrant,
> *Dictionnaire des symboles.*
> Paris, Robert Laffont/Jupiter, 1982.

The Centre de lecture et d'écriture (Centre for Reading
and Writing) — (CLE) has been opened since 1982. The
Centre is located in the Plateau Mont-Royal, a Montreal
working class neighbourhood where close to 30% of inhabitants have less than grade nine education. The CLE offers
literacy training to illiterate adults who live in the area surrounding its seven room offices on Mentana Street. In 1990,
the CLE reached some sixty participants.

CLE: a grass-roots literacy group

The Centre is a member of the Regroupement des groupes populaires en alphabétisation du Québec RGPAQ (Union of grass-roots literacy training groups of Quebec) since it was founded.[1] The well orchestrated visibility of the RGPAQ and its many contacts at the provincial, national and international levels have had tangible repercussions on the survival of its member groups and the CLE is among those.

Characteristics of the CLE Centre

Rhéo Desjardins, a member of the participants' committee of the CLE, previously took literacy training with a school board four nights per week. At the CLE, Rhéo also has taken literacy training for two nights per week (six hours) and this is how he explained it:

> At CLE, we learn more slowly, but better. We get a better quality of teaching. We are not only students, but active members of the Centre. We also improve our language. The teachers are special. They try to understand the human side of us. They are warm. Here, I realized that I was not only going to learn to read and write.

The CLE is a non-profit organization and a popular literacy training group, one where the literacy training is done in an environment and atmosphere very different from that of a school. The CLE is well established in its neighborhood and offers its services for free. The activities here take into account the learning capacities of the participants and their special needs such as their desire to learn autonomously and to feel supported and understood by all the staff members dealing with them.

The CLE is also important as a place where everyone can have their say and where the participants can meet other people in literacy training who are living through similar difficulties. With this focus, the participants are in a position to recognize their rights and the possibilities of exercising them. In this way, strong bonds are formed between the participants and staff.

The literacy workshops are given to small groups of about

ten participants where the interest and expectations of all are taken into account. There is also an attempt at establishing learning situations where peer competition is replaced by mutual help and respectful attention.

Within the community, the center aims at sensitizing the population to the reality of illiterate adults in order to lessen the prejudice surrounding illiteracy. The participants themselves are informed of this objective of demystifying illiteracy. They are key players at the CLE and they find there a means of improving their quality of life, of promoting and defending their rights.

In practising literacy training, the CLE promotes the less fortunate and the illiterate. Thus illiterate adults have the opportunity to read and write, so that they may express themselves culturally, politically and socially. Ideologically, literacy is perceived as a form of political and social intervention which brings illiterate people, who are often from the lower classes of society, to grasp the tool of literacy. There is an attempt at developing in them a better consciousness of their reality and their social situation. Historically, the original founders of the CLE were already active or had a background in popular movements such as in community press, political organizations or feminist groups.

The practices and reflections of other literacy training groups were a beacon for the CLE, especially the Carrefour training centre in Pointe-Saint-Charles as well as the Le Tour de Lire literacy training group of the Hochelaga-Maisonneuve district. Both these groups had a significant impact on the ideological perception of literacy, the pedagogical approach, the activities and even the location of the classes. At CLE, literacy training is done in apartments similar to that of Le Tour de Lire.

At CLE, literacy training is geared to learning the social tools of reading, writing and mathematical reasoning, but taking into account the following six elements:

1. The development of general knowledge (functional, political, social, personal);
2. The development of critical thinking;
3. The capacity to make individual and collective decisions;
4. An approach which integrates the individual into group dynamics;

5. The recognition of language, culture and values of the working class milieu;
6. The development of a feeling of belonging to a collective group, in order to better the quality of life of this population. (Gladu, 1988.)

Literacy training for the population at the CLE has four principles: the place where the students learn, the links with their natural environment, the links formed with community organization and a learning and thinking process aimed at the global facts of literacy, especially within their own social, political, cultural and economic space.

Another characteristic of the CLE is the fact that the teachers are called "animators." These people are there to guide the participants in their development. They help them to gain the skills necessary to take charge of their own learning. The teachers do not mystify their own knowledge. They accomplish these principles by working with the participants in the transmission of knowledge as a process of induction and discovery.

Involving the participants

The CLE practices popular literacy training with an emphasis on the participants within the literacy group. There is much consideration given to the participants' viewpoints, ideas and statements. For the teachers, involving the participants in their own literacy training process has many facets: acquired knowledge of basic French (reading and writing), mathematical reasoning and all that could be termed para-literacy training are taken into account.

Para-literacy activities in this case defines all other activities done on a voluntary basis outside of the literacy workshops. For example, at CLE, the participants are encouraged to participate in everything from political rallies to sidewalk sales in order to promote the realities of literacy training and to sensitize the people to the existence of illiteracy. Such promotion also helps the participants to exercise their rights to work, health and information services. Students have also distributed *Alpha Pop*, the RGPAQ journal published for the International Year of Literacy.

At CLE, school projects integrate knowledge and skills acquired within the literacy workshops. These collective school projects further link participants from the four CLE workshops and allow them to complete the finished product and to see tangible proof of their efforts and their progress in reading and writing. The projects are usually done over two sessions of three months, or six months, and are suggested, accepted, and accomplished by the participants of all the workshops at the CLE. Some examples of these are post card exchanges with another literacy group *A tout-Lire en Quebec* and the production of student newspapers, calendar, and agendas. The CLE also prepares a souvenir photo album of all the activities.

The committee of participants

Nicole Trudeau, a member of the participants' committee at CLE, defines their role as follows:

> A participants' committee provides a better quality of life to other participants. It helps also for sensitization. I participated in the Salon du Livre de Montreal (book fair), where I was able to explain to someone about the International Year of Literacy and about literacy training. A participants' committee helps us to express our demands. It helps the teachers also, by supporting them in their task.

The CLÉ provides a sense of belonging for everyone. Illiterate people feel at home there and they play a key role in the organization. The participants' committee is not elected. Anyone can take part. There is no hierarchy, no predetermined roles. The committee members can, with the committee's approval, choose to take on responsibilities individually. The participants' committee also oversees the organization of parties, outings and other special activities of paraliteracy. Decisions are made and elements for discussion are decided upon before the general assembly. Transcripts of the participants' meetings are available in simple, clear language for anyone who wishes to know what was discussed. The idea of tape recorded copies of the meetings was put forth to help those who have difficulty with concepts in writing. In this way, no one is excluded from the details of the participants' meetings.

The committee also tries to create continuity from one

meeting to the next between all members of the CLE. The members of the participants' committee are there to listen to the members of CLE and to generally promote a positive atmosphere and functioning of the center. The committee evaluates the level of satisfaction of the participants as to course choices, schedules, activities either within the literacy or the para-literacy training.

Committee members are the spokespersons for the participants both within and outside the centre. The committee is a solid, but not rigid nucleus. There is a minimum of structure. The committee is a venue for exchanges, dialogue, communication, information between the participants, employees — that is to say the teachers — other community groups within the neighbourhood, other literacy training groups and any other organization dealing with the CLE. The committee members also help out during fund raising campaigns, for example by helping with the mailings.

Here is a sampling of answers given by committee members who were asked: "What does your participation in the committee mean to you?":

> Now I have become involved in other groups, (Mount-Royal housing co-op). I work more on reading and writing. I am less solitary. I take classes on the meeting transcripts. (Richard)

> The committee gives me experience, it allows me to attend other meetings; I went to the general assembly at the adult education committee of the Petite Bourgogne and Saint-Henri (CEDA); I was representing the CLE (Iréne)

> The committee allowed me to be the delegate to the Forum on the rights of the illiterate. I am more proud of myself and my family is too. (Rhéo)

> I had many interesting experiences. I learned a new language(technical). Now I'm able to speak in public, to express my opinions without fear. (Nicole)

> I cannot learn if I don't give. Being part of the participants' committee gave me self-confidence. Now I know I can organize things. I hate to read. Reading for me is

> like eating fish that tastes off. Organizing activities is a
> reward for my efforts. In one way the participants'
> committee is the permanence of the CLE, in relation to
> the turnover of teachers. The committee members have
> closer ties to the participants. They understand them,
> they are in the same boat. (Alain)

Because they understand that the hired teachers don't
have enough time to organize all the para-literacy activities,
the committee members take on a share of the load. They act
as information agents and organizers for these activities. The
committee favors the free expression of each of its members.
They receive the ideas, suggestions and propositions of all
the participants. They then submit those for approval and
discussion.

The committee tries to find solutions to certain problems,
such as absenteeism which can disrupt the schedule at the
centre. According to one of its members, the committee
helps participants to integrate more smoothly into the CLE.
The committee also tries to prevent the insidious copying of
the traditional school style which has already failed most of
the participants. According to Pierette, one of the participants at CLE:

> I wanted to learn but I was having great difficulty.
> Nothing was getting through to my head. The classes
> were big. The teacher took care of the more advanced
> students and I was alone in a corner. Instead of taking
> care of me who needed help so much, she was paying
> attention to the others. I became discouraged and I left
> school in grade four.

Concluding comments
Bulletin de nouvelles d'action sur l'alphabétisation, No. 11,
August 1990, published a report on the participation of stu-
dents which was prepared during the third meeting of the
International Year of Literacy group in Chantilly, France, in
December 1988. Here is an excerpt which encompasses well
the vision of the CLE on literacy training:

Why have the students participated?

- The students are the ones who know their own problem and needs.
- The students are stigmatized and marginalized.
- Participation is an integral part of the learning process.
- A methodology aimed at the students must involve their participation. The participation of students changes the teacher-student relationship to one of joint learning.
- The participation of students enriches the programs and makes them more efficient.
- The participation of students fosters independence, self-confidence, self-determination and dignity.
- The participation of students changes everything.
  (Groupe d'Action sur l'alphabétisation, 1990.)

In short, the participation of students at the Centre is important at many levels, among them, in the collective efforts of all to make this beehive of activity which is CLE as welcoming as possible. Participants are encouraged to claim their rights, particularly their right to education. From the outset they are set on a path to self-affirmation. As Nicole Trudeau, a member of the participant's committee of the CLE puts it:

> Yes, we must remove our mask, stand up for ourselves. Not be afraid to say that we're in literacy training!

Notes

1. The RGPAQ is one of three provincial organizations recognized by the Quebec Ministry of Education to represent volunteer literacy training groups. The other two national organizations are the Mouvement d'éducation populaire et d'action communautaire du Québec (MEPACQ) and the Regroupement des organismes volontaires d'éducation populaire (ROVEP). The RGPAQ receives ministry of education grants due to its representative role of popular literacy groups, its promotion activities for literacy and education and because of its role in liaison and coordination of its members.

The RGPAQ plays this representative role at the provincial, national and international levels.

In Quebec, the RGPAQ represents its members at various committees under the ministry of education of Quebec (MÉQ). It represents its members and deals with various government levels to promote literacy. It is a part of the inter-ministerial committee on adult education. Different ministries and para-governmental organizations consult the RGPAQ regularly for expertise on the needs of certain groups or populations of illiterate adults. The RGPAQ collaborates with many organizations such as the Institute Canadien de l'éducation des adultes (ICEA), the MEPAQ, non-governmental organizations, intervenes in matters of international cooperation, of education related unions, (CEQ), National Federation of Teachers of Quebec (FNEEQ), and universities — the RGPAQ is a member of the certificate in literacy training review committee at the University of Quebec at Montreal (UQAM).

The RGPAQ maintains long-term relations with Canadian organizations which deal with literacy training in Canada (The Movement for Canadian Literacy, the Association of Community Colleges, le Regroupement ontarien des groupes d'alphabétisation francophone) and also with local francophone groups outside Quebec (Ontario, New Brunswick, Saskatchewan, Alberta, P.E.I.), not to mention its regular collaboration with the Canadian Commission for UNESCO. The RGPAQ often welcomes Canadian literacy groups who would like to develop their services much like certain situations in Quebec.

On the international level, the RGPAQ is a member of the international working group on literacy training set up under UNESCO. The RGPAQ also participated in the fourth UNESCO conference on adult education and literacy training. It also participates in literacy training projects in developing countries such as Peru and Nicaragua. The RGPAQ also participated in the fourth UNESCO conference on adult education and literacy training. It also participates in literacy training projects in developing countries such as Peru and Nicaragua. The RGPAQ welcomes guest representatives of literacy training groups from all over the world: Haiti, Senegal, Kenya, Latin America, France, Belgium, England, Scotland, New Guinea, Mali.

Discussion Questions

1. What are some of the distinguishing features of the Centre de lecture et d'écriture?
2. How would you describe the ideological approach towards literacy at the Centre?
3. What are the differences between the terms 'literacy teacher' and 'animator'?
4. How would you sum up the personal development skills acquired by the student members of the Centre?
5. List some of the obstacles students may face in program committee participation. What are the solutions?

CASE STUDIES
ON
LANGUAGE
AND
CULTURE

INTRODUCTION

James A. Draper

The case studies in this section discuss the influence of culture on literacy education and how such education can erode or enhance cultural identity. Culture is not inherited, it is learned, and the dominant expression and transmission of culture is through language.

Culture is also expressed through the traditions, values, symbols, and customs learned from early childhood. Such values and life traditions are integral to the language one first learns. Losing one's first language is also a loss of one's personal and collective history. It is easy to see that illiteracy can restrain the transmission of a community's cultural identity. To be acceptable and relevant, literacy programs need to be rooted in the culture of the adult students.

Many of the case studies illustrate the ways in which people have been deprived of their culture such as sending Native children to schools hundreds of miles from their parents and denying them the right to speak in their mother tongue. A dominant culture which disregards the cultures of minorities can be overwhelmingly destructive. Parents lose control over the education of their children; children and adults lose their rights, their identity, and confidence in their own abilities. People are marginalized. They may even feel ashamed of their culture, a sign of their submission to the dominant culture.

The first step to correcting these injustices is to understand the causes and their consequences. Through the efforts of literacy and other programs, people are assisted to regain what they have lost and to regain confidence with their own language by exploring their experiences. Speaking a language is an entry to writing and reading that language. Language is a collaborative effort to find and to make meaning and to transmit that meaning to others.

Tom Walker's case study, *Theatre as Literacy* illustrates the strong relationship between theatre, language and literacy. He points out that "the concept of theatre as literacy is not meant to be simply a metaphor" and that there are ways in which language is used beyond the many spoken and written forms. Each form complements the other in "achieving the widest and most complete knowledge of what is real." As pointed out, "Learning a particular language gives the individual a new way of knowing reality and of passing that knowledge on to others." Language therefore, is more than the acquisition of technical skills. Both theatre and language were and remain indispensable in teaching and communicating culture.

Using theatre to understand the broader issues of literacy and individual development, can enable people to understand and communicate issues that are important to them. It can provide a deeper level of understanding for the audience, the cast, and illiterate adults. What may result is a greater awareness of the roots of the problems of illiteracy, and its possible link to poverty, unemployment, the welfare system and the lack of affordable housing. Through theatre, controversial issues can be raised. Theatre can help to convey the many factors beyond a person's control, which perpetuate illiteracy and its other related human conditions. Theatre provides both involvement of people and an often uninhibited exposure of issues.

The continuation of a tradition, whether the survival of an entire culture or the survival of educational values, rests with the education of the child. Not surprisingly, many of the case studies comment on the importance of the child learning the heritage language. Family literacy and educational programs for Native people would be an example of this. Connecting with children through special events such as games, play readings and building confidence with their first language are some of the efforts which are mentioned. Contact with elders who have a pride in their traditions also provides the child with a role model.

Building a child's confidence in learning will greatly depend on the confidence which adults themselves are perceived to have. The continuity of one's culture, rooted in traditions, is best assured when adults have control over their own education. The case study *Native People Regaining Control* emphasizes that "true learning" occurs when a person learns in a holistic and balanced manner, encompassing the physical, mental, emotional and spiritual aspects of their culture.

Policies in the workplace also need to be re-examined, in some cases new ones developed. A number of successful examples of how this can be done are shown in the case studies in this section. The case study *Promoting Language, Literacy and Culture in an Arctic Community* illustrates that in order to sustain a people's culture, hiring procedures and job descriptions may need to be developed which encourage bilingualism, in this case, Inuktitut and English.

The "culture of the workplace" can be made to reflect the larger culture of society, in terms of language, work ethics, personal relationships and traditions. Helping others to construct meaning through their cultural traditions can take place on the job. *The Preservation of Franco-Ontarian Language and Culture* gives a number of examples of how the preservation of a culture can be reinforced through an employment site, helping to build cultural identity and pride in the French language. The important point made by the case studies is that the goal of cultural preservation can be integrated into all activities whether in job or non-job situations.

These examples have important implications for training programs for tutors and others, and urges them to review what they are doing towards respecting the cultures of others. The approach to take in enhancing cultural sensitivity is to emphasize that each and every person has a culture which appears right and rational. Self-reflection can be a forceful way to have someone appreciate their own culture and the cultural ways of others. From this approach should come appropriate teaching methods.

In spite of tragic historical circumstances, it is encouraging to see from these case studies the successes which are being achieved in assisting minority groups to revitalize their own culture, by encouraging cross-cultural interaction; the sharing of traditional and personal experiences through story-telling; reflections on the causes of human conditions; understanding the place of language in the daily lives of people; raising a person's consciousness; encouraging people to think and express themselves; making it possible for people to recover their history; and having people become involved in activities which may not involve reading and writing but which do involve language, such as folk theatre, music and story-telling.

The survival of minority cultural groups within a dominant culture involves compromise and adaptation but above all, the will to care and to understand. Language will be at the core. The challenge will be to develop harmony within individuals and groups. This cross-cultural understanding may involve a change in the way people think about others and about themselves. Culture encompasses all those forces and values which gives direction to our lives and language is the medium of that learning and its transmission. Literacy is never void of culture.

Chapter One
THE WHOLE PERSON APPROACH

Sheila Goldgrab

Place: *Indian Friendship Centre in Sault Ste Marie, Ontario*
Participants: *Native people*
Issues: 1. *Building self-confidence and self-identity*
        2. *Integrating literacy and life skills.*

Peer tutoring in an adult literacy class in the continuing education program at Sudbury's St. Thomas School where students are encouraged to be accountable for their own learning. With time, students are confident enough to coach their peers and the teacher is free to act as a resource person for learning pairs and small groups. As a result, the students are able to develop independent learning skills that are useful in and outside the literacy classroom.

Background
Sault Ste. Marie is a northern Ontario city situated between Lake Superior and Lake Huron on the American border. The industrial base is composed of primary steel, forestry, metal fabrication, pulp and paper, post-secondary and government research facilities, personal and business services and tourism. The largest private sector employers are Algoma Steel, Bell Canada, and LaJambe Forest Products. The Board of Education is the largest public sector employer in the city.

Sault Ste. Marie has a population of approximately 86,000 people. The ethnic origins of its population are British, Italian, French, Finnish, German, Aboriginal Peoples and Ukrainian. Aboriginal Peoples make up 1.57% of the city population. There were 3,575 non-institutional Aboriginal People in the city and surrounding area enumerated by the 1986 Canadian census. Batchewana of First Nation and Garden River of First Nation are the two Bands in the area. English is the first language for Aboriginal youth, the older adults over 60 speak Ojibway.

The Canadian Friendship Centre Movement

The Indian Friendship Centres currently provide a full range of social services to those in their communities. A review of the historical circumstances of the 1950's - 1960's is one way to understand the important role that the centres currently perform.

The Canadian Friendship Centre Movement began in the 1950's. The Friendship Centres were a response to increased migration of native people from reserves and rural communities into urban centres. The increased migration was a result of many factors. One significant cause was the 1951 amendments to the Indian Act that defined who was an Indian. The stringent application of the definition meant that many people left the reserves. There were requirements to "enfranchise" Indian people for their military service or for achieving a high school diploma. The Indian Act finalized policies that would discriminate against women who married non-Indians and forced them to live off the reserve. The requirement that all Indian children had to attend a recognized public school from the ages of six to sixteen, also facilitated migration as families wanted to be closer to their children.

In addition, a changing Canadian economy resulted in the development of are source industry which began to displace Natives from their traditional homelands and depleted the natural resources on which they had depended for their existence and survival. They were forced to look for employment in the urban centres.

With the increasing numbers of people in urban centres, Native peoples began to recognize that the existing mainstream social agencies were ill-equipped to meet their needs.

As well, the new urban Native residents were unfamiliar with their new foreign environment. Sylvia Maracle, the Executive Director of the Ontario Federation of Native Friendship Centres, described the situation in which many natives found themselves:

> A native person was generally not familiar with the Manpower Office and if by some fluke they contacted an Office, the staff didn't know how to address their needs. In those days, services were provided on the basis of benevolent paternalism. Native people were physically different, and they had language barriers and few skills that might apply to urban work situations. Those things together didn't encourage any positive interaction.
>
> Today, there is more of a recognition of the language and skill barriers preventing us from participating in meaningful employment. The system has evolved, but it marginalizes and ghettoizes Aboriginal issues. We have to go here for one thing and somewhere else for another thing. We don't live that way. The system still tries to force us to be like Dick and Jane. It is not willing to consider holistic approaches — the racism is more systemic.

This environment fostered the rise and the growth of the Friendship Centre Movement. Over the years, the Centres have evolved to provide direct counselling and programing in a broad spectrum of areas that effect urban living. Formal programs now exist in the areas of literacy education, housing, employment, day care, sensitivity and awareness training, youth programs, justice liaison, and alcohol and drug substance abuse support. There are programs for children, youth, adults and seniors which promote a positive self image about their native ancestry.

Education as a means of reclaiming control

The Niin Sakaan Literacy Program is one of 36 Native literacy programs in Ontario which are located on reserves and urban areas. Those in urban centres have Boards of Directors and programs on reserves are overseen by Band office administrators/counsellors. All of the literacy programs are members of the Ontario Native Literacy Coalition (ONLC).

According to Renee Abram, the Executive Director of the Coalition, literacy education is a way in which Native people can reclaim control over their lives and gain confidence to"address the issues that affect them, and become independent." The Coalition's statement of philosophy demonstrates a commitment to the student-centred approach. The Coalition believes that within the Native community, control over one's life will be increased through giving people control over the way they learn literacy skills, involving them in transmitting these skills to other members of the community and involving them in the decision making and other activities within the community related to literacy.

The Friendship Centre was established in 1972 and during this time, an Aboriginal education committee was formed. The committee was made of representatives from the Reserve in and outside the city, and all Native organizations within SSM reviewed the Native community's educational needs. They saw the need for Native adults to continue their education, to educate Native children to stay in school, to develop Native-relevant materials in school curricula, and to implement cross cultural training. When they assessed the situation, they recognized that illiteracy was holding back their community.

Last year, 61 students participated in the Niin Sakaan Literacy Program. The Centre's literacy group averages between five to eight students. Students at the Centre meet three times a week for three hours. Many students in the group are on fixed incomes, unemployed, are receiving disability benefits and lack employable skills. The majority are Native. As for many other students in literacy programs, self-confidence is a major obstacle to learning. The Friendship Centres develop their programing with this in mind. Renee Abram explained the priority placed on building self-confidence:

> Many literacy programs are basing a lot of work on rebuilding self-esteem in people. Before they can be comfortable in learning to read and write English, they have to be connected with their own culture and tradition. Centres offer different support services of a cultural kind, such as feasts, socials, and craft nights. They are

offering an opportunity for Natives to come together and talk.

The necessity of a whole person approach

The whole person approach is the foundation of literacy programing. The traditional Indian view of humankind includes the physical, mental, emotional and spiritual aspects of human life. Their ancestors viewed life in a manner that is called holistic. The concept of the holistic philosophy as applied to literacy can be described graphically with the shape of a circle. The circle is a significant symbol to Native people. It reflects the natural world: the sky, sun and moon, and the cycle of days and seasons. All these are circular. The symbol of the circle is used in all other phases of their lives, so as to act in harmony with nature. What the Native people call "true learning" occurs when a person learns in a whole and balanced manner when the physical, mental, emotional and spiritual dimensions are involved in the process.

The Niin Sakaan Literacy Program uses the whole person approach in dealing with clients. Sylvia Maracle elaborated on the imperative of self-identity as the centre of this approach:

> One has to understand the notion of how we see ourselves culturally as a people. Any program which is developed for Aboriginal People must consider the four aspects that we culturally believe we have as human beings. Those are: physical, mental, emotional and spiritual directions.
>
> In order for a literacy program to be acceptable and to have any chance at success it must be culturally based and respect these four directions. Any literacy initiative has to be supported by other services and programs in order to meet the needs of the learner in a holistic way as is consistent with these four directions.

For Florence Gray, the Coordinator of the Niin Sakaan Literacy Program, the holistic view is a natural part of literacy education:

> It is the Native mind-set. You can't categorize little bits and pieces of a person. Literacy is an extension. We don't put limits on anything here. It's not for us to do.

There are many instances which illustrate the holistic approach at work at the Native Friendship Centre:

Physical Doctor appointments are made as part of the learning curriculum. Explanations are given about medicine and dosages. Finances are discussed. A clothing depot is available to the clients.

Emotional Staff give support, encouragement and guidance to clients. Alternatives are given to help them overcome the "blank wall" syndrome. Referral to other specialized services based on the needs of clients are also done.

Mental Students are given instruction in reading, writing and computer skills.

Spiritual Students are encouraged to seek a better understanding of a higher Spiritual Being (through a traditional or an established Christian religion). Anyone can join the sweetgrass ceremony which takes place every morning.

Social Students are encouraged to socialize at the Friendship Centre. Friendships develop and students develop their own support system.

In addition to fostering self-confidence and self identity as a Native person, other reasons for this holistic approach to literacy education has to do with other needs. Illiteracy among Native communities is one among a number of social ills that effect Native people. Often, it is difficult to identify what the cause of the most visible problem is. Perhaps the person is unemployed because of poor literacy skills. Or maybe they are drinking heavily because they feel bad about themselves because they can't write. For that reason, it is difficult to provide literacy education in the absence of other supports. The Friendship Centres offer a variety of services from which the literacy student can benefit.

Working together with other programs
The two Friendship Centre Court Workers who specialize

in family and criminal law, accompany clients to court, help them get a lawyer and explain the law. The Employment Outreach Worker helps Native clients who are seeking employment. This program is funded by Canada Manpower and employs one full-time and one part-time worker. They meet with employers and prepare clients before the interview. They also provide them with direction and support but it is a service that is self-directed by the client.

The Health Promotion Program brings seminars to people to promote better health. Information sessions and workshops are also given about family violence. The Health Workers refer clients to non-Native services such as the Group Health Centre and Old Age Drop In Centre. The Little Beavers Program provides cultural, social, educational and recreational activities for children and youth.

Janet (not her real name), a Niin Sakaan literacy student, described how the Centre's other programs have helped her:

> Without the Friendship Centre, I would have gone to the welfare office alone. And to Children's Aid alone too. I come to school, that way I don't stay at home and think about my daughter all the time and worry about what will happen next. Here, if you have a problem, you go to the teacher or someone else. No pressure here.

According to Mary Desmoulin, the Centre's Director, regular staff meetings are an occasion where information about clients is shared. Previously, the staff did not discuss clients' problems because they wanted to respect everyone's confidentiality. Now, the staff discuss the problem or the issue without mentioning the clients name, and the other staff members are able to give advice and suggestions about what should be done. In this way, the programs work together for the clients of each of the Centre's programs.

The program workers are resource people for the clients of the Centre. When a literacy student, for example, approaches an Employment Referral Worker about a problem, the worker will admit not knowing the answer, but will help the student to find out. Terri Lynn Coulis, a Referral Worker and ex-literacy tutor explained that students are satisfied with this approach. In this way, the worker is able to build trust and develop a relationship with that student and others so that they are better able to accept the suggestions that are made.

Heather Pelky, a former literacy tutor, explained how she approached the technique of introducing a student to a new resource person at the Centre for the first time:

> They learn from not only me, but everyone else. If I introduce them to a person, I have to sit with them so that they're comfortable. Then they initiate seeing that worker on their own. This fosters independence.

Enlarging the circle of support

The social aspect of the Friendship Centre prevents a barrier between students and staff from forming. Friend-ships among students and tutors are formed. Marlene Antoniow, a Health Worker and former court worker and ex-literacy tutor, offered her interpretation of the relationship between students and staff:

> We just don't look at them and treat them as literacy students. We create a relationship with all of our clients and they feel comfortable coming here. They like to come.

The tutors are community members who have been trained by the Centre or by the ONLC. Mary explained that "we assume that a community person can relate to problems better than a professional teacher/tutor." Terri Lynn com-plained about the outside workshops on literacy that she's attended that did not locate literacy in the context of a whole person:

> I found it difficult, because I knew that there were a lot of special problems with shyness before they could learn. Learners learn literacy skills but their families had to learn about literacy too. No one zeroed in on those things. They were overlooked perhaps because it [the field] is so new. I would like to see more practical workshops with lots of new ideas.

Both Terri Lynn and Marlene agreed that a health confer-ence they attended in November of 1989 offered an excellent workshop on literacy. Terri Lynn thought highly of the conference because it dealt with literacy education within a larger context. Marlene added that she enjoys going to workshops that are held out of the Soo [the name for Sault Ste Marie] because it gives her a chance to rejuvenate, meet contacts, and it provides her with a break from a full workweek. Terri Lynn mentioned that the Ontario Federation of Indian Friendship Centres give annual workshops on many topics but that literacy is left out.

A satellite program — enlarging the circle

The Indian Friendship Centre also runs a literacy program one afternoon a week at Breton House, an alcohol and drug recovery home for women, owned and operated by the Algoma Substance Abuse Rehabilitation Centre. The literacy group averages about 7 - 10 women at one time and all the women who are staying at the house are obligated to attend. One woman explained that the literacy upgrading will help her communicate with her children. Another saw this course as a foundation for the rest of her life. She intended to go to college for a marketing diploma. Another woman believed that the literacy program was helping her keep sober:

> It's supportive. It helps you deal with being sober. You socialize and change old behaviours. I learn everyday life skills. Going to this class is part of my schedule.

Concluding comments

According to the Niin Sakaan Literacy Program, the definition of a "holistic philosophy" is "the satisfying of an individual's needs and wants in order to facilitate the development of a well rounded person." The holistic view to learning is not new. The Native people have used this concept for thousands of years. In fact, it is one of the twelve principles of Native philosophy. Making the connection of literacy learning to other needs that students might have, is not something especially new for community-based literacy programs in Ontario. What may be of special interest to those programs is, however, that the Indian Friendship Centre provides a full range of support services that complement the literacy program's role in its students' lives.

Discussion questions

1. How do you integrate literacy skills and life skills in an aboriginal program?
2. Learning activities in a native literacy program should be built around local issues and problems. Discuss.
3. Develop a curriculum theme using a holistic approach to literacy.
4. Identify three learning activities that promote the development of self-esteem and a positive native identity.
5. How would you encourage student generated materials in a native literacy program?
6. How will you know when program learners are empowered?

Chapter Two
THEATRE AS LITERACY

Tom Walker

Place: *Vancouver Community College in Vancouver B.C.
and Fraser valley College in Abbotsford B.C.*
Participants: *Adult students, theatre audience, college
instructors.*
Issues: *1. Alternate ways of communicating.*
2. Participation.

The view that theatre can be considered as literacy follows
from Augusto Boal's account of experiments he conducted in
1973 with the People's Theatre in Peru. These experiments
took place as part of a national literacy campaign in that
country. Boal (1979) outlines as one of the goals of that
project, "to teach literacy in all possible languages, especially
the artistic ones such as theatre, photography, puppetry,
films, journalism, etc."

Headlines Theatre of Vancouver, British Columbia has
evolved its Power Play workshops along lines established by
Boal in his Theatre of the Oppressed. The workshops use a
variety of theatrical games and exercises to build participants' confidence and dramatic skills and to begin to
explore problems faced in people's lives. Students at Vancouver Community College's King Edward Campus participated in a week long literacy Power Play workshop conducted by facilitators from Headlines Theatre. The
workshop activity culminated in a public performance of
two short problem plays in front of an audience of over one

hundred fellow students and faculty.

A more conventional approach to theatre involves the production of a play from a script. Students at Fraser Valley College in Abbotsford, B.C. have mounted twelve performances of the play *Marks on Paper* to raise public awareness about the issue of literacy and to raise funds for the operation of a workplace literacy program at the Matsqui, Sumas, Abbotsford Hospital. As of February, 1991, more than one thousand people had seen this production of the play.

Background

The two projects documented here highlight two different approaches to theatre. Each of these approaches has its advantages as well as its limitations. The Power Play approach would seem to have extraordinary value as a vehicle of reflection and self discovery, but may not result in a theatrical performance that is ready to be presented to a broader audience. While the more traditional performance of a play from a written script has more direct prospects for public presentation the impact that the rehearsal process has on the cast is largely incidental to the final product. Each approach, however, achieves both a way of knowing reality and a way of passing knowledge on to others.

The concept of theatre as literacy, as Boal presents it, is not meant to be simply a metaphor. In arguing for the "many languages besides those that are written or spoken," he insists that, "each language is absolutely irreplaceable. All languages complement each other in achieving the widest, most complete knowledge of what is real." Learning a particular language gives the individual a "new way of knowing reality" as well as a way of "passing that knowledge on to others."

Such a broad concept of literacy is attractive in its own right. It also serves as a corrective against the tendency to lose sight of the ends of literacy — enabling people to understand and communicate issues that are important to them and instead to view literacy solely in terms of the acquisition of a certified level of technical skill in the decoding and production of written text. Boal's concept of literacy redirects our focus on the purposes of literacy by clearly demonstrating, in the theatrical experiment, that there can be alternative means to achieving those ends.

Like writing, theatre uses ritualized codes to express meaning. An important difference is that theatrical codes "such as facial expression, gesture, movement, speech, and vocal inflection" can be more accessible because they typically are more concrete than the graphic, phonetic symbols used in writing.

When one considers the importance that dramatizations play in our daily lives — for example, the amount of time spent watching television or the careful attention given to scripting the performances of politicians — the fact that theatre occupies such a small place in education should be puzzling. This puzzle is only intensified if we recall that in pre-literate Greece, as in other cultures, theatre was the main vehicle for the initiation of youth. Throughout history theatre has continued to be an indispensable medium for communicating culture. Yet, with this century's mass media commercialisation and professionalisation of dramatic performance, popular theatre almost has to be introduced into adult education as an 'innovation'.

Headlines Theatre

Power Play is the name given by Vancouver's Headlines Theatre Company to their intensive five day theatre workshop. Headlines has been teaching popular theatre workshops since 1984. Members of the theatre company have worked on several occasions with Augusto Boal, originator of the Theatre of the Oppressed. The objective of the Power Play workshops is to "develop and then perform one or a series of very short plays which reflect situations in which people are oppressed and to explore ways to break these oppressive situations." Two notable features of the Power Play are the process of the workshops themselves and the form that the final performances take — what Headlines calls Forum Theatre.

Workshops begin with a variety of games and exercises that are designed to build a dynamic of working together amongst the members of the group. The first few days are spent loosening up, building trust, and learning new, non-verbal, ways of communicating. The second stage of the workshop involves drawing out deep feelings that the people in the workshop have about difficult situations from their own lives. In the group work, these personal concerns become something that "everyone can relate to and try to resolve."

The workshop facilitators help the group to shape the material from personal reflections into short plays. These plays are performed in front of a wider group, usually on the afternoon of the last day of the workshop. The short plays deal with experiences of oppression. Each play is performed twice. In the first performance, the play is done straight through to show the problem. During the second performance, members of the audience are encouraged to stop the action and enter into the play to act out their suggestions for how the problem might be solved. This opportunity for the audience to offer solutions is the basis for what is called Forum Theatre.

A literacy Power Play

In November, 1989, I approached Headlines Theatre with a proposal to do a literacy Power Play in connection with International Literacy Year. Sherri-lee Guilbert, Headlines' workshop coordinator enthusiastically endorsed the idea and encouraged me to pursue funding and to recruit a participating group of adult learners. Preliminary inquiries to the B. C. Ministry of Advanced Education, Training and Technology (MAETT) and to other potential sources of funding indicated likely support for a funding proposal.

The idea of doing a literacy Power Play was announced at two successive meetings of Project Literacy Greater Vancouver. A number of groups initially expressed some interest in participating, but they were unsure about scheduling or unable to commit themselves to mount a week long workshop involving at least fifteen students. Finally, Paulette Maglaque, Adult Basic Education Department Head at Vancouver Community Colleges' King Edward Campus took the idea back to her department. Their endorsement of the project enabled the submission of a successful application to MAETT for cost shared funding, scheduling of a Headlines workshop, and recruitment of student participants.

Student participants

The workshop took place in June, 1990. In December, I met with a group of the workshop participants to discuss their thoughts and recollections about their participation in the literacy Power Play. I had two discussion sessions with six of the participants: Gordon Balderstone, Betty Gladue, Angela Mati, Marie Montroy, Peter Moschopoulos, and Madeline Whitford. Initially several of the group described themselves as students — even though they felt some discomfort about telling people they were still in school.

A variety of goals and motivations had brought them back as adults to further their schooling. Gordon aspired to a career in computer graphics. Madeline hoped to work as a nurse's aide. Betty wanted to become a counsellor. Marie wanted to do something better with her life; she wanted, "to be able to teach [her] own kids and understand what they would be doing [in school]." Marie was also motivated by the difficulty she encountered functioning in day to day society. She resented being labeled as stupid because "you couldn't do things other people took for granted, such as add, subtract, read, and write."

When students came to the first organizing meeting for the workshop, they learned that a Power Play is different from other theatre. The fact that the Power Play didn't involve a script was important in convincing students to participate in the workshops. Many would have felt intimidated by the prospect of memorising a script in such a short period of time.

The workshop

The week long workshop ran from nine in the morning until three in the afternoon each day with an hour break for lunch. Workshop sessions took place in two class rooms that opened together into a large room. The facilitators, Patti Fraser and Victor Torter, moved at a comfortable pace.. On Monday morning the workshop began with everyone sitting around in a 'talking circle'. An earring was passed around, and as each person held the earring they had their own moment to speak without being interrupted. During the activity everyone else stayed quiet. "This is like the Native people do," Betty observed. Throughout the week long workshop, each day began with a talking circle.

The first day's exercises concentrated on exploring one's own body and senses and learning to trust and know each other. On the second day, people in the workshop began experimenting with new forms of non-verbal expression. These exercises showed the participants how much can be communicated without using words. They also helped correct the common misunderstanding that gesture, movement, and expression in theatre are meant to merely 'illustrate' the words of the script.

The hardest day emotionally for most participants was the third day. This was the day when people in the workshop began dealing with matters that were bothering them. The central activity of this day required people to lie on the floor and remember an event in their lives when they had been oppressed. They were told to make a sound that expressed just how that oppression had made them feel.

During this exercise, Betty remembered the racist attitudes of some teachers and how that made her feel when she was in school. It was painful to relive those experiences. But even as people had to confront negative thoughts, they were given the opportunity to see that the other people in the workshop had had the same kinds of things happen to them. People in the workshop were supportive and caring about each others' situation. They understood what each other had suffered through.Sharing the negative feelings helped build trust and compassion between the people in the workshop.

On the fourth day people in the workshop formed into groups and began work on developing the plays for performance. These plays evolved from the previous exercises. They involved role play to try to workout the problems that people had confronted the day before.

It is important to understand that the exercises required a great deal of trust and mutual respect from the people in the workshop. It can sometimes happen that someone gets the wrong idea about what the workshops are for. This is one instance where the skill and training of the facilitators is crucial. One participant apparently presumed that the workshop would present him with an opportunity to cuddle and try to pick up women. It was frightening to the women to have him there. His behaviour was quickly noticed by the facilitators and he did not continue in the workshop. It is not, however, the intention of the workshop to eliminate all friction between people. One participant confided that there was another woman whose high strung reactions in the workshop irritated her. However, the purpose of the Power Play was strong enough to put differences aside for the time and work together.

Public performance and reflections

At its conclusion, the workshop group presented two short plays. One dealt with obstacles that a second language English speaker encountered at the welfare office. The other portrayed a woman with reading difficulties being ridiculed by fellow students. The performance, in front of an audience of fellow students and instructors from King Edward Campus, generated a great deal of excitement. The audience readily participated in the Forum Theatre concept, producing many thoughtful interventions.

The confidence of the group on the day of the performance seems remarkable when one considers that not only do the performers present plays which they had put together just the day before, but they also have to improvise responses to the audience interventions. As one of the group pointed out, "During the interruption stuff my legs were rattling." In a way the interventions were, "like starting all over again."

But the audience's eager participation uplifted the cast. "People felt they weren't alone" For Marie, it was an inspiration to see the problem solvers coming from the audience. The incident portrayed in one of the plays where a student is ridiculed by other students actually happened to Madeline, "I thought this only happened to me but when I went to the play I saw many people there and they have the same problem." Angela also recalled that, "Sometime ago I was in that place when the teacher asked me to read. I'd feel like taking my book and going home." She realized that, "people are treated the same way as me and I'm not alone in these experiences."

The workshop also gave students an opportunity to explore unfamiliar roles. Betty felt that the workshop was valuable for bridging cultures. Several of the people in the workshop had come to Canada from less developed countries. Getting to know them helped her overcome her own earlier fears and suspicions about what motivates immigrants to come to Canada. Betty was also particularly moved by her opportunity to work closely with Peter, who has cerebral palsy. This experience convinced her of the need to deal openly with people's inhibitions about the disabled and the importance of overcoming the stigma of labelling.

In reflecting upon some of the things they had learned from the workshop, several students said that the term 'literacy' hid issues that were at the root of the problem — issues like racism, poverty, and unsupportive institutions. The label 'illiterate' is particularly maddening. It even sounds like it has something to do with sickness. Students felt that this word is shutting doors on people.

The timing of the workshop was one of the few drawbacks. Because the performance had come at the end of the school year, it wasn't possible to immediately capture the energy generated by the Power Play and direct it into ongoing activities. However, even six months after the workshop, participants still felt strongly about the issues that they had explored and presented in the plays. They hoped that this report would help to spread their message.

As Betty summed up:

> I am glad that I did the workshop because the feelings that I had for many years were dealt with there — with well trained people. It was hard for me to see myself — what made me fail in the school in my young years. It was good that we did the play because it tells the public something. I hope they learn from us. If they suffered from what they see in the play, I hope they understand that they are not alone.

Marks on Paper

Marks on Paper is a play about the problems faced by adults who have trouble with reading and writing. It opens with the actors speaking directly to the audience, telling about the inspiration for the play and about the extent of illiteracy in Canada. The second scene begins a discussion between the five actors who are now 'in character'. This discussion weaves its way through the play, introducing topics that are illustrated in each of five short dramatic sketches. In the first sketch, a shopper asks another shopper for help reading a shopping list left for her by her employer. She makes the excuse that she cannot make out his handwriting in order to cover up her inability to read. The second shopper is unable to help because, she claims, "I can't read things close up without my reading glasses, and I left them at home today."

The second sketch deals with the humiliation of an elementary school child who has difficulty when called upon to read in front of the class. As the similar scenes of hesitation and teasing are repeated through grades one, two and three, the young girl's frustration mounts until she throws her book on the floor and gives up. The remaining sketches illustrate the pain of a parent unable to read a bedtime story to her child and a conversation between a teacher and his student who is a competent mechanic but who has been placed in a 'special learning' reading class against his wishes. The last scene deals with the stress felt by an adult learner starting with a tutor, "Think of the one thing you were worst at as a kid, the thing you hated the most. Now imagine going back and starting to go through that whole torture all over again."

Written by John Lazarus in 1979, the play was commissioned by David Thomas of the Adult Basic Education program at Northern Lights College and Brian Paisley and Ti Hallas of Chinook Touring Theatre. It was first performed in April, 1979, by Chinook Touring Theatre in Fort St. John, B.C. As explained in the play's introduction, Lazarus wrote _Marks on Paper_ after visiting adult reading classes and talking to the students he met there. The stories in the play are their own stories, in their own words.

The Literacy Players

Since May, 1989, students from Fraser Valley College in Abbotsford, calling themselves The Literacy Players, have mounted twelve performances of _Marks on Paper_. Over one thousand people have seen the present production. Six future performances are scheduled at the time of this writing. The cast currently consists of Chris Grimson, Lisa Clark, Marg Short, Connoly Whitworth and Burc Colins. Former cast members include Mitch Smith, Wayne Hubley, Sheri McNeil, Bryan Wiebe and Neil Tanner. Wendy Watson and Cynthia Andruske, co-directors and co-producers of The Literacy Players production, work as adult basic education instructors at Fraser Valley College.

In 1989 they were thinking about how to involve students in a public awareness event at an upcoming regional learners' conference, scheduled for May at the El Rancho at Abbotsford. Having used media before, they were both tired of the usual videos. They brain-stormed on alternatives. Their main objective was that "awareness raising should focus around actual learners not experts or actors portraying learners." Wendy recalled seeing a videotape of a Vancouver Community College performance of *Marks on Paper* and wondered if a performance of the play could be done. They consulted Ian Fenwick, the theatre director at Fraser Valley College, who agreed that a student production of the play would be feasible.

The two instructors took on the tasks of producing and directing the play. Wendy had experience hosting a television show for the college and had done theatre in university. Cynthia has a background in television and video production from her undergraduate years at university. As they soon discovered, they were fortunate to have each other to share the responsibilities. Their advice to anyone else who is thinking of doing a theatre production, especially if this is in addition to a full time job: "you need at least two people to coordinate it, working together in a partnership." During our interview, as if to illustrate the preceding point, Wendy began, "We tend to..." Cynthia finished the sentence, "bounce off each other."

Putting on a theatre production is a complex and demanding enterprise. It is essential to be clear about costs, resources, and facilities. For The Literacy Players' production, a major part of those costs has been for travel. In order to maximize the fund raising potential of the out-of town performances, Watson and Andruske have cut down on expenses by arranging billets and being careful about going out to dinner. Cutting corners on travel expenses shouldn't be at the expense of the cast's morale, however. The occasional dinner out at a more expensive restaurant when touring can be a way of showing appreciation to the cast for all the hours they volunteer for rehearsals, traveling and performance.

It is also crucial to be familiar with the room where the performance will take place. The Literacy Players try to have a rehearsal at every new location. In any event, the producers must communicate to their hosts exactly what facilities they will need for the performance.

Getting the show on the road

The first auditions for the play took place informally. Chris

Grimson recalls that Cynthia approached her about doing the play after she had performed in a student skit. Cynthia looked upon the end of term skits as an ideal opportunity to scout for talent. Chris was invited to a meeting where she was shown a video of the Vancouver Community College production of _Marks on Paper_. At the meeting, Ian Fenwick elicited casting commitments from those attending. Rehearsals for the play took place three to four days a week for about three weeks.

Students are in the play for a variety of reasons. Chris told me, "It is really important to get the message across. I feel fantastic every time we do it." The only change the group did to the script was in the opening monologues. When they address the audience directly, as themselves, they tell about their own backgrounds and involvement with the production. This is the hardest part of the play — the part that is personal, and not rehearsed. Lisa Clark introduces herself and explains:

> I got to grade ten and found out that I had grade three or four level reading. I found out that I had dyslexia. — then I quit school. About six years later, I got really sick of doing assembly line jobs and realized I needed an education. I talked to Wendy Watson who set me up with a volunteer tutor to get to the fundamental levels. I just finished doing fundamental and I did it quite well. I'm now enrolled in regular adult basic education classes. This play is very important because I don't want other people to have to go through what I did. My goal is to be a teacher's aide for reading disabled adult learners. I am on the board of Literacy B.C. and Project Literacy Abbotsford-Matsqui.

Cast members agree that the language of the script is true to life. It comes from the words of literacy learners. In one of the scenes a young girl, Bonnie, is taunted by her classmates because she is having difficulty reading out loud. Lisa, who played Bonnie, has a hard time emotionally when she gets to the part where the other children say, "we're waiting Bonnie." But she knows it is too important to other people for her to quit. "People come up crying saying that was me in school". Some audience members have told her "I never want to see it again because it was too painful."

The co-producers recalled one performance of *Marks on Paper* that didn't go too well. The performance was booked at the end of a long day of meetings at a conference of adult educators. It also followed a professional troupe doing the play *Reading the Signs*. The audience was probably tired and obviously unresponsive. This upset the cast who had become used to playing in front of enthusiastic audiences. Cast members laboured through their roles as if they were carrying huge weights; one performer blew his lines and swore. When they got back to Abbotsford, Ian Fenwick gave them a pep talk and reassured them that difficult audiences were a fact of life in the theatre. The cast learned from this episode to carry on and not to be distracted by the audience's response.

The Literacy Players presented their first performance of *Marks on Paper* at the El Rancho in Abbotsford. At first, both the students and the directors expected to perform the play only once. But the producers received many requests for additional performances because the play was effective at presenting the message of learners. In addition to being an excellent way of raising public awareness, the play has helped raise money for a workplace literacy program at the Matsqui, Sumas, Abbotsford Hospital.[1] There has never been an admission charge to the audience. The performances have raised money directly through donations from the hosting organizations and indirectly when audience members are motivated to make donations to Project Literacy Abbotsford-Matsqui.

After a year and a half and twelve performances, The Literacy Players look forward to even more activity in the future. Lisa would like to start doing dress rehearsals for the play at local high schools, hoping, "to catch somebody going off the deep end a little." There is also some discussion of doing another play, perhaps one that they would write themselves. Even so, there remains a good deal of affection for *Marks on Paper*. Lisa insists, "I sure wouldn't want to give up doing the play. I feel like we're getting out to people. I would be happy to do it for 500 more performances."

Concluding comments

Students involved in both of the theatre projects discussed here have stressed repeatedly to me their confidence that their theatrical presentation has been effective in getting their message across. They have also made clear their convictions about the urgency of that message. This is all about communicating. Lots of times, as the scenes in these plays illustrate, what is taken by the school system as "literacy" isn't about communicating at all, but about control. These are difficult messages. They demand of us that we take another look at what we are doing as educators.

As I read over my manuscript, I am struck by a common incident that is referred to in both *Marks on Paper* and in the literacy Power Play: a character is called upon to read out loud in class and is made fun of by the others. This theme of public shaming — what Harold Garfinkel (1956) terms a "degradation ceremony" was recognized by both audiences and performers as recalling their own experiences. As so many of the performers I spoke to confirmed, "This happened to me." And they told me of audience members saying to them "That happened to me."

The irony here — and it is an irony of tragic proportions — is that the reading aloud ritual of elementary school is nothing less than an ill-conceived attempt to impose and induce a sort of dramatic performance of the text. A calculated bad performance: unrehearsed, uncomprehended, and insecure. Such an approach to drama is entirely backward. It suppresses the individual's concrete expressive capacities "again, gestures, facial expressions, movement, and vocal intonations; capacities that have already been acquired" and subordinates them to the abstract and alien text. Furthermore, through this suppression, the reading out loud ritual sets up a demonstration of inadequacy. It is not just the mastery of the text that is at stake. The subordination of all other powers of expression to the text makes the individual appear and feel completely unable to communicate, hence incompetent as a human being.

The incorporation of theatre into literacy programing may appear at first to be an interesting innovation with some fruitful possibilities. However, I would suggest an alternative view of the matter: the widespread absence of drama as a key aspect of literacy programing bespeaks a timidity in addressing the fundamentally oral nature of language, if not an unconscious denial to people of a powerful say in their own lives.

Notes

1. The workplace literacy program at the M.S.A. Hospital was among a number of projects that Project Literacy Abbotsford-Matsqui considered at the time it was formed in 1989. It was inspired by the success of a workplace program at the Royal Columbian Hospital in New Westminster. A partnership of Project Literacy Abbotsford-Matsqui, Fraser Valley College, the Hospital, the Hospital Employees Union, the B.C. Nurses Union and the Health Sciences Association, it began operations in January, 1991.

Discussion Questions

1. *In what ways can theatre be considered as literacy?*
2. *In what ways can theatre be used to build self-confidence?*
3. *What are some advantages and disadvantages of each of the two approaches to theatre illustrated in this case study?*
4. *How can a participatory approach be built into theatre production?*
5. *What approaches can be taken to identify issues that might be appropriate for a theatrical performance?*

Chapter Three
THE PRESERVATION OF FRANCO-ONTARIAN LANGUAGE AND CULTURE

Sheila Goldgrab

Place: *Le Centre d'alphabétisation de Prescott in Hawkesbury Ontario.*
Participants: *Franco-Ontarian adults.*
Issues: 1. *Preservation of culture.*
      2. *Building of self-identity.*
      3. *Minority groups.*
      4. *Social action.*

The Centre d'alphabétisation de Prescott is one of 27 French language literacy programs in Ontario. The Centre promotes pride in its language, traditions and culture. In this way franco-Ontarian learners are better able to understand the issues that concern them. The turbulent labour history in the united counties of Prescott-Russell in north-eastern Ontario played a major part in the discovery of the problem of illiteracy within the francophone community in this area.

Background
    The greatest concentration of people in the municipality of Prescott-Russell live in Hawkesbury. The city is located midway between Ottawa and Montreal and is situated on the Ottawa River upstream from the Long Sault rapids. One of the first Canadian pulp mills, Canadian International Paper (CIP) was built in Hawkesbury, and exports paper and lumber to the USA and the United Kingdom. Opportunities in industry meant that a considerable wage-earning class

settled in Hawkesbury, retail stores flourished and the area became prosperous. Thirty six manufacturing plants presently employ a major part of the population. Textile, metal, and plastic are among the industries in the region. Most of the residents of Hawkesbury are blue collar workers.

Of the 10,000 inhabitants of Hawkesbury, about 75% of are francophone. Only in the north- east and eastern Ontario do francophone communities represent a significant proportion of the regional populations. The years of 1971 to 1981 revealed a drop of over 2% of French language users in the Prescott-Russell region. Nevertheless, most francophones in the area use the French language on a regular basis at work and in their leisure time more often than any other francophone communities in the province (Savas, 1988).

The "discovery" of illiteracy among the area's franco-Ontarians

The creation of Le Centre d'Alphabetisation de Prescott (CAP), is tightly woven with the labour history of the region. Until the 1960's, Hawkesbury was considered a "one company town." The Canadian International Paper Company (CIP) in Hawkesbury employs 500 people. Only then did the Federal Expansion program and a community organization called Le Reveille des citoyens with a mandate of economic development, work to bring in new industry. As a result, the area underwent rapid expansion and twenty industries opened. The French population felt threatened by the newly located multinational American employers, as did the anglophone employers who had until this time allowed the francophone elite to manage the new industry in exchange for real control over the social, educational and cultural aspects of the region. As a result of such an arrangement, franco-Ontarian rights were held back.

In 1972, 1975 and again in 1981, the workers of a company producing undercarpets, walked out to protest bad working conditions. On all of these occasions, the heat had risen to an unbearable 110 degrees fahrenheit indoors. In 1975 all other plants in the area walked out in solidarity with the undercarpet workers. Prior to the 1981 strike, Richard Hudon, an "animateur social", applied for and received a grant to conduct a needs study about labour training issues concerning local unionized and non-unionized workers. When the strike began, union members took their questions to their community "animateur social" and shortly after, they asked him for help to organize a successful strike by utilizing committee structures.

Richard trained them to use faxes and computer printers, and organized a newspaper that was distributed on the picket line. It was then, when the newspapers were left unread, that a profound literacy problem was discovered within the union local. A great many of the membership and leadership of The International Woodworkers Union had inadequate reading skills. As an alternative to circulating reading materials, the union leadership decided to focus on visual strategies to educate the strikers. As an example, they showed films on important international strikes, and presented theatre plays by the strikers on the picket line.

French pride began to surface during the strike, evident both visually and during the negotiating process. Richard Hudon, presently the francophone coordinator of the Ontario Community literacy program, in the Literacy Branch of the Ontario Ministry of Education, described the signs of French pride on the picket line:

> All of the unilingual slogans on signs, such as "down with the company", were removed and repainted. They were taken away by the publicity committee of the union local and replaced with French slogans that affirmed their own language — that would click with them. They fought to get the work agreement translated to French. They tried to get acknowledgement that the French version would have the same legal validity in a court of law as the English version.

What was also being disputed was the manner in which the company imported a working ethic and style from outside the country and applied it to the employees without respect for the francophone culture and its own working ethic. Richard explained:

> The audacity of an American company naming an American with southern work ethics to be the new manager of the plant in 1978 was totally unacceptable to francophones. This manager modelled the work ethic he encouraged after the one he knew from the southern

United States. The company viewed franco-Ontarians as a minority and they worked the same way with the French as they (the company) did with the blacks from Alabama and South Carolina. Some of the problems in the workplace stemmed from using English as the only language of communication. The union local's newspaper was printed in French. To us as militants, we had to make people aware of their francophone pride and of being good workers. The more they went ahead into the strike, the more they were expressing themselves in French and reaffirming their culture.

Soon after, a brief needs assessment about literacy was done by the Association canadienne-française de l'Ontario (ACFO). This led to the formation of the Comité d'alphabétisation de Prescott and Russell, which in turn lead to the formation of Alfa Action, the first literacy group that was later renamed CAP. Richard Hudon and Lise Duval, a learner of Alfa Action, travelled to many other francophone regions in Ontario to try and start literacy groups. They began a publicity and recruitment campaign. Two years later the first literacy group opened in Prescott-Russell. The first literacy workers were Thérèse Jroleau, Chantal Kennedy and Maryse Pouliot.

Historical barriers to the French language in Ontario

Only as recent as 1989, twenty years after Premier Robarts promised franco-Ontarians the right to a high school education in their own language, was the école Secondaire Regional d'Hawkesbury/Hawkesbury Regional High School designated as a French school. Struggle for the accessibility of French language services in Ontario has been a long one. Currently, Bill 8 (Chapter 45, Statutes of Ontario 1986) guarantees French services where numbers in the province warrant. Finally, in 1986, the Ontario government began to support and promote literacy education in both national official languages. The Ministry of Education's literacy unit employs a French Coordinator, and literacy materials are developed for the French communities in the province, with their culture and traditions in mind. These publications and videos are more than just translations of English materials. Four French literacy groups opened in the first year that the government offered their support. There are currently twenty-seven francophone popular literacy groups in Ontario.

Le CAP

The CAP has six sites where it offers literacy workshops. The group's main office is located in a house called La Maison de l'ile on Ile du Chenail. The house is the only visual sign left of a francophone community that no longer exists. All of the inhabitants of the island, known to the locals as les Chenaielleurs, had their houses expropriated by Hydro Quebec when it flooded the island in 1965. The town council agreed to a cash settlement for damage compensation and the community was never restored.

The second site is in Le quartier Portelance-Taché-James, which is a neighbourhood of subsidized housing. Other sites are near the agricultural college where many learners live and in Curran, a small village where learners, including those with mental handicaps, come for literacy workshops. Recently, two new groups were started in St. Eugéne and L'Orignal. Although the francophone community in the area is large, it feels threatened by the proximity of the Association for the Preservation of English in Canada which is located only one hour away in nearby Cornwall.

French pride and popular education

Florian Levesque is the coordinator of the literacy organization for francophone literacy groups in Ontario. This movement is called le Regroupement des groupes francophone d'alphabétisation populaire de l'Ontario. The objectives of the Regroupement are to "promote, defend and develop popular literacy, popular literacy groups, and the rights of the illiterate." It began in December of 1988, and there are 22 groups that are currently members of the Regroupement. Florian views the creation of French popular literacy groups as the beginning of a process by which francophone literacy learners are able to feel in control of their destiny:

In Hawkesbury, as is the case throughout Ontario, literacy groups are giving the chance for people who are marginalized in society the opportunity to participate and make important decisions. People who were kicked out of schools, are now being brought into the literacy program and asked to think and express their ideas. My experience is when people feel responsible for things that touch their lives, they take responsibility and feel pride. Because of this, I consider this a movement not just an organization.

We push this, and we know that it will be an evolutionary process and that this type of thinking will blossom one day. By adopting this philosophy, and training workshop leaders and board of directors and coordinators and learners to work with this in mind, we may succeed to increase the awareness of the political, social and cultural awareness of literacy learners. Many local Board members will learn their role and be made aware of the impact that they can make in their community to defend the rights of the learners. The Regroupement is a resource for learners and for popular literacy groups. We explain their rights to them.

The movement for social justice that Florian talked about, is part of the mandate of the Regroupement. Florian described further the relationship of social justice to literacy educational workshops:

> We hope to bring in social justice as a part of the literacy programing for franco-Ontarians. For example, we're trying to affect changes in the Electoral Act so that the picture of the candidate will appear on the voting ballot. Although we're doing this for those francophones in the province who have difficulties reading, it will obviously have implications for everyone.

Diane Dugas, the coordinator of CAP, sees the centre as a place where learners are able to appreciate where their culture fits in:

> I would like to see learners re-define their relationship with the dominant class and see themselves as equals. I want them to improve their lives, to be full participants, and to understand that their culture is man-made and not inferior to the dominant culture. Many learners

believe culture to be formal, as in theatre, dance and literature. They don't relate to this culture. We want them to see culture in its larger perspective and feel that they have been participants in the larger culture — as everyone else has been. Once the learners can see that, they get a new sense of identity about where they come from, and what their contributions can bring to the future.

The literacy workers that I spoke to were unaware of their centre's mandate for social change. Diane explained that the former Board of Directors resisted this as part of CAP's agenda and that she hoped that now the process of conscientization would progress at a rapid rate.Right now "literacy workers are pre-occupied with methodology" said Diane, "And we, in the group, spend a lot of time trying to recruit literacy workers with qualifications to teach literacy.' As well, Diane believes that the fact that literacy workers at CAP work part time and not full time, is another reason that contributes to literacy workers not having a full understanding of the popular education philosophy that is basic to CAP.

The oral tradition and franco-Ontarian culture

The francophone literacy programs have acted as a means to discover their people's traditions and cultures. Foremost on everyone's agenda, is to learn how to read and write their mother tongue language. The literacy programs face the challenge of examining learners' shame about the language they call their own. Florian explained:

> Some francophones feel shame about the French language. Compare the language we speak in Ontario to the French language spoken in France. People here think that the language is not as good as European French. Really, a lot of the words that we use here are perceived to be anglicisms but are originally French words that the English language adopted.When the English came, we were cut off from France and the language remained very close to the old French of the first French settlers. Some of the words we use are very old ones no longer in use in other countries. Compare

this to the Europeans who had contacts with other French speaking cultures, such as Belgians, and their language was able to evolve differently. We're closest to the French from the past. It's history is rich and beautiful.

Diane added another reason why some Franco-Ontarians may feel ashamed about their language:

> It's a question of submission to the dominant language. In Sudbury, for example, where French people speak their own language in the schools, they speak English outside so that they will be accepted. Many people will speak English in the workplace to increase their chances of being promoted. In Hawkesbury, the French speaking people are a majority, but they still act as a minority in order to keep the peace with the anglophones in the area.

Recovering franco-Ontarian popular history is something else that takes place in literacy groups. The importance of the oral tradition is not lost on these literacy groups. Florian continued to explain:

> In francophone literacy programs they realize that the knowledge that these adults have acquired is important. My father is illiterate and he tells me stories about working hard lumbering on the waters.This historical information, based on personal experience, has more meaning to me than what is taught at a university. It's as important as what you learn there. Traditionally, we always had and still have story tellers. They communicate a lot of values within our community. We have to realize that the stories we're telling in Ontario were dying but now there's a move to have them survive.People who came from France long ago and came here had their traditional stories as part of their cultural background. Stories changed and adapted as time moved on and people changed.
> In those new stories the values that were carried were franco-Ontarian. Ti-Jean is always a character that comes up in the stories.He's poor, with many people in his family. He's always meeting the king, who

represents power, wealth, prestige and marries the princess, or tricks the king in order to survive. The French lumberers and miners didn't have a lot of money, that's Ti-Jean. He's always laughing even though he's out of luck. And he's smart. He cuts wood, and he's always looking to have a good time, and make a point somewhere and somehow. These stories are a form of literature but have not been written, until recently. These were kept alive by the illiterate, the learners. This is who we are as a culture.

The Regroupement is presently developing a program whereby they will be encouraging the learners to tell their own, traditional, personal and/or collective stories.

Historical events that effected the francophones of Ontario are discussed in the CAP's literacy workshops of five to eight students, as are contemporary news events heard over French language stations. These are all used as materials for reading, writing and discussion. News items from the local newspaper are also often discussed. Although the French language is spoken by all of the students, students come from different backgrounds, have different goals and work at different paces. Discussions about politics or other subjects is all interesting and helps the learners learn about issues that touch them as franco-Ontarians. They also work to strengthen people's arguing abilities, and powers of reasoning, since they don't always agree.

Learner involvement

Part of the philosophy of popular education that exists at CAP is the view that learners play an important role in the decision-making processes of the group. Diane offered many examples where this is the case:

Two learners sit on our Board of Directors of ten people and they are involved in all of the committees. They made their own television program — they initiated, wrote, and produced it in December of 1990. They organized the visit of a story teller named Pepere Cam.

They have their own fundraising committee for activities, such as visiting the Le Devoir newspaper, going to the theatre, and buying materials for the group.

The learners and their families participate in CAP's annual general assembly where learners, who were involved with the program for a long time, tell the story about how the literacy program began, and what it is doing now. The students are highly motivated to share their information and participate in the assembly in this way.

Concluding comments

For Diane, the connections between literacy, popular education and French cultural pride are essential for literacy to be meaningful:

> We want them to think of their literacy problem in a different way, to see it as it really is, a social phenomenon and not a result of their own incapacity.
>
> To do that they have to understand how society works, how the power is mostly distributed among elites. That is where popular education comes in. They have to know and experience that power belongs to the people who have the information and that the more they make themselves heard, the more they are able to play a key role in decision making.
>
> They have to feel that what they think is important and can make a difference. They have to be proud of who they are, where they come from, and know where they want to go as franco-Ontarians. We at CAP make the learners aware of their history as Franco-Ontarians, we teach them how to be full participants in the group, and to use their new skills to be aware of their newfound identity outside the group. It is a very long process because it implies a change in the way of thinking and in the way they see themselves.

Discussion Questions

1. *In what ways can literacy education assist in dealing with local socio-economic problems?*
2. *How would you go about creating suitable material for a literacy cultural-education program?*
3. *In what way is "culture" being used in this case study? Is it restricted to the specific group discussed in the case study?*
4. *What is the role of history in helping to build group identity?*
5. *What are the various ways in which adult students can be involved in taking control of their own learning? Go beyond the examples given in this case study.*

Chapter Four
LA PRESERVATION DE LA LANGUE ET DE LA CULTURE FRANCO-ONTARIENNE

Sheila Goldgrab

Lieu: Le Centre d'alphabétisation de Prescott, Hawkesbury, Ontario

Participants: 1. Le comité d'alphabétisation de Prescott et Russell et des apprenants

2. Le Regroupement des groupes francophones d'alphabétisation populaire de l'Ontario

Thème: La promotion et le développement de l'alphabétisation populaire dans le nord-est de l'Ontario

---

On conpte actuellement 27 programmes francophones d'alphabétisation en Ontario. L'histoire troublée des relations syndicales dans les comtés unis de Prescott-Russell dans le nord-est de la province a beaucoup fait pour mettre l'accent sur les problèmes d'analphabétisme dans la collectivité franco-ontarienne de la région. Le Centre d'Alphabétisation de Prescott encourage la promotion de la langue, les traditions et la culture. De cette façon, les apprenants franco-ontariens peuvent mieux comprendre les questions qui les touchent.

Historique

La plus importante concentration de population dans la municipalité de Prescott-Russell se trouve à Hawkesbury. La ville est située mi-chemin entre Ottawa et Montréal, en amont des rapides du Long Sault. L'usine de pulpe du Canadian International Paper, l'une des premières au Canada, fut construite à Hawkesbury, et exporte du bois d'oeuvre de

307

papier vers les États-Unis et le Royaume-Uni. Grâce à cette industrie, une classe salariale importante s'est établie à Hawkesbury, amenant ainsi, la prospérité aux détaillants locaux et à la règion entière. Une grande partie de la population se trouve actuellement à l'emploi de 36 usines manufacturières. La région compte des industries de textiles, de métal et de plastiques. La plupart des résidents d'Hawkesbury sont des cols bleus.

Une forte majorité des 10,000 habitants d'Hawkesbury, soit 75% de la population, sont francophones. Ce n'est que dans le nord-est et l'est de l'Ontario que les francophones forment une proportion considérable de la population régionale. De 1971 à 1981, on note une diminution de deux pour cent du nombre de gens qui parlent français dans la région de Prescott-Russell. Néanmoins, la plupart des francophones de la région parlent français de façon régulière dans leur lieux de travail et aux heures de loisir, et plus souvent que toute autre collectivité francophone de la province (Savas, 1988)

La «découverte» de l'analphabétisme parmi les Franco-Ontariens de la région

La création du Centre d'Alphabétisation de Prescott (CAP) est reliée de près à l'histoire syndicale de la région. Jusqu'aux années '60, Hawkesbury était considérée comme une ville à industrie unique. La Canadian International Paper Company (CIP) employait quelque 500 personnes. Ce n'est qu'à partir de cette époque que le programme fédéral d'expansion, ainsi qu'un organisme communautaire nommé le Réveille des citoyens et ayant comme mandat le développement économique, se sont mis à attirer de nouvelles industires dans la région. Il en résulta une expansion régionale rapide et l'ouverture de 20 industries. La population francophones se sentait menacée par l'arrivée de nouveaux employeurs multinationaux américains, tout comme les employeurs anglophones qui jusqu'alors avait permis à une élite francophone de gérer les nouvelles entreprises en échange du véritable contrôle des domaines sociaux, culturels et de l'éducation. Une telle situation ne pouvait qu'entraver le développement des droits des francophones.

En 1972, 1975 et encore en 1981, les employés d'AMOCO, qui travillaient à la fabrication de sous-tapis, ont débrayé pour protester contre les mauvaises conditions de travail. La température à l'intérieur de l'usine avait atteint un niveau intolérable, soit 110°F. En 1975, tous les autres travailleurs d'usine de la région ont débrayé par solidarité avec les travailleurs d'AMOCO. Avant la grève de 1981, Richard Hudon, un animateur social, avait obtenu une subvention lui permettant de mener une étude sur les besoins en matière de formation des travailleurs syndiqués et non-syndiqués dans la région. Une fois la grève déclenchée, c'est à l'animateur social de la collectivité que les syndiqués ont adressé leurs questions. Peu après, les grévistes ont sollicité son aide, lui demandant surtout de leur apprendre l'usage d'un système syndical de comités pour assurer la réussite de la grève.

Richard leur apprit l'utilisation des bélinographes et des imprimantes informatisées, et mit sur pied un petit journal qu'on distribua sur le piquet de grève. C'est à ce moment qu'on a constaté que plusieurs ne lisaient pas ce journal et donc, qu'un grave problème d'analphabétisme existait au sein de cette section locale. De façon générale, une majorité des membres et des dirigeants du Syndicat international des travailleurs du bois avaient atteint un niveau d'alphabétisme insuffisant. Comme solution de rechange, les chefs syndicaux ont décidé de renseigner les grévistes par des moyens visuels plutôt que par l'écriture. Par exemple, ils ont présenté des films sur des grèves internationales de grande envergure, ainsi que des spectacles dans la rue mettant en vedette les grévistes sur le cordon de piquet.

La fierté des francophones s'est mise à faire surface au cours de la grève, tant au plan visuel qu'au plan des négociations. Richard Hudon, qui est actuellement coordinateur francophone du programme ontarien d'alphabétisation communautaire dans la Direction de l'alphabétisation du ministère de l'éducation de l'Ontario, nous décrit les signes de fierté que l'on voyait sur le piquet:

> On a enlevé et repeint toutes les affiches portant des slogans unilingues (anglais), tels que "down with the company". Le comité publicitaire de la section locale du syndicate les a enlevées pour les remplacer par des affiches portant des slogans en français, des slogans pertinents pour les francophones. Ils on exigé la traduction vers le français de la convention collective. Ils ont demandé qu'on attribue à la version française une

validité égale à celle de la version anglaise devant les tribunaux.

On protestait également contre la façon dont la compagnie se permettait d'importer une éthique et un mode de travail peu ordinaire et cherchait à l'imposer aux employés sans égard à la culture francophone et a propre éthique de travail. Selon Richard:

> Les francophones ne pouvaient supporter l'audace d'une compagnie américaine qui en 1978 a nommé comme gestionnaire de l'usine un Américain pratiquant l'éthique de travail des états du sud. Il s'inspirait de l'éthique de travail qu'il avait apprise dans le sud des États-Unis. Pour la compagnie, les franco-ontariens était un groupe minoritaire, qu'on devait gérer de la même façon que les noirs de l'Alabama et de la Caroline du sud. Certains problèmes sur le lieu de travail étaient attribuables à l'usage exclusif de l'anglais comme moyen de communication. Le journal de la section locale du syndicat, cependant, était rédigé en français. Nous, les militants, cherchions à sensibiliser les gens pour qu'ils soient fiers d'être des francophones et des travailleurs compétents. À mesure qu'évoluait leur grève, ils s'exprimaient davantage en français et réaffirmaient leur culture.

Peur après, l'Association canadienne-française de l'Ontario (AFCO) a fait une évaluation sommaire des besoins dans le domaine de l'alphabétisme. Ce que a mené à la formation du Comité d'alphabétisation de Prescott et Russell, qui à son tour mena ensuite à la formation d'Alfa Action, le premier groupe d'alphabétisation qui fut ensuite rebaptisé le CAP. Richard Hudon et Lise Duval, une apprenante d'Alfa Action, ont voyagé dans plusieurs autres régions francophones de l'Ontario pour encourager la formation de groupes d'alphabétisation. Ils ont lancé une campagne de publicité et de recrutement. Après deux ans, le premier groupe d'alphabétisation a démarré à Prescott-Russell. Les premières enseignantes furent Thérèse Groleau, Chantal Kennedy et Maryse Pouliot.

Entraves traditionnelles à la langue française en Ontario

Ce n'est qu'en 1989, soit 20 ans après que le premier ministre Robarts ait promis que les franco-ontariens auraient droit à l'éducation secondaire dans leur propre langue, que l'école secondaire régionale d'Hawkesbury / Hawkesbury Regional High School est devenue une école de langue française. En Ontario, on lutte depuis longtemps pour obtenis des services en français. Présentement, la Loi 8 garantit des services francophones lorsque les données démographiques le justifient.

Enfin, en 1986, le gouvernement de l'Ontario s'est mis à encourager et à subventionner l'alphabétisation dans les deux langues officielles du pays. La section de l'alphabétisation du ministère de l'éducation emploie un coordinateur francophone, et on y élabore un matériel didactique d'aide à l'alphabétisation destiné aux collectivités francophones de la province, tenant compte de leur culture et de leurs traditions. Ces publications et ces vidéos ne sont pas de simples traductions de documents en langue anglaise. Avec les subventions gouvernementales de la première année, on a établi quatre groupes francophones d'alphabétisation. On compte actuellement 27 groupes francophones populaires d'alphabétisation en Ontario.

Le CAP

Le CAP offre des ateliers d'alphabétsation à six endroits. Son siège principal se trouve dans une maison qu'on appelle La Maison de l'île, située à l'île du Chenail. Cette maison est le seul signe externe d'une communauté francophone maintenant disparue. Tous les habitants de l'île, connus dans la région sous le nom de Chenailleurs, furent expropriés lorsqu'Hydro Québec inonda l'île en 1965. La ville accepta un paiement comptant en compensation, mais on n'a jamais rétabli la communauté. Le deuxième site est dans le quartier Portelance-Taché-James. Il s'agit d'un voisinage composé d'habitations à loyers subventionnés. D'autres ateliers se trouvent près du collège agricole, où habitent nombre de ces apprenants et à Curran, un petit village où les apprenants, y compris certains ayant une déficience mentale, assistent aux ateliers d'alphabétisation. Récemment, on a établi deux nouveaux groupes, l'un à St-Eugène et l'autre à l'Original.

Malgré son importance numérique dans la région, la population se sent menacée par la proximité de l'Association for the Preservation of English in Canada qui se trouve à Cornwall, à seulement une heure de route.

La fierté francophone et l'éducation populaire

Florian Lévesque est coordinateur du mouvement d'alphabétisation des organismes francophones d'éducation populaire dans la province. Ce mouvement s'appelle le Regroupement des groupes francophones d'alphabétisation populaire de l'Ontario. Les objectifs du Regroupement sont de «promouvoir, défendre et développer l'alphabétisation populaire et les organismes d'alphabétisation populaire, ainsi que les droits des analphabètes.» Débutant en décembre 1988, le Regroupement compte maintenant 22 organismes membres. Pour Florian, la formation de groupes francophones d'alphabétisation populaire signifie le début d'un processus qui permettra aux apprenants francophones — qui se sentent marginalisés par la société à cause de leur statut minoritaire dans la province et parce qu'ils sont économiquement défavorisés — de se sentir maîtres de leur destin:

> À Hawkesbury, comme partout en Ontario, les groupes d'alphabétisation offrent en effet aux gens marginalisés l'occasion de participer et de prendre des décisions importantes. Des gens qui autrefois ont été renvoyés de l'école font maintenant partie du programme d'alpha-bétisation, où ils doivent songer et exprimer leurs idées. Selon mon expérience, lorsque les gens se sentent responsables des choses qui les touchent de près, ils acceptent leurs responsabilités avec fierté. C'est pour-quoi is s'agit, selon moi, non seulement d'un organisme mais bien d'un mouvement.
>
> Nous encourageons une évolution en ce sens, sachant qu'un jour cette attitude se généralisera. En adoptant une telle philosophie, et en formant des chefs d'atelier, des dirigeants, des coordinateurs et des appre-nants selon ces principes, nous pourrons réussir à aug-menter le sensibilisation politique, sociale et culturelle des apprentis de ce programme. Plusieurs des membres du Conseil de direction découvriront le rôle qu'ils

peuvent jouer, et deviendront conscients de l'impact qu'ils peuvent avoir dans leur collectivité pour mieux défendre les droits des apprenants. Le Regroupement est une ressource pour les apprenants et pour les groupes d'alphabétisation populaire. Nous leur expliquons leurs droits.

Ce mouvement de justice sociale dont parle Florian fait partie du mandat du Regroupement. Florian nous décrit ainsi le lien entre la justice sociale et les ateliers d'alphabétisation:

> Nos programmes d'alphabétisation cherchent aussi à obtenir la justice sociale pour les franco-ontariens. Par exemple, nous cherchons à faire modifier la loi électorale pour que les photos des candidats figurent sur le bulletin de vote. Cette mesure favoriserait les francophones de la province qui ont de la difficulté à lire, bien entendu, mais elle aurait évidemment des effets partout dans la société.

Diane Dugas, coordinatrice du CAP, croit que c'est par le biais des groupes d'alphabétisation que les apprentis peuvent comprendre leur situation culturelle:

> J'espère que les apprenants pourront redéfinir leur rapports avec la classe dominante, et se considérer comme leurs égaux. Je voudrais qu'ils améliorent leurs vies, qu'ils deviennent des paricipants à part entière, et qu'ils comprennent que leur culture est une chose formée par la main de chacun, et qu'elle n'est nullement inférieure à la culture dominante. Pour un grand nombre des apprenants, la culture est une chose formaliste qui évoque le théâtre, la danse ou la littérature. Cette comception de la culture ne les rejoint pas. Nous voulons leur faire comprendre le terme «culture» dans un sens plus large, et les amener à comprendre qu'ils participent depuis toujours à cette grande culture — comme tout le monde, d'ailleurs. Aussitôt cette leçon apprise, les apprenants comprendront davantage à quoi ils ont contribué dans le passé et à quoi ils pourront contribuer à l'avenir.

Les travailleurs du programme d'alphabétisation auxquels j'ai parlé ignoraient ce mandat de leur organisme en faveur

du changement social. Diane a expliqé que l'ancien Conseil
de direction voyait d'un mauvais oeil cette partie du mandat
du CAP, et elle espère que le processus de sensibilisation
sera dorénavant plus rapide. Actuellement, «les travailleurs
des programmes d'alphabétisation se préoccupent de la
méthodologie», de dire Diane, «et dans le groupe, nous met-
tons beaucoup de temps à recruter des travailleurs compé-
tents qui peuvent ensigner l'alphabétiseme». De plus, Diane
croit que si certains enseignants ne comprennent pas très
bien la philosophie d'éducation populaire sur laquelle le
CAP se fonde, c'est parce qu'ils sont des travailleurs à temps
partiel et non à temps plein.

La tradition orale et la culture francophone

Les programmes francophones d'alphabétisation ont
permis à un peuple de mieux comprendre ses traditions et sa
culture. Les gens veulent d'abord apprendre à lire et à écrire
leur lange maternelle. Les programmes d'alphabétisation
doivent faire face au problème des apprenants qui ont honte
de leur propre langue. Florian nous explique pourquoi certains ont honte de se servir d'une langue qui est bien la leur:

> Certains francophones ont honte de la langue française.
> Comparant la langue parlée en Ontario à celle de la
> France. Certains croient que leur langue est inférieure
> au français européen. En réalité, beaucoup de mots que
> nous employons sont perçus comme étant des
> anglicismes mais en effet, ce sont des mots d'origine
> française que l'anglais a adoptés. Avec l'arrivée des
> Anglais, nous avons perdu contact avec la France, et la
> langue est demeurée très près de celle des premiers
> colons francophones. Certains des nos mots sont
> d'anciens termes qui ne sont plus utilisés ailleurs. Si
> vous comparez notre situation à celle d'autres cultures
> francophones, les Belges par exemple, vous verrez que
> ces cultures one connu une différente évolution. Nous
> sommes plus près des français d'autrefois. Et cela fait
> partie d'une histoire riche et intéressante.

Diane nous offre une autre explication: une sorte de
sentiment de honte que les franco-ontariens éprouvent
envers leur langue:

Il s'agit d'un esprit de soumission envers la langue dominante. À Sudbury, par exemple, les francophones parlent français à l'école, mais ailleurs ils parlent anglais afin d'être acceptés. Plusieurs parleront anglais au travail pour améliorer leurs chances d'obtenir une promotion. À Hawkesbury, les francophones majoritaires agissent en minorité pour ne pas créer de conflit avec les anglophones de la région.

Les groupes d'alphabétisation tentent aussi de redécouvrir l'histoire populaire des franco-ontariens. Ces groupes n'ignorent pas l'importance des traditions orales. Florian nous explique:

Dans les programmes francophones d'alphabétisation, on comprend la valeur des connaissances que ces adultes ont acquises. Mon père est analphabète et il me raconte des histoires du dur travail qu'il faisait comme bûcheron sur la rivière. Ces renseignements historiques extraits de sa propre expérience me sont plus précieux que les choses que j'ai apprises à l'université. C'est tout aussi important, comme connaissance. Traditionnellement, nous avons toujours eu beaucoup de raconteurs, et nous en avons toujours plusieurs. Ils nous aident à communiquer les valeurs de notre collectivité. Il faut comprendre que les histoires que nous racontons disparaissaient en Ontario, mais nous leur donnons une nouvelle vie. Les gens qui sont venus ici de la France il y a longtemps avaient des histoires qui faisaient partie de leur culture. Les temps ont changé, les gens ont changé, et les histoires aussi. Ces «nouvelles» histoires véhiculaient les valeurs des franco-ontariens. Ti-Jean est un personnage qui figure dians plusieurs histoires. Il es pauvre, et issu d'une famille nombreuse. Il rencontre souvent un roi, symbole du pouvoir, de la richesse et du prestige, et il épouse la princesse, ou bien il assure sa survie en trompant le roi. Ti-Jean représente les bûcherons et les mineurs défavorisés. Il est toujours de bonne humeur malgré sa mauvaise fortune. De plus, il est intelligent. Il coupe du bois, il cherche toujours la bonne aventure, et il cherche à s'affirmer d'une façon ou d'une autre. Il en est de même dans la culture acadienne. Voici une culture qui aime le rire et les farces. Ces histoires sont un genre de littérature, mais jusqu'à récemment, on ne les avait jamais écrites. Ce sont les analphabètes, les apprenants, qui les ont fait survivre. Voilà notre identité en tant que peuple.

Le Regroupement développe actuellement un programme qui encouragera les apprenants à raconter leurs propres histoires, qu'elles soient traditionnelles, personnelles ou collectives.

Dans les ateliers d'alphabétisation du CAP, composés de 5 à 8 étudiants, on discute des événements historiques qui ont formé les francophones de l'Ontario, ainsi que des actualités qu'on a entendu à la radio francophone. Ces sujets servent tous de matériel de lecture, de composition et de discussion. Souvent, on discute également des reportages dans les journaux. Les étudiants discutent de sujets tels que le carnaval d'hiver, et le collège francophone de la région d'Ottawa qui serait construit en face de l'île. On se préoccupe aussi de l'Accord du Lac Meech et de ce qu'il signifie pour le Québec. Pour l'une des classes, le sujet méritait qu'on passe aux gestes. Ils se sont réunis, en tant que groupe, avec leur député pour discuter de l'Accord. Bien que le français soit la langue commune des étudiants, ils sont issues de différents milieux, ont différents buts et différents emplois. Les discussions sont toujours intéressantes et permettent aux apprenants de se renseigner sur les questions qui les touchent en tant que franco-ontariens. Ils servent aussi à améliorer leurs capacités de débat et de raisonnement, puisque les participants ne sont pas toujours d'accord.

L'engagement des apprentis

Selon la philosophie d'éducation populaire du CAP, les apprentis ont un rôle important à jouer dans la prise des décisions par le groupe. Diane nous en offre bien des exemples:

Deux apprentis siègent au Conseil de direction, qui est composé de dix membres, et ils font partie de tous les comités. Ils ont réalisé leur propre émission de télévision — ils l'ont initiée, en ont rédigé les textes, et en ont fait la mise en scène en décembre 1990. Ils son organisé la tournée d'un raconteur du nom de Pépère Cam. Ils ont leur propre comité de financement pour subventionner leurs activités, comme, par exemple, une visite au journal *Le Devoir*, l'assistance au théâtre, et l'achat de matériel didactique pour le groupe.

Les apprenants et leurs familles participent à l'assemblée annuelle générale du CAP, où les apprentis chevronnés du programmes racontent ses débuts et ses réalisations actuelles. Les étudiants sont très bien motivés pour participer de cette façon à l'assemblée.

Conclusion

Selon Diane, l'alphabétisation réussit dans la mesure où il existe un lien entre l'alphabétisme, l'éducation populaire et la fierté francophone:

> Nous voulons leur faire voir leur analphabétisme d'un oeil différent, et comprendre qu'il s'agit vraiment d'un phénomène social qui ne relève pas d'une incapacité personnelle. Pour ce faire, ils doivent comprendre le fonctionnement de la société, et le fait que le pouvoir est surtout entre les mains des élites. Voici le rôle de l'éducation populaire. Ils doivent apprendre et ressentir que le pouvoir appartient à ceux qui ont des connaissances, et que c'est à force de faire valoir leurs opinions qu'ils pourront avoir un mot à dire dans la prise des décisions. Ils doivent croire que leur opinion a de la valeur, et n'est pas sans conséquence. Ils doivent être fiers de leur identité, de leurs origines, et doivent définir leur destin en tant que franco-ontariens. Au CAP, nous les rendons conscients de leur histoire franco-ontarienne, nous leur enseignons comment participer pleinement au groupe, et comment se servir de leurs nouvelles capacités à affirmer leur nouvelle identité à l'extérieur du groupe. C'est un processus lent, car ils doivent modifier leur façon de penser et la façon dont ils se voient.

Questions de discussion

1. *Comment décrire le statut minoritaire des analphabètes francophones? À quels problèmes sont-ils confrontés?*
2. *Quel lien établissez-vous entre vos activités d'alphabétisation et des actions de sensibilisation politique, sociale et culturelle?*
3. *Comment aidez-vous les analphabètes et la population en général à comprendre la situation culturelle des minorités francophones canadiennes?*
4. *Quelle place accordez-vous à la tradition orale, cette "littérature jamais écrite", dans vos groupes d'alphabétisation?*
5. *Comment encouragez-vous les apprenants à ràconter leurs histoires traditionnelles, collectives, personnelles?*
6. *Comment établissez-vous des liens entre l'alphabétisation, l'éducation populaire et la fierté francophone dans votre groupe d'alphabétisation?*

Chapter Five
PROMOTING LANGUAGE, LITERACY AND CULTURE IN AN ARCTIC COMMUNITY[1]

Mary Norton

Place: *Inuktitut Literacy program in Arviat Northwest Territories.*
Participants: *Inuit.*
Issues: 1. *Preservation of language.*
2. *Cultural identity.*

> ...*it's the only thing [we] have left. [Our] way of living is gone, like living out on the land... Language is the only thing that is left and language and culture go hand in hand. If you lose your language, you also lose your culture.*
>
> Joy Suluk

Joy's language, Inuktitut, is one of the few aboriginal languages in Canada which is considered to have a good chance of survival.[2] Yet Joy and others in her community of Arviat, in the Northwest Territories, are aware of changes in their language and of its declining use. At the same time, English is needed for formal education, employment and commerce. So in Arviat, adult literacy programing is directed at promoting Inuktitut as well as supporting English language and literacy development.

This case study is about the Inuktitut program.[3] To prepare the study, I spoke with Stu Mackay, the Adult Educator at the Community Learning Centre in Arviat; Joy Suluk, the Adult Educator trainee; Mark Kalluak and Mary K.

Pameolik, the current and former coordinators of the Inuktitut Literacy program; and Thomas Aniksak and Campbell Atatsiak, students in a part-time adult upgrading program in Arviat. En route to Arviat, I had met with Michael Kusugak, an author, and the Director of Community Programs, Arctic College (Keewatin Region).[4]

Background

The Northwest Territories cover a vast span of land and water. It shares borders with three and a half provinces to the south, and stretches almost the width of Canada at some points. Fifty-eight percent of the territories' 52,000 people are aboriginal, including Dene, Cree and Inuit. In 1990, the Government of the Northwest Territories (GNWT) passed legislation which recognized eight aboriginal languages as official ones, along with English and French.[5]

The NWT is comprised of two large areas, called the Western and Eastern Arctic, and is also divided into six regions. The 22,000 Inuit live mainly in the northern part of the Western Arctic and throughout the Eastern Arctic.[6] Arviat, an Eastern Arctic community, is situated on the western shore of the Hudson Bay.[7]

Traditionally used as a summer camp by local Inuit, Arviat began to develop as a permanent settlement after the Hudson's Bay Company established a trading post in the 1920's. Settlement in the community was also supported by the establishment of Christian missions about the same time. In the 1950's, Arviat and other Eastern Arctic communities began to be affected by post-war northern development. Mining, military defence, telecommunications and related projects initiated economic change, and the provision of federal government services introduced changes in health care, social services and schooling.[8] More and more, Inuit who had been living on the land moved into settlements such as Arviat.

Today, with a population of about 1300, Arviat is a major settlement in the Keewatin Region. Employment in the community is provided by about 30 businesses, three levels of government, and a number of non-profit agencies. However, almost half of the available jobs are part-time, and except in the construction industry, full-time employment is directly related to having higher levels of schooling or further education. Fluency in English is necessary for most jobs, but with Inuit comprising 95% of the population, the ideal employee is bilingual and literate in both English and Inuktitut.

Inuktitut literacy development

Missionaries in the Eastern Arctic adapted Cree syllabics to translate the Bible into Inuktitut, and they used the translations in their mission work.[9] Literacy spread quickly and people began to use syllabics for correspondence and record keeping, as well as for religious purposes. At first, people learned to read and write from the missionaries, but later generations also learned from their parents or taught themselves. Michael Kusugak, who was living in Repulse Bay at the time, recalled:

> ...the front of the [Roman Catholic prayer] book had the Inuktitut alphabet and [we had] calendars that showed the Inuktitut alphabet. I remember lying in bed with my mother, and one of the calendars was hanging on the wall, and she was teaching me to read.

Michael could read and write Inuktitut when he started English school and recalled that he and his classmates used Inuktitut syllabics to record the words of English songs: "If you would read it in Inuktitut it wouldn't make any sense, but all the sounds were there."

Joy Suluk, who grew up in Arviat, taught herself syllabics because "when we were in church everybody would be reading and I couldn't." At about age seven, she "decided I'm going to learn how to read." She studied a syllabics chart and started reading sentences: "If I got stuck I'd go back to the chart, that's how I learned."

Mary K. Pameolik recalled learning to read by following along as her mother or the church minister read Bible stories. Her mother also taught her the syllabics from a chart, and once she learned the syllabics she started reading everything: "At first it was just signs, like at the nursing station: It will be open on..."

Mark Kalluak learned syllabics out of necessity to communicate with his family. He contracted polio when he was about four or five, and spent four years in a Winnipeg hospital:

Everyone else was getting letters from home, and they could read it, and I couldn't, so I decided to learn to read. They had those little syllabics on the back of the Bible, so I learned that, and I wrote my first letter home.

Schooling and English language/literacy development

Christian missions established schools in the Eastern Arctic as early as 1894. However, schools didn't begin to have a major impact in the region until after the Second World War, when the federal government started funding churches to operate boarding schools. Michael recalled starting school in 1954:

...in the fall before the ice came, an airplane would come and land on the sea [at Repulse Bay] and take a whole bunch of us kids, load us on the plane and haul us off to Chesterfield Inlet, about 250 miles south. We'd stay there the whole year until the ice left, around July.

Michael is one of the few Inuit of his generation to finish high school and doing so meant being away from home for many of his school years.Although the federal government started building day schools, the one in Rankin Inlet where Michael's family moved went only to grade five. Michael completed grade six by correspondence then went to Yellow-knife (for grades seven and nine), to Churchill Manitoba, (for grade ten), and finally to Saskatoon where he graduated from high school and started university.

Joy was able to attend school in her own community Arviat, but the school only went as far as grade six. Unable to leave home to continue her schooling, Joy started working as a classroom assistant and continued learning English through various jobs. (Joy has since attained a GED-12, and a Diploma in Adult Education, which she completed by distance education.) However, she explained that there are "a lot of people who can't read and write...They never went to school or they dropped out of school."

Michael and Joy were not allowed to speak Inuktitut in school,and Joy recalled that pupils were punished if they spoke their language. Michael recalled that his first year of school was very hard, because "you don't understand any English at all. You're six years old and you're hauled away from your parents..." And despite the title, "it wasn't much fun learning with Dick and Jane: I didn't have the foggiest idea what fences were... [I'd] never seen trees before, never seen cows or cats... horses or barns."

There have since been a number of changes in the school system. In 1970, responsibility for education was passed from the federal government to the GNWT, and a 1972 Department of Education *Survey of Education* recommended that aboriginal languages be given precedence in schooling. As well, the report recommended that education be controlled locally and that curriculum be relevant to pupils' lifestyles.[10] Community Education Councils were established to oversee the school programs and facilities.

Schooling to higher grades is now more widely available in the community although Arviat students do have to go to Rankin Inlet to complete high school. Inuktitut is one of the languages of instruction for the first four years (k-4) of school and an Inuit teacher training program has prepared teachers to teach in the Inuktitut classes. The education system is aiming to help young people maintain their identity while preparing for the new way of life in their communities.[11] Still, Joy explained, there are young people leaving the school system without full fluency in either English or in Inuktitut.[12]

For example Thomas Aniksak, now in his early 20's, left school when he was in grade six because there were "too many problems. They were teaching too fast." He worked as a carpenter for four years, has taken carpenter training, and was enrolled in basic education upgrading so that he could "have enough training to get a job." Campbell Atasiak, a comtemporary of Thomas, went as far as grade seven. He said that he was attending upgrading because he has forgotten much of the math and reading and language which he had learned in school.

Both men spoke Inuktitut when they started school but Thomas said that, "In school I didn't learn much about Inuktitut." Campbell added, "I don't know how to spell [in] Inuktitut, I don't know the symbols." Thomas said that he would like to be able to read Inuktitut so "I can have my own traditional ways... [so] they won't disappear."

Challenges to Inuktitut language

Although Thomas and Campbell both expressed a need to

learn to read and write in Inuktitut, they said that their oral Inuktitut is fluent. Thomas explained that"I'm an Eskimo, I can speak whatever I want. Whatever I say, I don't even need to learn it." However, older people in the community are concerned that young people are not developing the traditional level of fluency. Even Thomas suggested that some of the younger people need to learn Inuktitut "before they forget the language of the Eskimos…"

Language is changing as young people develop their own terms. Vocabulary related to traditional ways is no longer used and the structure of the language is being simplified. From the point of view of elders, young people's speech is like "baby talk."

Joy explained that "when I talk to my grandmother, I talk the way we talked when we moved here in '57 or '58, but when I talk with my children its different, it's not as sophisticated." Mary K. commented that she has to "correct [her children] so many times a day." She suggested that her children's Inukitut usage reflects the mix of dialects in the community as well as the influence of English.

Michael suggested that"dialectical differences are disappearing at quite a rate because on the radio every day we listen to people from the Baffin," who speak a different dialect. Whereas at one time, people in the Keewatin wouldn't have understood some of the words in the other dialect, "today you take [them] for granted." Mark explained that when,

> …people lived as tribes in the old days [with] one or two people camping out, their language was in no danger of being lost. But when people started moving into the community, people moved from all over. Our language started to get mixed…that's one way that our language is deteriorating.

Although Joy and Michael were not allowed to speak Inuktitut in school, neither of them lost their first language. Both credited their strong command of Inuktitut as the reason they were able to learn English so readily. Joy said that

> when the school opened, I was one of the first to go. What we had going for us [was that] we were already fluent in Inuktitut. Our values and our principles were

already based in Inuktitut, so it was easier for us to learn another language.

Joy and her husband made a commitment to speak only Inuktitut at home, and Joy said that she has never heard her children speak English. However, some children may not be getting a strong grounding in their first language, and Joy suggested that this could have an impact on children's confidence in learning. As well, Mark explained, there are concerns that "even though they're trying very hard to teach Inuktitut in schools, the Inuit teachers are not that fluent."

Challenges to Inuktitut literacy

Forty years ago, people learned to read and write Inuktitut by reading along in the Bible, by studying syllabics, and by using the newly acquired literacy. Today, it seems, Inuktitut literacy instruction has been left to the schools, a reflection of what has happened generally regarding children's education. Mark explained that:

> All they've known for the last ten years is the school system that their children go through day after day. Our way of teaching was living on the land, teaching our daughters and sons how to behave among people, how to excel, to be good hunters, to be good sewers...All those kind of values, they're gone. Children believe in other values now.

As well, Joy explained, the schools and the workplace supports English language use and development, rather than Inuktitut.

> Everything supports English...look at the workplace. Even though Inuktitut was declared one of the official languages...all the materials support English, the education supports English.

Legislation requires that GNWT materials be translated, but Michael, who worked as a translator, wondered whether anyone was going to read "99.9%" of what he translated. Further, Mark and Mary K. both explained that if they have a choice of reading Inuktitut or English materials at a meeting, they will usually choose the English version. They said that they can scan the English more easily...they are used to reading English, and it's harder to pick out key words when scanning syllabic symbols.

What is needed, Michael suggested, are more resources that people would read for enjoyment. "I write books", he said, "and I would dearly love to be able to write them in Inuktitut." However, the small audience for Inuktitut makes commercial publication almost unviable. As an example, the royalties from sales of the Inuktitut version of one of his books amounted to less than one tenth of the royalties from sales of the English version.[13]

Developing the Inuktitut literacy program

The Community Learning Centre was started in the early 1970's as part of a territory-wide move to provide upgrading and employment training for adults. The centre is now affiliated with the recently formed Arctic College, but continues to take direction from an elected Community Education Council (CEC) and a Community Training Advisory Committee (CTAC).[14]

Although English literacy development has been a component of basic education and employment preparation courses, the CEC and the CTAC identified literacy as the "number one training need for Arviat." The committees "directed the Community Learning Centre to encourage awareness of literacy and to work towards its attainment."[15] In 1989 the CLC initiated an Inuktitut and English Literacy project called Partners in Learning. Part-time coordinators were hired to develop the English and Inuktitut aspects of the project.

One of the coordinators' initial tasks was to create interest in the project. Mary K., who coordinated the Inuktitut program for the first year, described how she and the English coordinator worked at promoting awareness through a weekly radio show:

> We would take short stories or articles we thought were interesting, copy them and distribute them at places where people would pick them up and...We would read them out on Tuesday night and if people wanted to read along they could.We knew people were picking

them up because they were gone the next day.

Although interest in English literacy development emerged, there was limited response to the call for Inuktitut tutors and few people turned out for an Inuktitut class which was offered. Joy suggested that although the "[Inuktitut] program was considered important, there was no initial interest, maybe because people are confident in their abilities." Joy said that they started to realize that reading and writing in Inuktitut was not the place to start:

> I guess we thought about reading and writing...we thought that's what the community needed. People were interested, but when we actually offered the course one or two people came, so we knew that wasn't working.

The English component of the literacy program has developed as a tutor based mode and it was initially thought that the Inuktitut program would develop in the same way. Mary K. recalls that although there were manuals for English literacy tutoring, there were no resources for teaching Inuktitut. She attended training for English tutors and adapted approaches for Inuktitut. But on reflection, Stu suggested, they had tried to impose an English literacy programing model to address Inuktitut needs, with rather frustrating results. In the new approach, Mary K. began to promote language awareness as a base for literacy development. As Joy explained, "we had to change our approach. What we have today is not what we started out with."

Promoting language and culture

Mary K. introduced an Inuktitut version of "Balderdash" on the radio. Each week, she broadcasted old Inuktitut words, and people were invited to phone in their definitions. Mark recalled that even some older people commented that they hadn't realized they had forgotten some of the old words. This project generated a good deal of interest.

Mark described two activities which are being planned to build on this interest. One is to gather fluent Inuktitut speakers together so they can carry on conversations with others. In this way old vocabulary can be highlighted and language use can be corrected. The other, Mark explained, is to

> ...build an igloo [which the elders can use] for what-
> ever they want to do...cooking, fixing skins, drum
> dances, story telling...Having an igloo and using it
> year round will bring back many of the memories and
> the knowledge that we don't even think about because
> we're so modern.

Joy explained that while the activities planned for the igloo "don't involve reading and writing" they do involve language, and language and culture, you can't separate them. If we make our culture interesting, there will be more interest in our language too."

There is also a need Mark explained, to get elders' "stories in printed form [so they] will be available instead of being told and forgotten." Documenting stories and information is also a way to develop a collection of local Inuktitut resources. Mary K. said that elders had stressed the need for printed resource materials and stories, and she added that, "when I first started...there were very little reading materials." When Mark took over the role of Inuktitut coordinator, his first task was an elders' syllabic writing project.

Mark has worked as an interpreter and translator for many years, so he started by "doing what I do best...going around, visiting the elders [and] recording what they have to say." He transcribed the stories, songs and rhymes which he collected and translated them into English as well. These materials are available for the community.

The involvement of elders has become a key component of the Inuktitut program. Mary K. said that the elders are the best resource people in Inuktitut. She suggested that she had some difficulties developing the program and getting started because she "didn't actually start meeting them until later." Her advice to others starting aboriginal language programs is to "go to the elders right away."

Concluding comments

Arviat and other Eastern Arctic communities have experienced massive changes in fewer than forty years. Overnight, as Joy said, parents lost control of their children's education.

Younger people are not developing Inuktitut literacy the way their parents did, and their oral language use is declining as well.

The Arviat Community Education Committee and the Community Learning Centre have taken back responsibility for Inuktitut development, and are turning to traditional ways to promote language and cultural awareness. At the same time, as Joy said, "we have to realize that we are not living in the past, we are different." If Inuktitut is to be maintained and used, it has to "have all the support that English has."

Mark said that if the language is lost, then the history will be lost. And this could happen soon, because there are not enough people promoting Inuktitut. Mark's view is that:

> ...the legislative assembly has told us that the Inuktitut language as well as other languages are recognized. To support that, the government should fund language development. [They should] give it more funds to operate and to promote it, so it is used...put signs up in Inuktitut, use Inuktitut more in the workplace, and look for people who can use their own language and function and work among people. That way people will begin to see [that they can] be part of their own language.

Mark ended by saying that "I'm not trying to say do away with English or French, I'm just saying if they really mean that, give us a chance to work."

Notes

1. The Government of the Northwest Territories requires that all research in the territories be done under licence from the Science Institute of the NWT. Prior to completing the research for this report, I was granted a 1991 Scientific Research Licence, No. 11009.

2. In its fourth report (December, 1990) The Standing Committee on Aboriginal Affairs cites information on aboriginal language speakers which was gathered by the Department of the Secretary of State. Of 53 aboriginal languages listed

in this information, 43, or 81%, are considered to be on the verge of extinction, seven are considered "endangered" and only three are thought to have "excellent chances of survival." These three are Cree (55,000 speakers in a population of 92,875), Ojibway (30,000 speakers in a population of 62,545) and Inuktitut (16,000 speakers in a population of 22,000).

3. Another case study in this report, *Linking Literacy and Health: A Popular Education Approach*, describes one of the English literacy projects in Arviat.

4. In preparation for my visit to Arviat, I also met with Elizabeth Biscaye, the Assistant Deputy Minister of Culture and Communications. Ms Biscaye outlined some of the challenges to aboriginal language maintenance and literacy development in the NWT. I also spoke with Jean Reston, the Consultant, Adult Education, with the Department of Education, who provided background about the Arctic College system and adult literacy provision.

5. The official languages include five Dene languages (Chipewyan, Dogrib, Gwichin, North and South Slave) Cree and Inuktitut. Variations of Inuktitut include Inuvialuktun and Inuinnaqktun.

6. The Inuit in the Western Arctic include the following groups: Inuvaluit, Inuinnait, and Netsilingomuit.

7. The community has also been called Eskimo Point, but Arviat is the preferred Inuktitut name.

8. Spread of disease and food shortages in the north were also a factor in the settlement of some communities. As Stu Mackay explained, "starvation and disease became a major news event and the subsequent public outcry forced the Federal Government to respond to the health crisis. Re-location of families to centralized distribution points for food, shelter and medical aid led to the development of the settlements."

9. Missionaries in the Western Arctic used Roman orthography to write Inuktitut or its variations. Western Arctic Inuit continue to use this orthography for their writing.

10. Patterson, D. The Challenge to Northern Education. Inuktitut. Volume 63, Summer 1986. A later *Report of the Task Force on Aboriginal Languages* (GNWT, 1986), noted that these recommendations "marked a major change in attitude towards aboriginal languages. However, it has never been fully

implemented in schools in the Northwest Territories." According to Lyn Fogwell the GNWT Literacy Program Manager, "real change didn't occur until the 1980's, and then only in the Eastern Arctic."

11. Shouldice, M. Making Education Work for Inuit in the Modern World. *Inuktitut*, Summer 1986, Volume 63.

12. In the above cited article, Mr. Shouldice explained that "the number of young people who complete high school is low and few have gone on to university. In some communities many students drop out of school before completing grade 9 [and] these young people unfortunately often have poor communication skills in Inuktitut as well as English."

13. *A Promise is a Promise*, published in English and Inuktitut, tells a story about the Quallupillut who live under the sea and grab children who aren't with their parents. Michael collaborated with Robert Munsch to write the English copy, and both versions are published by Annick Press (Toronto, 1988).

14. The GNWT Department of Education began to provide for adult education in the territories by establishing community Adult Education Centres. Adult educators worked with local community committees to plan and deliver adult programs, including basic education, employment preparation courses and other courses of interest to the community.

The Arctic Vocational Training Centre opened in Fort Smith in the late 1960's, also under the auspices of the Department of Education to provide trades training. The range of courses offered by the AVCT were expanded during the 1970's and in the early 1980's, the centre was renamed Thebacha College. The 1985 Colleges Act initiated the formation of Arctic College, with Thebacha as a campus. Other campuses have since been developed in the six NWT regions, and responsibility for the Adult Education Centres has been transferred to Arctic College. The Adult Education Centres continue to provide adult upgrading and pre-employment training, while the college campuses provide trades training and other courses for the region.

15. Mackay, S. Arviat Literacy Project: Built Upon Strength from Within and Help from Without. *Arctic College Dialogue* Volume 4 number 6. November 1990.

Discussion Questions

1. How can an educational program accommodate the needs of both minority and dominant language learning?
2. Give examples of how a dominant culture can threaten the continuation of a minority cultural group.
3. In what ways does "full fluency" in one language assist the learning of second language?
4. What contribution can older people play in helping to preserve the culture of a minority group?
5. What can be done to increase community interest in cultural education programs?

CASE STUDIES ON WORKPLACE LITERACY

INTRODUCTION

Maurice C. Taylor

The growing phenomenon: the job skills gap

Recently in Canada the term workforce literacy has been receiving considerable attention. This activity which is sometimes referred to as the basic skills needed to function effectively in the economy, has become a concern for human resource executives, union personnel, training and development managers and others in private and public organizations throughout Canada. As suggested by the term, it pertains to the other half of the adult literacy population specifically those workers who have seriously limited basic skills. With the changing workplace now requiring a different type of labour force than in the past, literacy advocacy groups are now challenged by this new phenomenon — the job skills gap or the mismatch between job demands and worker skills.

Understanding solutions to this national problem means in part, understanding the reasons why our workplace is changing. One factor affecting this change is that fewer young people are now entering the world of work which means that over the next decade older Canadians will make up a larger part of the labour market. Another trend facing the economy is the growth of the service sector. Community, business and personal services are now the main sources of job opportunities.

These employment shifts coupled with the fact that knowledge has become a very important national resource have added their own dimensions to the changing economy. Along with these trends, the labour force is also experiencing technological change. In almost every Canadian industry some type of automation has been introduced. As well, with the increased use of technologies in such areas as robotics and statistical control procedures, more sophisticated skills and knowledge will be required. It is now evident that these various changes and conditions in the economy are calling for workers with a higher and broader range of skills in almost every job.

The need for new training strategies.

As a result of these changes new training strategies such as workplace literacy programs are now being introduced by employers and employees as opportunities to learn the necessary skills required for fuller participation in work life. This section describes how some organizations have initiated partnerships to bridge education and training with a new emphasis on basic skills training. Most experts in this field would agree that workplace literacy requires a knowledge of the world of work and an understanding of how basic skills instruction relates to the unique characteristics of the workplace.

As illustrated by the following case studies, these two characteristics are vital ingredients for the planning of any such initiative. As well, the reader will note that there also seems to be a common set of guiding principles for developing and implementing a workplace literacy program.

Knowing the structure of the organization

For practitioners who have already determined a readiness in the business community for initiating a workplace literacy intervention, the first important principle is related to knowing the structure of the organization which will be collaborating in the program. It is essential to become aware of the chain of command, the role of unions, the commitment of the organization to employees, the overall goals of the organization and whether or not there are internal or external conflicts within the company. All of this foundational information will provide an awareness of the organizational process which is at the heart of any basic skills training program.

As pointed out in the following case studies, this organizational process is unique to each workplace. For example, in the Vancouver Municipal Workplace Language Training Program, the Equal Employment Opportunities Committee was the guiding structure which supported the overall development of the initiative whereas in the Weston Bakery program a Reclassification and a Manpower Adaptability Committee provided the thrust and direction for the literacy training. In a slightly different basic skills program called Occupational Knowledge, which is for youth between the ages of 18-24, it was the Employment Liaison Worker who developed the partnerships with local employers. Becoming aware of the various companies and organizations and their specific responsibilities and tasks helped the worker to match trainee interests with job placements.

As a rule of thumb, getting to know the organizational process and identifying support and potential barriers seems to be a fundamental principle in the development of a workplace literacy intervention.

Conducting a situational analysis

A second important principle for developing a workplace program is understanding the rationale for conducting a situational analysis. This entails an examination of the perceived needs of an organization to determine if the problems have educational solutions and if the educational solutions have a literacy component. In the case of the Weston Bakery program both the company and committee structures had determined that to introduce the new technology, a pre-training component was required which included basic skills in literacy and numeracy. In the Vancouver language program, based on a needs assessment of middle managers, union representatives and previous unsuccessful experiences, it was determined to offer integrated

English Second Language (ESL) and literacy training.

As well, instructors at Learnex which operates out of the Saint John Learning Exchange also conducted needs assessments for interested companies. This information provided the foundation for their ongoing program development in basic skills training. Practitioners will most likely find that for each workplace a different type of situational analysis will be required. However the information from this examination of the organization provides a clearly marked road map for guiding the program development. As can be seen from the case studies, by conducting a needs assessment both the climate and resources of the organization become apparent.

Negotiating to provide literacy services

Thirdly, any effective workplace intervention involves negotiation and a contract with the organization to provide the literacy services. Deciding on who the partners are, the services to be offered, the content of the program, participation details, program structure and schedule, resource commitment, assessment strategy, and evaluation procedures are all important components of a program that require some type of contractual agreement.

The reader will find in the following descriptions an interesting mix of program features, some of which were negotiated and some of which were not. After an agreement has been made to proceed, the actual program planning can begin. As part of the planning strategy, it is important to consider a program that meets the need of the organization and at the same time is perceived by participants to be worthwhile. By soliciting input from management, labour, trainers and workers, as was the case in the following programs, an agenda for partnership building can be initiated at this early stage and further developed throughout the intervention.

The circular process of effective evaluation

A final principle worthy of consideration in developing and implementing basic skills training is the continuous, circular process of an effective program evaluation. This exercise should not be at the end of program planning but actually be an integral part of it. Measuring the effectiveness of a workplace literacy program should involve thinking through some of the following steps:

- What are the goals of the program?
- What objectives will be set to reach those program goals?
- What testing procedures will be used?
- What is the time line of these goals?
- Who will be involved with the evaluation, and how will the results of the evaluation be used?

In the following descriptions the reader will observe numerous attempts to incorporate some of these strategies. As is often the case though, stakeholders in a program will have very diverse opinions about the purposes for evaluation. However, a well articulated strategy helps lay the groundwork for longer ranged programing.

Chapter One
COLLABORATION IN WORKPLACE LITERACY

Richard Darville

Place: *Municipal Workplace Language Training Program in Vancouver, British Columbia.*
Participants: *Program staff, students and company personnel.*
Issue: *Management and unions working together in basic skills training.*

Workplace literacy programs have been actively promoted in British Columbia for several years. There have been public panel discussions as well as a one-day conference on workplace literacy. An official of the Business Council of B.C. has been active in literacy advocacy and discussions in trade union circles are increasingly intensive. The Council of Forest Industries and the International Woodworkers of America have studied language difficulties in provincial sawmills and the B.C. Federation of Labour is examining workplace literacy needs and program possibilities. Nevertheless, workplace programs have only slowly been organized in B.C.

Literacy advocates often feel that workplace literacy raises sensitive issues, especially in a province with a history of intense labour-management antagonism. Even raising the literacy issue may threaten workers with blocked advancement or even dismissal. Furthermore there are difficult questions of control over curriculum, recruitment and reporting. In addition training for workers is limited and the politics involved are difficult in Canada as a whole, not only in B.C. (Davis, Huot and others 1989 and Muszynski and Wolfe 1989).

This case study aims to document how workplace literacy programs can be made to work, and how circumstances and forces promote or hinder them. We look at the issue of collaboration between management and unions in workplace literacy,in conjunction with questions of workplace literacy needs analysis and recruitment. We also examine this issue within the organization of the Municipal Workplace Language Training Program, operated under the auspices of the Equal Employment Opportunities Program (EEO) of the City of Vancouver. The story told here is largely based on the information and even the words of the EEO officer most concerned with the program, and the program's chief teacher. Even when the text is not sprinkled with quotation marks, the case studies should be read together. (For interesting accounts of other workplace programs (see Añorve 1989; and Levine, 1991).

Background

There are many immigrants and speakers of English as a second language in Vancouver. In the Vancouver population as a whole, 26% are visible minorities. Of the roughly 8000 employees of the City of Vancouver, about one in five speak English as a second language. Within the city government, there is special attention to problems that arise between immigrants and minorities, as well as women, and the dominant groups in Canadian society. The city's Equal Employment Opportunities program has a mandate to find and to reduce institutional racism and sexism, and racial and sexual harassment. This includes, among other matters, people's access to city employment, and to promotions. The EEO is also concerned with the equitable provision of services for the public. It is often seen throughout the city government as "the fixer" for racial, cultural and language problems. Its general philosophy is to work with members of cultural and linguistic minorities,and listen to how they identify problems and envision solutions. To fit the EEO mandate, literacy and language ability determine access.

EEO officials recognize "a strong political commitment to equity in the city," under mayors of the 1980s and from the city manager. There's a management belief that fairness is in everybody's best interest. This support is key in EEO efforts, and it gives leeway for experimentation in identifying and addressing problems.

Getting started

The beginning of the City of Vancouver Workplace Language Program can be seen in phone calls and reports to EEO, about language difficulties. For example:

> A superintendent of one department phoned in to say that many of the Indo-Canadian men that worked under him had failed a brake test, and couldn't become truck drivers. Could somebody come and teach the brake test? (Superintendents are under some pressure to see minority promotions).

> In another department, one woman (Canadian-born, with two years of community college) had six times failed a personnel exam which was a standardized language skill test, couldn't get permanent status, and never built up any seniority. Yet she trained other people in her worksite.

> In another department, workers were writing documents with legal implications for the city, and supervisors were worried about the workers' language skills. In another situation, a clerical worker didn't take phone messages adequately. In both cases there were concerns about union conflicts if workers were let go.

> An Italian foreman had ordered seven yards of cement, about one truckload, for the next morning's job on the seawall. He was puzzled in the morning to find ten trucks parked and waiting. This is what had happened: he spoke in the manner of many Italians who have learned English, adding vowel sounds to the ends of words. So his "seven" came out more like "sevenee." It was heard as "seventy" on the other end of the phone. Another use was found for the extra cement.

The accumulation of workplace language and literacy trouble stories defined a problem. The mandate of the Equal

Employment Opportunities office defined who might attempt to address it. In mid-1989, EEO official Norma Jean McLaren was instructed to set up a program, in response to departmental demands.

There had been two earlier efforts to set up a language and literacy program. One effort involved meetings with the local community college, whose management said students could be referred to their regular, ongoing programs. But the EEO wanted something specifically related to the workplace. A second effort saw students sent to a private training company with computer-assisted instruction, using the IBM PALS program. Students found the computerized training patronizing, and made comments like "I'm not a child and don't want to deal with cartoons;" or simply, "This isn't what I wanted." It was clear that a computer-based program, operated away from the worksite, wasn't the program needed. There had also been an earlier experience with a specific air brake curriculum at a community college; workers had not gone.

Norma Jean McLaren now saw that she needed to follow her gut instincts, towards what she later came to call "flexible" and "learner-centred" programing. The EEO drafted a call for proposals for conducting a needs assessment, and developing and implementing a learner-centred workplace language and literacy program.

The successful proposal was submitted by the Invergarry Learning Centre, a school board-sponsored, community-oriented program in the working-class suburb of Surrey. The Invergarry program publishes the widely circulated magazine of student writing, *Voice*, and it had experience conducting an ESL literacy course and job-creation project for immigrant women who were experienced seamstresses. The Invergarry program shared the EEO view that second-language issues should not be excluded from the treatment of "literacy." A teacher-consultant from the Invergarry program, Gary Pharness, had become the chief teacher in the city program which has now run for three complete sessions. Support for the program has come from several sources. The City of Vancouver budgets $80,000 a year for employee release time, and provides EEO staff time. In different sessions, funding has been provided by the Ministry of Advanced Education, Training and Technology; a local school board; and the province's Open Learning Agency.

Workplace literacy needs assessment

In the five-week needs assessment, the project consultant and EEO staff contacted middle management designated to deal with the language program, in eleven city departments. The departments anticipated to have the greatest needs were Housing and Properties, which included building service workers, long-term care workers, and janitors; Health, with clerical workers and medical and dental assistants; Licensing and Inspection, again with many clerical workers; and Engineering, where most "outside workers" are situated. The Park Board and the Vancouver Public Library were contacted as well. There were also contacts with unions, and some with individual workers, but it was felt that workers' views which favoured a non computer-based program and small classes, were already known from evaluations of earlier programing efforts. With limited time for needs assessment, the focus was on managers.

There were two aspects of the needs assessment. One focused on learning what needs and what people the program could serve. The other focused on promoting the program, especially with managers and supervisors. Both these processes worked through hearing stories, and turning them into anecdotes to be repeated which often provoked others to reflect on their experience. Needs assessment brought many stories to light like those described above. There were, for example, stories of good clerical workers who couldn't do all facets of their jobs, such as dealing with the public on the phone or over the counter; or dicta-typists whose work required many corrections because they weren't hearing the inflections in words.

Needs assessment was not a simple matter of asking managers what skills they wanted workers to have. It was never said that the program would increase productivity. Some managers did ask how job tasks would be transposed into a formally defined process of curriculum, instruction and assessment. The response was, "That's not how it works." Managers were urged to accept that in the long run it's important for workers to decide what to study. An effective study process begins in open-ended speaking, writing and reading, and brings in specific workplace materials when learners decide to bring them. There was however, an agreement with managers and supervisors to discuss halfway through each session, how the program was going and what workplace materials it might be helpful to introduce.

In the program promotion process there were explicit discussions with managers and supervisors of "What's in it for you?" Health and safety issues were raised, especially with Housing and Engineering. Supervisory responsibility for errors that might arise from workers' language difficulties were discussed. As well the detrimental effects on the working atmosphere of the isolation of workers in ethnic ghettoes was considered.

The needs assessment was completed in the fall of 1989. It called for classes to meet six hours a week, with teacher-student ratios possibly as low as one to five. Workers could be involved in the program one-half on city time and one-half on their own for one 12-week session; then one-quarter on city time and three-quarters on their own for another session; and thereafter entirely on their own time. Classes would be held at the centrally-located City Hall, at the Trout Lake Community Centre in the east end, and at the Manitoba Yards in south Vancouver, the central facility for the city Engineering department. The program would involve 100 students a year.

The unions that organize city employees first responded to the program proposal with uneasiness about what management wanted. After some discussion and reassurance that management was willing not to direct curriculum, and that they would receive no evaluations of individuals, unions "concurred" with the program. This term was used within the city administrative process to indicate no opposition. "Concurrence" changed to active involvement at a later date.

The program's curricular autonomy has been important in two ways. It is essential for the program's learner-centred teaching. But also in practice, the autonomy of the program was the necessary basis for collaboration between management and labour.

Recruitment

As literacy workers know, literacy programs always address inequalities in language skill and opportunity to use language. These inequalities exist in larger social contexts. They are often intertwined with gender and ethnic relations. Within workplaces, these inequalities are embedded in specific workplace hierarchies. To promote literacy is to struggle against these inequalities. Recruitment to literacy programs should be understood in this broad context.

To describe recruitment within the city of Vancouver requires looking again at the EEO. The EEO's mandate to reduce institutional racism and sexism commits it to aspects of the struggle against inequalities. In this effort it forms a central part of an informal network in the city government. Some individuals in this network have come to the city with commitments against inequality. Others are graduates of a central EEO training program, the Kingswood Training Model which offers intensive week-long residential workshops for middle and upper management.

The workshops, which have been attended by individuals from all city departments and boards, deal with multiculturalism and employment equity. At the end of the workshops, managers contract with EEO regarding changes in their areas of responsibility. Graduates often become reflective about cross-cultural relations, language and people's abilities, and many work supportively with the EEO.

Initial recruitment efforts focused on areas of the city government where managers were expected to be advocates of the language program. Nine-tenths were graduates of the Kingswood program. This was done within a long-range strategy of establishing selected bases for the program and its credibility before moving on to other areas. Recruitment has worked best where there was direct contact between the language program and supervisors who know the individual workers.

Consider just one example. A woman we can call Lois, who worked as a Library Assistant 1 ("the bottom of the heap," as she said) came to the program. She explained that her supervisor, a woman two years from retirement, who was like a mother to her, sent her to the program so that she would be able to keep her job in the library.

There are of course people who see language and literacy inequalities as natural, and the struggle against them as troublesome. For example, there is some ongoing resistance to the very idea of education for manual labourers. Some say things like, "It's better for the Italians to be on the streets anyhow." Although the vast majority of supervisors have been supportive, a few obstructed recruitment. They kept papers on their desks for months, or said, "None of you guys want to go back to school, do you?" "We've got one guy from here going there already, it would be really hard to send somebody else." "Sure you can go, you'll just have to make up your time later on."

The program staff recognize that supervisors who refer students need ongoing support and encouragement, since they may be under pressure, for example if it takes longer to get jobs done because workers are away studying. Similarly, in class there is talk with students about asserting the right to study and about handling kidding by other workers.

Emerging recruitment issues

As the program matures, certain problems in the recruitment effort have become clear, and the organization of the effort for recruitment is changing. Although there isn't precise data on the number of people referred by supervisors, and the number who come independently, it is clear that most students have come through supervisor referrals. The number coming independently increased slowly in the second and third sessions, as people responded to posted notices, or heard about the program through worker-to-worker communications.

In the third session, enrollment was somewhat down, perhaps because there was less EEO staff time available than before for recruitment work. In the fourth session, however, enrollment was high again as more people saw notices on bulletin boards and in union newsletters and as there was increased communication about the program through union counsellors, shop stewards, and health and safety officers.

Another problem which has only become clear with experience, is that nine students out of ten have been second-language speakers of English. Those operating the program expect that increased union involvement, along with word-of-mouth recruitment by program graduates, will bring more Canadian-born students and native speakers of English. It appears that this shift began to occur, in the fourth session.

Developing collaboration, and the program as a model

The EEO, through its affiliated organization — the Hastings Institute, and the Canadian Union of Public Employees

(CUPE) — which represents the city's "outside workers," have come together as partners with a shared intention to expand workplace literacy and language programing. They are working to develop a program that can be made available to other employers and employees. CUPE along with the B.C. Federation of Labour will help to identify possible sites. The Hastings Institute will work with employers and proposed teachers in implementing programs.

Within both these organizations, there have already been changes and learning.Likewise the forms of collaboration are already changing. EEO has asked City Council to approve a policy that language development is an ongoing concern. That approval has been secured and the program is now "permanent."

CUPE now clearly perceives the program as a way to serve workers' interests,for example in gaining access to the seniority system. CUPE support has also been stimulated by the interest in literacy of the Canadian Labour Congress and the B.C. Federation of Labour. The union now dedicates staff time to program publicity, and provides a language program space away from the worksite. In this space there is a two-hour-a-week service that assists workers in dealing with forms and complaints and an off-site class for workers who do not want management to know of their language problems.

New questions will certainly arise as the program is developed in other settings. Consider here just one. Many workplaces have less amicable labour-management relations than the city of Vancouver, and most workplaces do not have an internal unit like EEO, which stands somewhat apart from both management and labour, while promoting both management interests in clear communication and workers' interests in self-development, job security and advancement. Specific organizational forms, to provide the program autonomy that is necessary for collaboration will have to be devised in each organizational setting.

Concluding comments

This case study of collaboration in a workplace language and literacy program has told at least a part of one program's story. The case study reflects the time constraints of its production — a few days for interviews, classroom observations, and reviewing documents, a few more days for analyzing interviews, and few more days for writing.

Almost everything in this case study I have learned from the EEO official most concerned, the teacher who operates the program on a day-to-day basis, and a number of students. The write-up tells the program's story largely as it appears to them. It would have been easy to spend a month, interviewing others in the EEO office and the city management, trade union officials, administrators in other sponsoring organizations, more students in the program, workers who didn't come to the program or even know about it, leaders and members of various community ethnic organizations, and so on. The write-up could have been a very much richer and denser description.

As noted at the outset, this case study aims to contribute to the documentation of ways that workplace literacy programs can be made to work, and of the circumstances and forces that promote or hinder them. The study has described processes that could be explored in thematic analyses of a number of workplace literacy programs. For example, any workplace program will involve an organizational process that puts together funding, physical space, staff time, and information flow. It will involve an understanding that promoting literacy is a goal that can be shared by the diverse interests at play in a workplace setting, without suppressing their differences. These organizational processes and these understandings need not always be the same.

> Here, the telling and exchange of workplace language trouble stories helped provoke the reflection that led to the program. Must it always?

> Here, the program has operated through an internal equal opportunities unit with a mandate that encompasses language and literacy activities. The program has been supported by a management belief that visible fairness is in everybody's interest, and by pressures for minority hiring and advancement. Under what other auspices and what other pressures can programs be established?

> Here, an equal opportunities unit has secured the program autonomy that allows for labour-management

collaboration, and for a flexible response to workers' needs. How else can this program autonomy been secured?

That such questions arise demonstrates the careful analysis and planning in one remarkable effort in workplace programing.

Discussion Questions

1. What are some of the signals of a need for workplace literacy training in your community?
2. How could you tailor-make a needs assessment for an organization or company experiencing literacy problems in your community?
3. What are the ingredients for a successful recruitment strategy?
4. Program autonomy that is necessary for collaboration will have to be devised in each organizational setting. Discuss.
5. If you were going to document an existing workplace literacy program, what major section headings would you use in the report?

Chapter Two

S'ALPHABÉTISER
EN MILIEU DE TRAVAIL

Hélène Blais

Lieu: *La Compagnie Weston, Longueil Quebec*
Participants: *La Commission scolaire régionale Chambly et les travaileurs de chez Weston.*
Thème: *La sensibilisation de tous les partenaires a un contexte de formation.*

Le pain joue tant de rôles! Nous avons appris à reconnaître, dans le pain, un instrument de la communauté des hommes, à cause du pain à rompre ensemble. Nous avons appris à recommaître, dans le pain, l'image de la grandeur du travail, à cause du pain à gagner à la sueur du front [...] La saveur du pain partagé n'a point d'égale.

Antoine de Saint-Exupéry, *Pilote de guerre*,
Paris, Gallimard, 1948 «Blanche»).

Quelques données historiques

Dès 1984, les employés de chez Weston, en particulier ceux affectés à la production des pains — on parle icic de 298 employés sur 670 — ont été aiguillés sur l'instauration d'une nouvelle usine munie d'équipements à la fine pointe de la technologie. Comme ce changement peut provoquer des coupures de postes, un comité de reclassement est chargé d'élaborer un jugement diagnostique de la situation. Ce comité en arrive à la conclusion que 50% des employés affectés au secteur de la production pourraient perdre leur emploi : boulangers, contremaîtres, travilleurs manuels, travailleurs spécialisés (pétrin, four), travailleurs affectés à la réception des matières premières, à l'emballage des pains dans les sacs, à la salubrité et à l'expédition.

En 1988, les représentants syndicaux font appel aux services d'organismes spécialisés en alphabétisation des adultes et en informatique dans le cadre d'un projet intitulé ABC INFO. On procède ainsi pour que les employés dont les postes sont les plus touchés par le déménagement dans d'autres locaux soient en mesure de se réorienter professionnellement, de rafraîchir leurs connaissances ou de négocier le virage technologique.

En février 1989, la boulangerie Weston annonce officiellement qu'elle changera de lieux et modernisera ses équipements. Pour faire en sorte que les perturbations dues au déménagement de la boulangerie Weston entraînent les décisions administratives les plus impartiales, un comité d'adaptation de la main d'oeuvre (CAMO) voit le jour au sein de la compagnie pour prendre les meilleures décisions possibles. La compagnie Weston requiert alors les services de la Commission scolaire régionale (CSR) Chambly pour qu'elle prenne en charge des activités de préformation, c'est-à-dire des cours de français et de mathématiques d'appoint, un rafraîchissement des connaissances générales et une révision générale de base. La CSR Chambly offre des services d'alphabétisation depuis 1976 et de la formation sur mesure en entreprise depuis 1987.

Les travailleurs s'inscrivent sur une base volontaire aux activités d'alphabétisation sur leur lieu de travail, afin de contrer un futur critère de sélection du personnel : posséder un diplôme d'études secondaires. Ce critère, pris au pied de la lettre, aurait éliminé du jour au lendemain une bonne partie des employés disposant en moyenne de 15 ans d'ancienneté.

Distribution des rôles

Le partenaire éducatif : la CSR Chambly

La CSR Chambly a pour mandat d'offrir une formation-éclair de 24 heures en mathématiques (à raison de 6 heures par semaine pendant 4 semaines) et de 42 heures en français (à raison de 6 heures par semaine pendant 7 semaines). Après avoir visité les lieux et déterminé les besoins de formation, les «responsable-matière» administrent des tests-maison pour évaluer les connaissances de 70 travailleurs en lecture et en mathématiques :

> compréhension de consignes, déchiffrage des commands propres au fonctionnement des nouvelles machines avec lesquelles les employés auraient à travailler, décodage des informations liées à la sécurité dans l'usine;

> quatre opérations de base, compréhension du système métrique, des fractions décimales, lecture d'un graphique, de plans, d'un talon de chèque de paye, calcul du cumul des heures de travail.

À partir de besoins précis, de restrictions quant au nombre d'heures disponibles, la CSR Chambly bâtit un programme de formation en tenant compte des exigences de la compagnie Weston et de l'évaluation des connaissances des travailleurs. Il a toujours été très clair que cette évaluation des connaissances des travailleurs ne serait jamais remise entre les mains de l'employeur par souci d'équité et pour s'assurer qu'elle ne puisse en aucun cas porter préjudice aux employés qui décideraient de «s'afficher» comme ayant besoin d'alphabétisation. On procède ensuite à l'engagement des formatrices en leur proposant de travailler en équipe.

Le partenaire industriel : la compagnie Weston

En plus d'une liste d'objectifs à atteindre pour que ses employés puissent être capables d'intégrer les cours de formation technique, la boulangerie Weston fournit les locaux nécessaires aux activités d'alphabétisation sur les lieux de travail, le matériel et l'équipement essentiels au bon fonctionnement des cours, par exemple, l'accès aux services de photocopie.

La consultante en gestion de la formation

Conseillère dans le dossier, la consultante en gestion de la formation collabore à l'élaboration du plan de la «préformation». Cette préformation sera suivie d'une sensibilisation au monde de l'informatique, d'une durée de quinze heures et assumée par un formateur du Cégep Édouard-Montpetit. Les employés seront alors en mesure d'aborder la formation technique proprement dite.

Au moyen d'interviews individuelles, la consultante jauge les besoins des travailleurs n'ayant pas atteint la scolarité d'une première, deuxième ou troisième secondaire. Environ 84 personnes sont conviées. Quatorze personnes qui auraient eu le plus besoin de services d'alphabétisation n'ont pas suivi la formation pour des raisons d'ancienneté, d'ententes avec l'employeur quant à des préretraites anticipées.

Ces entrevues ont pour objectif principal de mesurer les connaissances des employés : raisonnement mathématique, opérations mathématiques de base, lecture de plan, déchiffrage de graphiques, familiarité avec la technologie générale, liée à la vie quotidienne. On pense ici, entre autres, à l'utilisation d'une calculatrice électronique, à la fréquentation d'un guichet bancaire automatisé, à la programmation d'un appareil vidéo, au maniement d'un four micro-ondes. On évalue aussi les habiletés acquises dans des emplois antérieurs, le curriculum vitae des employés et leurs motivations face au processur d'alphabétisation proposé.

Les travailleurs de chez Weston

Au total, 41 employées ont bénéficié des services d'alphabétisation en milieu de travail: 41 personnes en mathématiques et 23 personnes sur 41 en français. Certains participants ont suivi la formation à la fois en français et en mathématiques. Les travailleurs composaient des groupes de 13 à 15 membres sous l'égide de 3 professeures en mathématiques, 3 professeures en français, en plus d'une formatice chargée de l'apprentissage intégré du français et des mathématiques auprès d'un groupe de 3 participants considérés comme «débutants».

Les formatrices de la CSR Chambly

Grosso modo, les formatrices ont mis en pratique le plan de formation planifié par les deux responsables-matières (français et mathématiques). Le programme de formation en français a été élaboré à partir de quatre thèmes adaptés aux niveaux d'apprentissage des travailleurs:

1° *Les matières dangereuses* : comprendre les pictogrammes, lire et comprendre les instructions simples, lire et comprendre les étiquettes des produits de nettoyage et de désinfection, lire et comprendre les instructions concernant les matières dangereuses utilisées pour les besoins du travail.

2° *La santé et la sécurité* : lire et comprendre des instructions simples concernant les premiers soins, lire et comprendre les consignes de sécurité simples, rédiger un rapport d'accident en quatre ou cinq phrases courtes, dans un langage assez clair pour qu'il soit compris du lecteur.

3° *Les habiletés pour effectuer les tâches de travail* : lire des instructions simples permettant d'effectuer le travail demandé, lire et comprendre la planification de production, lire les étiquettes et les noms des produits, lire la liste des prix, lire les températures, remplir ses cartes de temps, remplir les formulaires de réquisitions (sacs et étiquettes), remplir les formulaires de suivis de production, lire les recettes (produits et quantités), faire des réquisitions.

4° *Les habiletés connexes au contexte du milieu* : lire les formulaires et les mémos informatifs, lire les documents affichés sur les babillards, remplir les formulaires de demande d'emplois pour pouvoir poser sa candidature aux emplois affichés, remplir des formulaires de «demandes de vacances».

En mathématiques, le programme de formation a misé sur les apprentissages suivants:

1° *La numération* : lire des nombres de 1 à 1000.

2° *L'utilisation de la calculatrice électronique* : connaître les principales commandes.

3° *Les quatre opérations de base à l'aide de la calculatrice* : connaître le sens de l'opération à effectuer, être capable de manipuler la calculatrice pour faire une opération.

4° *La notion de temps* : lire l'heure dans le système métrique, la date en notation numérique, faire des équivalences et transformer par exemple les heures en minutes; additionner, soustraire, multiplier, diviser des mesures de temps.

5° *Le système international* : lire les thermomètres gradués en degrés Farenheit et en degrés Celsius, lire des mesures liquides, des mesures solides, des mesures de poids sur une balance.

6° *Les cartes de temps* : remplir sa carte de temps de travail, calculer les taux horaires (tarifs de travail à temps simple, temps et demi et temps double), comprendre les déductions effectuées sur le chèque de paye.

7° *Les fractions décimales* : lire des nombres décimaux, connaître le rôle du point dans les fractions décimales, lire en dixième, centième, millième, connaître la valeur de position, calculer avec la calculatrice électronique, lire des quantités métriques, évaluer des pourcentages et le sens du pourcentage, calculer des quantités.

Évaluations

Évaluation des formatrices

Les formatrices sont très satisfaites des apprentissages effectués par les participants. Elles ont remarqué chez eux un souci constant de respecter les horaires, beaucoup de motivation à apprendre, une volonté opiniâtre de s'en sortir, malheureusement trop souvent liée à la peur de perdre leurs emplois. Les travailleurs démontrent une capacité d'auto-discipline et détiennent des habiletés importantes liées à leur expérience de vie personnelle. Cet état de fait pallie un niveau de scolarité assez sommaire qu'on aurait jugé inadéquat dans l'exercice de nouvelles fonctions dans l'usine transformée.

Compte tenu du temps très court consacré à la formation proprement dite, c'est-à-dire la préparation et la planification des activités d'alphabétisation, les formatrices ont décidé de s'en tirer en axant particulièrement leurs interventions sur l'utilisation maximale de la calculatrice électronique et sur la pratique de la lecture. De façon générale, les formatrices ont apprécié des étudiants qu'ils sachent ce qu'ils voulaient, qu'ils soient exigeants, assidus (certains travailleurs n'ont pas pris leurs vacances pour terminer leur formation).

Les formatrices se sont par contre sentie plus ou moins à l'aise avec le programme de formation qui leur était demandé. Ne connaissant pas le logiciel précis qui serait utilisé par les employés, il leur était difficile de les préparer concrètement, avec des outils pédagogiques «réels».

Les formatrices avaient quelquefois l'impression de travailler à l'aveuglette. Elles souhaiteraient donc, à l'avenir, pouvoir bénéficier d'une bonne préparation préalable, visiter des lieux où leurs futurs étudiants travaillent pour se familiariser avec l'écriture qui y est présente (signes écrits mais aussi toutes sortes d'autres signes lisibles par les travailleurs). Elles voudraient aussi rencontrer les travailleurs, pouvoir établir avec eux un premier dialogue pour jauger la nature de leurs attentes et planifier un peu plus l'aspect matériel du travail (locaux, éclairage, matériel didactique, dictionnaires, classeurs, ardoises).

Elles insistent aussi sur la nécessité de connaître clairement et en profondeur le milieu où le travailleur aura à transférer ses apprentissages afin de bien déterminer les prérequis essentiels à ce transfert. Elles seront ainsi mieux armées pour acclimater le travailleur à son futur environnement de travail, à ses nouvelles fonctions.

Une fois la formation achevée, les formatrices ont pu témoigner de l'autonomie et de la capacité d'assimilation des travailleurs qui son généralement plus développées que celles des autres adultes en processus d'alphabétisation non insérés dans le monde du travail. À leurs yeux, les travailleurs sont capables de faire des liens, des transferts d'apprentissage et d'apprendre des trucs. Pour les formatrices, l'une des forces majeures de l'expérience de «former sur mesure» (expression qui leur semble plus juste que l'«alphabétisation» qu'elles peuvent exercer ailleurs) a été d'augmenter la confiance des travailleurs en leur capacité d'apprendre du nouveau.

Évaluation des participants

Les travailleurs considèrent que l'expérience d'une formation sur mesure «condensée» sur leur lieu de travail, a concouru à rafraîchir des connaissances qui, pour certains, étaient enfouies ou inutilisées. En effet, les apprenants recrutés sont soit des travailleurs âgés, ayant beaucoup d'années d'expérience mais très peu de scolarité, soit d'ex-décrocheurs embauchés très jeunes. Ce sont des employés qui, selon leur expression, «ont gagné leur vie avec leurs bras plutôt qu'avec leur tête». Confinés à des tâches manuelles, souvent répétitives, n'exigeant aucune connaissance ou usage approfondi de la lecture, de l'écriture ou du raisonnement mathématiaque. Ils ont tout simplement appris à fonctionner sans lire ni écrire ni compter ou en exerçant ces activités de façon tout à fait approximative.

Le fait de suivre des cours après leurs heures de travail a fait naître de l'entraide, de la coopération entre les travailleurs. Revenir étudier les a poussés à vaincre leur honte, leur timidité. Ils ont apprécié l'approche des formatrices qui pratiquaient des corrections collectives, expliquaient les raisons de certains de leurs blocages dans les apprentissages. Pour les travailleurs, les formatrices sont vite devenues des amies, des complices suscitant leur intérêt à continuer à apprendre. Voici quelques témoignages éloquents de travailleurs:

- Tu commences à travailler à 6 heures du matin pour finir à 7 heures le soir, c'est dur.
- La formation a été donnée trop vite pour approfondir.
- Un vrai bourrage de crâne.
- Les points positifs de la formation a été l'enseignement du système métrique puis en français c'a été des rappels.
- Le système métrique ne s'enseignait pas dans notre temps. On l'a appris en travaillant, à peu près. J'ai aussi révisé les décimales. On a parlé des produits dangereux, c'a été intéressant.
- Je suis moins nerveux parce que j'ai une base pour

commencer. C'est dur. Il a fallu apprendre à écouter et à déchiffrer les livres. Ca nous donne une idée.

- Moi au commencement j'aimais pas ça. Après avoir appris, j'étais content.
- Tu ne peux pas apprendre quelque chose que t'as jamais voulu apprendre mais que tu dois apprendre.
- On s'est supporté, on s'est aidé. Les gens sont moins gênés de poser des questions, par exemple, lorsqu'il faut lire les affiches au tableau.

Évaluation de la CSR Chambly

Pour concevoir un programme de formation adéquat, il est essentiel de connaître les futurs outils des travailleurs. On doit s'assurer que la nouvelle machinerie, les logiciels dont l'utilisation est prévue à court ou à moyen terme, les données d'utilisation réelle du système de calcul métrique soient disponibles quand la formation se donne. En d'autres mots, cela souligne toute l'importance de favoriser la cohésion dans les équipes de travail, d'être sur la même longueur d'onde quant aux modes de fonctionnement d'une telle formation d'appoint.

Le personnel lié à la formation des travailleurs doit posséder une solide expérience dans le domaine de l'alphabétisation des adultes. Il doit aussi axer son action éducative sur une approche de travail fonctionnelle plutôt que sur un travail de conscientisation aux problèmes globaux de l'analphabétisme. L'approache conscientisante est impossible à imaginer dans le couloir étroit et précis de réponses spécifiques à des besoins «pointus» et liés à des impondérables temporels.

On a procédé à un cataloguage d'«habiletés de base» déjà acquises ou à acquérir par les travailleurs : savoir classer des documents, interpréter des signaux, interpréter des symboles, prévoir des délais, établir l'ordre de ses tâches, l'ordre des tâches d'autrui, analyser une situation, faire preuve de jugement, prendre une décision, en évaluer son efficaçité, justifier sa décision, être capable d'argumenter logiquement. On a aussi cerné quelques «habiletés sociales de base» : être constant dans sa présence physique au travail, être attentif et consciencieux au travail, être capable de bonnes relations avec les autres. Ces «habiletés de base» ont fait l'objet d'un examen attentif de la part des formatrices tout au long de l'apprentissage et d'une évaluation en bonne et due forme à la fin de la formation sur mesure.

Évaluation de la compagnie Weston

Pour une entreprise privée, la rentabilité d'une formation continue est intimement liée à une qualité continue des produits fabriqués par des travailleurs formés, impliqués dans ce que la compagnie Weston appelle «la qualité totale» de ses produits. Un sentiment d'appartenance plus net aux destinées de la compagnie a été sensible chez les employés. À plus long terme, l'employeur prévoit réduire les accidents de travail, les pertes matérielles, le taux d'absentéisme et augmenter la productivité.

Évaluation des représentants syndicaux

Des représentants syndicaux font le bilan de l'experience d'alphabétisation en milieu de travail:

- Ça été un acte de bravoure car ils ont été identifiés à des analphabètes s'exposant aux prèjugés des autres. Les retour aux études c'est difficile avec les responsabilités familiales en plus. Ils n'ont pas eu le choix, leurs emplois étaient en jeu.

- J'ai été surpris du nombre d'employés avec ce problème. Je les trouve courageux. Si la formation ne s'était pas donnée au travail, les trois quarts n'y auraient pas été.

- Le plaisir des gars en français ça été la manipulation du dictionnaire et du Bescherelle (*L'art de conjuguer*). D'ailleurs ils ont acheté les manuels et ont été heureux de le faire. On nous avait dit que le déménagement c'était pour septembre. Ca n'est pas le cas. Avoir su, on aurait prévu une formation plus longue. Il fallait un éveil, pour, éventuellement, suite à ce premier pas, poursuivre en allant à l'école des adultes.

- Le travailleur de Weston ne sera plus un travailleur de shop mais un travailleur spécialisé.

Il est certain aussi que la préformation offerte chez Weston ne peut en aucun cas remplacer un processus d'alphabétisation complet, échelonné à plus long terme et offert soit à travers le réseau des groupes populaires en alphabétisation, soit à l'intérieur du réseau d'alphabétisation pour adultes offerts par les commissions scolaires. Les représentants syndicaux sont bien conscients que certains des employés de la boulangerie gagneraient à poursuivre leur formation dans l'un ou l'autre de ces réseaux.

Évaluation de la consultante en gestion de la formation

Le test de classement de la CSR Chambly, évaluant les connaissances, a été pour certains employés une source de stress, de peur, de difficultés. Cela veut dire qu'il faut bien préparer les candidats en leur assurant que les résultats de ces tests ne viendront jamais à l'encontre d'une promotion possible au sein de la compagnie ou new joueront jamais rôle discriminant. La spécificité du fonctionnement d'une boulangerie occasionne un travail à entrées continues. Cela a eu pour effet de rendre la planification horaire un peu ardue, les cours se donnant en dehors des heures de travail. Une dizaine d'employés ont dû abandonner leur formation à cause de l'effort soutenu et très exigeant qu'impliquait l'obligation de s'alphabétiser après de longues heures de travail.

Conclusions, prospectives

Une formation liée à une gestion particulière

Une idée qui semblait faire consensus auprès des intervenantes et intervenants interrogés était de ne pas nommer «programme d'alphabétisation» la formation très ponctuelle qui avait été offerte au sein de la boulangerie Weston. L'on a aussi tenu à mentionner que ce type de formation offerte dans les entreprises est très lié à la philosophie de gestion participative prônée par la Centrale des syndicats démocratiques (CSD) et partagée idéologiquement par la compagnie Weston.

Le fait d'offrir des activités d'alphabétisation au sein de l'entreprise a permis de saisir la grande importance du travail d'équipe, de l'entraide entre les employés. Des activités de ce genre démystifient l'apprentissage. Elles sont même une condition sine qua non à une formation professionnelle plus spécialisée. Il faudrait aussi que le même type d'expérience tentée dans d'autres usines se fonde sur l'accessibilité universelle à la préformation, sans tenir compte de la scolarité déclarée des employés. Il faut penser qu'une expérience de vie et de travail (par exemple, l'expertise de la fabrication de la pâte à pain) mariée à une bonne formation sur mesure peut donner naissance à une main-d'oeuvre qualifiée, spécialisée.

Les travailleurs comme ressources

Le concept d'une usine hautement infomatisée a été instigué pour réduire les coûts de production et pour pallier les effets nocifs du libre-échange (l'usine de Longueuil est géographiquement située à environ 120 kilomètres de la frontière américaine) et de la saturation du marché par les compétiteurs québécois.

Dans cette optique, les employés sont considérés comme des ressources riches de qualités qui importent autant que tout l'équipement neuf et hautement performant qui fera progresser l'entreprise. C'est ainsi que l'ancienneté et des connaissances pratiques indéniables en production du pain ont pu faire contrepoids à une scolarité restreinte.

Un contexte de formation

Processus de longue haleine, l'alphabétisation doit être insérée dans les plans de carrière globaux des travailleurs, dans ce que nous convenons d'appeler une formation continue. Par voie de conséquence, une attention particulière doit être apportée à la sensibilisation de tous les partenaires à un contexte de formation plus qu'à des activités éducatives passagères qui pallient momentanément des états d'urgence. Il ne faudrait donc pas confondre préformation et formation technique.

Sensibilisation et coûts

Une alphabétisation pratiquée en milieu de travail nécessite des efforts de sensibilisation à l'analphabétisme vécu par des travailleurs salariés. Du côté patronal, il est primordial que l'on accepte que l'analphabétisme est une réalité indéniable, qu'il existe des travailleurs analphabètes qui ont besoin d'une formation adaptée à leur réalité. Il faut aussi tenir compte des coûts que ces démarches entraînent et aller chercher le financement adéquat auprès de la Commission de la formation professionnelle (CFP), du Secrétariat d'État à l'alphabétisation.

Alphabétisation en milieu de travail : un créneau d'avenir

Toutes les personnes impliquées directement ou indirectement dans des efforts de démystification du phénomène, dans le «dépistage» des travailleurs analphabètes, devront être informées des implications globales de tels projets : négociation possible de congés-éducation, alphabétisation continue, échelonnée à moyen et à long terme plutôt que dans des structures d'urgence, exercise facilité des droits des travailleurs analphabètes. Nous pensons, entre autres, à la simplification souhaitée par nombre d'employés du jargon très lourd qui constitue la mie des textes des conventions collectives.

Questions de discussion

1. *D'après vous, quels seraient les rôles des partenaires éducatifs (patronat, employés, syndicats, commissions scolaires, groupes d'alphabétisation populaire) dans un programme d'alphabétisation en milieu de travail?*
2. *Comment tenir compte des compétences de travail des employés analphabètes en processus d'alphabétisation? Comment considérer les travailleurs analphabètes comme des ressources dans ce même processus?*
3. *Vous voulez exercer des activités d'alphabétisation dans un milieu de travavil donné. Pouvez-vous inventorier les activités qui nécessitent de lire et d'écrire dans ce milieu de travail?*
4. *Comment bien se préparer avant d'aller alphabétiser en milieu de travail?*
5. *Comment insérer l'alphabétisation dans des plans de formation continue en milieu de travail?*
6. *Quels liens établir entre les congés-éducation, l'alphabétisation continue et les droits des travailleurs analphabètes?*

Chapter Three
LITERACY TRAINING IN THE WORKPLACE

Hélène Blais

Place: *Weston Bakery in Longueuil Quebec*
Participants: *Chambly Board of Education literacy staff and Weston Bakery personnel and trainees.*
Issue: *The importance of teamwork and cooperation in delivering workplace literacy training.*

> *Bread has so many uses! We have learned to recognize, in bread, a tool of the family of man, as in the bread broken and shared among us. We have learned to recognize, in bread, the image of the grandeur of hard work, because of the bread earned with the sweat of one's brow... There is nothing quite like the taste of bread shared among friends.*
>
> *Antoine de Saint-Expuery, 1948*

Background

In 1984, approximately 300 employees of Weston Bakery who worked at bread production were selected to work in a new factory equipped with the latest high technology machines. As the changeover would result in a loss of jobs, a reclassification committee was asked to evaluate the situation. The committee's findings were that 50% of production employees could lose their jobs, including bakers, foremen, manual labourers, specialized workers in raw material receiving, bread wrapping, cleaning and shipping.

In 1988, union representatives called upon literacy and computer training specialists for adults and ran a program called ABC INFO to help those employees whose jobs were most likely to be affected with the move and the new technology.

In February 1989, Weston bakeries officially announced the move to a new location and the new technology. To ensure total impartiality in management decisions related tothe move, a manpower adaptability committee was created within the company. The Weston company then sought the services of the Chambly regional school board to take over the pre-training; basic French and mathematics and upgrading of general knowledge and basic skills. The Chambly Board of Education has offered literacy training since 1976 and specifically tailored training for companies since 1987.

The workers were invited to register on a voluntary basis for literacy training in the workplace in view of a future selection criteria for all personnel:a high school diploma. This criteria if applied absolutely would have eliminated overnight the better part of all employees with an average of fifteen years of seniority.

Assigning the roles

The educational partner: Chambly Board of Education

The Chambly Board was asked to provide a twenty-four-hour crash course in mathematics (six hours per week for four weeks) and forty two hours of French training (six hours per week for seven weeks). After visiting the factory and evaluating the training needs, the "course content teachers" administered in-house tests to seventy of the workers to gauge their skills in reading and mathematics.

The following skills were tested:

- Comprehension of instructions,understanding commands for the new machinery they would be using,understanding workplace safety information;
- Four basic operations,understanding the metric system, decimal fractions, graph reading, reading blueprints, paycheck stubs, and calculating work hours.

With limited hours available, the Chambly Board designed a tailored training program with Weston's needs and the workers knowledge in mind. It was made clear from the beginning that the results of the evaluation would never be turned over to the employer.This was done in order to guarantee that those workers who were found to require literacy upgrading would not be fired. The next step was to set up a team approach for the project and to select the teachers.

The corporate partner: The Weston Company

Beyond a list of objectives for training workers to use the new technology, Weston bakery provided on-site literacy training rooms, materials and equipment for the classrooms. As well, other services such as access to photocopy services were provided.

The training management consultant

The consultant was in this case, a training management consultant, who collaborated in preparing the pre-training plan. This pre-training was to be followed by a 15 hour introduction to computerization given by a training specialist from the CEGEP Edouard-Monpetit. The employees would then be in a position to begin further technical training.

With one-on-one interviews, the consultant determined the training needs of those workers who had not reached the first, second or third level of secondary school. About 84 people were interviewed. Fourteen people out of the 84 who needed the literacy training the most did not take the courses because of seniority agreements and deals with the employer for early retirement.

These interviews were designed to measure the employees' knowledge in mathematical thinking, basic mathematical operations, blueprint reading, reading and understanding graphs or diagrams, and becoming familiar with the general technology linked to daily life such as using an electronic calculator, using an instant teller machine, programing a VCR, and using a micro-wave oven. Skills learned at previous jobs were also evaluated as well as the workers' curriculum vitae and their motivation for literacy training.

The Weston employees

A total of 41 employees received literacy training in the workplace: Forty-one people in mathematics and of this number 23 people also received training in French. Some participants took both French and mathematics. The workers were set up into groups of 13 to 15 people with three teachers each for French and three for mathematics, and one special teacher for a selected group of three participants who were considered beginners.

The instructors from the Chambly Board

For the most part, the instructors followed the training plan devised by the two course-content teachers (French and mathematics). The French language training program was developed based on four basic categories, and adapted to the learning skills of the workers.

1. Hazardous substances: understanding pictograms, reading and understanding simple instructions, labels on cleaning products and disinfecting substances, and instructions about hazardous products used in the workplace.
2. Health and safety: reading simple instructions for first aid, safety rules, filling out an accident report in four or five short sentences in simple clear language.
3. Working skills: reading simple instructions in order to complete the required task, reading and understanding production plans, reading labels and product names, price lists, temperatures, filling out time cards, order forms (bags and labels), filling out production reports, reading recipes and request forms.
4. Skills related to the workplace: reading memos and forms, reading various documents on the bulletin board, filling out job applications to apply for jobs posted, filling out request forms for vacation time.

In mathematics, the program was aimed at teaching the following skills:

1. Numeracy: reading numbers from one to 1000.

2. Using an electronic calculator: knowing the main functions.
3. Understanding the four basic operations on the calculator, including the operation required for the task, and executing the operation on the calculator.
4. The concept of time: telling time in the metric system, the date in numeric notation, calculating equivalence of an hour into minutes; addition, subtraction, multiplication, dividing time measures.
5. The international system: reading thermometers with Fahrenheit and Celsius degrees, liquid and solid measures, weight measures on a scale.
6. Time cards: filling out time cards, figuring out hourly wages (at time and a half, double time), understanding payroll deductions.
7. Decimal fractions: reading decimal fractions, understanding the meaning of a period in decimal fractions, reading in tenths, hundredths, thousandths, understanding the meaning of positions, calculator functions, reading metric quantities, evaluating percentages and their meaning, calculating quantities.

Evaluations

Instructor evaluation

The instructors were quite satisfied with the learning accomplished by the participants. They noted a keen interest in the student participants in keeping on schedule, motivation to learn and a sheer determination to get through it. Unfortunately, this was all too often linked to the fear of losing their jobs. The workers showed self-discipline and a remarkable use of skills that had been acquired in their personal lives. Although their lack of formal education might have caused them to be judged inadequate for work in the high-tech factory, their assets acquired through the training far outweighed this possible judgement.

Due to lack of time spent on planning and preparing the literacy training program, the instructors decided to concentrate their efforts especially on the use of electronic calculators and on reading skills.

Over all, the instructors appreciated that the students

knew what they wanted. They were demanding of themselves and all went to great lengths to be there. Some of the workers didn't even take their holidays so that they could complete their training.

The instructors were less than happy however, with the training program which they were asked to devise. Because they did not know exactly which software the employees would be using, it was difficult to prepare them with actual tools of learning. They sometimes felt that they were working in the dark. They wished that in the future they could have more time to prepare by visiting the site where their students would be working, reading what types of signs the workers were faced with (written signs as well as all other types of visual information), meeting with the workers in order to better understand their expectations and more planning time to set up such things as the classrooms, lighting, dictionaries, files, and blackboards.

The instructors also emphasized the necessity for them to clearly understand the work environment into which their students would be transferred so that they could determine the requirements for a successful integration. Having done this they would then be better able to help acclimatize the worker to the new environment and to the new job. Once the training was completed, the instructors were witness to the autonomy and assimilation skills of the workers. They observed that the workers were able to correlate, to transfer skills and to learn new techniques. In addition, one of the major benefits from this experience was that they were able to increase the workers' confidence to learn new things through the design of "tailored training."

Participant evaluation

The workers expressed that this condensed on-site "tailored training" provided the opportunity to review the skills and knowledge that for many of them, had been buried. Most of the recruits were older, with many years of work experience but with very little formal education. Or some were dropouts who entered the workforce at a very young age. The employees described themselves as, "having earned their living with their backs rather then their heads." Confined to manual, often repetitive tasks requiring little knowledge or use of reading, writing or mathematical skills, they simply learned to function without these skills and had relied on guesswork when it was necessary.

The fact that they were attending these courses after work hours encouraged mutual help and cooperation. Going back to school helped them to overcome their shame and embarrassment. They appreciated the teachers' approach, such as the collective correction of the work and the explanation of reasons for some of the mental blocks that people can encounter. The teachers quickly became friends with their students. The following comments from the workers provide some insightful information about their experiences as students.

- When you start to work at 6: AM and you finish at 7: PM, it's hard.
- The training time was too short to really get deep into it.
- A real cram session.
- The best thing about the training was the teaching of the metric system and in French it was a revision.
- Back in our day they didn't teach the metric system. We learned it at work, hit and miss. I also brushed up on the decimal system. We talked about hazardous products, it was interesting.
- I'm less nervous now because I have a base from which to go on. It's hard. We had to learn to listen and to decipher books: that gives us good ideas.
- Myself, in the beginning, I didn't like it. After having learned, I was happy.
- You can't learn something that you never wanted to learn but that you have to learn.
- We helped each other, we supported each other. People are less embarrassed for example when we have to read something on the board.

Evaluation of the School Board

As the teachers themselves recognized, in order to create an adequate training program, it is essential to know which tools the workers will be using and to make sure they are available when the training is taking place. As was experienced in this workplace program, it is very important for cohesion within the different work teams, each one informing

the other of their participation. As well, the people involved
with training the workers should have a solid background in
literacy training for adults as was the casein this program.
Using the functional context approach to training is also a vital
ingredient for a successful program.

In order to assist the instructors in program evaluation a
list was prepared identifying basic functioning skills which
the workers already had or needed to have, such as filing
documents, interpreting signals, symbols, establishing dead-
lines, deciding the order to tasks for oneself and for others,
analysing a situation, showing good judgement, making a
decision, evaluating its impact, justifying a decision, and
arguing logically. Certain basic social skills were also identified: being physically present consistently at work, being
attentive and conscientious at work, and being able to maintain good relations with others. These basic skills were
closely monitored by the teachers throughout the training
and in the follow-up evaluation after completion of this
made-to-measure training program.

Evaluation by Weston

In private enterprise, the value of ongoing training is
closely linked to the quality of the products made by trained
employees. This is what the Weston company calls the 'overall quality' of its products. This training principle was made
evident to all the trainees. In the longer term, the employer
foresaw a reduction in on-the-job accidents, material losses
and absenteeism as well as an increase in productivity all due
to the intensive workplace training program.

Evaluation by the Union

Union representatives also expressed their opinions about
the workplace training experience.

> It was an act of bravery since they were identified
> with other illiterates and exposed to the prejudices of
> workers not in the program. Going back to school is
> difficult with family responsibilities as well. They had
> no choice, their jobs were on the line.
>
> I was surprised at the number of employees with this
> problem. They are brave. If the training had not been

given at work, three quarters of them would not have gone.

The best part for the guys in the French class was working with the dictionary and the Bescherelle (conjugation manual). Besides they bought the books and they were happy to do it. We were told that the move would be in September. This was not the case. Had we known, we would have tried for a longer training period. We needed a starting point to help us. After this first step, we could continue with adult education.

The Weston employee will no longer be a shop employee but rather a specialized worker.

Of course the pre-training offered by Weston can never replace a complete literacy training process, extended for a longer time period and offered either through the network of popular literacy training groups or within the framework of literacy training programs offered by various school boards. The union representatives were well aware that some of the workers of Weston bakeries would benefit from continuing their training through either of these networks.

Evaluation by the training management consultant

The Chambly Board evaluation test was, for some employees, a great source of stress, fear, and hardship. This indicates that the candidates should be reassured that the results of these tests will never interfere with their promotion within the company or be used in a discriminatory fashion. The very workings of the bakery business demands shift work which made planning class schedules difficult at times. About ten of the employees were forced to drop the classes because of the difficulty of coming to class for literacy training after a long work shift.

Concluding comments

There was a consensus among all those asked that the program should not be called a 'literacy program' since it was highly specialized training within Weston Bakery and designed specifically for them. It was also noted that this type of training offered by companies is closely linked to the participatory management philosophy advocated by labour organizations and shared by the Weston company.

The fact that the literacy training was offered within the company highlighted the importance of teamwork and cooperation among the employees. This kind of project worked to demystify learning. It also is a condition to further specialized professional training. Projects such as this in other factories should be founded on the universal accessibility to pre-training, without basing it on the formal education of the employees. It seems that life experience, combined with work experience, together with good specific training, results in qualified, specialized manpower.

The workers as a resource

The concept of a computerized factory was adopted to reduce costs and to counter the effects of the Free Trade Agreement. With this in mind, the employees are considered a valuable resource, equal to the now highly technological equipment of the company. In this way, years of experience and undeniable skills in bread production outweighed limited formal education.

The context of training

Literacy is a long-term process and as such it must be part of long range career plans for employees. Consequently, the involvement of all partners in the training is more important then implementing temporary educational activities to meet an emergency situation. One must not confuse pre-training and actual on-going technological training.

Literacy training in the workplace requires sensitivity to illiteracy through the actual life experience of the workers. From the corporate standpoint it is essential that the existence of illiteracy be recognized and that there are some illiterate workers who need training tailored to their real situations. One must also take into account the cost of such training and obtain adequate financing from CFP (Professional Training Commission) and other agencies, such as the National Literacy Secretariat.

All those directly or indirectly involved in the demystification of this phenomenon of 'uncovering' illiterate workers will have to be informed of the overall implications of such projects. In other words it will become important to explore the possibilities of negotiating such activities as educational leave, working holidays and on-going literacy training as opposed to quick fix emergency training. Aiming toward the future, it will be an empowering experience for workers when they can read and understand the collective agreement that has been written in plain language.

Discussion Questions

1. *How would you describe the partnership that existed between the company and the literacy providers?*
2. *Would a literacy task analysis have been useful in determining the curriculum for the program?*
3. *What other kinds of work documents could have been used in the program?*
4. *What is your opinion of an assessment portfolio as an alternative form of student evaluation?*
5. *As opposed to calling the service a literacy program, what other names could have conveyed the purpose of the program?*

Chapter Four
COLLABORATIVE LEARNING IN TIMES OF CHANGE

Marion Wells

Place: The Learning Exchange in Saint John, New
Brunswick.
Participants: Staff and students of the various programs.
Issue: Responsive programs for youth and adults.

The Saint John Learning Exchange is so named because
from its beginning in 1984 it has been committed to the
principle of collaborative learning. In collaborative learning
people do not necessarily learn the same things but they
participate as mutually supportive equals.Learning takes
place as an exchange of ideas and skills. Programs based on
this or similar approaches need a strong philosophical base if
they are going to withstand the fluctuating philosophies of
policy indecision which affects literacy programing
throughout Canada. The Learning Exchange has always
compared new ventures with its mission statement and the
basic principles for operating in responding to the needs of
the community.

Background

The Learning Exchange operates in Saint John, New
Brunswick and has had its share of funding uncertainty
since it began. It now offers a wide range of literacy and

educational services to a city of 120,000 inhabitants. In responding to identified community needs it has diversified and broadened its approach. Its programs are delivered from a downtown location, a block away from the harbour in the heart of the city. The original Core Literacy program provides full or part-time learning opportunities for fifty people, males and females from ages sixteen to sixty plus.

This core program has remained basically the same over the past eight years.Literacy staff are called "animators," a term borrowed from the French word "animateur." It describes best what learning facilitators do at the Exchange, which is to bring learning to life. The other programs and activities operated by the Exchange all adhere to the same learner-centred philosophy of the original core program because it works.

The youth program is called Occupational Knowledge (O.K.) and it helps young people who want to work to develop the attitudes and skills employers are looking for. The Exchange matches learners' needs, interests and developing skills with job exposure experiences which eventually leads to actual jobs. Two newer programs operated by the Exchange for people still in conventional schools are the Stay in School program and the Homework School. Each of these abide by the same overarching philosophy, except that in the Homework School learners work on regular school assignments as part of each session. The Stay in School program consists of two adult learners visiting Junior High and Elementary schools and talking about their experiences and the problems they encountered as undereducated young adults.

The Exchange also runs Learnex which promotes worker literacy and develops workplace literacy programs.

In becoming a diversified service provider, the people at the Exchange understood the dangers of doing "too many things at once." At the Exchange the eighteen full time and three part-time employees view ongoing training as crucial. Staff in all programs operated by the Exchange review the basic principles of the agency frequently.

Such training sessions need not be formal or costly, but they need to be continuous and taken seriously. Training is not the best word. What is really happening is learning,relearning and reaffirming the fundamental values of the agency in balance with professional development topics.

After three initial weeks of training all staff get one day each month plus a full week each year of in-house training sessions. They also attend, on a rotating basis, outside workshops on such topics as time management, youth issues, health and leadership.

Learner-Centred or Learner-Inspired?

Jean Peters, animator-trainer at the Learning Exchange says:

> I like to think of my work as learner-inspired. Since the starting point for us to participate in collaborative learning is that people come here voluntarily, we know we are involved in a mutual experience. I am nothing without active learners. My function has no purpose at all if they are not here for learning, ready to learn.

At 55 Canterbury Street, people arrive every day full of troubles and preoccupations which interfere with their self-set learning goals. The Learning Exchange has two counsellors on its payroll and both are there to listen, to reassure and to suggest options. Both have received Learning Exchange training in non-directive counselling techniques appropriate to the people who attend. The Exchange Counsellor Mary Snow has an open heart and a creative mind; she works very closely with all staff to maximize appropriate areas of support. She is skilled in identifying those whose needs and problems go beyond the scope of a literacy program. As well she helps people to find the special services they may require and often goes with them if they feel the need for her company.

> I will never send anyone to an agency I don't know about. I find out who cares, who I can trust in an organization. My job is to maximize the support-side of the Learning Exchange so that people can continue learning. Similarly, I see that they get the help they need if they can't continue. This is my part of the collaborative learning contract that we have with learners.

The principle of learner-centred education has become something of a discussion point recently, and the Exchange has its own view of what is meant by learner-centred.

Marion Wells, Director of the Learning Exchange has no
difficulty with the various and often differing interpretations
of the meaning of the term.

> It's a fascinating discussion. For instance, whether
> "learner-centred" means something different from
> "women-centred" and "adult-centred?" The politics of
> linguistics is exciting.

> For me, a learner-centred approach is extremely rele-
> vant to the collaboration between animator and learner,
> especially regarding the recognition of individual learn-
> ing styles and needs. But I do not go along with the idea
> that, because a learner is interested in one particular
> thing, she and I will spend three hours focusing only on
> that interest. I am much more concerned with how she
> learns, what she tells me, what she understands, what
> she reads, what she writes. Together, we build a curricu-
> lum out of a two-way process of showing, knowing and
> sharing. We exchange ideas about learning goals and
> how to accomplish them.

> Whether you believe your efforts are directed towards
> empowering people, or assisting people to empower
> themselves, the issue remains: How can you accom-
> plish your end goal? How you do it remains the single
> most important question, once you have settled why.

The Stay in School program

The Stay in School program, in which two former literacy
learners visit schools, leaves students with the message that
they should remain in school. Sometimes students are suf-
fering with insensitive and indifferent environments at
school and being told they are 'stupid' or 'trouble-makers'. By
thinking about schools in a learner-centred way, the
Exchange's Stay in School workers give a clear, straight-
forward message.

Their own personal stories are compelling, and they provide examples of courage and endurance. The Stay in School
project workers talk about trying to build self-determination
when life is tough. If students want to stay in school but feel
the odds are against them, they learn that there are people in

the community who understand and care and can help. Exhorting kids to stay in school and take more of the same is not learner-centred. Reaching those students who need some objective guidance, something to inspire them, or specific information on services, is another example of how we define learner-centred.

The Stay in School program is popular with students and teachers mostly because its message is directed at the students' own feelings. One problem for the Exchange workers is that sometimes students confess that they are failing because they cannot read well. Others telephone the project workers for advice on personal problems. These needs will have to be addressed or at least managed in some way before they become unbearable. For now, as much moral support as possible is given as well as information on available services.

The Homework School and Occupational Knowledge (O.K.)

To date, the Exchange has developed two other direct services for youth, which in different ways respond to what the Stay in School program has identified as needed services. The Homework School and Occupational Knowledge (O.K.) which is now entering its third year are attempting to meet some of the needs. Young people out of school are especially vulnerable in a rapidly changing society. Without concrete support the prospects of undereducated youth entering and staying in the workforce are slim. Those who have not been esteemed by their schools, parents or peers are looking for ways to feel powerful. If they are interested in trying the idea of employment they need the kind of help that will not take away from their frequently-fragile sense of individuality and independence.

Help with homework assignments

For students still in school the Homework School offers help with homework assignments and literacy problems. Students in grades six to nine attend the program from 4:PM to 7: PM This is after the day learners leave and before the evening program begins. Teachers and parents are involved to varying degrees but students must attend voluntarily. They tell us they have more confidence in themselves, ask for help more often in class and feel more optimistic about their futures with this program.

The Occupational Knowledge (O.K.) program opens its doors and its heart to youth who are eighteen to twenty-four years of age, and who have limited education and no employment experience. The only other criterion at the entry stage is that they must want to get involved in paid work. In O.K.young people are welcomed to join small groups of seven learners. Each group is led by a salaried animator, trained in Learning Exchange philosophy and approach. Intake is on a continuous basis and participants can stay for up to a year.

The expectation is that they learn about work, try it, and learn about themselves as well. Empowering young people means giving them a chance to learn the individual skills they need. The program as a whole must support them personally and make counselling promptly available. The strong, practical focus on learning workplace skills and attention to supporting learners individually, attracts students who have dropped out of the school system or who have no marketable skills. The O.K. program operates right through the summer.

Setting up individual study programs

O.K. learners set up their own individual study programs with their animators.They work together in small groups to role-play interviews, discuss issues, create and edit O.K. copies of the regularly produced newsletter, *The Exchange*. By taking more and more control the students build up their own self-esteem which is a fundamental concern of the program.

It is important to remind ourselves that the individual is what programs are really about. Trouble occurs when we turn students off by forgetting their needs in the scramble to reach curriculum goals. Other danger signs for programs are when staff become less motivated, or lose their focus which must always be on the individual, and his or her needs.

Canada Employment gives learners small allowances while they attend the O.K.program. Money for babysitting, childcare and transportation is also available. Learners are restricted to a year in the program. However, when learners are placed in permanent jobs, staff continue to work in a supportive role on the job with students and employers for another full year. O.K. helps learners to refine their understanding of what paid work is and how they might become a part of it. Young people come to O.K.because they want to work but they don't know how to go about it. They have not succeeded in the school system and therefore do not want more school. They want first of all, to discover who they are. Then they want successful working lives.

Being at O.K. seems to help change people's way of looking at themselves and their skill levels. Learners often come in saying simply that they will give it a try. Later, they are defining their goals and figuring out how to achieve them. One learner goes to a nursing home to study the issues there, issues she may encounter in that line of work. Another learner job-shadows, and then works for a photography studio. Job exposures of one or two weeks have been established with more than fifty local employers.

The employment Liaison Worker

Don Peters, the program's Employment Liaison Worker is the main link to the outside world of work for O.K. learners. He is on guard against the type of boss whose indifference will doom learners to failure. Don has to know each learner job trainee very well. For this reason he swims or bowls with all learners twice a week, plays chess with them at lunchtimes and holds frequent job-thinking sessions for those preparing to go out on job exposures. All of the animators set up job exposures jointly with their learners. They go with learners on the first day, having already visited the job site. They keep careful watch for problems, and evaluate the entire experience with learners.

Learners articulate their goals and make changes with the direct assistance of animators. Students come from nine to four every day and are expected to call in before 9: AM if they cannot attend that day. Everyone on staff encourages students to keep trying. Students are called if they don't show up, or are visited at home if they have no telephone. Staff at the Exchange call this caring, and caring also means knowing when to back off.

This type of counselling is especially important for youth. Extending messages of support through the grape-vine also helps to break down barriers of mistrust and of disillusion. Learners take on more job- related activities as they become more confident. They reach a crucial point when they are able to define what kind of work they want to do. Often this in itself propels them towards developing more literacy skills.

Within the program they have opportunities to work with cash registers and Visa machines, take inventory or do regular office jobs. As well they run a fruit stand in the program and discover their purchasing, marketing and organizational skills. The animators pay attention to giving students more control of the program as they are ready to take it; control they are more than willing to assume.

The Employers' Role

The role of employers is to provide workplace print material, job descriptions, and information on specific responsibilities and tasks. Employers also show staff and learners the worksite in which the job trainees will work.

Don Peters had some thoughts on the importance of frequent communication with employers about their job placements:

> Frequent face-to-face communication with employers increases their committment to helping the job placements succeed. They know that the trainees come to them prepared, having an understanding of the work ethic as well as the work environment. Employers begin to invest time and effort in the job trainees, knowing they can call on our assistance should the need arise. The feedback we receive from participating employers helps us to develop specific areas of emphasis in our individual training objectives.

The staff role as supportive resource

Once a program participant has acquired sufficient confidence, skills and know-how to commit him or herself to a job, the staff role is to act as a supportive resource for both the job trainee and the employer. Confusion, misunderstandings and negativity from co-workers may occur in the crucial early days of the job. Such pressures are often enough to make the job trainee panic and resign. Students are always trained to call Don or their animator immediately if something happens which may impel them to quit.

By talking with the trainee and then the employers, ninety per-cent of problems are resolved. Employers appreciate the interest shown by program staff in problems and the suggestions made for the resolution of these problems. Says one O.K. student,

> It was real good to know that when I had problems at my job exposure site that all I had to do was to call my animator and he was there. John talked with me and also the manager of the store the very next day. Later on in the week, I had enough confidence to run both the produce and fish departments by myself.

The Exchange and local employers: a partnership

The partnership between the Exchange and local employers is still a developing one. Much effort is required to make a long term success of it, and recognizing the cooperation and interest of employers is important. The Exchange knows that employers have trouble finding young workers for lower paying jobs and therefore will collaborate with O.K. But the quality of the service is what really sells the program. Employers sometimes invest a great deal of time, effort and money into the people who work for them. O.K. hopes that its students will be treated this way and there are already some encouraging signs.

A long term goal is to see employers really pick-up on the training issue and appreciate the relationship between training and work. If they come to see it this way, worker training and upgrading will become an essential part of a company's operating expenses.

Learnex for workplace literacy programs

The adult workplace literacy programs envisaged by the Exchange have been slow in coming. Employers say they know they have problems with employee literacy and unions state they are addressing the issue. For Learnex, the unit at the Exchange which develops programs for workers, several initiatives are being developed to meet the needs of companies.

Learnex has made inroads mostly through individually funded sponsorships of workers by companies, and three workplace classrooms are in the planning stage. Although there are other government operated training institutions, the Exchange is attempting to convince employers that they must look at educational philosophies and hear the positive evidence which exists for flexible and humanistic programs. Learnex has to sensitize employers to the plight of those who are afraid of the more curriculum-driven approach of the institutions.

Concluding comments

The original Core literacy program enacts our philosophy in an intensive and upbeat schedule of activities which change frequently as needs are determined. Groups work on topics such as newsletter production, letters to employers, questionnaires for a survey, categorizing jobs, discussing parenting tips, and planning a variety show. Often trips to places of a controversial or interesting nature occur spontaneously, as well. Outside group activities such as swimming at the aquatic centre, picnics and scavenger hunts are valued by learners and staff as social and learning activities. Anyone who has witnessed about 50 learners and staff arriving back from a three string bowling tournament knows the renewed sense of community such an activity brings to a program.

But has this anything to do with learning? Do the faces filled with enthusiasm and 'team-spirit' signify that any learning has occurred? Measuring success is a necessary part of a program's survival, not only to satisfy funders, but for staff and learners to see where they have come from, and where they are going. Core learners get jobs because they can read and write more effectively. Their confidence and self-esteem is heightened and they like themselves more. The life-benefits seem obvious, but are sometimes subtle. Learners become leaders, they help others, they peer-tutor, they take hold of problems and they begin to control their own environment. All of this can be, and is, measurable, and all of this means that learning has occurred for everyone involved.

Programs feeling the economic pinch may feel pressured to abandon or relax their basic philosophy, but the Exchange has decided it would close down rather than be swayed from its principles. Financially sound at present, the Exchange plans its activities well ahead and watches for signs of organizational stress. Diversification within an organization presents major challenges, but there are significant benefits to be accrued from adding new things, even though the initial stimulus may be the question of survival.

Learning about the new enterprises and sharing knowledge from program to program within the agency broadens everyone. The Exchange maintains itself financially by a grid of supportive partnerships: federal/provincial/municipal funding, industry sponsorship, and private contributions. As well, networks of educators and community workers, friends and families of staff and learners, and media recognition supply crucial moral and psychological support.

As the Exchange embarks on new relationships with its supporting funders in the various levels of government, it is very conscious of its reputation for flexibility and responsiveness. But the agency draws a clear line between the needs or demands of its funders and the needs of the consumers of its services. The qualities of creativity and sensitivity can only be maintained when certain program elements are in place.

At the Exchange these essential elements are prompt, accessible in-house counselling, continuous staff training and partnerships with other players such as private sector interests. Programs like the Exchange, which have long ago settled their philosophy and approach, need to identify the principles they will never give up. If a program broadens its activities it must decide what it will abandon in the face of funding shortages.The Exchange has made up its mind about its own bottom line. Being relevant and responsive to youths' and adults' needs determine that line.

Discussion Questions

1. How would you describe the role of staff training at the Learning Exchange?
2. What is your definition of learner-centred?
3. What are some of the reasons why the O.K. program appears to be successful?
4. What kind of groundwork is required before launching a workplace literacy program?
5. How do you know when your programs have been relevant and responsive to the needs of the students?

EPILOGUE

CONTINUING THE DEBATE

James A. Draper

The many cases presented in this book have implicitly or explicitly, touched on a wide variety of issues relating to adult literacy and basic education. The presence of issues (meaning that which is disputed or under discussion) within literacy programs is due to both internal and external forces. There are challenges to be met, differing viewpoints to be dealt with, limited resources to be prioritized and alternative ways of reaching goals to be developed. All of these need to be discussed. Ignoring these issues is one way to deal with them but this attitude is usually self-defeating. Generally speaking, those programs which are innovative and exemplary of good practice are those which articulate and creatively deal with issues and do so regularly. In fact this would likely be a major criteria for assessing good practice.

Practitioners experience many areas of concern. For example, early in 1991 Betty-Ann Lloyd, a Nova Scotia literacy practitioner brought together twelve literacy workers in Nova Scotia for a one day workshop to talk about the issues they perceived. (Draper, Taylor and Goldgrab, 1991) Some of these included:

- Permanent and adequate core funding;
- More program time, flexibility, variety and counselling as well as more follow-up with students;
- Increased awareness of the long term needs of adult students by adult educators, program administrators and government bureaucrats;
- Better working conditions for adult educators such as: paid time for preparation and continuous learning, administrative and counselling support, professional level of pay plus benefits as well as practical training opportunities for adult educators;
- Regular exchange between public school teachers, adult educators and literacy practitioners;
- Better assessment instruments to help improve programs for both adult students and agencies.

Her group concluded that "Literacy work is complex, multi-faceted and accomplished on several levels simultaneously." They found it difficult to focus on some issues to the exclusion of others especially when there had been no opportunity for small literacy groups to develop a sense of solidarity that could bridge differences in programs between adult students, and differences in geographic locations and regional needs.

In reality, the actual number of issues facing literacy workers is in itself an issue. To describe the issues is to describe the complexity of this developing field.

Like the issues collected by Betty-Ann Lloyd, most of these issues are not just local but can be generalized to the larger literacy field. Similarly, while collecting data for the Ontario case studies, Sheila Goldgrab had many conversations with practitioners and noted these issues which also have critical importance for many:

The issue of labour law and paid literacy practitioners. Certified teachers in community-based literacy programs, for example, are not paid according to their qualifications and certification. In labour law, a teacher is someone who is certified and who holds a contract. Because many teachers who teach literacy education in the schools and in community-based programs do not have contracts, they earn considerably less than a usual teacher's salary. Is there a way to pay teachers fairly?

The issue of professionalization is one that concerns many in the literacy field and particularly program coordinators. Practitioners have asked how they can achieve the level of respect and funding enjoyed by their colleagues in the English as a Second Language (ESL) field. At the same time, there is concern that if certification is made obligatory, uncertified qualified tutors may be left out.

The issue of community-based literacy programs. Many adults who wish to upgrade their reading, writing and numeracy skills are doing so in community-based literacy programs. Will community-based literacy programs (in some cases the only available ones in a large rural area) continue to be funded by the Ontario Ministry of Education? Are these programs well understood by the present funders?

The issue of future funding. The changing of ministries responsible for funding literacy education has literacy program coordinators concerned about the future direction of funding. Currently, one-to-one tutoring in the home or at a program centre seems to be more favoured than group literacy education. Will one-to-one literacy, popular among many students for its privacy and personal attention, continue to be funded?

The issue of the student-centred approach. Many literacy tutors and students favour this approach where students are given the opportunity to create their own learning plans and are active participants in all aspects of their learning. Will this continue or will province-wide curriculums and standardized evaluations be the norm?

The issue of racist attitudes. Urban centres in Ontario as in many other areas, have a large ethno-cultural mix of participants in their programs. Literacy practitioners are facing many questions about how to deal with racist attitudes that emerge within the program, between tutors and students for example, or from student's experiences outside the program. Such incidents require exposure and discussion and equitable resolution. Is there a link within society between racist attitudes and illiteracy among minority groups? Do programs respond to everyone's needs? In what ways can they be made more sensitive? Few seem to be engaging in dialogue on these topics.

The issue of the future of adult basic education. International Literacy Year (1990) is over and the future direction of adult basic education is a matter that everyone involved in literacy education is talking about. For example in Ontario, coincident with the end of a concentrated international focus on illiteracy, is the new relationship that has begun between the literacy field and the Ministry of Education, newly responsible for literacy funding. As responsibilities for funding shifts, in what new directions will adult basic education go?

Still other issues that emerged from the Ontario region but which have implications elsewhere, included: learning styles, learning disabilities, student self-perception, assessment and evaluation, organizational structures, dealing with organizational changes, oral-based literacy, tutor training and support, tutor involvement, tutor expectations, literacy and social change, staff development, and funding partnerships. Nor do the range of literacy concerns end there. Other issues presented in discussion groups across the country related to team teaching, continuous intake of students into a literacy program, the optimum number of students in a given literacy class especially as a program moves away from a one-to-one approach to teaching, the place of volunteers in a literacy program, and the deep-seated issues relating to philosophy and language. Some of these emerge and are dealt with in some detail in other parts of this book.

Let's take a closer look at a few of these areas of concern. Hopefully this will provoke a continuing discussion not only in each community but also as literacy practitioners meet in larger networking groups and conferences.

Social Change or Status Quo?

The goals of a literacy program are its philosophical statements. They deserve careful and periodic scrutiny. Do these goals express the desire to bring about social change or to retain the status quo? What do these statements really mean? Social change in what context and from whose point of view and to what end? Does change mean within the classroom, within an organization (such as the workplace or the school) or change within a larger community? We need to discuss openly and frequently the implications of trying to bring about social change. Can we help to bring about social change through a one-to-one teaching approach, as compared to a group approach to education? What do we mean when we speak of "literacy education as a social movement?"

An essential component of a social change or radical approach to literacy education is the raising of personal critical consciousness. That is, developing and nurturing the individual's ability to think critically through an ongoing questioning of assumptions and the status quo, questioning information sources, and reflecting on possibilities and their consequences. But there is a danger that this approach can also be used to manipulate adult students by literacy workers or agencies. While involving adults in discussions on social issues such as unemployment, welfare, taxes, free trade,racial and gender inequality, and the constitution, are we careful to encourage a discussion that considers the complexity of differing viewpoints?

It is always important to examine the implications of any social changes being proposed. For example, what are the implications of developing critical thinking in employees who are working within a hierarchical industry? Or in an adult whose spouse does not understand the process of critical thinking? Or within a literacy agency whose funding comes from a traditional bureaucracy? What are the consequences of immersion in a radical approach to literacy education when that adult leaves the program and enters an environment which has limited tolerance for such thinking or behaviour?

The Process or the Product?

The term process is widely used in the field of adult literacy education. It can become an issue when there is a conflict with the stated goals of a program. One area of misunderstanding is to think that the achievement of a product (or an outcome) is synonymous with the specific method employed to achieve such outcomes. Take for example the training of a worker to do a particular task. There is little dispute over the end goal of preparing a competent and qualified worker (or an engineer or a medical doctor). Over the years, the education or training of such people has become associated with the belief (more like a tradition or a mythology) that to achieve the end goal only one method is appropriate without realizing that different methods for teaching can be used in order to achieve similar goals.

The process (what happens on the way to the goals) has especially become an important and recognized part of many literacy and other educational programs. The process may best be thought of as the journey of discovery to be valued in itself, without the obsession of achieving the goal. Experience can be valued for the sake of learning about the exploration, the discussion and the reflections. Time is required to do this. The process is especially important in attempting to bring about social change and in developing critical thinking. Many issues can arise, determined by the depth to which we are willing to explore specific literacy programs.

Who Advocates for Whom?

Many of the case studies in this book touch on the issue of advocacy (meaning to speak on behalf of). Who speaks for students? For tutors? For a program? It is widely acknowledged today that people should have the opportunity to speak on their own behalf. But there are still many examples in literacy and other programs of "professional authorities" usurping that right by professing to speak on behalf of "the disadvantaged." But speaking for oneself requires specific skills, attitudes and knowledge. These are not to be taken for granted. Support and practice is usually required to develop such qualities. Still, there are examples of administrators and coordinators of literacy programs making judgements on behalf of students while at the same time expounding on the participatory quality of their programs.

A person can advocate on his or her own behalf but this also demands collaboration with others. Is there opportunity to participate in an agency's program? The statement "we have students on our board" needs probing. Why are the students on the board? A number of answers could be given, some of which may not be related to students advocating for themselves at all. In this way, questioning causes further issues to emerge.

Understanding the Learning Process

Many issues which arise in the field of literacy education are due to a lack of understanding or a misunderstanding of learning. Learning is at the heart of what all educators do and is the essence of all educational programs. The whole point of education, educational materials, programs and teachers, is to facilitate learning. Unless learning occurs, there is no education. It is interesting to note that in spite of this, educators often assume that they understand how their own learning has happened and how it occurs for their students. Not only is such an understanding important in the planning of programs, it is also helpful in guiding students and in helping them to assess where they are in their learning. Thelma Barer-Stein's *Learning about Learning* elaborates on this topic.

The Management of Literacy Education

Many issues in literacy education relate to the management of the programs. The non-formal education of adults through literacy education programs is quite different from the management of formal education programs for children. Management refers to all those skills and functions which are necessary to plan, implement, sustain, and assess an educational program. Management also includes the acquisition and effective use of resources, both human and material. Many issues arise when we ask: What specific skills are required to manage literacy programs? How wisely are literacy education programs managed and how can we assess this? Could the resources be managed more effectively? How does the management of a program affect overall organizational development and those within it?

The management of time is also an important factor in operating an educational program. Since we cannot create time, it is important to use it creatively, wisely and efficiently. Planning and managing a literacy program requires particular skills, and time management is definitely one of them.

Funding Literacy Education

There is a multitude of issues which relate to the funding of educational programs and their desperation to survive. Obtaining funds requires a disproportionate amount of energy, anxiety and paradoxically, just to survive with existing programs, often an inefficient use of resources. One of the great challenges to literacy education in the immediate future will be to deal with the major issues centring around funding. Such a discussion must not focus exclusively on the continuing dependency on government funding but creatively find and use other resources. The issue of funding should be seen in its relationship to other issues such as the management of literacy programs, public relations and fundraising skills, and teaching practices. Removing the obstacle of funding literacy programs may not automatically lead to more effective programs.

Broadening the Perspective on Literacy

More and more, linkages are being made between illiteracy and other societal dimensions. Illiteracy may be related to poverty, unemployment, under-employment, poor housing, malnutrition, infant mortality, violence, and other social, economic and psychological factors. Illiteracy is also used as an important indicator of a nation's growth and development. However, it is important not to overgeneralize these linkages nor to see them as cause and effect relationships. That is, of one being the direct cause of something else. These relationships help to emphasize the complexity and the fragility of many human conditions and lead us away from viewing each in isolation from the other. Also, it is wise not to overemphasize the "illiteracy issue." In setting priorities to deal with the complexity of these linkages, while yet retaining a holistic view of the individual, it may be necessary to begin with the problems of shelter, employment, and food and not with literacy. Literacy education may come in due course.

Learning Through Research

The essence of research (re-searching) is to discover what we do not know. In examining what we need to know, we can improve our literacy programs and improve our own skills and effectiveness. To deny research as part of a literacy program can be interpreted to mean "I'm not really interested in improving myself or my program." Research, even in the loose sense in which it is used here, should be an integral part of all literacy programs. Research might include keeping simple records in order to document changes over time or trying out different ways of running a training program or examining alternative teaching methods. Documentation, discussion, reflection and analysis are the key components of research.

There are a number of issues which relate to a person's perception and use of research. We still hear comments such as "Why is the government wasting money on research?" "Why not just give us the money for our programing?" "Money spent on research is not money well spent." Such narrow and misinformed points of view exemplify a crucial issue in literacy education. A good literacy program comprises more than organizing classroom space and recruiting students. The lack of research and a negative attitude toward its value is one cause for inefficiency and wastage in some literacy programs.

It is true that a literacy program must guard against inundation by people wanting to do research, including research on students, but this can be controlled. Each agency should be encouraged to develop a policy on research and the extent to which they can undertake research internally or in cooperation with outside agencies. Being involved in research begins with questions which are relevant to a specific agency. Recently, a literacy education agency was asked if a person from outside the agency might meet with students to talk about a research project. The coordinator of the program refused without asking the students if they would like to be involved. Since research is intended to expand our knowledge, perhaps the students might have enjoyed and benefitted from the involvement. An often-overlooked but basic assumption about research is that anyone can participate.

The above comments and related issues also apply to evaluation (valuing) as a particular kind of research. Evaluation is a form of research and is intended to enhance our knowledge. It can be either non-formal or formal in nature. When evaluating, we can ask: From whose point of view are we evaluating: The student, the teacher or the funding agency? The field of literacy education illustrates many issues relating to evaluation.

Supporting Innovations

Introducing an innovation into a literacy program may raise a number of issues and requires more than a new idea. In order to take root and grow, an innovation needs to be nourished and sustained. To introduce a new idea means to change and thus to challenge the status quo which in turn alters the power relationships between people. One of the major issues which relates to introducing change is the differences in perceptions of alternatives. An openness to dialogue is required to explore possibilities widely and this should include all who are involved.

It is not surprising that there is often opposition to change. Failure to sustain innovations in the past often overlooked the point that the process required to introduce an innovation is essentially a learning process. Innovation introduces something new, something different, something unfamiliar. People need to be given the opportunity to approach innovation as a learning process and need to be given the time to progress through its steps. Following Barer-Stein's *Learning as a Process of Experiencing the Unfamiliar*, they need:

- A period of time *to be made aware* of issues
- A chance *to observe* similar changes elsewhere
- A non-threatening opportunity *to try out* the new ideas and *to practice* them
- A time *to confront* their own doubts and anxieties together with others
- And finally to take the time *to reflect* on their own place in the change, and to reach an understanding of *the personal relevance* of the innovation and its place in their program.

In spite of what we know about it, introducing change is always fraught with anxiety and differences of opinion, as we've seen in some of the case studies presented in this book. But these case studies also confirm that participation in change decreases that initial anxiety and increases understanding and cooperation.

Policies and Bureaucracies

A series of issues arise from bureaucratic policies (often those of government and other funding agencies) which may impede the effectiveness of literacy educational programs. Such policies are often formulated by non-practitioners for purposes of control and defended on the basis of accountability.

If policy makers understood the realities of adults struggling with literacy education, they may be more flexible in their expectations and attempt to accommodate the daily life concerns of many of these adults. Time consuming and unnecessary record-keeping are often required by bureaucracies and becomes an issue for some literacy education agencies. There are examples of funding being cut off from a student because, while enrolled in an adult basic education course, the student was also working on a correspondence course for secondary school credit. There are also policies which set quotas or fixed number of hours for program completion. Other examples could be given of external authorities interfering with the implementation of student-centred programs.

It should be recognized however, that non-government literacy education agencies also have their own bureaucracies and politics. Some of these too, are incompatible with the goals which they expound. An agency might profess a student-learner approach to education but have policies in actual practice which contradict this. Students and tutors in such agencies might not feel free to express how they feel about the program or its directors, and may feel that suggestions for change would not betaken seriously. A task for many organizations could be to critically examine their own policies and day-to-day practices in light of their stated goals.

It goes without saying that the sources of conflict and the resultant issues which arise can come from within as well as outside an agency's program. When examining the causes of an issue it is important to analyze the degree of actual control assigned to the agency.

Those who practice in the field of literacy education are especially sensitive to which ministry within the government is given the mandate for adult literacy education. To varying degrees, literacy is the responsibility of all ministries within government, for example education, labour, citizenship, immigration, correctional services, fishing, technical education, colleges, skills development. Similarly, as we have seen, literacy is more than an educational issue.

Organizational policies can also be the cause of problematic issues relating to certification and the professionalization of the field. The role and influence of teacher unions would be examples of such current policies. What evidence is there that uncertified teachers are poorer teachers? Or that certified ones are better? The question of certification looms as a continuing issue.

Beyond Training

All of the topics mentioned so far have implications for training programs, including the training of volunteers. Considering all of these educational implications broadens the approach to education and is desirable for everyone associated with a literacy education program, including adult students, in order that people understand the issues at hand, especially those which concern them personally.

The training of tutors is as complex as the tasks expected of them. Tutors do more than teach. They also advocate, counsel, advise, plan, evaluate, research, reflect and defend. There are different points of view regarding these functions. What is required, is both a generic as well as a specific program for training and education, often centring around the issues mentioned above.

The Larger Context of Local Practice

International Literacy Year 1990, helped to relate local practice in literacy education with an international world view. It is important that this should happen since the linkage acknowledges that there is a viable international network in literacy education through which ideas can be exchanged and political support can be acquired. The various world declarations on literacy, and the Canadian Cedar Glen Declaration, all tie together and not only help to raise the profile for basic education for adults but also help to provide some political clout. National organizations like the Canadian Alliance for Literacy (CAL), an umbrella group comprising most national and literacy groups helps to provide political strength from the field. The 1990 international conference *Education for All*, held in Thailand helped to raise many international issues relating to education, including the inter-relationship between non-formal and formal education.

Mention could also be made of the contribution of the Canadian Commission for UNESCO, including the *Future Contributions to Literacy in Canada* conferences which it has organized. When the planners first met to organize the second conference(held in Toronto 1987) on literacy in industrialized countries, one of their first decisions was to invite colleagues from developing countries to share their extensively rich experience in literacy education. Although not without its own issues, there is now a much greater openness for sharing, locally, regionally, provincially, nationally and internationally. Literacy education, wherever it occurs in Canada, must now be seen within the international context. Many such programs now use an international vocabulary such as "lifelong education", "continuous learning" and "education as a human right", all of which are also part of the vocabulary of the larger field of adult education.

Concluding Comments

Literacy education is a growing and maturing field of specialization within the field of adult education. It is not surprising that the field is undergoing growing pains which are part of this maturation process. The refinement of a vocabulary to describe practice is also part of this process, as are the increasing concerns and examination of literacy issues. The growth of a specialized field of practice, such as literacy education, parallels the growth of its own specialized body of knowledge based on research, reflection and critical thinking. Articulating, clarifying and refining a practicing philosophy of literacy education becomes a unifying link to this growth.

A number of other issues and questions arise when attempting to understand and direct the expansion of the literacy education field. For example: What does it mean to be a professional literacy educator? What balance is required between the formal accreditation of an individual and good literacy practice? How can teaching and management philosophies best be matched with student learning goals? What do these philosophies imply in terms of evaluation (of programs, teachers, students) and how can these be conveyed practically and effectively to funding agencies? What is the basic theory and knowledge required of literacy practitioner-educators? What funding arrangements, from which sources, can best and most fairly give security to the on-going presence of literacy education programs? What distinctions can be made between "educators of adults" and "adult educators;" the latter referring to someone who has a basic understanding of the theory,literature and research within the specialized field of adult education?

Various issues also arise when we articulate some of the trends which seem to be apparent within the literacy education field. For instance, we can see that there is a decentralization of literacy programs. The workplace, for instance, is being rediscovered as a site for education, a fact which programs in developing countries have always practiced. What skills are required to make decentralized programs effective?

Our questions seem to be endless, but the effectiveness of a literacy education program is greatly dependent on the extent to which issues are questioned, defined, discussed and hopefully solved. These functions in turn help to shape exemplary practice. Involving all the stake holders can be challenging. But it is only such involvement that can enrich the practice and study of literacy education and help to raise the voices to be heard from the literacy field.

SELECTED REFERENCES

SELECTED REFERENCES

General References

Alpha Consultants Inc. (1992) *Literacy in rural communities: Proceedings from the International Conference*. Ottawa, May 10-13,1991. Toronto Ontario.

Barer-Stein, T. (1989) Reflections on Literacy and the Universal Learning Process. In M. Taylor and J.A. Draper (eds.) *Adult Literacy Perspectives*. Toronto: Culture Concepts Inc.

Barer-Stein, T. (1987) On the Meaning of Learning: Reflections with Dewey. *The Canadian Journal for the Study of Adult Education 1* (1).

Barer-Stein, T. and Draper, J.A.(eds.) (1988) *The Craft of Teaching Adults*. Toronto: Culture Concepts Inc.

Boud, D. and Griffin, V. (eds.) (1987) *Appreciating Adults Learning: from the Learner's Perspective*. UK: Biddles Ltd.

Council of Ministers of Education, Canada. (1990) *Adult Literacy Canada: Report to the 42nd Session International Conference on Education, Geneva*. Toronto: Council of Ministers of Education.

Council of Ministers of Education, Canada. (1988) *Adult Illiteracy in Canada: Identifying and Addressing the Problem*. Statement of the Council of Ministers of Education, Canada.

Council of Ministers of Education, Canada. (1988) *Adult Illiteracy in Canada*. Toronto: Council of Ministers of Education, Canada.

Draper, J.A., Taylor, M.C. and Goldgrab, S. (1991) *Issues in Adult Literacy and Basic Education: Canada*. Toronto: Department of Adult Education, Ontario Institute for Studies in Education.

Draper, J.A. (1990) *Writings Relating to Literacy*. Toronto: Ontario Institute for Studies in Education.

Draper, J.A. (1986) *Re-Thinking Adult Literacy*. Toronto: World Literacy of Canada.

Duff-McCracken, D. and Fretz, B.(1992) *Learner Involvement in Community-Based Literacy Programs*: A discussion paper. Kitchener Ontario: Core Literacy.

Griffin, V. (1988) Holistic Learning / Teachingin Adult Education: Would You Play a One-String Guitar? In T. Barer-Stein and J.A. Draper (eds.) *The Craft of Teaching Adults*. Toronto: Culture Concepts Inc.

Herman, R., Moore, L. and Ryan, F. (1984) *A Social Services Model of Adult Basic Education (A.B.E.): A Case Study of Urban and Rural Applications*. Toronto: The Department of Adult Education, Ontario Institute for the Study of Education.

International Council for Adult Education. (1987) Literacy in the Industrialized Countries: A Focus on Practice. *Convergence*. XX.

Jones, J. (1989) *Annotated Bibliography: Communications Level 1: Evening Literacy, Adult Basic Education*. Ottawa: Algonquin College.

Literacy Research Center, Graduate School of Education, University of Pennsylvania. (1990, Spring) *Literacy Research Newsletter* 6 (1). Philadelphia: University of Pennsylvania.

Lloyd, B.A. (1988) *Adult Literacy, Basic Education and Academic Upgrading in Nova Scotia: The Role of the Community College.* Halifax: Literacy Nova Scotia.

Newman, A. and Beverstock, S.C. (1990) *Adult Literacy: Contexts and Challenges.* Newark, Delaware: International Reading Association.

North York Public Library Program. (1987) *A New Start: Adult Literacy Resource Materials.* Toronto: Libraries and Community Information Branch, Ontario Ministry of Citizenship and Culture.

Norris, S.P. and Phillips, L.M. (1990) *Foundations of Literacy Policy in Canada* Calgary: Detselig Enterprises Limited.

Open File From Literacy to Education for All: The Critical Decade. *Prospects XIX (4).*

Ryan, J.L. (1989) *Literacy Collection Development in Libraries: A Bibliography* (Second revised edition). Syracuse: Laubach Literacy International.

Street, B. (1984) *Literacy in Theory and Practice.* Cambridge University Press.

Taylor, M. and Draper, J.(eds.) (1989) *Adult Literacy Perspectives.* Toronto: Culture Concepts Inc.

Thomas, A. (1989) *Exemplary Adult Literacy Programs and Innovative Practices in Canada.* British Columbia: Ministry of Advanced Education and Job Training and Ministry Responsible for Science and Technology.

Thomas, A. (1990) *Encouraging Adults to Acquire Literacy Skills.* Ottawa: National Literacy Secretariat (K1A 0M5).

Wagner, S. (1985) Illiteracy and Adult Literacy Teaching in Canada. *Prospects XV (1)*

UNESCO. (1990) *UNESCO Adult Education, Information Notes 2.* Paris: UNESCO.

Vélis, J.P. (1990) *Through a Glass, Darkly: Functional Illiteracy in Industrialized Countries.* Paris: The UNESCO Press.

Community Building

Alden, H. (1982) *Illiteracy and Poverty in Canada: Toward a Critical Perspective.* Thesis, Toronto: University of Toronto, Department of Educational Theory.

Añorve, R.L. (1989) Community-Based Literacy Educators: Experts and Catalysts for Change. In A. Fingeret and P. Jurmo (eds.) *Participatory Literacy Education.* New Directions in Continuing Education 42. San Francisco: Jossey-Bass.

Association of Canadian Community Colleges. (1988-1989) *Literacy in the Colleges / Institutes.* Toronto: Literacy Task Group, the Association of Canadian Community Colleges.

Brookfield, S. (1988) *Developing Critical Thinkers.* San Francisco: Jossey-Bass Publishers.

The Canadian Centre for Philanthropy. (1989) *The Canadian Directory to Foundations and Granting Agencies and the Canadian Index to Foundation Grants.* Toronto: The Canadian Centre for Philanthropy.

Carpenter, T. (1986) The Right to Read: *Tutor's Handbook for the Student*

Centred Individualized Learning Program. Miria Ioannou and Gilda Mekler (eds.) Toronto: Frontier College.

Chobot, M. (1989) Public Libraries and Museums. In S.Merriam and P. Cunningham (eds.) *Handbook of Adult and Continuing Education.* San Francisco: Jossey-Bass.

Chynoweth, J. (1989) *Enhancing Literacy for Jobs and Productivity.* Washington D.C.: The Council of State Policy and Planning Agencies.

Compton, L. and McClusky, H. (1980) Community Education for Community Development. In E. Boone, R. Shearon, E. White and Associates (eds.) *Serving Personal and Community Needs through Adult Education.* San Francisco: Jossey-Bass.

Ferrell, S. (1990) Adult Literacy Programs in Rural Areas. *Journal of Reading.* (ERIC ED321966).

Gaber-Katz, E. and Watson, G. (1987) *Libraries for Literacy: The 1987 Toronto Public Library Literacy Study.* Toronto: Toronto Public Library.

Gaber-Katz, E. and Watson, G. (1989) Community-Based Literacy Programing The Toronto Experience. In M. Taylor and J. Draper (eds.) *Adult Literacy Perspectives.* Toronto: Culture Concepts Inc.

Gaber-Katz, E. and Watson, G. (1990) *Community-based Literacy: An Emerging Practice and Theory.* Toronto: OISE Press.

Gaber-Katz, E. and Watson, G. (1991) *The Land That We Dream Of: A Participatory Study of Community-based Literacy.* Toronto: OISE Press.

Godin, J. (1991) *Words of Promise: Voluntary Organizations' Experience with Literacy.* Ottawa: National Literacy Secretariat (Multiculturalism and Citizenship Canada).

Hamilton, E. (1984) Adult Education and Community Development in Nigeria. *Graduate Studies Journal 2.*

Hamilton, E. and Cunningham, P. (1989) Community-based Adult Education. In S. Merriam, and P. Cunningham (eds.) *Handbook of Adult and Continuing Education.* San Francisco: Jossey-Bass.

Kearns, L.J. (1989, June) Libraries and Literacy Programs: Get Educated Before Getting Involved. *Canadian Library Journal 46 (3).*

Lobley, G. (1985) *Adult Basic Education: Organizing Provision in the Inner London Education Authority* (ILEA). Richmond, British Columbia: The Opening Agency, Marketing Department.

Metro Toronto Movement for Literacy. (1987) *Good Materials and Where to Find Them*: A Literacy Resource Guide. Toronto: The Curriculum Work Group, ALO.

No Name Brand Clan and Tanya Lester. (1990) *Under the Line.* Winnipeg, Manitoba: Popular Theater Alliance of Manitoba and Journeys Education Association.

Ontario Ministry of Culture and Communications.(1989) *Libraries and Literacy.* Toronto: Ontario Ministry of Culture and Communications.

Padak, N.D. and Padak, G.M. (1991, February) What Works: Adult Literacy Program Evaluation. *Journal of Reading 34 (5).*

Pemik, L. (1990) *Learning for a Healthier Future: A Polite Project in Health and Literacy.* Arviat, NWT: Arctic College.

Roach, R. (1990) *Branching Out: Tutor's Guide to Purposeful and Creative Writing.* Saint John, N.B.: Laubach Literacy Canada.

Shuttleworth, D.E. (1989) Adult Basic Education and Community Development. In M. Taylor and Draper (eds.) *Adult Literacy Perspectives*. Toronto: Culture Concepts Inc.

Slonosky, C. (1990) *Looking Ahead: Tutor's Guide to Lesson Planning*. Saint John, N.B.: Laubach Literacy of Canada.

Thomas, A.M. (1989) *Adult Literacy Volunteer Tutor Evaluation Kit*. Victoria, B.C.: Ministry of Advanced Education and Job Training, and Ministry responsible for Science and Technology.

Thomas,R. (1990) *A Short History of the Saskatoon Literacy Coalition*. Saskatoon, Saskatchewan: Unpublished.

VanHorn, B.H., Hart, B. et al. (1987) *Planning Adult Literacy Services, Options for Library Involvement*. Pennsylvania: Institute for the Study of Adult Literacy. (ERIC ED317761)

World Literacy of Canada. (1990)Reading the Signs. Toronto: World Literacy of Canada.

Alderson-Gill andAssociates Consulting Inc. (1989) Study of Literacy and Learning Disabilities. Ottawa: The Learning Disabilities Association of Canada.

Bingham, M. (1989) *Learning Differently: Meeting the Needs of Adults with Learning Disabilities*. The University of Tennessee, Knoxville: Center for Literacy Studies.

British Columbia Ministry of Education. (1987) *Learning Together: A Handbook for Teaching Adults with Learning Disabilities*. Victoria, B.C.: The Ministry of Education.

Canadian Congress for Learning Opportunities for Women. (1990) *Guide to Good Canadian Materials for Women Learning to Read*. Toronto: CCLOW.

Canadian Women Studies. (1988) *Women and Literacy*. Downsview, Ontario: York University Publication.

Conger, S.D.S. (1989) Life Skills. In M. Taylor andJ. Draper (eds.) *Adult Literacy Perspectives*. Toronto: Culture Concepts Inc.

Fisher, J.C. (1987) *The Literacy Level Among Older Adults: Is It a Problem?* Adult Literacy and Basic Education 11 (1) (ERIC).

Gillette, A. (1989) Youth's Participation in Literacy Work. In Taylor, M. and Draper, J. (eds.) *Adult Literacy Perspectives*. Toronto: Culture Concepts Inc.

Goldstein, R. (1989) *Taking the Mystique Out of Learning Disabilities: A Practical Guide for Literacy Tutors*. New Brunswick: Laubach Literacy of Canada.

Horsman, J. (1989) From the Learner's Voice: Women's Experience of Il/literacy. In M. Taylor, and J. Draper (eds.) *Adult Literacy Perspectives*. Toronto: Culture Concepts Inc.

Horsman, J. (1990) *Women and Literacy — Something in My Mind Besides the Everyday*. Toronto: Women's Press.

International Council for Adult Education.(1990) *Voices Rising. The Literacy Issues — Feminist Perspectives on Reading and Writing* 4 (1). Toronto: ICAE Women's Program.

Karassik, J. (1989) *Literacy and Learning Disabilities: A Handbook for Literacy Workers*. Ottawa: Learning Disabilities Association of Canada.

Klugerman, P. (1989) Developmentally Disabled Adult Learners. In S. Merriam and P. Cunningham (eds.) *Handbook of Adult and Continuing Education*. San Francisco: Jossey-Bass.

McGivney, V. (1990) *Education's for Other People: Access to Education for Non-Participant Adults*. United Kingdom: National Institute of Adult Continuing Education (NIACE).

Ontario Literacy Coalition. (1991) *Women, Literacy and Action: A Handbook*. Toronto: Ontario Literacy Coalition.

Rockhill, K. (1987, Spring) Literacy as Threat/Desire: Longing to Be Somebody. In J.S. Gaskill and A.T. Mclaren (eds.) *Women and Education 5* (3).

Rutherford, J. (1989) Illiteracy and Older Canadians. Ottawa: *One Voice — The Canadian Seniors Network*, Department of the Secretary of State. National Literacy Secretariat.

Selman, G. and Dampier, P. (1991) *The Foundations of Adult Education in Canada*. Toronto: Thompson Educational Publishing.

Thomas, D. (1985) Older Adults and Lifelong Learning. *Convergence* XVI (11).

TV Ontario. (1989) *Lifeline to Literacy: People with Disabilities Speak Out*. Canada: The Ontario Education Communications Authority.

Activating Student Participation

Arnold, R. and Burke, B. (1983) *A Popular Education Handbook: An Educational Experience Taken from Central America and Adapted to the Canadian Context*. A joint publication of: USO, Development Education Centre, Ontario Institute for Studies in Education.

Association Canadienne d'éducation de langue française (ACELF). (1989, été et automne) *Revue éducation et francophonie*, nos 27 et 28.

Balmuth, M. (1987) Essential Characteristics of Effective Adult Literacy Programs. Albany Adult Beginning Reader Project. New York: State Education Department. In S. Brookfield (ed) (1988) *Developing Critical Thinkers*. San Francisco: Jossey Bass.

Business Council for Effective Literacy. (1986) Developing an Employee Volunteer Literacy Program. *BCEL Bulletin* (1). New York: BCEL.

Chisman, F. (1990) *Leadership for Literacy: The Agenda for the 1990's*. San Francisco: Jossey Bass.

Fingeret, H. (1989) The Social and Historical Context of Participatory Literacy Education. In H. Fingeret and P. Jurmo (eds.) *Participatory Literacy Education*. San Francisco: Jossey-Bass.

Gladu, N. (1988) *L'approche du centre de lecture et d'écriture*. Montreal: Centre de lecture et d'écriture, document polycopié.

Groupe d'action sur l'alphabétisation. (1990, août) *Le Bulletin de nouvelles du groupe d'action sur l'alphabétisation*, No. 11. Numéro spécial avec la contribution de nouveaux apprenants.

Haigler, C. (1990) Building Ties Among Literacy Programs: Achieving Strength Through Co-operation. In F. Chisman and Associates (eds.) *Leadership for Literacy: The Agenda for the 1990's*. San Francisco: Jossey-Bass Inc.

Hunter, C.S.J. (1987, Spring) *Literacy/Illiteracy in an International Perspective*. World Education Reports.

James, S. et al. (1987) *Meeting Half Way. Some Approaches to Educational Work with Single Homeless People by the Basic Education Development Scheme*. London (England) North Lambeth Day Centre, Limited (ERIC ED290907).

Jurmo, P. (1989) The Case for Participatory Literacy Education.

In H. Fingeret and P. Jurmo (eds.) *Participatory Literacy Education.* San Francisco: Jossey-Bass.

Jurmo, P. (1987) *Learner Participation Practices in Adult Literacy Efforts in the United States.* UMI Dissertation Information Service, 300. N. Zeeb Road, Ann Arbor, MI 48106 (Order No. 8805934).

Labrie, V. et les mots de bien du monde (1990) *Par-dessus le fossé des lettres. Des lieux pour des personnes fières, Dialogues entre des étudiante-e-s an alpha et des intervenants-e-s,* Bureau de consultation en alphabétisation, Québec, Commission des écoles catholiques de Québec.

Labrie, V. (1990) *Activités a vivre en classe pour souligner l'Année international de l'alphabétisme,* Bureau de consultation en alphabétisation, Québec, Commission des écoles catholiques de Québec. Photocopied document.

Labrie, V. (1989, août) «De l'automobile à la soupe à l'alphabet: réflexion culturelles sur l'indispensable alphabétisation, *education et francophonie* 17 (2).

Lytle, S. (1988) *From the Inside Out: Reinventing Assessment.* World Education, 2 (1).

Picon, C. (1988) Literacy and Popular Education: A Latin American Experience. In *Literacy in the Industrialized Countries: A Focus on Practice.* M. Gayfer (ed.) Toronto: International Council on Adult Education.

Smith, E.T. (n.d.) Advocates for Literacy? *The Librarian Situation,* Catholic Library World 52 (2).

Thomas, A. (1990, November) The Reluctant Learner: A Research Report on Non-Participation and dropout in Literacy Programs in British Columbia. In the *Movement for Canadian Literacy Newsletter.* (Available from: Provincial Curriculum Publications, Marketing Department, Open Learning Agency, P.O. Box 9400, Richmond, B.C., V6Y 2A2).

Turcot, K. (1987) Kolette, Paris et Montréal, *Science et Service Quart Monde.*

Van Horn, B.H., et al. (1987) Planning Adult Literacy Services. *Options for Literacy Involvement.* Pennsylvania: Pennsylvania State University, University Park. Institute for the Study of Adult Literacy.

Language and Culture

Anderson, K. (1989, Summer and Fall) Native Women and Literacy. *Canadian Women Studies.* (10).

Anderson, K. (1990) *Minutes of Proceeding and Evidence. Issue No. 39:30.* Standing Committee on Aboriginal Affairs. Ottawa: House of Commons.

Añorve, R.L. (1989) Community-Based Literacy Educators: Experts and Catalysts for Change. In A. Fingeret and P. Jurmo (eds.) *Participatory Literacy Education.* New Directions in Continuing Education 42 San Francisco: Jossey-Bass.

Assembly of First Nations, Education Secretariat. (1990) *Towards Linguistic Justice for First Nations.* Ottawa, Canada.

Baldwin, R. (1984) *Clear Writing and Literacy.* Toronto: Ontario Literacy Coalition.

Barer-Stein, T. (1988) Culture in the Classroom. In T. Barer-Stein and J.A. Draper (eds.) *The Craft of Teaching Adults.* Toronto: Culture Concepts Inc.

B.C. Ministry of Education. (1984) *Native Literacy and Life Skills Curriculum Guidelines: A Resource Book for Adult Basic Education.* British Columbia:

Ministry of Education. Reprinted by Ministry of Advanced Education and Job Training, and Ministry Responsible for Science and Technology (1989).

Bell, J. and Burnaby, B. (1984) *A Handbook for ESL Literacy*. Toronto: OISE Press.

Boal, A. (1979) *Theater of the Oppressed*. London: Pluto Press.

Canadian Institute of Adult Education, Institut Canadien d'éducation des adultes. (n.d.) En toutes lettres et en français. Montréal: ICEA. (Available at 506 Catherine St. East, Room 800, Montréal, Québec H2L 2C7)

Church, S., Gamberg, R., Manicom, A. and Rice, J. (1989) *Whole Language in Nova Scotia. Our Schools/Our Selves 1 (2) and (3)*. Toronto: Education Foundation and Garamond Press.

Collectif. (1991, hiver) Dossier autochtone, interviews avec Georges E. sioui et Cleary. *Revue Québec français 80.*

Cummins, J. (1986) Empowering Minority Students: A Framework for Intervention. *Harvard Educational Review 56 (1).*

Davies, P. and McQuaid, A. (1990) *Whole Language and Adult Literacy Instruction*. Prince George, B.C.: College of New Caledonia.

Davis, J., Huot, J. et al. (1989) It's Our Own Knowledge: Labour, Public *Education and Skills Training. Our Schools/Our Selves*. Toronto: Education Foundation and Garamond Press.

ERIC Clearinghouse on Language and Linguistics. (1990, March) *ERIC/CLL News Bulletin*. 13 (2). Washington DC.: ERIC/CLL.

ERIC National Clearinghouseon Literacy Education. (1990, October)

ERIC Digest: *Developing Native Language Literacy in Language Minority Adult Learners*. Washington DC.: Center for Applied Linguistics.

Epskamp, K.P. (1989) *Theater in Search of Social Change: The Relative Significance of Different Theatrical Approaches*. Translation from Dutch under the direction of G. Hooijmans, CESO Paperback No. 7. The Hague.

Faulk,J. (1990) *Minutes of Proceedings and Evidence. Issue No. 35:20.* Standing Committee on Aboriginal Affairs. Ottawa: House of Commons. *Focus on Basics*. (1988) Special Issue on ESL Literacy 1.

Gabriel Dumont Institute of Native Studies and Applied Research Inc. and the Metis National Council. (1990) *Literacy for Metis and Non-status Indian Peoples: A National Strategy: A Final Report on a Comprehensive Strategy for Aboriginal Literacy* Presented to Department of Secretary of State Canada.

Garfinkel, H. (1956) Conditions of SuccessfulDegradation Ceremonies. *The American Journal of Sociology.*

Gee, J.P. (1989) Orality and Literacy: From The Savage Mind to Ways with Words *Journal of Education 171 (1).*

Hamilton, E. (1987) Popular Theater Teaches Skills and Motivates Inuit Young People of Canada's Arctic. *Convergence XX (2).*

Hamilton,E. (1987, Summer) Theater for Education. *Women's Education des Femmes.*

Heath, S.B. (1990) The Fourth Vision: Literate Language at Work. In *The Right To Literacy*. New York Modern Language Association.

Hughes, K. (1990) *Aboriginal Literacy and Empowerment*. Standing Committee on Aboriginal Affairs. Ottawa: House of Commons.

Mackay, S. (1990) Arviat Literacy Project: Build Upon Strength from Within and Help from Without. *Arctic College Dialogue* 4 (6).

McCracken, R.A. (1987) *Stories, Songs, and Poetry to Teach Reading and Writing: Literacy Through Language*. Winnipeg: Peguis.

McNaughton, L. (1990) International Year of Literacy Helps Native Community. *Windspeaker* 7 (49)

Millard, E. (1987) Development of Literacy Education in the Yukon. *Literacy/Alphabétisation*. 12 (2).

Monteith, L., Gaber-Katz, E. et al. (n.d.) *Guide to Resources for ESL Literacy Facilitator*. Toronto: Toronto Board of Education, ABE Unit, Bickford Center.

National Association of Friendship Centres. (1990) *National Literacy Survey*.

Northwest Territories Department of Advanced Education. (1989) *Literacy Initiatives in the Northwest Territories*. Yellowknife: Northwest Territories Department of Advanced Education.

Restakis, J. (1988) *Native Literacy Training Report*. Toronto: Community Literacy Unit, Literacy Branch, Ministry of Skills Development.

Rodriguez, C. and Sawyer, D. (1990) *Native Literacy Research Report* Salmon Arm, B.C.: Native Education Resource Centre, Okanagan College.

Ross, E.P. (1989, October) *How to Use the Whole Language Approach*. Adult Learning 1, 2 (ERIC EJ396202).

Roy-Poirier, J. (1989) The Case of the Franco-Ontarian Illiterate: A Historical Perspective. In M. Taylor and J. Draper (eds.) *Adult Literacy Perspectives*. Toronto: CultureConcepts Inc.

Saskatchewan Indian Institute of Technologies Asimakaniseekan Askiy Reserve. (1990) *Aboriginal Literacy Action Plan: A Literacy Practitioners Guide to Action*. Saskatchewan: Saskatchewan Indian Institute of Technologies.

Savas, D. (1988) *Profile of the Franco-Ontarian Community*. Toronto, Ontario: Office des affaires francophones.

Shearwood, P. (1987, May) Literacy Among the Aboriginal Peoples of the Northwest Territories. *Canadian Modern Language Review* 43 (4).

Stewig, J.W. (1983) *Informal Drama in the Elementary Language Arts Program*. New York: Teachers College Press.

Wallerstein, N. (1983) *Language and Culture in Conflict: Problem-Posing in the ESL Classroom*. Reading, Mass.: Addison-Wesley.

Standing Committee on Aboriginal Affairs. (1990) *You Took My Talk: Aboriginal Literacy and Empowerment. Fourth Report of the Standing Committee on Aboriginal Affairs*.

Workplace

Añorve, R.L. (1989) Community Based Literacy Educators: Experts and Catalysts for Change. In A. Fingeret and P. Jurmo (eds.) *Participatory Literacy Education*. New Directions in Continuing Education 42. San Francisco: Jossey-Bass.

Askov, E. (1989) *Upgrading Basic Skills for the Workplace*. Pennsylvania State University: The Institute for the Study of Adult Literacy.

Bohnen, E.D. (1988) *Effective Proposal Development: A How-To Manual for Skills Training Programs*. Toronto: George Brown College and St. Stephen's Community House.

Braverman, H. (1974) *Labour and Monopoly Capital.* New York: Monthly Review Press.

Business Council for Effective Literacy. (1987) *Job-Related Basic Skills, A Guide for Planners of Employee Programs.* New York: BCEL.

Canadian Business Task Force on Literacy. (1988) *Measuring the Costs of Illiteracy in Canada.* Toronto: CBTFL.

Carnevale, A., Gainer, L. and Meltzer, A. (1990) *Workplace Basics Training Manual.* San Francisco: Jossey-Bass.

Carnevale, A., Gainer, L. and Meltzer, A. (1988) *Workplace Basics: The Skills Employers Want.* Virginia, Alexandria: The American Society for Training and Development.

Chynoweth, J. (1989) *Enhancing Literacy for Jobs and Productivity.* The Council of State and Policy And Planning Agencies. Washington, D.C.

Corporation Postes Canada. (1990, September) *A Flight for Freedom. Témoignage de Réne Lefebvre (French) (Chambly, QC), Productions Forevergreen. (47 min. 50 sec. VHS).*

Davis, J., Huot, J., Jackson, N., Johnston, R., Little, D., Martell, G., Moss, P., Noble, D., Turk, J., and Wilson, G. (1989) *It's Our Own Knowledge*: Labour, Public Education and Skills Training. Toronto: Our Schools/Our Selves Education Foundation and Garamond Press.

Draper, J. (1991) Understanding Values in Workplace Education. In M.C. Taylor, G. Lewe and J.A. Draper (eds.) *Basic Skills For the Workplace.* Toronto: Culture Concepts Inc.

Drew, R. and Mikulecky, L. (1988) *How to Gather and Develop Job Specific Literacy Materials for Basic Skills Instruction.* Bloomington, Indiana: The Office of Education and Training Resources, School of Education.

Fabiani, C. (1989-1990, décembre-janvier) Nouvelle expérience au Québec: Alphabétisation en millieu de travail au Boulangeries Weston. *Alpha-Pop.*

Goddard, R.W. (1987,December) The Crisis in Workplace Literacy. *Personnel Journal* 66 (12).

Hull,W. and Sechler, J. (1987) *Adult Literacy: Skills for the American Workplace.* The National Center for Research in Vocational Education. Columbus, Ohio: The Ohio State University.

Lee, C. (1986, September) Literacy Training: A Hidden Need. *Training: The Magazine of Human Resource Development* 23 (9).

Levine, T. (1991) BEST Project: Ontario Federation of Labor. In P. Bossort et al (eds.) *Literacy 2000 — Making the Next Ten Years Matter*: Conference Summary. NewWestminster, BC.: Douglas College.

Muszynski, L. and Wolfe, D.A. (1989) New Technology and Training: Lessons from Abroad. *Canadian Public Policy/Analysede politiques, 15 (3).*

Noel, D. (1990, Septembre) L'alphabétisation en millieu de travail, *L'ABC de la prévention. Prévention au travail 3 (8).*

O'Connor, P. (1991) *Pitfalls and Possibilities: Women and Workplace Basic Education.* Redfern: New South Wales Adult Literacy Council Inc.

Ontario Ministry of Skills Development.(1989) *How to Set up Literacy and Basic Skills Training in the Workplace.* Toronto, Ontario.

Pershing, J. (1988) *Bridging Education and Employment with Basic Education Skills, The Work Education Bridge,* The Office of Education and Training Resources, School of Education, Indiana University,

Bloomington, Indiana.

Philippi, J. (1988) Matching Literacy to Job Training: Some Applications from Military Programs. *Journal of Reading* 31 (7).

Philippi, J. (1989) *Developing Instruction for Workplace Literacy Programs.* Springfield: Performance Plus Learning Consultants Inc.

Rush, T., Moe, A. and Storlie, R. (1986) *OccupationalLiteracy Education.* Newark Delaware: International Reading Association.

Soifer, R., Young, D.L. and Irwin, M. (1989) The Academy: A Learner-Centered Workplace Literacy Program. In A. Fingeret and P. Jurmo (eds.) *Participatory Literacy Education*, New Directions in Continuing Education 42. San Francisco: Jossey-Bass.

Taylor, M.C., Lewe, G.R. and Draper, J.A. (eds.) (1991) *Basic Skills for the Workplace.* Toronto: Culture Concepts Inc.

Taylor, M. andLewe, G. (1990) *Literacy Task Analysis: A How to Manual for Workplace Trainers.* Ottawa: Algonquin College.

Zuboff, S. (1988) *In the Age of the Smart Machine.* New York: Basic Books.